Pittsburgh
Series in
Social
and Labor
History

The

Shadow

of the

Mills

Working-Class Families

in Pittsburgh, 1870–1907

S. J. Kleinberg

University of Pittsburgh Press

Published by the University of Pittsburgh Press,
Pittsburgh, PA., 15260
Copyright © 1989, University of Pittsburgh Press
All rights reserved
Baker & Taylor International, London
Manufactured in the United States of America
Paperback reprint 1991

Library of Congress Cataloging-in-Publication Data

Kleinberg, S. J.
  The shadow of the mills : working-class families in Pittsburgh. 1870–1907 / S. J.
Kleinberg.
    p.   cm. — (Pittsburgh series in social and labor history)
Bibliography: p.
Includes index.
ISBN 0–8229–3599–6 — ISBN 0–8229–5445–1 (pbk.)
  1. Pittsburgh (Pa.) — Economic conditions.   2. Family — Pennsylvania — Pittsburgh
History.   3. Women — Employment — Pennsylvania — Pittsburgh History.   4. Labor
and laboring classes — Pennsylvania — Pittsburgh History.   I. Title.   II. Series.
HC108.P7K64   1989
305.5′62′0974886 — dc19   88–23627
                                                                                            CIP

For
Nic,
Kinnie,
and
Peter

Contents

Tables
and
Figures

Tables

xi

Figures

Preface

Over this manuscript's long gestation period, I have accumulated many debts that it is a pleasure to acknowledge. My overall approach to the subject of class and gender relations has been shaped by the tutelage of Samuel P. Hays and David Montgomery. Their concern about the distribution of power and control in the city and in the workplace pointed my research in the direction it has taken. They encouraged these investigations into the lives of working-class women, the family, the city, and the industrial economy when I was a graduate student and have continued to do so.

Many other scholars have made valuable suggestions and comments upon successive drafts of this manuscript. The late Herbert Gutman, and Tamara Hareven, Joan Scott, John Modell, and Daniel Scott Smith commented upon papers presented at conferences. Milton Cantor, Glen Elder, Jr., Bruce Laurie, Donald Hastings, Claudia Goldin, Richard Jensen, Maris Vinovskis, Peter Williams, Alice Kessler-Harris, Dudley Baines, Nigel Walford, Anne Hockey, Sara Arber, Joan Jensen, Paul Johnson, August Giebelhaus, Howell Harris, and Janet Hunter read all or parts of this work in progress, making much appreciated suggestions. Gerda Lerner's and Joan Scott's encouragement and recommendations have sustained me during the process of turning a dissertation into a book. Daniel Walkowitz made incisive comments upon the penultimate version of this work. Maurine Greenwald's continued interest in the project and penetrating observations have been invaluable. Colleagues at both the University of Tennessee and the London School of Economics helped to refine and shape the ideas presented in these pages. I have been especially fortunate to benefit from the suggestions of the historical community on both sides of the Atlantic and am immensely grateful to all those who made themselves part of this project through giving their time and ideas.

Historians rely heavily upon libraries for access to their raw materials. The staff of the Pennsylvania Division of the Carnegie Library of Pittsburgh, Frank Zabrosky of the University of Pittsburgh's Archives of Industrial Society, and John Pinfold of the British Library of Political and Economic Science have been immeasurably resourceful in a project that has frequently been conducted long-distance. The computer centers of the University of California, San Diego, and Miami University of Ohio, provided assistance in the initial stages of data processing. The Sociology Department of the University of Surrey, where I enjoyed three years as an honorary visiting research fellow, supplied a stimulating setting as well as access to their mainframe.

The Western Pennsylvania Humane Society, the Pittsburgh Association for the Improvement of the Poor, and the Allegheny, St. Mary's, and South Side cemeteries permitted me to scour their records for useful material and kindly provided me with places to work. Various Pittsburgh and Allegheny County agencies, particularly the Division of Biostatistics and the Marriage License Bureau, allowed me to make time- and space-consuming investigations into their holdings. I am grateful to the staffs of these busy institutions for accommodating me as I worked through their materials.

This work has enjoyed the cooperation, moral support, and editorial suggestions of Jenny Law, Tess Truman, Rosemary Hudson, Helen Denore, and Linda Sampson, who converted mangled, handwritten drafts into neatly typed text. Tracie Dyer, Samantha Lambley, Suzanne Clift, Janet Blythman, and Cathy Monger provided loving care for Kinnie and Peter Kleinberg Flemming at various times, freeing both their parents to work.

Nicholas C. Flemming has sustained this project from its beginnings as a dissertation to its completion as a book. His incisive editorial eye and scientific precision tightened my prose and focused my arguments. In many ways this work is a product of our time together. It has certainly taken up much of our time and has benefited enormously from Nic's faith in it and his willingness to read draft after draft. Kinnie and Peter Kleinberg Flemming have contributed immeasurably, if intangibly, to this book. Their presence helped sensitize me to the intricacies of family relationships and the family economy. It is thus to my own family, to Nic, Kinnie, and Peter, that I dedicate this book about families in Pittsburgh.

Introduction

Writing in 1909, the director of the Pittsburgh Survey described Pittsburgh as "not primarily a woman's town."[1] Yet without the labor of women, Pittsburgh could not have existed as the leading iron and steel producer in the United States. To be sure, female employment levels were lower in the Steel City than in all other U.S. cities, other centers of heavy industry excepted.[2] No women poured molten metal, but they were as necessary to industry as if they guided the flashing iron bars through the great rolls. Women's place in Pittsburgh's main industries was completely peripheral but absolutely vital. Peripheral because, with a few exceptions, they did not hold industrial jobs, and vital because they undertook all the daily work in the home, which enabled men to toil intolerably long hours in the mills. Although economists ignored this work, it underpinned this extreme form of the industrial economy and made it possible to wring every last drop of effort from the millhands.[3]

The separation of home and workplace and a longer working day and working week accompanied industrialization. The family reacted to these dislocations by concentrating domestic responsibilities upon women, freeing men to focus their efforts upon income earning. In Pittsburgh the switch to steel from iron exacerbated this situation in the 1880s as the twelve-hour day replaced the ten-hour one and working every other Sunday became the norm. In such circumstances women's domestic labors were crucial to family survival. Millworkers could not have endured the grueling work routines demanded of them unless someone cared for all their personal requirements. As either wives or lodging house keepers, women cooked, cleaned, and made homes for the iron- and steelworkers at a time when all those tasks were vastly time-consuming. It was almost inconceivable that a man would be able to work a twelve-hour day and provide his own domestic services or spend much time looking after his children. Thus it can be said that the economy that emerged in Pittsburgh at this time depended as much upon women's labor in the home and total responsibility for looking after the family as upon men's work outside it. This was not, of course, unique to Pittsburgh, but the physically debilitating and dangerous nature of men's work and the lack of nonhousehold employments for women represented an extreme version of the male-as-breadwinner, female-as-domestic-manager dichotomy.[4] It also contributed to a separate and seemingly unequal division of power within the family.[5]

This study examines the development of Pittsburgh, in 1900 the nation's eleventh largest city, and its primary enterprises. It details the consequences of the industrial transformation and rapid urban growth for laboring families' daily lives and life chances. It provides an opportunity to see how gender constraints influenced the inhabitants of heavy industry cities and towns and, conversely, how the industrial structure influenced gender roles. It examines women's response to the urban industrial setting itself, as they attempted to make their homes into comfortable and safe places for their husbands and children. It looks at the family economy, efforts to reform the city, its industry, and family relationships, while at the same time tracing the working-class response to the grand forces affecting the lives of workers and their families.[6]

The issues raised here concern the ways in which industrialization and urbanization changed family life and gender roles. To what extent was the individual affected by the grand forces of the age? What did urbanization, industrialization, migration, and immigration really mean to the people who lived through these processes?[7] These forces were the backdrop to the everyday dramas of proletarian existence. Everywhere one looks in Pittsburgh, the mills forged daily life as well as molten metal. The developments in the economy, the shift from iron to steel production, and the coming of the white-collar era altered the employment prospects of the men in the mills, their sons, and their daughters. The mills shaped male and female employment patterns, mobility into and within the city, and the home environment. As in other rapidly expanding urban areas, the need for services, particularly sanitation, outstripped the available expertise and political willingness to provide them. The consequences for health were grave indeed.[8] The expansion of steel production lured tens of thousands of people into the city, turning it into a whirling vortex of humanity, frequently ill-housed and poorly served by outmoded physical structures. Rapid population turnover severely stressed the sanitary services and cultural homogeneity of the city, provoking responses from reformers and workers alike. Newcomers suffered great hardship in this period of extreme exploitation, but they also searched for their own solutions to the problems of urban, industrial life. As steel replaced iron as the linchpin of Pittsburgh's economy, longer working days, devaluation of skills, and higher occupational mortality rates affected all phases of the working-class life cycle: the interaction between parents and their children, the life chances of the very young, their education, employment prospects, marital relationships, and the lives of the elderly.[9]

The years between 1870 and 1907 witnessed the shaping of urban industrial life before regulation and reform blunted the rougher edges.[10] This era is vitally important to historians seeking to understand the interaction between industrialization, urbanization, and gender roles since it shows the extent to which previous understandings about gender structured working people's response to new economic modes and residential environments. They are particularly crucial ones in Pittsburgh's history. The city grew rapidly in these years, and the economy began its transition from skill-based to capital-intensive. Massive immigration from Southern and Eastern Europe changed the demographic composition, and the flow of blacks into the city also began in these years.[11] The population thus diversified as the industrial pace quickened.

Epitomizing reformers' concern over the problems of urban industrial society, several Progressive investigations focused on Pittsburgh. Lincoln Steffens condemned its politics as corrupt in *The Shame of the Cities*, first published as a series of articles in the muckraking *McClure's*

Magazine in 1902.[12] In 1907–1908 a group of concerned Progressive reformers clustered around *Charities and the Commons* magazine launched a study of the working and living conditions in the Pittsburgh district, by which they meant the city itself, Allegheny City, and neighboring steel mill towns including Homestead. This classic study, the Pittsburgh Survey, shows the concerns of that important group of reformers, while it documents and analyzes life, work, and politics in Pittsburgh at the height of its industrial might. The results of the Pittsburgh Survey were published in six volumes devoted to the steel mills, workplace accidents, industrial households, women's employments, wage earners, and the politics and infrastructure of the area.[13] The Survey chose Pittsburgh because it was the "capital of a district representative of untrammeled industrial development." It was not merely a scapegoat city for all the illnesses of that development but also an area that was "rampantly American" and representative of the problems and potentials of urban industrial society.[14] The social workers, academics, and reformers who comprised the Survey team believed it was possible both to measure the social effects of industrialization and to suggest remedies for the ills they believed characterized that society.[15]

Subsequently, Pittsburgh has been the subject of several biographies and specialized studies, as befits its status as a major industrial city.[16] A recent group of books have focused on various aspects of working-class life in the late nineteenth and twentieth centuries. One examined the experiences of groups of migrants to the city after 1900, contrasting the employment, housing, and mobility patterns that developed as blacks, Poles, and Italians adapted to urban life. Another compared working-class standards of living in Pittsburgh with those of workers in heavy industry settings in Britain. A third explored the artisan culture that grew up around the city's iron mills and was submerged by the industrial shifts accompanying the switch from iron to steel manufacturing.[17] These works either look at the industrial and family economies in the twentieth century, after they had reached their mature form, or neglect women's work at home and in the labor force by emphasizing the culture of skilled workers and industrial employment. Most of Pittsburgh's wage workers were unskilled, and most women performed non-wage labor inside the home after marriage.

The issues of gender, industrialization, and the family economy are intertwined in Pittsburgh in two ways. It has been suggested that women's employment outside the home before and after marriage, especially in large units with other women, determines the degree of equality in family relations and extends women's interests beyond the house and family.[18] In addition, the type of paid wage labor prevalent in a heavy industry setting rested upon certain social and economic assumptions, namely that women would devote themselves exclusively to domestic services for their families while men and older children provided a cash income.[19] Girls and women were expected to serve their families, even if this meant the eldest daughter stayed home from school to watch her younger siblings while her mother did the family wash and baked.[20] Many impoverished new residents carried their assumptions about housework to the new country with them. New World emphasis on the importance of education notwithstanding, they assumed that the daughter's schooling took a back seat to the overall needs of the family. She might be enrolled, but she was kept home on the days when her mother needed an extra pair of hands.

Social engineers responded in these decades to the problems highlighted by the Pittsburgh Survey, condemning the family economy that sacrificed the individual for the group. New methods replaced older, less formal approaches to problem solving, engendering more interference into family relations. This reflected the willingness of many reformers to impose their values and perspectives on the less comfortably circumstanced and those from alien cultures. Such ventures directly affected the women and children of the city, who were more likely to become dependent through the premature death of the breadwinner, nonsupport, and the inability to find steady work in Pittsburgh's narrow economy. The institution of new forms of charity and social services has been amply documented on the national level.[21] These new services impinged upon the family, trying to transmit the values of the dominant cultural group. Municipally funded charity was utterly inadequate in this era; thus self-help efforts of newcomers existed along with new charities and welfare agencies.

Pittsburgh also illustrates the class-based divergence in women's ability to participate in public affairs, which became more exaggerated as industrialization progressed. Freed from rigid domestic routines by domestic servants and household technology, middle-class women moved into political and social activities outside the home, joining a panoply of clubs, agitating for temperance, civic reform, and suffrage. The arduous nature of proletarian women's domestic tasks meant they remained primarily engaged in the service of their families inside the home.[22] This was particularly the case for the wives of unskilled workers, who lived in the most crowded and least sanitary dwellings. Their men's long working hours, the dirt of the city, and the struggle to make ends meet complicated their housekeeping chores.[23] Because their husbands and boarders worked varying shifts in the mills and they were expected to service their needs, these women had little time to venture outside the home.

As married women and, to a lesser extent, children were excluded from production, they became men's economic dependents. State-mandated school attendance and protective labor legislation, for which Progressive reformers struggled, reinforced this tendency.[24] In Pittsburgh older working-class children joined the labor force in growing numbers throughout this era, but married women remained outside it. Secular changes in the structure of work, middle-class ideologies of domesticity and childhood, and intensified assumptions that men should receive wages sufficient to support their families reinforced married women's exclusion from the economy.[25] In Pittsburgh many women tacitly accepted the domestic and family wage ideologies but still tried to make economic contributions to their families by taking in boarders, bringing money into the household without going outside it.[26] These economic endeavors capitalized on women's domestic abilities but buttressed the separation of spheres of the sexes by, in effect, restricting women to the home.

This book focuses on the private side of industrialization, on how the mills structured the everyday existence of the women, men, and children who lived in their shadows. The women appear in few historical records. They did not participate in politics; they were too busy making ends meet and meeting their families' needs to join in the club activities of their more affluent sisters. Their lives were, nevertheless, indicative of their times and as affected by Pittsburgh's mighty industries as those of their husbands. In order to understand them, one must look first at men's work, for the family was organized around it and could be destroyed by it, and the children's life chances were powerfully affected by it. Only then is it possible to explore the environment in which the working class lived, their health, and well-being. Families existed in this urban industrial environment, making choices about their children's education and employment within it. They got on with the daily relations between husband and wife while the mills roared around them. Their lives, as they aged, were powerfuly affected by the role allocated to them as workers, in the mills and at home.

The organization of the data would have made sense to the people of Pittsburgh—work comes first. Most people migrated to Pittsburgh in search of employment or to join kin who had found jobs there. The population ebbed and flowed in response to business cycles. Once one has examined men's lives at work, the development of the physical world of the working class, and their homes and health, it is then possible to turn to family life: to children's prospects as shaped by class and gender, to gender roles themselves, and to family members' progression through the life course.[27] The proletariat, reformers, and government all perceived industrialization and densely crowded living conditions as engendering problems for the citizens of the Steel City. Although death logically forms the final chapter in the examination of the life course, it is not the last chapter of this book, since one needs to consider the reaction of the family and the community to the problems brought not only by death but also by the adversities of life in the steel mill milieu.

The working class was not passive in response either to death or to the problems of urban life, despite the overwhelming forces at work. They united into trade unions to concentrate their efforts against those of their employers. More significantly for unskilled workers and their families and the new immigrants pouring into Pittsburgh at the turn of the century, they formed religious, social, benevolent and self-help organizations to provide solidarity, aid, and assistance.[28] The working class turned first to members of their own community both to celebrate the good times and to assuage disaster. When informal familial and neighborly resources proved insufficient, they relied upon their own class and ethnic organizations. Outside agencies, middle-class charities, and city services were the last resort for Pittsburgh's less affluent citizens. Reformers tried to rationalize family relationships, to manipulate them like so much molten metal to be poured into new castings, seeking the same efficiency in charity and welfare as Andrew Carnegie sought in his mills. But the women and men of the industrial districts sought their own solutions to the challenges of life in the industrial city as they molded their family relationships around emerging work patterns and opportunities.

The term *working class*, as used here, denotes all manual workers, regardless of skill level or affluence. The differences between the classes were real, though not entirely financial.[29] A member of the labor aristocracy might earn more than a clerk, but he was subject to much the same working conditions as a laborer. He might die in an industrial accident; he endured the same intolerably long hours and came home as tired. Nevertheless, significant discrepancies existed between skilled and unskilled workers' place in the labor force and their families' prospects. Wherever the data permit, I draw distinctions within the working class, notably in standards of living, role of children in the family economy, and infant mortality. I also refer to widows as a class. Although a few were comfortably situated, most were not. The lack of an adult male breadwinner seriously impaired children's life chances in a city that provided few employment opportunities for women. Not all widows were elderly, but the two groups are treated together because they shared certain characteristics, most notably a high degree of economic marginality and dependency. Because they are less central to this study, I frequently lump the middle and upper classes together. Where they are differentiated, *upper class* refers to professionals and the owners and upper-echelon managers of the means of production, large stores, and banks. *Middle class* refers to petty proprietors and entrepreneurs, lower- and middle-level white-collar workers.[30]

This investigation largely ends in 1907, the year of both the Pittsburgh Survey and the amalgamation of Allegheny City into Pittsburgh. Later data for Pittsburgh, for example in the printed tables of the United States Census from 1910 onward, also included Allegheny City's rather broader economic base. I draw material from the Survey itself, as it describes the culmination of three decades of economic and social upheaval, occasionally moving beyond the geographical boundaries of the Steel City when such information illuminates the lives of iron- and steel-making families. The most notable instance of this is Margaret Byington's investigation for the Survey of Homestead, a small mill town immediately east of Pittsburgh.[31] Homestead was Pittsburgh distilled into its purest form, wholly dependent upon the steel mills for sustenance, a small industrial community with no counterbalance to the might of the Carnegie Steel empire. Byington analyzed the daily lives of millworkers' families, with particular attention to the penetration of the mill into family life and the discrepancies in standard of living between Slavic and English-speaking millworkers. Although outside Pittsburgh's political boundaries, Homestead was a microcosm of the Pittsburgh experience.[32]

My concern in this work is to root the development of family economy into a particular urban industrial setting and to examine how urbanization and industrialization each shaped the lives and living conditions, work, and family and gender relationships of Pittsburgh's working class. The Survey provided a snapshot of Pittsburgh, whereas this study explores the development of class and gender relations as the nature of male and female employments changed and formal institutions emerged to cope with worsening urban conditions. Pittsburgh epitomized heavy industrial settings in the United States with their limited employment opportunities for women and brutal working conditions for men. Its families struggled to make a world for themselves where each member's contribution was vital, but strictly limited by gender.

The
Shadow
of the
Mills

Bessemer Converter at Andrew Carnegie's Pittsburgh Steel Works, 1886, by Charles Graham for *Harper's Weekly*

Iron and Steel in Pittsburgh's Economy

The Nature of Industry

Visitors to nineteenth-century Pittsburgh agreed that it looked like "hell with the lid off," its skies colored by the fire and dust spewing forth from the teeming iron and steel mills.[1] The mills dominated the city and the lives of its inhabitants, reaching into the very households of the working class to structure their daily lives, relations within families, and the life cycles of both males and females. The organization of work and power in the iron and steel industries affected almost every aspect of working-class family life: relations between husbands and wives, the role of women in the family, attitudes toward education, marriage, and widowhood, and the nature and extent of family mobility. The mills molded time and space, family life and leisure. The city's wealth originated with its industrial might, but in Pittsburgh, as in other mill towns, the "outpourings of smoke and soot suggested the ruthlessness with which great industry consumes the city's working people," and the wealth produced by the mills was distributed most unequally between millworker and magnate.[2] This chapter explores the dynamics of the iron and steel industries and the consequences of industrial employment, particularly the high accident rates that characterized the steel industry in this era.

The mill penetrated the household in each phase of the industrial economy as it developed in Pittsburgh between 1870 and 1907. Frequent unemployment engendered insecurity and diminished standards of living.

3

Rotating shifts disrupted household routines. The lengthening of the working day left men exhausted. Sex-segregated occupational patterns curtailed women's employment outside the home even if they wanted or needed to work. Industrial accidents impoverished working-class families, leaving them dependent upon their respective ethnic communities and external agencies for assistance. At the same time, technological innovations and the shift from iron to steel production devalued the position of many skilled workers, which contributed to the demise of the Amalgamated Association of Iron and Steel Workers (AAISW) in Pittsburgh and increased economic uncertainty for millworkers' families.[3]

The iron industry itself grew gradually in Pittsburgh through mid-century, the first local attempts to manufacture iron occurring in 1792. By 1813, Pittsburgh had a diverse iron industry with a rolling mill, blister steel furnace, iron foundries, and nail factories. Entrepreneurs constructed three or four mills each decade, so that by 1840 there were nine rolling mills, eighteen foundries, many engine factories, and machine shops. Iron manufacturing in Pittsburgh expanded as railroads spread across the United States and the demand for iron surged. Five new rolling mills appeared in the 1850s and ten in the 1860s, by which time subsidiary light industries such as cotton textile manufacturing had disappeared, although the glass industry persisted.[4] Pittsburgh's mastery of heavy industry in the United States intensified during the second half of the nineteenth century, leading the Pennsylvania Bureau of Industrial Statistics to declare that "in steel, as in iron, Pittsburgh is the preponderating manufacturing community of the United States."[5] In 1900, Pittsburgh ranked fifth among U.S. cities in the amount of capital invested in manufacturing, with more than half its assets located in iron and steel production. It produced one-fourth of the nation's iron and steel in its forty-eight mills and nearly three hundred metalworking establishments.[6]

The nature of Pittsburgh's industries structured the sexual composition of its labor force. In both 1870 and 1900 the iron and steel industries employed more than one-third of the male labor force but almost no women. In fact, the entire labor force in Pittsburgh was predominantly male, unusually so for a large U.S. city. In 1870, 14 percent of Pittsburgh's workers were female; by 1900 this proportion had risen to 18 percent, at a time when women comprised 30 percent of the labor force in other major U.S. cities.[7] The lack of employment opportunities for women in Pittsburgh should be placed in its cultural context, for in other heavy industrial settings women did labor in the metal trades. Thus in Birmingham, England, nearly 20 percent of the women workers toiled in the metal trades compared with less than 1 percent in Pittsburgh. Nearly 25 percent of the metalworkers were female in the English city compared with 1 percent of Pittsburgh's iron- and steelworkers.[8]

The production of iron required a strong, skilled labor force. The first step was to convert iron ore into pig iron in a blast furnace, a huge barrel of masonry and steel plates into which layers of ore, coke, and limestone were loaded from the top, and the resultant molten pig iron tapped from the bottom.[9] Small carts carried the raw materials to the top of the furnace, where laborers known as top fillers dumped the contents into the giant barrel. By 1900 top filling was done automatically in many blast furnaces, eliminating the top fillers' position altogether.[10] After the oxides of iron in the ore reacted with the coke and limestone to form pig iron and slag, men tapped the furnace (let the molten ore out) by drilling partway through the fireclay bung, then hitting it with a metal rod. The pig iron roared out, burning anyone who did not jump quickly, while molders channeled it into forms prepared by pattern makers in the sand in front of the furnace. Manipulating the molten metal was difficult, dangerous work that had to be done with care lest the molds be ruined. Molders and pattern makers needed years of training acquired as helpers or apprentices and were highly skilled workers.[11]

The next stage in iron making was the elimination of carbon impurities from the pig iron. Until the middle of the century, this had been done manually by alternately heating and beating the iron, but three innovations mechanized the procedure. Ironmasters substituted hotter-burning coke for charcoal. Reverberatory furnaces separated the iron from the fire, reducing contamination and permitting the use of the less pure coke. Lastly, iron-bottomed furnaces reduced wastage previously caused by spilling liquid pig iron. The new fuel and machines put an end to manual purification, increased output, and improved the quality of the iron.[12]

Highly skilled puddlers stirred the molten pig iron through a small opening in the furnace until the impurities separated. John Fitch, author of *The Steel Workers*, likened the process to churning butter from cream.[13] James J. Davis, a former puddler who became Warren Harding's secretary of labor, described the puddler's job as similar to a cook's stirring gravy to keep it from scorching. As the iron solidified, the puddler worked it into flaming balls, which he then pulled through the door. The puddler stood exposed to the furnace's full heat and glare, stirring his iron stew with a rabble weighing twenty-five pounds.[14] The work required skill as well as strength; if the balls were removed too soon, they could not be worked and would need reheating, slowing down production. Nor could the procedure be hurried; iron makers never discovered a way to mechanize the puddler's judgment, and puddling remained an impediment to the rapid manufacture of iron until the adoption of the open hearth for making steel in the 1880s displaced wrought iron in Pittsburgh's economy, a transition completed by 1890.[15]

The next stage of the iron-making process squeezed the remaining impurities from the puddled iron balls. The flattened billets were rolled through a series of muck or roughing rolls, rather like old-fashioned clothes wringers, which flattened them. The resulting muck bars went to a furnace where the heater reheated them so they could be welded together in the finishing rolls. Rolling was the most skilled operation in the mill. Rollers served long apprenticeships learning to guide the iron bars through the rolls without jamming them. They also had significant supervisory posts in the mills, being responsible for the machines and production from furnace to finishing.[16]

Despite technological innovations, iron making remained a skilled trade in which key artisan workers, particularly puddlers and rollers, exercised control over critical processes and trained their own successors. During the years between 1870 and 1907, as steel replaced iron as the basic product of the Pittsburgh mills, the balance shifted from significant worker autonomy in the iron mills to owner control of the steel industry.

Increased mechanization meant fewer skilled workers and apprenticeships, a relative loss of differentials between the skilled and unskilled, larger mills, and a speeding up of production. It also meant, in many cases, that new methods outmoded the knowledge of older workers, so that one aspect of control in the workplace, the training of new workers, passed to supervisory personnel. Managers pushed men in the less mechanized departments to keep pace with machines elsewhere in the mill, and new devices replaced workers altogether or divided complex, skilled tasks into easy-to-learn unskilled jobs.[17]

The expansion of the railroad network, which led initially to increased use of iron, resulted in a demand for steel as heavier, high-speed trains quickly wore out wrought iron rails. Railroad magnates experimented with steel rails imported from Great Britain, but the adoption of the Bessemer process in the United States in 1865 provided a domestic source of relatively inexpensive steel, most of it produced in Pennsylvania, and much of that in Pittsburgh. A decade after the first steel rails had been rolled in the United States, the railroads used more steel than iron in their tracks, and by 1883 the manufacture of iron rails virtually ceased. Total iron and steel production figures reflected shifting demand, so that by 1892 U.S. mills turned out more steel than iron.[18]

The technology of the steel industry made it more highly integrated than the iron industry had been, with production concentrated in a relatively few large firms. Before 1865 the transformation of iron ore into pig iron and then into wrought iron had been accomplished by separate firms, so that the integration present in steel firms can largely be attributed to the Bessemer process itself.[19] In 1876, Pittsburgh had ten steel works, all larger than its thirty-three iron rolling mills. Over time, the size differential between iron and steel mills grew. Whereas the average blast furnace employed 71 hands in 1869 and 176 in 1899, the typical steel mill employed 119 men in 1869 and 412 in 1899, with the large integrated firms employing many more hands than the smaller individual ones.[20] The extreme integration of the larger works, such as Andrew Carnegie's, contributed to the callous attitude prevalent in the steel industry that workers were merely another factor in the cost of production, to be bought as cheaply as possible. Steel manufacturers did not regard their workers as individuals, only as anonymous providers of the commodity known as labor. The success of the U.S. steel industry lay in its ability to reduce labor costs, largely through the substitution of machines for men and the elimination of skilled workers, whom the manufacturers perceived as impediments to production and unionized troublemakers.[21]

Of the long list of technological innovations in the steel industry, a few are particularly illustrative of the general trend toward economy of labor cost and the undermining of the position of skilled workers who might hold up production through strikes or restrictive practices. Engineers and new machines operated by interchangeable unskilled workers replaced many skilled and semiskilled workers as first the Bessemer process, then the open-hearth furnace made it possible to fabricate steel directly from pig iron without the intervening step of wrought iron production. The contrast between the two methods of making steel was elaborated in a 1908 book designed to make steel making intelligible to the lay reader. "Instead of the puddler raking for hours his little puddle of iron into a viscous ball, later to soak for days in the charcoal bath to be recarbonized, Bessemer ran tons of molten iron into a great pear-shaped retort and through holes in the bottom air, under pressure, was blown."[22] This air blast burned carbon impurities from tons of iron in about twenty minutes whereas it took a puddler thirty minutes to purify a hundredweight. The open-hearth furnace, which supplanted the Bessemer converters in the 1880s, was essentially an extremely hot puddling furnace that operated without puddlers. These two innovations rendered puddlers' skills obsolete by the mid-1880s with the result that many puddlers and boilers could not find work in those mills and were forced to take any job, whether skilled or not.[23]

Puddlers and boilers were not the only uprooted workers. The shift from iron to steel nails and the introduction of automatic nail-making machines displaced many nailers and nail feeders. As the production of steel nails rose, so did unemployment and idle mills. The nail trade suffered from a classic "speed up and stretch out" situation as employers forced workers to keep pace with the new machines and to operate more of them. Nailers and nail feeders resorted to wage cutting among themselves to obtain employment, and the nailers' skill became unimportant in the manufacturing process. Overall, the introduction of machinery dislodged skilled workers in the fabrication of many small hardware items including nuts, bolts, chains, and forgings and resulted in the employment of a few women in some of the fabrication processes.[24]

The introduction of natural gas in the iron and steel industry in the 1880s also resulted in unemployment, this time for unskilled workers. In one Carnegie Steel Company boiler house, a single man tending a gas flame replaced ninety firemen shoveling four hundred tons of coal a day.[25] Whether the particular innovation displaced skilled or unskilled workers, the overall trend was clear to workers and industry analysts alike. In 1885 the iron- and steelworkers' union, the AAISW, protested the inroads steel had made upon iron and urged a return to iron nails in order to reemploy displaced puddlers and boilers. A decade later the Pennsylvania Bureau of Industrial Statistics estimated that one man produced as much iron or steel as six or eight had in 1840, before the use of the new fuels and new machines.[26] The overall effect of this shift was to introduce more instability into working-class life as workers and their families moved in search of work.

Another factor contributed to the increased output per hand in the steel mills: the hours of labor actually rose at the end of the century. Most iron- and steelworkers toiled ten hours a day in the 1870s for an average working week of sixty hours. The iron furnaces of the 1870s did not run continuously, and custom fixed daily output at five or six heats (about ten hours) per day, so that puddlers fired their furnaces early in the morning, made their heats, and went home after a long, but not shattering day's work. The lengthening of the work day occurred with the shift to direct steel production. The steel mills could not be shut down easily, for the large furnaces cracked unless kept hot, even if idle. In 1879 this led steel magnates to employ three eight-hour shifts, since "it was entirely out of the question to expect human flesh and blood to labor incessantly for twelve hours." Captain William R. Jones's statement notwithstanding, most Carnegie plants turned to a twelve-hour day in the 1880s as further mechanization somewhat reduced the physical effort required of the workers. Hands then labored eleven hours a day on the day shift (or turn) and thirteen hours on the night turn, or seventy-two to eighty-nine hours a week. The longer working day remained standard through the first decades of the twentieth century until a coalition of church members and reformers successfully pressed for its abolition in 1923.[27]

Steelworkers in the 1890s endured longer working weeks as well as longer working days then had ironworkers earlier in the century. Although a seven-day week had been the norm in 1870, the Amalgamated successfully fought in the mid-1880s to eliminate Sunday work. Following the Homestead Strike in 1892, employers reinstated Sunday work, so that most men labored twelve hours a day, six or seven days a week. The hands alternated day and night shifts biweekly, the switch occurring on Sunday night as men from the day turn stayed on through the night, laboring twenty-four hours without respite. A character in Thomas Bell's novel of life among the steelworkers, *Out Of This Furnace*, said of this shift, "At three o'clock in the morning of a long turn, a man could die without knowing it."[28]

Most workers reacted negatively to the longer working day and the long turn, which left them too exhausted to enjoy their nonworking hours and disrupted their family life. Many wrote to the Bureau of Industrial Statistics to support a return to the eight-hour day. Jim Barr typified the hands in this regard. A skilled worker with a comfortable home, he believed: "I've got as good a home here as a man could want. It's comfortable and I enjoy my family. But I only have these things to think about. I'm at work most of the day, and I'm so tired at night that I just go to bed as soon as I've eaten supper. I have ideas of what a home ought to be, all right, but the way things are now I just eat and sleep here." Home was food, bed, and a family seen in passing for Barr and countless others.[29] They had little time with their children and wives because they spent so much time in the mills. Longer hours of labor burdened wives, whose husbands were too exhausted to do much at home, leaving the women most of the work and responsibility for running the home. This form of industrialization removed men from their families and reinforced gender role distinctions.

Shift and Sunday work complicated family life and made domestic arrangements more difficult. It fell to the wives to keep the children quiet so that men could sleep during the day, to organize their household routines around the men's schedules so that their needs for food and sleep could be met in the crowded homes. With the men gone twelve hours a day and too tired to do more than eat and fall into bed, the mill reached into the household to determine the activities of all its members and deprived women and children of whatever household and child care duties the men might have performed had they not been so tired. The mills thus made their contribution to emerging gender roles in which a man's main contribution to the household was his wages rather than his presence, the passing on of skills to his sons, or participation in the daily events of family life.[30]

The various technological innovations that were responsible for the longer hours of labor also contributed to the decline of the AAISW in the Pittsburgh district, although unstable economic conditions and the desire of the employers to break the unions also played critical roles. The Amalgamated enrolled approximately two-thirds of the eligible skilled workers at its peak, but it excluded the laborers, who comprised a growing proportion of the industry. The union concerned itself chiefly with wages and struck repeatedly to force manufacturers to sign the scale of wages it set. Most strikes lasted a matter of weeks, but some dragged on for months, depleting the union treasury and workers' resources.[31]

Large numbers of nonunion men in many mills limited the effectiveness of the Amalgamated's strikes. When some AAISW members walked out over the number of heats per day in 1878, its *Journal of Proceedings* stated that the unorganized hands manifested no interest in the question but continued to work and thus broke the strike. According to the Bureau of Industrial Statistics, the iron and steel mill strikes had been unsuccessful more often than not in the years preceding the debacle at Homestead in 1892. In that strike skilled and unskilled, union and non-union men banded together but lost in the face of the force exerted by the Carnegie Steel Company's hired Pinkertons.[32] Previously union membership ebbed and flowed with the business cycle. Membership stood at 16,000 in 1882 but fell to 6,000 in 1885, a reflection of unemployment and reverses suffered in strikes during the depression. It peaked at 24,000 in 1892 and plummeted after the Homestead Strike failed, leaving former AAISW members in Pittsburgh with no organization to turn to in hard times and, as I shall show in the last chapter, enhancing their dependence upon private and public welfare agencies.[33]

At the end of the nineteenth century, technological innovations and cost-conscious capitalists converted iron and steel making from a highly skilled, unionized craft into an enormous industrial enterprise with large numbers of unskilled, unorganized laborers. The general skill structure of Pittsburgh's labor force mirrored these industrial transformations (see table 1) as the proportion of unskilled workers rose from 37 percent in 1870 to 41 percent in 1900, while that of skilled workers dropped sharply from 45 percent to 36 percent. During the same interval the proportion of white-collar workers in the labor force climbed from 18 to 23 percent, a reflection of the increased paperwork and professionalization that accompanied urban industrial life at the turn of the century.

Ethnic Composition of the Labor Force

As the city's labor force became more sharply differentiated by status at the end of the nineteenth century, so did the ethnic composition of the population. Southern and Eastern European immigrants poured into the United States at this time; many of them sought employment in the mills and mines of the Keystone State, in the anthracite region of Eastern Pennsylvania and the bituminous fields at the western end of the state. The expanding steel mills of Pittsburgh, Homestead, and numerous towns up and down the Monongahela and Allegheny rivers attracted a new work force searching for greater economic rewards than their home fields could offer. For many, money compensated for the dreary brownish-red pall hanging over the mills and the fire shooting from the furnaces that disturbed the night sky and blotted out the stars. The new immigrants took their places at the bottom of the economic hierarchy. Relatives and former neighbors from the old country used their toeholds in the mills and construction gangs to get work for their landsmen.[34]

By the beginning of the new century, the older ethnic groups had largely been assimilated. Though native-born white men continued to occupy most of the white-collar positions, both the British and the Irish had moved into clerical and professional employments and away from

Table 1. Occupational Level of Male Workers
(In Percentages)

	Unskilled[a]	Skilled[b]	White-collar[c]	N
1870	37	45	18	25,606
1900	41	36	23	107,902

Sources: U.S. Census, Ninth Census, 1870, vol. 1 Population, pt. 1, p. 795; U.S. Census, Twelfth Census, 1900, vol. 2, Population, pt. 2, pp. 582–85.
a. Unskilled includes laborers, gardeners, domestic servants, launderers, soldiers, operatives, and other unskilled workers. Where unskilled and white collar were grouped together in the 1870 census, as in hotel and restaurant owners and employees, the categories were separated using the proportions given in the 1900 census as guidelines.
b. Skilled includes craft occupations specified in the "Manufacturing" category of the census but omits occupations requiring little or no training. The largest category, iron- and steelworkers, was included as skilled since "in manufacturing districts unskilled workmen are often reported simply as 'laborers' " rather than as, say, iron- or steelworkers.
c. It was assumed that in the domestic and personal service and manufacturing categories, the unitemized workers were unskilled and skilled workers, respectively. White-collar workers were taken as the residual labor force after the unskilled and skilled positions were itemized.

unskilled labor (see table 2). The newest migrants into Pittsburgh, blacks and Southern and Eastern Europeans, were concentrated in laboring positions with little white-collar or professional employment among them. German immigrants also moved into white-collar work, but not proportionately to their numbers in the populations, which may be partially explained by the census practice of designating some Slavic immigrants, notably those from "German Poland," as Germans rather than Poles. As a result those people listed as German in the census show a bifurcated pattern with, presumably, the older German-speaking immigrants moving into the nonmanual positions and the newer, Polish-speaking ones taking jobs in the steel mills.[35]

As Pittsburgh's major employers, the mills reflected the city's diverse population, though not completely, for some migrant groups opted out of the mills while others were not permitted into them. At the beginning of this period, 1870, the mills and laboring population of the city (since unskilled millworkers were usually designated as laborers in

Table 2. Ethnic Composition of the Male Labor Force
(In Percentages)

	Laborers		Iron & Steel		Clerks		Professional		Total Labor Force	
	1870	1900	1870	1900	1870	1900	1870	1900	1870	1900
N	5,533	23,430	2,542	9,646	1,547	5,824	793	4,429	25,772	107,902
Native-born white	23	11	50	16	83	52	74	54	51	26
British	5	6	20	13	2	10	5	10	7	9
Irish	49	22	21	21	7	18	9	12	23	18
German	20	17	8	22	7	15	8	14	16	21
Black	NA[a]	12	NA	4	NA	1	NA	2	NA	7
S. & E. European	—	30	—	20	—	2	—	4	—	15
Other[b]	3	2	1	4	1	2	4	4	3	4
Total	100	100	100	100	100	100	100	100	100	100

Sources: U.S. Census, Ninth Census, 1870, vol. 1, *Population*, pt. 1, p. 795; U.S. Census, Twelfth Census, 1900, vol. 2, *Population*, pt. 2, pp. 582–85.

a. Not available, as the 1870 Census did not separated native blacks and whites.
b. Northern European, Canadian, and unknown.

the census, rather than by industry) reflected the older immigration pattern. In that year, nearly one-half Pittsburgh's laborers had been born in Ireland, the rest came equally from Germany and the United States, and a few came from Great Britain and other Northern European nations. The iron- and steelworkers listed in the census were mainly semiskilled and skilled workmen; one-half were U.S. born, Great Britain and Ireland each contributed one-fifth, and the rest were of German or Northern European origin. As a group they probably would have agreed with the poem published in the *Irish Pennsylvanian,* "The Dignity of Labor," that their trade gave them status as well as a living, for even the unskilled among them could aspire to advance within the mill.

> The master of a trade may proudly sing:
> "I am a power on earth, and may earn
> the right to call myself a man. I turn
> The wheel of progress, and I feel a king
> Among the useless drones. The shame and sting
> of charity I know not for I learn
> to use my gifts. The highest plane I yearn
> To reach, to merit all that life may bring."[36]

The steel industry into which the new immigrants moved at the turn of the century differed greatly from the iron and steel industry prior to 1870. It had no place for skills acquired through long years of assisting older workers. By the time of the Pittsburgh Survey in 1907, nearly three-quarters of the hands working in the steel industry were unskilled or semiskilled. The decline in status coincided with a shift in ethnic composition of the mill labor force. The proportion of native-born whites in the mills decreased dramatically; it was one-third what it had been in 1870, and the proportion of native-born whites and Irish doing laboring jobs dropped by half. Although the Irish continued to hold skilled and supervisory jobs in the mills, these were increasingly as foremen rather than as the puddlers, heaters, and rollers of the earlier period. John Fitch, who visited every mill in the Pittsburgh district for the Survey, wrote that it was surprising to see a (white) American, German, or Irishman among the unskilled millworkers. He also said that he knew of no Slavic men working as rollers or heaters; in other words, none held skilled positions in the steel works.[37]

Polish immigrants to Pittsburgh at the turn of the century moved into the mills in large numbers, assisted by relatives and fellow countrymen to find work in the labor gangs. They toiled with their kin and friends within the steel works, serving what amounted to an ethnic apprenticeship that helped acculturate them into the industrial world. Bodnar, Simon, and Weber's study of Italians, Poles, and blacks in twentieth-century Pittsburgh demonstrates the way in which the lack of opportunity for advancement within the mills impeded Polish upward mobility. They found that as many as "two-thirds of Pittsburgh's Poles" became mill-hands and thus had little chance to move up the hierarchy. In 1905, Polish and Italian men experienced roughly the same lack of mobility, 76 percent of the Poles and 78 percent of the Italians holding the same level of job as they had in 1900. But by 1910 the Italians, who eschewed the mills in favor of construction jobs and petty entrepreneurship, began to pull ahead; only 62 percent had the same level of job as in 1900, compared with 71 percent of the Poles.[38]

Though some of those Poles who stayed on in the mills eventually achieved upward mobility through longevity in the workplace, mill owners at the turn of the century assumed that ethnic segregation in the mills was "quite natural." One steel company official justified this opinion by saying that the skilled men were the ones from whose ranks foremen were chosen, that they needed to know English and be literate, which many of the new immigrants were not. In 1899 more than one-fifth the immigrants to the United States were illiterate and the proportion was much higher among Southern and Eastern Europeans. The mill official believed that this group had no "stake in the country" and did not expect to remain in the United States. He predicted that those who did stay and sent their children to the public schools would "in the second and third generation, be absorbed into the general mass of 'Americans' whose progress in the steel industry or any other will depend solely on individual fitness and adaptability." Though this prediction was not wholly accurate, either as to the assimilative power of education or as to the disappearance of ethnic prejudice, it also ignored the changing structure of employment within the iron and steel industry, which constricted opportunity altogether at the skilled level.[39]

Recent immigrants found it to their advantage in obtaining employment to look as "American" as possible. As soon as one got to Pittsburgh, his relatives spent $15 to buy him American style clothes. According to John Kaczyski, a retired millworker, straw bosses handpicked the crews each morning from men lined up outside the mill gate and often turned away more than they hired for the day. In this man's recollection, those who worked regularly were the ones who slipped the straw boss a dollar on payday. But even the Slavs' position at the bottom of the mill hierarchy could be insecure. During the depressed years of 1907 and 1908, foremen and superintendents gave out-of-work English-speaking skilled workers the unskilled jobs previously held by Southern and Eastern Europeans, displacing the new hands until, with better times, the skilled men went back to their higher-paying, higher-status employment.[40]

The mills may have been open to the new immigrants depending upon the business cycle, but blacks migrating to Pittsburgh at this time found them less hospitable. In the 1880s a few black men managed to cross the color line into the mills but were never able to consolidate their position. By 1900, when blacks comprised 7 percent of the labor force and 12 percent of the laborers, they were less than 4 percent of the iron- and steelworkers. Most black steelworkers migrated to Pittsburgh in search of work, getting into the mills by dint of their own efforts, rather than through the assistance of friends or relatives. A large number of them worked at just one plant, the Clark Mills. Blacks comprised a greater percentage of the labor force in the Pittsburgh mills than they did in some of the surrounding towns. In Homestead, where only 2 percent of the millworkers in 1907 were black, some managed to move up the mill hierarchy. Of Homestead's labor force, 2 percent were black, but 17 percent of those had skilled jobs. By contrast, only 2 percent of the Slavic hands at the Homestead works in 1907 had skilled jobs, though 35 percent of the English-speaking Europeans and 40 percent of the native-born whites had advanced up the skill ladder. The experience of blacks in Homestead paralleled that of Pittsburgh blacks, with some of the men who had been at the Clark Mills for a number of years managing to work their way up from the ranks of the unskilled. Three actually became rollers, the most skilled and highly paid job in the mills.[41] These limited successes notwithstanding, blacks remained a tiny fraction of the mill labor force. One man, who arrived in 1906, summed up the situation nineteen years later by saying that "all the best jobs were for the white men. Plenty of hard work here but there is no chance to get anywhere. Colored men work at the same jobs from year to year while white men and foreigners are promoted in 2 or 3 months after coming here."[42]

Blacks encountered hostility from white foremen, who did much of the hiring in the mills, from their co-workers, and from the unions. Although tradition had it that blacks entered the mills first as strikebreakers, as they did at the Clark Mills in 1883, some belonged to unions.[43] The black hands at the Black Diamond Mill, who may have gotten their jobs there originally in the wake of a strike in 1878, organized themselves as Garfield Lodge No. 92, Colored, of the AAISW in 1882. They stood fast with the union in refusing to "learn green hands," or train inexperienced, nonunion men. As a result, two Garfield Lodge members were fired and had trouble finding work in other mills, which demonstrates both their solidarity and the precarious nature of their situation within the steel industry. Their presence within the union and the mill itself was by no means universally accepted. The union from which the Amalgamated was formed, the Sons of Vulcan, limited membership to whites only. In 1885, however, the annual meeting of the AAISW rejected a proposal that "no colored person of any trade or occupation be eligible to hold membership." Some delegates termed the attempt to insert the words *white male persons* into the constitution absurd and ridiculous. Still, J. H. Carter and other black union members complained of ill-treatment from white co-unionists in various mills in the Pittsburgh district. By the beginning of the new century, black steelworkers believed that white union members would not protect them in controversies with the mill owners, nor were whites willing to admit them to the union on an equal basis. So despite some occupational mobility within the mills, blacks never became a significant proportion of the mill work force, for racial prejudice led foremen to rely upon informal communication among the Slavic immigrants to provide the fluctuating supply of inexpensive labor they required.[44]

Wages, Working Conditions, and Unemployment

The old immigrant groups, concentrated as they were in the skilled positions in the mills, enjoyed a considerably higher standard of living than the new immigrants or most blacks in the mills. Great disparities existed between the wages of the most and least skilled workers in the iron and steel industry of the 1870s, those of the labor aristocracy averaging many times those of common laborers. Rollers, the most highly skilled workers, had the fattest pay packets, which made them, according to Jesse Robinson, an early historian of the Amalgamated, "the highest-priced workmen, naturally the object of envy of other workmen." With steady employment, assuming thirty weeks of work in depression years and fifty weeks during good times, rollers might earn as much as $1,200 to $2,000 per year; puddlers and other skilled workers averaged between $600 and $1,000 and semiskilled hands between $400 and $750, but laborers made as little as $300 to $550 per year. To relate this to other occupations, the aristocracy of labor earned more than lower-echelon white-collar workers, skilled workers about the same, and the semiskilled and unskilled considerably less.[45] Skilled workers could afford to send their children to high school, to buy homes, and to purchase some of the new labor-saving devices for their wives. Unskilled workers depended upon the labor of their children and the boarders their wives took in to make ends meet.

By the end of this era, mill owners narrowed the differential between the wages of the skilled and unskilled as technological innovations and the defeat of the Amalgamated during the Homestead Strike undermined the position of the skilled workers. Although overall wage rates remained fairly stable in the years between 1880 and 1907, manufacturers cut the amounts paid to rollers and heaters while actually increasing the remuneration of laborers from $0.14 to $0.15 or $0.16 an hour. As the new machines increased output, employers lowered the tonnage rates paid to skilled men, effectively reducing their income despite rising productivity and profits. The beginnings of this tendency can be seen in an action taken to reduce the wages of heaters in the mid-1880s following the switch from coal to gas at the soft rolls. Management lowered the wages of heaters belonging to the Soho Lodge of the A AISW from $2.25 to $2.00 per day, claiming that the new fuel meant less effort was required to heat the steel; therefore the heaters should be paid less.[46] Following the Homestead Strike, other mills in the Pittsburgh district ousted the union and hence cut the wages paid to the skilled, unionized workers. Since green hands could be trained to operate the new machinery, management could, and did, dispense with many skilled workers whom they regarded as a "tax on improvements."[47] Thus the discrepancy between the wages of the skilled and unskilled, which typified the early years of steel, declined somewhat as technological innovations in the industry outmoded the very skills that made rollers and puddlers into the aristocracy of labor.

As the range of earnings between prosperous and depressed years suggests, unemployment was a major factor in determining the income of Pittsburgh's working class. Idleness in the iron and steel industry had a number of components. Manufacturers responded to the business cycle, but they also used unemployment to control unruly workers. Thus Henry Clay Frick gave orders to "stop Works if necessary" to prevent the formation of a new union lodge at Homestead in 1899. The integration of the steel industry with many mills under one management, as typified by Andrew Carnegie's holdings and later by United States Steel, meant that production could be shifted from one plant to another in order to control worker unrest through short time or shutting down a particular mill. Conversely, nonunion mills might have steadier employment. Thus Margaret Byington found that after the defeat of the union at Homestead, the mill ran steadily from 1893 until 1907, when an industrial depression brought short time.[48] Since the vast furnaces could not be run efficiently at half speed, employers preferred to run at maximum production levels, then close down entirely when enough steel had been produced to meet their orders. This approach pertained in good times as well as bad, so that overall prosperity of the economy did not necessarily determine the amount of work an individual would get or the wages he would be able to turn over to his family.[49]

In 1880, as Pittsburgh recovered from the depression of the preceding decade, 30 percent of all working-class men suffered some unemployment and 15 percent were jobless for more than four months. The proportion unemployed for more than one month of the year climbed slightly higher during the rest of the century, being 34 percent in 1890 and 32 percent in 1900. Iron- and steelworkers endured more slack time than some construction workers, a group famous for their seasonal booms and slumps, but less than glassworkers, whose factories shut down for two to six weeks each summer when it became too hot to blow glass. Approximately 23 percent of the carpenters, 39 percent of the iron- and steelworkers, and 65 percent of the glassworkers endured a month or more of enforced idleness in 1890 (see table 3). But whereas the glassworkers expected to have an annual unpaid summer holiday and the carpenters anticipated slack time in the winter, unemployment in the iron and steel industry occurred randomly and unevenly. It was not uncommon for one mill to close although its neighbor ran around the clock, or for a company to concentrate production in one works and temporarily shut down its others. The net effect was to exacerbate insecurity and make financial planning difficult for all working-class families, but especially those of iron- and steelworkers. Laborers' families were hit hardest of all, their low incomes severely stressed by unstable employment.

Table 3. Male Unemployment, 1890

Occupation	Number	Number Unemployed	% Unemployed
Clergy	257	5	1.9
Physicians	344	3	0.9
Bankers	432	15	3.5
Agents	999	41	4.1
Merchants	3,573	157	4.4
Carpenters	2,466	471	23.2
Laborers	20,081	5,516	27.5
Iron- & steelworkers	10,019	3,866	38.6
Masons	954	394	41.3
Glassworkers	3,671	2,402	65.4

Source: U.S. Census, Eleventh Census, 1890, vol. 1, Population, pt. 2, pp. 712–13.

The insecurity engendered by frequent employment crises did not extend to members of the middle class. Less than 1 percent of Pittsburgh's physicians and 2 percent of its clergy had been unemployed for any length of time in the year preceding the census. The figure for professional men as a whole was about 1 percent. It was slightly higher among those engaged in trade, about 4 percent. The jobless figure among working-class men hovered around 33 percent, suggesting that some of the affluence enjoyed by the middle classes stemmed from the security of their jobs as well as their higher rates of remuneration. Certainly, at the turn of the century, the professional classes nationally had lower unemployment rates than other groups in the population. Slightly more than 1 percent of all professional men had experienced one or more months out of work in 1890, which compared very favorably with the national average of 28 percent for manufacturing and mechanical workers.[50]

The unemployment pattern in Pittsburgh mirrored that of other heavy industry centers in the United States. In 1890, 23 percent of all Pittsburgh men had been out of work for more than one month, giving the city one of the highest rates of inactivity in the nation. Only three of the fifty-six U.S. cities with more than fifty thousand inhabitants had more men out of work. Troy, N.Y., Lynn, Mass., and Scranton, Pa., with economies dominated by iron and shoe manufacturing and mining, had in excess of 26 percent of the male labor force out of work for more than one month. As in Pittsburgh, where one or two industries held sway over a city's economy, they made the workers more vulnerable to downturns in the business cycle and shifting and seasonal patterns of demand.[51]

Family Responses to Unemployment

Joblessness in most mill communities rather than wage rate variations gave Pittsburgh's working-class families extremely unstable incomes during the last decades of the nineteenth century, as was also the case for iron- and steelworkers' families in Troy and shoe workers' in Lynn. Alan Dawley has written of the shoe workers at midcentury that "the wages of unemployment were debt and destitution. Going into debt during the winter layover was a normal experience for shoemakers, but every year since the Panic of 1857 getting out of debt in the spring had been unusually difficult."[52] If the shoe workers in Lynn, like the glassworkers in Pittsburgh, knew when their idle times would come, the iron- and steelworkers did not. Contemporary analysts described the irregular income of working-class families as one of their major economic dilemmas. The holder of the family purse strings never knew if the same amount "however high or low would come into her hands for three or four successive weeks of the year." These women never knew how much money they would have for their shopping and frequently went into debt for necessities and paid it off when work picked up.[53] Although Byington found that the Homestead mill provided steady work, atypical of Pittsburgh district mills, she nevertheless concluded that "regularity no less than rate of wages determines what a family's annual receipts amount to, and the family adjusts its grade of living more or less closely to this expected income."[54]

As the family money managers, women had to make the requisite household economies in order to keep the family afloat during these repeated bouts of unemployment. Some did this by buying cheaper cuts of meat, finding meat substitutes, or sticking to basic food items required to sustain men in the mills, even if other members of the family went without. Millworkers' diets were heavy on meat, fats, and sweets. Immigrant families purchased more potatoes (which were cheap) and fewer fresh fruits and vegetables (which were relatively more expensive). Laborers' wives spent between 46 and 48 percent of the family income on food, whereas those of skilled workers spent about 10 percent less of their husbands' larger pay packets to feel the family.[55] The more affluent had more margin to cut expenses, as two family budgets from the mid-1870s demonstrate. One family had an income of $22.50, a puddler's weekly wage; the other lived on $38.00, the wage of a roller. The two adults and five children in each family consumed about twenty pounds of meat weekly, much of which went onto father's plate. They used two or three pounds of lard and four or five pounds of butter for frying the meat, spreading on bread, and mixing with sugar and flour in cakes and sweets. In each case the more affluent family used larger quantities. Each family consumed six or seven pounds of sugar in its sweets, coffee, and cooking and drank about eight quarts of milk.[56] In hard times they followed the advice printed in the labor newspapers on "how to prepare cheap cuts" of beef by boiling, braising, then baking each piece, but did not need to curtail the amount of meat in their diets severely. They purchased cheaper meats, restricted milk and fresh vegetable purchases, and used more lard and less butter. Where careful shopping and cooking did not suffice, as they frequently did not in the poorer segments of the working class, women resorted to draconian measures.[57] A dietary study made during the depression of the 1890s discovered a mother and her children living on bread and tea. Settlement house workers found that the men continued to eat meat while the women and children went without.[58] The earnings of men were not always an accurate guide to the living standards of the women and children. In Pittsburgh, as in other industrial areas, the man customarily handed his pay packet over to his wife after withdrawing his beer and tobacco money. If he took a fixed amount each week, regardless of his actual earnings, there was less for other family members.[59] Unemployment, then, complicated the housewife's task of feeding her family and could lead to hunger for some or all of the family.

The effects of unemployment on Pittsburgh's working-class families may have been more marked than it was in most cities because fewer jobs were available to ancillary wage earners. The labor force participation rate of married women was extremely low in most U. S. cities at the turn of the century—less than 6 percent—though it varied with the type of work available, the ethnocultural values of the woman, and the economic status of the family.[60] Unlike the Italian-American women documented by Miriam Cohen in New York City, the wives and daughters of Pittsburgh's laboring class had few trades to which they could turn temporarily to help the family through men's unemployment, although white-collar and sweated employment did expand at the turn of the century. Women in Steelton, Pennsylvania, sought work in the local cigar factory or dress factories in nearby Harrisburg. Some married women worked in the textile factories in Manchester, N.H., and Lawrence, Mass.[61] Married black women in most northern and southern cities entered the labor force in large numbers. In Pittsburgh, the labor force participation rates of married women ranged from 1 to 3 percent between

1880 and 1900 and surpassed 10 percent only for blacks. As will be discussed in greater detail in the chapters on women's work, married women's supplemental earnings were almost always domestic, that is, they sewed, washed, or took in boarders. The resulting dependence upon men's wages was due, wrote Byington of Homestead in 1907, "to the simple fact that the one industry cannot use the work of women and children."[62] This starkly reinforced gender roles by restricting women's economic contribution to the private sphere while thrusting men firmly outside the home.

The burden of family support fell primarily upon the adult male in Pittsburgh. With the exception of the glass houses, almost none of Pittsburgh's heavy industries employed children under the age of sixteen or women. Of Pittsburgh's 1,984 glassworkers, 12 percent were under sixteen and 6 percent were female in 1900, but only 4 percent of the iron- and steelworkers were in that age group, and there were almost no females among them.[63] Some women did work in the ancillary metal manufacturing trades, however. After the turn of the century, Elizabeth Butler's pioneering study, *Women and the Trades,* found about two thousand women in Pittsburgh, Allegheny City, and surrounding towns employed in subsidiary processing in the metal trades. These women had "nothing to do with the great ingots or with the fashioning or assembling of involved machinery; rather they handle the small pieces of brass or aluminum or steel which are needed in such quantities that the process of making them can be turned into a mere series of repetitions, or they tend machines which they do not control or understand."[64] In the iron and steel industry as a whole, women comprised 1 percent of the labor force in Pittsburgh, a proportion that forced reliance upon the male breadwinners. The relative lack of employment for women and children differentiated Pittsburgh from other U.S. cities. A survey conducted by the Massachusetts Bureau of Statistics of Labor in 1875 reported that 25 percent of the earnings of all families and 40 percent of those of unskilled families came from children's work.[65] Modell, Furstenberg, and Hershberg concluded that most urban families operated "with a margin of comfort to the degree that they could count on a steady contribution from their laboring children of both sexes."[66]

The relative lack of job opportunities for ancillary wage earners in Pittsburgh reduced that margin of comfort. The structure of Pittsburgh's economy coupled with traditional notions of women's work and women's place reinforced the limitation of women to domestic pursuits. Simultaneously, because the mills required great physical strength, Pittsburgh's children entered the labor force later than those in other cities. The net effect was that Pittsburgh families depended heavily upon the wages of adult men. In a study that compared the contributions of women and children to the family economies of Birmingham, England, and Pittsburgh, Peter Shergold found that they were two-thirds higher in the English city than in the U.S. one, even when the monetary contribution of taking in boarders was included.[67] Clearly, this made Pittsburgh's working-class families extremely vulnerable to the business cycle and accentuated the differences in standards of living between the skilled and unskilled segments of the working class, even as these differences narrowed at the turn of the century.

The responses of the industrial working class to unemployment demonstrated that belt-tightening rather than reliance on auxilliary wage earners was the standard solution to notices such as those distributed to 1,640 employees at Jones and Laughlin's American Iron Works in the depression of the 1870s that there was to be "another reduction of ten percent" of their wages.[68] The testimony of workers to the Bureau of Industrial Statistics regarding the depression of 1883–85 stressed the number of workdays lost and the financial reverses suffered, but few sent their children to work. A puddler living on the South Side with five children had earned $2.50 a day before the depression and $2.00 a day thereafter when he could find work. He lost ninety days because of "want of trade" and sixty days because of strikes, but none of his children had jobs. Other millworkers had their wages reduced by a tenth with the mills running two-thirds time, which resulted in a sharp drop in income. Typical of this group was a boiler with six children, one of whom, a 14-year-old son, worked. The family also had two children in school and three at home. In 1885 the father earned about $350, much below his annual wage in prosperous times, because of the reduction in wage level and slack trade. Assuming his son worked the same number of days as the father, he might have added about $85 to the family coffers. A hooker (a semiskilled mill occupation) with two school-age children lost a total of sixty-nine days, costing him $207 in wages in addition to the $0.30 a day reduction exacted by his employers because trade was slow that year.[69] Unskilled workers, with their lower incomes, had less ability to set aside money to tide them over hard times. One laborer wrote to the *National Labor Tribune*, the newspaper of the AAISW, that he could not provide a decent standard of living for his family on his income. This man earned about $300 per year during the depression, about half what the Bureau of Industrial Statistics estimated as necessary to keep a family of six without going into debt.[70]

Pittsburgh families then had a number of alternatives open to them when depressions or strikes undercut their income: they could send another person out to work; economize; go into debt; rely upon family and friends for assistance; take in boarders; leave the city in search of work; return to their place of origin; or turn to public or private charity. Most used a combination of strategies, but public relief tended to be a last resort in Pittsburgh, as elsewhere. Moreover, it was primarily reserved for U.S. citizens, which excluded many of the very poorest people, in particular the new immigrants to the city from Southern and Eastern Europe.[71]

Industrial Accidents

Some facets of industrial life were difficult, if not impossible, to ameliorate at the family level, despite their dire impact upon household life. Metal processing was dangerous work with high accident and death rates. Families lived with the uncertainty of the breadwinners' return home from the day's toil. Molten metal spattered the millhands. Unstable piles of iron billets stood everywhere. Hot floors burned feet through wooden-soled shoes. Molds and furnaces exploded. The machinery had no protective guards. The noise deafened or impaired millworkers' hearing; the heat sapped their strength. Standing next to a hot furnace all day stirring iron, guiding it through the rolls, carrying it, dumping materials into blast furnaces, and pouring steel into molds drained workers, especially during the summer, when the mills resembled infernos.[72] In the summer it took three men to produce the iron two made in winter since there was, as one puddler described it, "a liability to be overcome by the heat ... and some danger from explosion."[73] Manufacturers recognized the extra exertion entailed when they briefly granted puddlers and boilers an extra or "hot" dollar, in addition to the regular price per ton during the summer months. Economic hardship and the declining importance of the skilled workers left mill owners less amenable to workers' demands. The hot dollar disappeared as the mills grew larger.[74] The pressure to produce continued regardless of the weather. British experts visiting Pittsburgh during the summer declared the men "were certainly selling their lives" by toiling in the sticky heat. The millhands themselves, more troubled by the loss of wages than by the heat, rejected the notion of an annual summer shutdown similar to that of glassworkers when the issue arose at AAISW conventions in the mid-1880s.[75]

The heat wore men out, but the mills could be fatal as well as exhausting places to work. The Department of Public Safety noted in 1893 that "Pittsburgh being a great manufacturing and railroad centre, naturally has an excessive number of deaths from violent causes."[76] Other cities had higher overall mortality rates, but few experienced such substantial mortality among men in their prime working years. In 1900, Pittsburgh ranked eighth among large cities in general mortality levels, sixth in overall male mortality, but third for men between the ages of 15 and 54. The city's industries were largely responsible for this excessive male mortality: Pittsburgh's industrial mix—iron, steel, and railroads, with mining on the periphery—resulted in a remarkable concentration of potentially lethal occupations in one area. Women's mortality levels generally resembled those of other cities in both age and cause of death, but men's did not. Men between the ages of 15 and 24 were half again as likely to die as their counterparts in other large cities, and the death rate of 25–34 year old men was one-third higher.[77]

A number of comparisons highlight the importance of accidents as a cause of death in the heavy industry setting. Overall the death rate fell in Pittsburgh between the 1870s and the 1900s from 27.7 per 1,000 in 1871 to 19.57 per 1,000 in 1900.[78] Despite the overall decline, the accidental death rate rose as steel replaced iron as the mill's primary product. As table 4 shows, in 1870 there were 123 deaths due to accidents per 100,000 residents; by 1900 this figure rose to 214. Overall rates are suggestive, but the sex composition of accidental mortality points to industry as a main culprit in male mortality. Women's accidental death rates ranged from about one-sixth to two-fifths of men's throughout this era. One-fifth of all adult men died as a result of mishaps; in contrast only one-twentieth of the women did so.[79] Most accidents happened to men in their prime working years. About one-third of the female accidental deaths were under the age of 15, but only one-eighth of the male accident victims were in that age group. Accidental deaths were thus a primary cause of adult male mortality.

Most accidental and violent deaths occurred in the workplace. At a conservative estimate, work processes or hazards in the workplace caused between one-fourth and one-half of all accidental deaths. The proportion of work-related accidents must be estimated since the death certificates themselves did not always specify the conditions under which the mishap transpired.[80] It seems likely, however, that an even larger number of accidents were due to work hazards since working-class men were the primary sufferers of deaths due to accidental causes. Three-fifths of all such deaths among adult men happened to unskilled and semiskilled workers, although they accounted for less than one-half of the total number of deaths (see table 5). About one-half of the industrial fatalities

Table 4. Death Rate Due to Accidents
(Per 100,000 Deaths)

	Female	Male	Annual Average
1870	42.3	200.6	122.7
1875	85.1	204.5	102.9
1880	66.0	249.1	157.9
1885	56.5	195.3	127.5
1890	49.4	310.4	185.5
1895	64.2	279.9	176.0
1900	68.9	349.6	213.5

Source: Pittsburgh death certificates, 1870–1900.

in Allegheny County in 1906–1907 came from the ranks of unskilled workers earning less than the $15.00 per week needed to sustain a family of five at the minimum acceptable standard of living.[81] The slight under-representation of skilled male workers among accident victims stemmed from their experience and the safer nature of some skilled jobs, particularly in the artisan trades. Men from the middle and upper classes, on the other hand, comprised one-fifth of the adult male dead, but only one-eighth the accidental deaths.

The iron, steel, railroad, coal, and construction industries had the highest proportion of accidental and violent deaths among adult men, accounting for two-fifths of the accident fatalities. Construction workers included bricklayers and others in the mills themselves. Almost two-fifths of the workers involved in accidents were laborers, many of whom worked in the iron, steel, and railroad industries. These industries, then, accounted for approximately four-fifths of the total accidental and violent deaths among adult men.[82]

Accidental deaths, moreover, varied with the business cycle, being highest during prosperous years and lowest during depressions, when the steel mills operated on reduced schedules or not at all. The accidental death rate for men declined during the depressions of the 1880s and 1890s, but not in the 1870s. Iron production, with its greater concentration of skilled and experienced workers, entailed fewer accidental deaths than

Table 5. Occupational Level of Adult Male Accident Victims, 1870–1900

	Accident Victims		All Male Decedents		Accidental Deaths
	N	%	N	%	%
White-collar	52	12.5	415	20.1	12.5
Skilled	98	23.6	552	26.8	17.8
Unskilled	251	60.5	977	47.4	25.7
No occupation/unknown					
occupation	14	3.4	116	5.7	12.1
Total	415	100.0	2,060	100.0	20.2

Source: Pittsburgh death certificates, 1870–1900.

steel, with its large gangs of unskilled workers and longer hours. As a result, when steel replaced iron as the city's principal industrial commodity, the accident rate fluctuated with the business cycle. A *Pittsburgh Dispatch* headline indicated cause and effect: "A let up in accidents—the Rolling mills being shut down the probable cause."[83] The *National Labor Tribune,* as official newspaper for the AAISW, observed the industry closely and pointed out that "anybody who knows aught of the mills knows that there are at least as many mishaps unreported as are reported. There is probably as long a list of killed and wounded in all the mills of the country in a busy year such as was 1889 as there was in one of the smaller battles of the American Civil War."[84] But the decline in accidental deaths during depressions really had three causes. First, the mills operated on reduced schedules, which meant fewer accidents could take place. Second, fewer operating days permitted workers to get more rest and be more alert when on the job. Third, during depressions less experienced hands were let go, so that even laboring jobs might be performed by workers familiar with the intricacies of steel production and less apt to be caught unaware by unguarded machinery.[85] Accidents were a macabre indication of prosperity in Pittsburgh's steel mills.

Immigrants bore the brunt of the fatalities in the steel industry. Between 1870 and 1900 accidents accounted for 20 percent of the total adult male mortality but 40 percent of the deaths among Southern and Eastern European immigrants to the Steel City. An investigation at the Carnegie South Works between 1907 and 1916 discovered that 25 percent of the recent immigrants employed there had been injured or killed. Herbert Gutman suggested that the immigrants did not protest these conditions because they did not plan to stay long in the United States, but if the workers had protested, it is likely they would have been fired and replaced by others desperate for work.[86] The steel industry used the immigrant workers to do the physically most demanding and most dangerous work, and they died in large numbers as a result, leaving families bereft and dependent upon children, charity, and goodwill for support.

The proletarian press recounted these accidents in detail, as a warning to workers and a commentary on the steelworkers' way of life. The

National Labor Tribune reported the following incident at the Edgar Thomson Steel Works in Braddock in which immigrants were sent to correct an extremely dangerous situation and lost their lives when the furnace exploded.

> The blowout or explosion occurred at the top of the furnace. In dumping the ore into the huge bell, the barrow, weighing some 1500 pounds, was accidentally allowed to topple over into the receptacle for the ore and was bearing its weight on the bell, which was impossible to raise. In the meantime the gas was accumulating rapidly between the bell and what is known as a "hang in the furnace." It was to take this load from the bell that a gang of laborers under the foremanship of James Harrison were called to the top of the furnace. They were all supplied with huge iron crowbars and were in the act of raising the heavy weight from the bell when the "hang" gave way.
>
> The effect was horrible. Without a moment's warning immense volumes of burning lava and gas surrounded the unfortunate victims. The flames of burning gas belched from the top of the furnace to a height of fully 300 feet. . . . The men on top of the furnace were taken so unawares that they had no time whatever to make any attempt to escape.[87]

And so they died, horribly burned, in agony, because the steel companies had been experimenting with a cheaper ore and had not learned the necessary variations in technique to prevent clogging the furnaces. The Slavic immigrants in the labor gang died, but the foreman, Harrison, wise in the ways of the furnace, survived.[88]

When the explosions occurred, women and the men on the other shift would run to the mills, hoping against hope that no one had been injured and praying that their menfolk and friends had not been hurt. These accidents became part of the folklore passed from one generation to the next. According to Mrs. Ann Haver, the daughter of a Slovak steelworker in Pittsburgh, the immigrants of her parents' generation described accidents in detail at home. Women overheard their husbands talking about the dangers of their work and lived in constant fear that the dangerous mills would maim or kill their men. The children of immigrants learned that the mill owners "didn't believe in safety," at least not for the immigrant laborers at the bottom of the mill hierarchy, who were the industrial equivalent of cannon fodder.[89]

The workers on the railroads and in the mines also labored under dangerous conditions. Railroad brakemen walked on the tops of cars to adjust couplings and turn switches. They jumped on and off moving trains, ran alongside them, or jumped in between to set the coupling pin. Not infrequently they fell between the cars and were injured or killed.[90] In cold weather their fingers froze, and numb hands led to accidents. The *Commoner and Glass Worker* repeatedly published lists of railroad accidents in the Pittsburgh district with details of the mishap and the damages sustained by the men. In one issue alone it related that:

> G.W. Jones, front brakeman on the Panhandle, fell from the train on Friday morning last and a number of cars passed over his body. He was instantly killed. His body was found shortly afterward terribly mangled. Deceased had been married but a short time and resided at Burgettstown.
>
> Fireman James Walters of the PV and C Road, while leaning out of his cab window on Saturday afternoon last, came in contact with a box car standing on a side track and was knocked out under the moving wheels, having both feet severed above the ankles. The unfortunate man was taken to the West Penn Hospital, where he died a few hours later.
>
> Edward Moon, conductor of the local freight between Mansfield and Washington, fell from the top of a box car on Thursday of last week and sustained a severe fracture of a leg. The accident was caused by pulling out of a draw head.
>
> Robert Parkinson, Panhandle Brakeman, had two fingers crushed while coupling cars in the yard on Sunday morning.[91]

And yet there were more men looking for work as brakemen, conductors, and firemen than there were positions to fill.

The Federal Safety Act of 1893 mandated the use of automatic couplers on trains used in interstate commerce. Since the private railroads of the steel companies traveled only within the state, they were not subject to federal jurisdiction and did not use the new safety devices. An engineer on one of these trains said that several brakeman had been killed and the fingers and hands of countless others smashed during his twenty-five years of driving the dinkey.[92] Employers striving to keep costs down did not install safety devices unless legislation required them, leaving their employees at risk unnecessarily.

Coal miners in Pittsburgh's outlying districts also suffered from the hazards of their trade.[93] Their lanterns ignited the gas trapped in the mines; slate and rock fell on them; the buggies used to carry ore to the surface ran over them. In 1880 the Pennsylvania Bureau of Industrial Statistics estimated that one miner in six "is eventually maimed or killed in the mines, making about 17 percent, of which 3 percent are fatal."[94] Following a series of accidents, one coal miner penned a short funeral poem.

> Each sad remembrance of the past
>   Hast brought forth sorrow and distress
> On those sad days they little thought
>   When to their work they went
> That unto death they should be brought
>   Before the day was spent.[95]

The poem might serve as the epitaph for all those in the Steel City's dangerous trades, for the men knew the dangers of their work. They and their families lived with uncertainty.

Four themes dominated working-class responses to accidents and the deaths that resulted from them. The first was a fatalism imbued by the fortuitous nature of the accidents themselves. Chains broke and hot metal dropped on workers; freight trains jumped their tracks and the firemen, engineers, and brakemen died. A miner in the bituminous coal fields of central Pennsylvania described the hazard underground.

> Beneath a solid rocky mass
> Surrounded by some deadly gas
> He hides himself from nature's light
> And works away with all his might.

A stone may fall upon his head
And lay him motionless and dead.
A car may on his body roll
And send away his precious soul
Or water may secrete him where
His life is taken in despair.[96]

Workers never knew when they might die or what would cause the accident; they accepted the dangerous nature of their work.

A second theme in these accounts of work-related deaths was their gruesome nature, which the labor press delineated graphically. Daniel Fahey, an assistant engineer at the Anderson Steel Works, died as a result of "being caught in the machinery. He was thrown into the pit of the driving wheel, the lower part of which cut through his body tearing away the flesh so that his entrails protruded." Elaborate accident descriptions warned of danger and lauded those who risked their lives in the mills, mines, and railroads.[97]

Third, these accounts emphasized dying well, going bravely to the end, and being a manly man. The proletarian press celebrated these virtues and so encouraged the efforts of those who risked their lives to save others. In describing a colliery disaster, the editors of the *National Labor Tribune* applauded the "rare heroism" of one George Dixon, who stayed with an injured miner who could not move.[98] The *Commoner and Glass Worker* remarked upon the nobility of a Pennsylvania Railroad engineer who "asked if the passengers were safe and was then prepared to die. Such heroism doesn't often creep into the daily papers."[99] Men were supposed to die manly deaths, suffering bravely to the end, more concerned for the welfare of others than for themselves. The steelworker who said "he had to look out for himself" earned the condemnation of his fellows, and the emphasis on manliness reflected pride in the very danger of the work, which only "real" men could understand.[100]

The fourth theme was that workers had a responsibility to protect themselves from the hazards of their jobs. Accident notices in trade newspapers and incidents recounted in the homes and taverns near the mills, mines, and railroad yards warned native and foreign-born workers of their trades' potential dangers. Workmen had to exercise constant vigilance to avoid what *Commoner and Glass Worker* described as an "indisputable fact that workmen who labor at dangerous work get used to the danger and in time see no danger in that which may cost them their lives." A lapse of attention could prove fatal, so workers in the hazardous trades needed to be alert at all times. The detailed narration of accidents in the workplace helped maintain this attentive state. Skilled iron and steel men also discussed new safety devices, urging their utilization. They called for frequent and rigorous safety inspections of workplaces, steam boilers, and ventilation systems and the installation of heat shields in front of furnaces and automatic shut-off switches on electrically powered machines.[101]

As employees lost control of the productive processes, they requested legislative regulation of working hours and conditions. Industrial workers needed the protection of the state as a matter of general policy. The *National Labor Tribune* maintained that "the government, state or national, owes working men all the protection possible." Nevertheless, legislative safeguards could be and were vitiated, as hasty mine inspections and incompetent inspectors demonstrated. State officials colluded with mine operators to protect the interests of the owners at the expense of the workers. Judicial interpretations of existing legislation afforded little protection to employees, and employers evaded the letter of the law as well as its spirit in order to keep costs down.[102]

Prior to 1907 the courts ruled that a person who contracted to work in a steel mill, coal mine, railroad, or steam laundry voluntarily assumed risks arising from the ordinary and extraordinary dangers of the job as well as the carelessness of his or her fellow employees. In practice, this meant that the laundry workers who complained about a loose protective device but continued to work could not collect damages after an accident. Although the employer did not fix the device, he was not liable because the laundry worker "assumed the risk of a condition which she ought to have known was dangerous." All those who worked for the same employer were held to be fellow servants, which limited employer liability for damages caused by another worker's negligence. For example, the steel mill owners evaded responsibility for the death of the 27-year-old Italian laborer run over by a railroad car in the mill because a fellow employee drove the car. Judicial decisions, then, reduced the mill owners' responsibility for dangerous conditions and weakened their incentive to make the workplace safe. The doctrines of contributory negligence and fellow employees' responsibility were nothing but a "club," stated the *National Labor Tribune*, "with which large employers of labor beat the unfortunate in a heartless manner."[103]

Employers themselves attributed accidents to employee carelessness and drinking, so they stressed sobriety as a cure for industrial mishaps. During the 1880s many railroad managers forbade their employees to drink on the job. Nearly one-fourth of the 3,644 manufacturing concerns surveyed by the U.S. Commissioner of Labor in 1897 prohibited the use of liquor during working hours. Few industrial concerns bothered about safety regulations or equipment, however, until the twentieth century, when the United States Steel Corporation began an industrial safety movement. The steel company initially stressed the need for physical safeguards around machinery but quickly emphasized employee responsibility, "carelessness, ignorance, inexperience, and drinking" as the root causes of most accidents, thus shifting the onus from capital to labor. Though employers did not benefit from work accidents, they did little to prevent them, nor did they accept liability for them. Moreover, mill, mine, and railroad owners did almost nothing to compensate the families who lost their entire livelihood through the death of the principal breadwinner.[104]

Toward the end of the century, a few employers tacitly acknowledged responsibility for accidents through contributions to pension funds or funeral expenses. Some companies gave a lump sum if the relatives lived in the United States but required the grieving family to sign a waiver of responsibility before payment was made. The Westinghouse Machine Company subsidized a mutual aid society with a $250 donation in 1884 and contributed one-third of the injury and accidental death benefits. This practice was not widespread until after the turn of the century, when Andrew Carnegie established his relief fund, making "first use of surplus wealth upon retiring from business as an acknowledgement of the deep debt which I owe to workmen who have contributed so greatly to my success."[105] Carnegie's profits derived partially from pushing his men like machines and shaving costs by installing no safety devices in his mills. His relief fund upon his own retirement hardly compensated for the abuse of his employees while he was owner of the Carnegie Steel Company.

Many industrialists in the years between the Civil War and World War I disregarded their workers' well-being. Employers and mill superintendents shared the ethnocentrism of their times and had callous attitudes toward their immigrant work force. When a load of hot steel fell from a crane and killed four Slavic men, the superintendent remarked that "Americans would know enough to keep out from under these loads."[106] Given the absence of warning signs in their languages, the lack of proper training, and the dearth of safety devices, it is little wonder that the primarily unskilled Southern and Eastern Europeans had an accidental death rate twice that of the general male population. Employers could afford to be especially negligent toward aliens without relatives in the United States, for these were not entitled to compensation in the event of an accident. One-third of the immigrant steelworkers surveyed by the U.S. Immigration Commission were single; the wives of three-fourths of the married men resident in the United States for less than five years still lived in the old country. According to Crystal Eastman's study, the employers of resident aliens "suffered practically nothing from these fatalities. One man lived seven days, costing the company $7.00, besides his funeral expenses. In the other cases the funeral was the only expense, amounting to $75.00 apiece."[107] The availability of a disposable labor force to whom the state afforded little or no protection encouraged employers' irresponsible attitude toward workers.

Although some employees tried to sue the steel mill owners for physical injuries sustained on the job, they rarely received just compensation. The courts refused to entertain the litigation or deprived working people of their rights by refusing, in the words of *Commoner and Glass Worker*, "a fair trial before a jury and the securement of a verdict if they have a just and legal case."[108] A suit against Delworth, Porter and Company took nine years and six trials before the court awarded the Spike Mill employee $1,500 for his injuries. The exposés of the Pittsburgh Survey shamed some employers into improving conditions in the workplace, but as John Fitch noted, prior to 1910 the major economic loss in over one-half of the accidents studied "stayed where it first fell—on the families of the men killed at work."[109] Steel companies rarely lost suits, and their assumption of hospital and funeral costs hardly compensated the bereaved families. Even the proliferation of funeral aid and death benefit societies, while performing a valuable service, showed that the workers accepted the burden because they knew there was little appeal against the steel mill owners' negligence.

Most victims of industrial mishaps were young family men. Crystal Eastman's study of work accidents for the Pittsburgh Survey found that 68 percent of those who died as a result of such fatalities were between the ages of 21 and 40, and the rest came equally from those age groups immediately younger and older. Of those who died, 64 percent were the sole or primary breadwinners and an additional 19 percent contributed regularly to the family finances. The men most likely to be injured or killed in mill accidents were precisely those who had young families to support and no one else who could shoulder their burdens. Widows with young children were even more limited in their employment prospects than women generally, since live-in domestic service was virtually closed to them. The poorest families were most vulnerable. Of the accident victims, 44 percent had no insurance or savings; 62 percent of those with incomes under $15.00 per week had no resources to fall back on in such a crisis.[110] The net effect of the technological shifts, reliance upon un-skilled workers, and longer hours in the mills was to increase the accidental injury and mortality rates, to exacerbate uncertainties of unemployment, and to increase the vulnerability of the working-class family to the vagaries of the industrial system.

By 1907 the iron and steel industry had evolved into a bureaucratically organized workplace with large labor gangs composed mostly of new immigrants, with proportionately fewer skilled workers than in the halcyon days of AAISW in the 1870s and 1880s. The differentials between skilled and unskilled remained large but were being undercut by the mill owners. The hours of labor increased in these same years, so that iron and steel men put in longer days and work weeks than previously and than did workers in the building trades, printing, or even retail stores. In effect, the industrial system withdrew men from their homes for longer and longer periods of time. It associated prosperity (a full working week) with men being out of the home, and poverty (short time or unemployment) with their being at home. Working-class families in Pittsburgh were unusually dependent upon men as breadwinners as a result of the industrial structure of the city because so few nondomestic jobs were open to women. This reinforced the reluctance among some ethnic groups for women to work and confined others to poorly paid, poorly regarded labor in other women's homes.

The mills dominated the daily lives of the working class. They structured employment opportunities for men and the lack of them for women. They loomed over the millworkers' households, spewing grit into the air, while the middle class moved away from the crowded downtown and inner city neighborhoods as transportation permitted, distancing themselves both from pollution and physical contact with the working class. This physical shift helps explain the demise of informal charitable assistance and the emergence of more formal, institutionalized social services toward the end of the century. Though this regularization occurred in most U.S. cities at this time, it has particular significance for those with large immigrant populations. They developed their own fraternal and benevolent societies largely because they were so vulnerable to the swings of the business cycle and, in Pittsburgh, the hazards of the mills, but were neglected by most helping institutions, which preferred native-born or English-speaking recipients, with whom they could communicate easily and who shared their cultural assumptions. The uncertain employment provided by the mills influenced mobility patterns within and out of the city, and their physical presence, along with urbanization and the development of municipal technology and public services, fashioned the daily environment of the working-class family. Newcomers to the city experienced the most dangerous jobs and inhabited the least healthy areas of the city. Women's work within the home ameliorated insofar as possible the worst aspects of urban life but could little compensate for the death of the breadwinner.

2 | Population Growth and Mobility

The end of the nineteenth century witnessed a reorganization of inhabitants and industry in Pittsburgh similar to that experienced by other rapidly growing urban centers. Its population tripled between 1850 and 1880 and then doubled by 1900, making Pittsburgh the eleventh largest city in the nation. Rapid economic growth inspired by the burgeoning steel industry caused the city and its industries to spill over the original settlement, a narrow wedge of land known as the Point, at the confluence of the Monongahela and Allegheny rivers. The enormous size of the new steel mills led manufacturers to look east along the river banks and across the rivers into the surrounding towns for cheap land on which to build new plants while maintaining central offices downtown. This spread of manufacturing establishments prompted Pittsburgh's annexation of neighboring towns in 1872, when it added the iron-, glass-, and steel-producing districts across the Monongahela River, subsequently known as the South Side, and in 1907, when it incorporated Allegheny City despite strong protests from the citizens of what came to be known as the North Side. The remaining suburban communities successfully fought attempts to create a "Greater Pittsburgh," although some regionalization of functions inevitably occurred later in the twentieth century.[1]

The processes of urbanization and industrialization altered the environment within which the family existed. Between 1870 and 1907 the compact walking city gave way to a sprawling industrial metropolis, significantly more segregated by class and ethnicity than its predecessor. The concentration of middle-class employments in the downtown headquarters of the local iron, steel, coal, coke,and glass industries contrasted sharply with the dispersal of manufacturing throughout the district, resulting in distinct residential patterns for the working and middle classes. The middle class took advantage of the streetcars and railways to escape from the polluted center to homogeneous suburbs, well served by transportation to the central business district. Roads radiated from the Point along well-defined axes. As the mills scattered across the district, they drew concentrations of workers and their families after them into separate communities poorly connected, if at all, with one another or the city's center. Working-class families crowded into small houses built on scraps of land not required by the mills, up steep hills or next to busy roads. Lack of transport, unstable employment, and shift work precluded a suburbanization pattern similar to that of the middle class and contributed to much higher rates of geographic mobility among Pittsburgh's workers, who frequently had to change neighborhoods if they changed jobs. The city's economic development patterns thus contributed to the physical separation of the working and middle classes while differentiating the relationship between housing and employment they experienced.[2]

Typifying the expansion of industry to outlying districts, Andrew Carnegie and his partners broke ground for the Edgar Thomson works in Braddock in 1873. The town was named for Major General Edward Braddock, who received a fatal combat wound there at the start of the French and Indian Wars.[3] The stark contrast between sylvan and steel inspired Frank Cowan, a local historian, to describe the transition in verse.

> Where the guns of the foe were revealed by a flash—
>   A report—and the fall of the killed and wounded,
> Till the woods were ablaze, and a deafening crash
>   With the wail of the wounded and dying resounded;
> There the ingot aglow is drawn out to a rail,
>   While the coffee-mill crusher booms, rattles, and groans,
> And the water-boy hurries along with his pail,
>   Saying Braddock be blowed! he's a slouch to Bill Jones.[4]

Other mills occupied the farmland surrounding Pittsburgh, though none evoked such poetic outpourings. In 1881 the Kloman steel mill opened in Homestead; it was subsequently known as the Homestead Works following its takeover by the Carnegie Steel Company in 1886. Steel manufacturers established mills in McKeesport, Monessen, Duquesne, Donora, and other small towns in Allegheny County and up the Monongahela Valley. Some expansion also took place on the outskirts of the city, as Jones and Laughlin opened plants in Hazelwood and on the South Side. The net effect was to disperse iron- and steelworkers into small communities throughout the district in which the mills provided virtually the only employment.[5]

Population Composition

As a manufacturing center, Pittsburgh attracted an ethnically diverse population. In 1870 32 percent of Pittsburgh's residents had been born abroad; they were predominantly Irish, but with a sizable German and British component. Blacks formed a considerably smaller segment of the population, about 2 percent. By the end of the century, the older immigrant groups had largely been absorbed, only to be replaced by Southern and Eastern Europeans. The actual proportion of foreign-born residents declined to 26 percent of the city's population, while the proportion of blacks more than doubled, to 5 percent. Prompted by population pressure on the land, searching for new opportunities, and aided by family and friends who had already moved away from home to find employment, newcomers flooded into Pittsburgh. By the end of the century, ''new'' immigrants, particularly Poles and Italians, constituted the largest group of foreign-born residents.[6]

Though the process of chain migration and immigration has been amply documented elsewhere for Pittsburgh and other cities, several points are worth noting here. As migrants and immigrants assisted friends and relatives from their old homes to find both work and housing, they reinforced patterns of residential clustering and ethnic occupational segregation.[7] By 1900, Poles in Pittsburgh had consolidated beachheads in various steel mills, and more than 90 percent lived either within a mile of the mills on the Allegheny River in a district that came to be known as Polish Hill, or beneath the smokestacks of Jones and Laughlin and the Oliver Iron and Steel Mills on the South Side.[8] Lithuanians lived near the National Tube Works and the American Steel and Wire Company on the South Side where many worked; Slovaks clustered in Soho (the Sixth Ward), and Croations and Serbians congregated around Jones and Laughlin's works.[9]

The process of chain migration for blacks approximated that of Southern and Eastern Europeans, but black migrants were much less successful in penetrating industrial establishments or obtaining jobs for family and friends in them. White foremen gave jobs to recent immigrants in preference to blacks, particularly those recently arrived from the South. Black communities in Pittsburgh depended upon domestic and service employments based upon individual ties to whites. They thus lacked the group work focus that the new immigrant communities quickly developed. The work-home nexus also differed between the races, since domestic-based employment for most black women and many black men actually withdrew them from their own neighborhoods and thrust them into white ones, effectively isolating them in all-white environs. Black Pittsburghers lived in scattered enclaves in the Hill District, Lawrenceville, and Homewood-Brushton.[10]

As Pittsburgh's newcomers swirled farther from their homes in search of work, they followed the examples set by earlier migrants. They came in response to job opportunities reported back in glowing terms by neighbors or relatives who had already made the trip. They stopped along the way to earn money, picking up casual work and skills en route. Some Eastern European immigrants viewed the trip to Pittsburgh as an extension of seasonal migrations in search of work within Europe. They came to earn money to improve their condition at home, not to stay.[11] Others viewed the move in permanent terms, differing little in this respect from earlier generations of immigrants, who had already established themselves. Former Pittsburgh steelworker James J. Davis described his family's peregrinations from Wales to the United States in the serial fashion that characterized Southern and Eastern European immigrants at the turn of the century. The family had planned to travel from New York to Pittsburgh, "but the mill father was working in had shut down. And so he had sent us tickets to Hubbard, Ohio, where his brother had a job as a muck roller—the man who takes the bloom from the squeezer and throws it into the rollers." They then moved to Sharon, Pennsylvania, and, once his father earned enough money to make another trip, they went on to Pittsburgh.[12] Many of the forty-two Slavic families visited in Homestead by Margaret Byington had a similar pattern of aiding or depending upon relatives during their migrations. Several had nieces or nephews living with them, a child living with kin in the old country, a husband who emigrated first, and assistance from relatives during spells of unemployment.[13]

The employment-based settlement pattern had several consequences for women migrants and the city's demographic structure. Given Pittsburgh's occupational structure and the persistence of male beachhead migration, it is not surprising that Pittsburgh had more men than women. In fact, it had one of the highest male to female ratios of any U.S. city, with 106 males for every 100 females, when the average large city had about 97 men for every 100 women in 1900.[14] Although Pittsburgh offered limited employment opportunities to women, the sex ratio facilitated marriage for them. It may be that the lack of jobs coupled with the preponderance of males actually reinforced marriage as a goal for women. It certainly was the case that men tended to come first to the city, to be older than their wives, and to learn some English at work (in the case of European immigrants), whereas the women did if they worked as domestics before marriage, but not if they immigrated to join their husbands. Thus men's position as interpreter of the external world to the household and as head of the household was strengthened by their longer domicile in the city and their ability to communicate with the world outside the ethnic community. Black women who worked as domestics in white people's homes before (and sometimes during) marriage were as familiar with the world beyond their own neighborhoods as black men, though how enjoyable they found the contact obtained in such menial positions is debatable.[15]

The constant infusion of young men into the city and the dangerous nature of the occupations distorted Pittsburgh's demographic structure by age as well as by sex. Pittsburgh's population was unusually young even for a U.S. city. The Steel City had as low a percentage of men over 65 as any city in the nation, about 2 percent, although the elderly comprised 4 to 6 percent of the population of other large urban centers. Pittsburgh's female population, with fewer young women coming to the city in search of work, had a slightly higher proportion of elderly, about 3 percent in 1900. Because of the ebb and flow of immigrants from various countries, the proportion of elderly in Pittsburgh's population remained almost constant during the last half of the century. In 1860, 2.3 percent of all Pittsburgh residents were over 65, and in 1900 the figure was 2.4 percent.[16] The continual migration of men seeking work in the mills, alone, accompanied, or followed by their relatives, meant that the population as a whole retained the same general age structure throughout these years.

Most of Pittsburgh's older residents were foreign-born, both in 1860 and 1900. In 1860, 70 percent of those 65 and older had been born abroad, mostly in Ireland and Germany; when the new century began, 64 percent were of foreign origin. The age structure among blacks reflected the surge of migration into the city at the turn of the century. In 1860 blacks accounted for 3 percent of the elderly (roughly in proportion to the total number of blacks in the population). By 1900, when blacks comprised 5 percent of Pittsburgh's residents, they were only 2 percent of those over 65. There are several reasons for this discrepancy. Most of the black migrants to the city from the South had been young women and men. As this migration accelerated near the end of the century, the black population had not yet aged as much as either native or foreign-born whites. Blacks also suffered higher mortality rates than whites, so that they died before they had a chance to grow old. It is also possible that some blacks, as with some foreign-born whites, returned to their place of birth as they grew older, but without any method of tracing out-migration, this must remain speculation.[17]

Residential Expansion

The modern city, poorer at the center and more affluent at the periphery, took shape during these decades. As the spatial relationship between housing and employment changed, there was a complete redistribution of the socioeconomic classes that, almost literally, turned the city inside out. Where the traditional city mixed commercial, industrial, and residential functions, the modern city separates them, so that density decreases at the center and increases at the margins. Urban growth brought with it greater physical distances between the classes and age groups in Pittsburgh, a reflection of the general trend toward suburbanization and class homogeneity present in U.S. cities at the end of the nineteenth century.[18] The very size and unpleasantness of Pittsburgh's mills exacerbated these trends. In Pittsburgh, where laboring men needed to live near their work, the great expanses of land occupied by the mills kept ancillary employments out of many working-class districts. The resulting class and occupational homogeneity lessened opportunities for female employment near mill neighborhoods while the physical expansion of the city meant they lived at a great distance from the expanding white-collar sector downtown.

Before the development of public transportation in Pittsburgh, the middle and upper classes resided in the center of the city, the working class lived on the outskirts, although still within walking distance of the Point. Approximately 80 percent of the population in the outer wards were laborers or skilled artisans at midcentury, but only 40 percent of the inner ward residents were. Of the downtown residents, 45 percent came from the middle class, and the remaining 15 percent were drawn from the city's elite—professionals, manufacturers, merchants, and bankers. Since the central business district contained industrial as well as residential, governmental, and religious buildings, even the most fashionable neighborhoods endured the dreadful soot and smoke that hung over the Point like a thick black cloud.[19] Yet "tradition and convenience still held the older inhabitants of the city in its most cramped sections" at midcentury, since the paucity of transportation facilities and proximity to work outweighed pollution and traffic to make downtown the preferred residential area.[20]

This concentration of middle- and upper-class, principally native-born white inhabitants downtown disappeared after the Civil War as increased industrialization evoked an emotional longing for things rural in many cities at the same time as public transportation made it possible to move beyond the perimeters of the walking city.[21] The omnibus, commuter railroad, and streetcar networks introduced in Pittsburgh in the 1850s and expanded throughout the latter half of the century enabled those with time and money to escape the smoke and noise. As the middle and upper classes moved to the eastern suburbs, they abandoned their downtown mansions to the "encroachments of the railroads and the noise and clatter of numerous trains."[22]

Five factors influenced the patronage of mass transportation and suggest that the middle and upper classes, rather than the working class, were the primary beneficiaries of the new systems. The location of routes, the amount of the fare, the length of the workday, the regularity of employment, and the number of family members in the labor force determined who could afford to live beyond walking distance of their employment. The omnibus lines charged twelve cents per ride, about 10 percent of a laborer's daily wage. Joel Tarr suggests in his transportation history of Pittsburgh that, "while some skilled workers probably used the omnibus, ads in the Pittsburgh press for 'country residences' for businessmen located near omnibus lines suggest that the well-to-do and growing middle class made the most extensive use of this form of public transit."[23] Although the streetcar and horsecar fares were not as high, they, too, were beyond most working-class pockets.

Low wages for unskilled workers, high unemployment rates among all mill hands, irregular hours, and long working days all precluded widespread utilization of mass transit among Pittsburgh's working class. A study of New York City's manufacturing and clerical workers published in 1911 by Edward Ewing Pratt demonstrated that the longer the workday and the lower the wage, the more likely a person was to walk to work.[24] Pittsburgh millhands laboring on rotating twelve-hour day and night shifts eschewed the streetcars and lived close to the mills. Margaret Byington captured the flavor of the men's march into the mills when she wrote that "if you are near the mill in the late afternoon you will see a procession, an almost steady stream of men, each carrying the inevitable bucket, hurrying towards the great buildings for the night's work. A little later the tide turns and back come the day men, walking slowly and wearily towards home and supper."[25] Decades later, immigrants and their children recalled that no one wanted to spend time commuting to and from work after a twelve-hour day.[26]

Since they often changed jobs in response to the business cycle or technological innovations, millworkers would have needed to live on transportation lines that would carry them to a variety of mills if they had lived in the suburbs. The original horsecar lines in Pittsburgh ran downtown from the outer wards. In 1869, three horsecar lines connected the eastern suburbs with downtown, two ran from fashionable Allegheny City to the central business district, but only one served the entire industrial district south of the Monongahela River and another traveled through the iron and steel neighborhoods near the Allegheny River. By 1890 streetcar lines proliferated in the suburbs of Allegheny City and to the east, but few traversed the mill districts, and only one connected one steel mill area with another.[27] Millworkers and their families, then, were excluded from urban transit by the location of the routes as much as the cost of the fares and the length of their workdays.

The transportation revolution in the city led to segregation by class and function through homogeneous residential developments and the specialization of land usage. Homes, churches, and schools disappeared as commerce and industry took over the downtown wards. Extensive building occurred along the streetcar and railroad lines into the eastern section of the city as business and professional people moved from mixed-class neighborhoods into essentially homogeneous middle-class suburbs. White-collar expansion was heaviest within an hour's ride of the central business district, whereas outlying areas, dependent upon railroad transportation, grew more slowly and attracted more upper-class residents. At the same time, the working class remained heavily concentrated in the areas surrounding the mills and on the edge of downtown, into which many recent immigrants poured.[28] The Hill District and the outer fringe of the central business district became the centers of Pittsburgh's sweated trades, tenement factories, and stogy (cigar) industry. These burgeoned at the beginning of the twentieth century, and, though still occupying a small proportion of Pittsburgh's workers, they were the locus of much of women's industrial employment.[29]

The new suburban districts showed greater residential class and age segregation than the old downtown wards, making the middle and upper class who lived on the outskirts more isolated from the working class than previously had been the case. Fewer laboring families lived in the new areas than had resided downtown either in 1850 or 1880. Since the new wards were much larger than the old, the various population strata lived farther apart in the suburbs than they had downtown. Table 6 shows that in 1880, 30 percent of the most exclusive downtown ward came from the manufacturing, banking, professional and merchant classes, and 43 percent of the elite suburban wards did so; in comparison only 11 percent of all Pittsburgh's household heads belonged to the upper class, and a mere 6 percent of the residents of the iron and steel wards lining the rivers came from the elite. The South Side had the lowest proportion of upper-class residents, a paltry 4 percent.[30]

By 1900 improved transportation facilities and the consequent development of the outer wards and residential suburbs as far away as Sewickley (twelve miles from Pittsburgh) accentuated the trend toward housing segregation by class. Some groups participated less in the general urban expansion than others. More than four-fifths of the residents in the mill neighborhoods were skilled and unskilled workers who, although

Table 6. Socioeconomic Class Distribution of Household Heads, 1880 (In Percentages)

	N	Unskilled	Skilled	Middle-class	Upper-class	Total
Wards 1–3	173	42	14	33	11	100
Ward 4	59	21	24	24	31	100
Suburban elite wards						
20, 22, 23	185	27	18	12	43	100
Riverfront mill wards						
6, 9, 10, 14, 15	468	52	28	14	6	100
South Side	722	53	32	11	4	100
Citywide average	1607	48	27	14	11	100

Source: 1880 census sample.

they moved frequently, did so between one mill district and another either in the older industrial sections or into the mill towns that lined the rivers. Widows and the elderly in general remained concentrated in the older sections of the city.

The people who moved into the suburbs in the last decades of the nineteenth century tended to be younger than those who remained downtown. In this they prefigured the suburbanizing trends of the twentieth century. Approximately one-fourth the household heads in the newly fashionable districts and the city generally were over 50 but nearly one-third of those who remained downtown came from that age group. The age differential among household heads suggests that the younger members of the elite moved to the suburbs seeking privacy and green space in which to raise their children. They surrounded their homes with fences that symbolically separated them from the urban scene, and they hung heavy curtains over their windows to keep out inquisitive glances. A swath of green lawn provided a modicum of the rural ideal, acted as a buffer from the street, and gave the children a traffic-free play area. The steel mill wards, like the new suburbs, had more young household heads, iron and steel millworkers also beginning their families, but raising them in the shadow of the mills rather than under the oak trees for which Oakland was named, or Shadyside, Squirrel Hill, or Highland Park, whose very names were redolent of country vistas. Older residents remained downtown in homes opening directly onto the pavement, surrounded by the hurly-burly of the city, under its smoke-laden skies.[31]

The mill wards differed significantly in demographic composition from the suburban sections of Pittsburgh in one other way: they had a much higher proportion of widowed household heads, even though they had the same general age structure. More than twice as many mill district household heads were widows. Only 10 percent of the suburban household heads were widows, as compared with 19 percent downtown and fully 22 percent of the mill ward household heads. The generally older age structure of the central business district suggests that these women (and a few men) had lost their spouses because of the natural aging processes and diseases. The relatively younger population of the mill wards implies that being a widow there was not solely a function of age but was due also to the nature of the industries themselves. The widows in the iron and steel districts were, in many cases, young women with families to support rather than older ones with grown children who could help out.[32]

The problems of widowhood and work accidents are recurring themes in this book, just as they were in Pittsburgh's iron and steel districts. As a boy, James J. Davis occasionally delivered telegrams bearing bad news. His autobiography described the devastation accidents brought to the survivors. "And when a man was killed, it often meant his wife and babies would face hunger, for the jobs were not the kind for women and children; muscular men were needed. Aside from the occupation of housewife, there was nothing for a woman to do in those days except to take in washing or sewing."[33] The relative isolation of the mill districts, brought about by inadequate transportation facilities, exacerbated the problems widows faced in supporting their families. The class homogeneity of their neighborhoods meant that there were few local people who could afford the services of a washerwoman or a seamstress.

Population Mobility

The preceding overview of residential expansion has shown the general pattern of age and class segregation within the city. The middle class, aided by municipal transit systems, purchased comfortable environments removed from noise and pollution. In the years between 1870 and 1907, geographical mobility increased within the city, but the tendency to move varied by sex, class, ethnicity, age, and marital status. The pattern of geographical mobility for various socioeconomic, sex, and age groups in Pittsburgh can be compared to those established for men in other cities, although there are no comparable data for women. The traditional method of tracing men through census records and city directories is more difficult to use for women, who tended not to be listed in the directories and changed their names upon marriage, making record linkage through the census a laborious task.[34] One unusual source permits analysis of female mobility patterns and comparison with male movement into and within Pittsburgh. The death certificates filed in Pittsburgh from 1870 onward contained residential information, place of birth, location at time of death, length of time at that place, and previous domicile. These certificates have two flaws as a data base for mobility studies: they exist only for people who died within the city, hence one cannot trace out-migration; and working-class men, because of the dangerous nature of their occupations, were more likely than others to die in the prime of life, when they were most mobile. This may overemphasize the degree of movement experienced by iron- and steelworkers, miners, and railroaders, whose trades were the most likely to result in fatal job-related injuries. Middle-class men in sedentary occupations moved into the suburbs during these years but had lower death rates. As a result these records would not reflect their mobility entirely. The death certificates compensate for this bias by providing detailed information on where all people lived before they came to Pittsburgh (if their last move was not within the city) and the length of time between moves. They are invaluable for the comparisons they permit between women and men.[35] The definition of mobility as it derives from these sources is moving in the year prior to death, which is idiosyncratic but does provide scope for contrasting urban mobility between the sexes.

Regardless of the sources used, researchers have found that nineteenth-century cities had highly mobile populations. The first studies relied on city directories. They focused on out-migration and found urban Americans to be restless indeed. Stephan Thernstrom described workers in Newburyport, Mass., as "permanent transients," for whom that New England town was only "one more place in which to carry on the struggle for existence" before moving on.[36] More recent studies of other cities confirm the picture of an urban maelstrom. In Omaha, Neb., for example, 40 percent of the males resident in 1880 departed after three years, and nearly 70 percent had gone by the end of the century. About 50 percent of the male workers in Poughkeepsie, N.Y., in 1860 lived elsewhere a decade later. Other studies computed nineteenth-century urban persistence rates as varying between 40 and 60 percent.[37] Bodnar, Simon, and Weber's study of the black, Italian, and Polish experience in Pittsburgh in the twentieth century found that these recent immigrants were particularly volatile. A mere 24 percent resident in Pittsburgh in 1900 persisted through 1905. Many of those who left were young men without family ties. Those who remained for at least five years tended to stay much longer, a tendency that led these authors to suggest that "migration may be a function of a stage in the life cycle. As workers grew older and took on family obligations, they became more settled, less likely to pick up and leave a city to escape adverse conditions."[38]

While out-migration was not calculated for the present study because of the data source, internal migration figures and literary evidence suggest that the young and the single were the most mobile and that overall mobility in Pittsburgh approximated that of other large U.S. cities at the turn of the century. High rates of unemployment, technological shifts within the industry, and the widely scattered location of the steel mills meant workers virtually had to move from one section of the city to another or leave town altogether in order to locate work. "Even in the Pittsburgh district," David Brody wrote in *Steelworkers in America,* "mills were too distant for a man conveniently to live in the same residence after changing jobs."[39] The workers themselves were aware of the impact of technological unemployment in the iron and steel industry of the nineteenth century. The conversion from iron to steel left boilers and puddlers drifting "from one place to another in search of work of any kind," according to a report from a Pittsburgh local to the AAISW.[40]

The most restless individuals in the city were young, male, unmarried, recent immigrants, blacks, and unskilled workers, whereas older Pittsburghers, women, the married and widowed, old-stock immigrants, and the upper class moved least.[41] Male and female mobility patterns diverged in a number of ways (see table 7). Most obviously, men were more likely to move within and into the city than women as they searched for work. The data source is most likely to distort the mobility pattern at this point, simply because the new worker in a mill was most vulnerable. Male mobility responded to the business cycle in two seemingly contradictory ways. Internal movement in the city slackened for men during depressions. Mobility out of the city, however, increased as those less entrenched in the occupational hierarchy—recent immigrants for example—responded to hard times by re-emigrating.[42] Women's mobility in the year prior to death seemed less affected by the business cycle, climbing steadily from 32 percent in 1875 to 47 percent in 1900. The only exception to the pattern of decreased internal mobility for men during depressions came in 1885, when there was an upsurge of such movement. William Weihe, president of the Amalgamated, noted that trade picked up by August 1885, and with this came an increase both in men moving in search of work and in work accidents, which would affect the most mobile groups within the population, the young worker and the green hand.[43]

Decreased male mobility within the city during depressions, then, reflects increased departure rates from the city to other places in search of work or a return to the workers's point of origin, whether in the rural United States or overseas, in the hopes that times would be less hard there. An enquiry into the cost of living in U.S. towns conducted by the Board of Trade of London concluded that "in times of severe depression the immigrant aliens do, in fact, return to Europe in large numbers" particularly if they had no ties in the United States—that is, were young, single men, or married men who had left their families in the old country.[44] Those who were more established or who had found a niche within the immigrant community tended to stay on. Men who had work or friends or landlords who would extend credit to them might well remain. The solidarity of the ethnic community helped sustain some immigrants who might otherwise have left the country. An investigator for the Pittsburgh Survey asked Koval, a poor Ruthenian, why he kept twelve boarders,

Table 7. Adults Moving in Year Preceding Death, by Sex

	Females		Males		Total	
	N	% Moving	N	% Moving	N	% Moving
1870	193	46	252	47	445	47
1875	205	32	211	34	416	33
1880	179	34	229	42	408	38
1885	202	37	265	49	429	43
1890	214	42	347	56	561	50
1895	204	45	294	51	498	48
1900	227	47	312	58	539	53

Source: Sample of Pittsburgh death certificates, taken every fifth year, 1870–1900.

only one of whom could pay. He replied, "Why, what else could I do? They have no work and no other place to go. I cannot throw a man into the street. They will go themselves when they can."[45] Yet, as Michael Anderson points out in his study of textile workers in Lancashire, the amount of time a man could live off his friends was limited. Eventually the men of Preston, England, went tramping in search of work or returned to the villages of their birth until the employment situation improved.[46] During the depression of 1907 and 1908, Pittsburgh's immigrants "returned home by the thousands" rather than remain in a city that had no work for them and in which they were the first to be fired.[47]

Women's movements within the city seemed less affected by economic downturns than men's. Except for an initial drop during the depression of the 1870s, women moved about the city more during every five-year period than they had in the last as figure 1 shows. The differential impact of economic crises on male and female mobility was most apparent during the depression of the 1890s, when women's mobility within the city continued its upward trend at the same time as men's declined. The nature of male and female employment explains some of this difference. Young women, working as domestic servants, may have found their jobs less secure when hard times struck and moved to another employer's house or back to their parents. Their mobility would thus have taken place within the city rather than out of it, as was the case for young men or those who left their families back in Europe. Some of the apparent differences in movement within the city may be artifacts of the source used in this investigation, but without comparable studies of women's mobility in other cities, there is no way to ascertain this.[48]

Some women's employment could tie them to one location rather than encouraging or forcing them to move in search of work. Carolyn Schumacher's study of education in Pittsburgh revealed a lack of mobility for women teachers. She traced the movements of male and female high school students from the opening of Pittsburgh's high school in 1867 through the turn of the century, finding that men moved from one address to another and from one occupation to another but that women, even if working, did not. Instead these women, principally teachers, resided at one address and had one job year after year. These women taught in the

Figure 1. Mobility in Year Preceding Death, by Sex

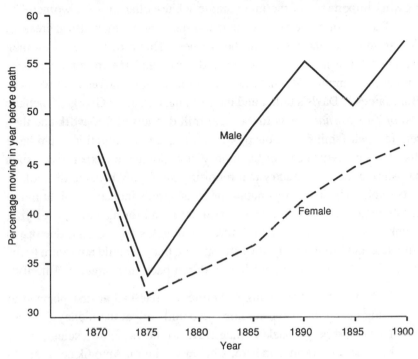

Source: Pittsburgh death certificates, 1870–1900.

same ward school for many years, with few promotions and encountering little occupational or geographic mobility.[49] Although professional and employed women were a decided minority among Pittsburgh's female population, their experiences demonstrate another way in which work influenced persistence.

In 1870 women and men of the same marital status had very similar persistence patterns, with nearly three-fifths of the single and two-fifths of the married and widowed of both sexes moving that year (see table 8). By 1900 the male and female patterns had diverged as men of all marital statuses became rather more restless than their female counterparts. The greatest discrepancy occurred between single men and women, a reflection of the increased immigration from Southern and Eastern Europe, which brought large numbers of young, single men into the city, the increased insecurity of employment in the iron and steel mills, and the growing importance of the more stable white-collar jobs for women.[50]

The rate of movement for married men and women also increased, though more for the men than the women. This reflected the way men searched for work in Pittsburgh's industries and the migration pattern among new immigrants, in which men made more moves than women. Both James J. Davis's father and the fictional character George Kracha in *Out of This Furnace* went to the steel mill districts to find work and then sent for their families.[51] This process of sequential migration could have disastrous consequences for the family unit. Some men experienced such hardship in the new country that reuniting the family became difficult or impossible. The dangerous nature of Pittsburgh's industries might maim or kill a man before he had saved enough to send for his family. A flying chunk of scrap metal crushed Andrew Antonik's leg, forcing doctors to amputate and leaving him with a stump, and thus he could not return to the steel mill. He had a wife and five children back in Hungary. Antonik

> looked at the future blankly, helplessly. He had at first planned to bring his family here, but now he could not get the money for that. Nor could he go back to them. He would be more useless, more helpless, on a farm than here. The only solution Antonik could see to the lifelong problem suddenly thrust upon him by that flying piece of scrap, was for him and his family to remain indefinitely apart, he

Table 8. Adults Moving in Year Preceding Death, by Marital Status (In Percentages)

	1870		1900	
	Female ($N=193$)	Male ($N=252$)	Female ($N=227$)	Male ($N=312$)
Single	57	59	55	67
Married	43	43	52	57
Widowed	42	40	35	41

Source: Pittsburgh death certificates, 1870 and 1900.

working at whatever poor job and at whatever low wage he could get, and sending a little to Hungary to help out, his wife to continue working on a farm at 12 or 15 cents a day.[52]

For Antonik and others like him, the steel mill accident assured his continued movement for work in the district, though his wife would never join him. He swelled the number of married men who moved but whose wives did not accompany them on their travels.

Widows and the elderly were the most persistent groups in the population. Their immobility helps explain the trend toward residential segregation by age in Pittsburgh during this period. While the elderly stayed in one place, the city expanded beyond them. Again a divergence developed: widowers' mobility increased slightly, whereas that of widows decreased. In 1870, 42 percent of the widows in the sample had changed residences in the year preceding death, but by 1900 the proportion had fallen to 35 percent. Since the percentage of older women moving remained almost constant, one would expect that it was the young widows, mostly those of steelworkers, who became less mobile as the century ended, or who left the city altogether, perhaps to return to their homelands, and thus were beyond the scope of the records used here to examine movement within the city.

Though exhibiting lower mobility rates than younger men, older men nevertheless grew more mobile as the century ended (see table 9). The problems of older men in retaining their employment in the mills will be discussed in the chapter on aging, but certainly some of this increased movement can be attributed to occupational instability, the devaluation of skills in the mills, and the longer workday demanded by employers. Since the persistence rate remained stable among widowed men, it would seem that movement in search of work was more prevalent among those with families to support. The widowed and the elderly remained in the older districts of the city, staying close to their remaining friends, ethnic community, and occasional sources of employment, but more removed from their children, who took up residence in the newer sections of the city and beyond in search of work.[53]

Difference in mobility patterns existed among racial, ethnic, and class groups (see table 10) as well between the sexes and age groups. People at the bottom of the socioeconomic ladder and newcomers to the city (frequently the same groups) changed residences more often than those who had higher prestige jobs or who had been in the city longer. The mobility rates for native and foreign-born whites in 1870 clustered closely between 42 and 47 percent, with the exception of the British, 54 percent of whom had moved in the year preceding death. Since many of the British were iron- and steelworkers, they shared the flux associated with those trades. The few blacks in the sample had a very high rate of mobility, 58 percent having moved in the year preceding death. Low wages, the personal nature of employment in domestic service, and the irregular work of the unskilled laborer all contributed to the greater residential turnover among Pittsburgh's blacks.[54]

By 1900 mobility within the city had declined for the older immigrant groups as they aged and acquired skilled jobs in industry. German-born immigrants seemingly were an exception to the noticeably decreased mobility. As artisans and shopkeepers they were more stable geographically already in 1870. By 1900 their mobility rate exceeded that of other northeast Europeans, an indication of continued immigration and lower occupational status.[55] The persistent instability can be attributed to the way in which ethnicity was determined in these records. The death certificates listed some Eastern Europeans as German although their names indicated that they were Slavic rather than German. This misattri-

Table 9. Adults Moving in Year Preceding Death, by Age and Sex
(In Percentages)

	1870		1900	
	Female (N=193)	Male (N=252)	Female (N=227)	Male (N=312)
15–34	57	59	59	64
35–54	37	48	56	66
55+	34	33	33	42

Source: Pittsburgh death certificates, 1870 and 1900.

bution accounts for the seeming constancy of German mobility within Pittsburgh.[56]

Southern and Eastern European immigrants had the highest mobility rates of any group in Pittsburgh at the end of the century; 75 percent had moved in the preceding year. In many cases they were new residents of the city, but some of their relative lack of persistence is an artifact of the mortality records, since they were new to industrial work and suffered a disproportionate share of mill, mining, and railroad accidents.[57] They also tended to be young and single, and, like the native-born whites in this sample who also had a high mobility rate (58 percent), of an age characterized by a rapid turnover in search of work.

The actual persistence rates of blacks in Pittsburgh, as opposed to movement within or to the city (which is all that the mortality records can show) have been found to be higher at the turn of the century than was the case for Southern and Eastern European immigrants, who were also moving into Pittsburgh in large numbers at this time. Bodnar, Simon, and Weber found that approximately 35 percent of the black men in Pittsburgh in their 1900 sample were still there in 1905, but that only 27 percent of the German Poles and 15 percent of the Russian Poles stayed in the city over that five-year span.[58] Although measuring continued presence within the city rather than at an address, their figures are roughly comparable with

Table 10. Adults Moving in Year Preceding Death, by Race and Ethnicity

	1870		1900	
	N	% Moving	N	% Moving
Native-born white	180	47	264	58
Irish	142	44	79	39
German	65	42	83	41
British	37	54	29	35
S. & E. European	2	100	44	75
Black	19	58	40	60
Average	445	47	539	53

Source: Pittsburgh death certificates, 1870 and 1900.

those derived from the death certificates, which showed that 60 percent of all blacks (women as well as men) changed residence in the year preceding death—that is, 40 percent had not moved. The lower persistence rates of Poles and Italians that these researchers found between 1900 and 1905 are similar to the high rates of mobility uncovered within the city in 1900. Many of the Southern and Eastern European immigrants were young, geographically restless men. Like the blacks, Poles and Italians became more persistent as the twentieth century progressed, so that by 1915 they exhibited a similar stability within the city. As the population aged, families and communities were formed, both of which helped newcomers to establish roots within the city.[59]

Thus the period under examination here, 1870–1907, was one of remarkable fluidity into, out of, and within the city. There was a particularly strong relationship between occupational turnover and residential mobility in these decades for those at the bottom of the economic hierarchy: those in the least secure positions moved most often. As table 11 shows, three-fifths of the working class but only two-fifths of the middle

Table 11. Socioeconomic Class of Movers[a]

	1870		1900	
	N	% Moving	N	% Moving
Upper	36	39	18	39
Middle	81	41	78	58
Skilled	132	57	113	50
Unskilled	208	63	268	68
Widows[b]	21	38	58	31
Class unknown[c]	143	58	121	60
Total	621	55	656	58

Source: Pittsburgh death certificates, 1870 and 1900.

a. Includes children as well as adults in order to increase sample size.

b. A residual category; widowed women with occupations were assigned to the relevant class; this group was therefore older and more persistent.

c. Because children were included and their fathers' occupations traced through the city directories, a large portion could not be designated by class.

and upper classes moved in 1870, with slightly more unskilled than skilled workers and middle- than upper-class individuals changing residence in that year. By 1900 the correlation between economic status and residential stability lessened. More members of the middle class moved into the suburbs, and those skilled workers who had managed to retain their positions despite changes in industry became more firmly entrenched in their own neighborhoods. At the same time, the proportion of unskilled workers and their families who moved increased.

Since the death certificates included the previous residence of the deceased, it was possible to plot the pattern of geographical mobility. In 1870, prior to the proliferation of suburban dwellings, there were few significant distinctions in the network of moves made by individuals from different socioeconomic strata. By 1900 the working and middle classes had very distinct mobility patterns. The affluent tended to move farther into the suburbs, while members of the working class changed residences within a neighborhood or moved to another just like it. The laboring population searched for work within its present district or, not finding it, moved farther afield to a different section or outside the city altogether. The middle class, less neighborhood-oriented in employment, moved within certain desirable sections of the city, so that by 1900 they were largely resident in the outer wards and rode the trolleys to work.

The middle class removed themselves to a "safe" zone, one free from the obvious negative side effects of urban industrial expansion: crowding, pollution, and contact with the forces of disorder. The increased mobility of the middle class in 1900 reflected both a desire to leave the noise and dirt of the city behind and the means to do so. Manual workers and their families remained concentrated in the older sections of the city, moving more frequently than the affluent, but not leaving the mills behind them. If anything, the collective standard of living declined as working-class neighborhoods grew more crowded and uncertainty over employment, even for the skilled, increased. Pittsburgh remained a mecca for those seeking employment in its expanding steel industry, but many stayed only a short time, either failing to reach their goals or returning to their point of origin when they achieved them. In many cases families were left behind as men sought work. The growing discrepancy in male and female mobility patterns suggests that insofar as the family unit was concerned, urbanization and industrialization augmented the differentiation of the male and female experiences during these years. Young, single women were less mobile than their brothers in 1900, though they had not been in 1870. Older, married women were less mobile than their husbands at the start of the new century, though they, too, had the same overall mobility level in 1870. Men's increased geographical mobility was a metaphor for the changes wrought by industrialization. They moved farther from home than did women, searching for work and, once finding it, left the household daily to earn the family's bread. Women were more rooted within their homes. They responded to male occupational imperatives: he moved for work, she moved to be with him. This reinforced the domestic, responsive aspect of women's lives. His day's (or night's) work took him outside the home; hers kept her within or very near it.

As the middle class moved to the urban periphery, they left behind the conditions with which the working class continued to grapple: unsanitary housing, dirty streets, and polluted neighborhoods. Their new homes gave them more peace, more privacy, and more space. The city grew more heterogeneous, but neighborhoods were more homogeneous by class at the turn of the century than they had been earlier. Residents of the new suburbs demanded, and received, services from the city. Millworkers moved frequently in search of work. They crowded into the older, unsanitary, unserviced sections of the city with their wives and children. The hallmark of the new city was a growing separation and segregation, by class, by age, and by gender, so that each group's experience was increasingly differentiated from that of the others.

3 | # Home and Neighborhood

The nature of Pittsburgh's industries, rapid population growth, the suburbanization of the middle class and the high residential turnover of the working class, when overlaid by certain political decisions regarding the provision of municipal services, resulted in cramped housing in unsanitary neighborhoods for the majority of the city's laboring population. Differentiation and segregation of the classes highlighted the inadequate nature of much of the housing near the mills and the unhealthy conditions in these districts. Although Pittsburgh's laboring families experienced less overcrowding than those in Manhattan and other very large cities, the divergence in population density, housing soundness, safety, and sanitation between socioeconomic groups existed to the detriment of working-class comfort and health while complicating women's domestic routines. As they battled with inadequate weapons against the pervasive dirt and grit produced by the mills, women played a crucial role in the transition to a consumer economy within the constraints of industrial poverty. They ameliorated the noxious side effects of the urban industrial environment through their housekeeping efforts, including careful financial management and taking in boarders. Their efforts enabled some working-class families to make the highly valued transition from tenancy to home ownership, although this was more common after the close of this era.[1]

The iron and steel mills made bad neighbors. Indeed, "dirt, and noise were inseparable adjuncts to life in a mill district."[2] Dense volumes of black smoke poured from hundreds of furnaces, prompting a correspondent for *Harper's New Monthly Magazine* to claim that the "true Pittsburgher" gloried in the city's wealth and dirt. He believed that "the great Iron City's mills and her wonderful furnaces are inspiring to the dullest."[3] Contemporary photographs and panoramic views of the city in this period invariably showed belching furnaces and haze obscuring the workers' housing nearby.[4] The mills usurped large tracts of level ground, polluted the atmosphere, scattered grit everywhere, and absorbed municipal resources to the detriment of the working-class women and families who lived nearby. Though they might have excited the men who made great profits from them, they created unpleasant, perhaps intimidating surroundings in which to live and raise a family.

Housing Density

As industry required more land, the families of the millworkers and glassworkers squeezed into the remnants, interspersed with the works or perched onto the hillsides above them. Pittsburgh's topography complicated workers' housing: the steep hills placed a premium on flat land for industrial development, and industrial expansion left little room for dwellings.[5] Thus the mills preempted prime building land, leading one steelworker to believe that laboring families paid high rents for poor accommodations because "the available building ground except in the elevated portions is all occupied."[6] The progressive increase in housing density reflected the shift in the nature of working-class housing. At midcentury most unskilled workers and their families had rented their own cottages; by the 1870s they lived in small terraced houses with little yard space; at the end of the century many inhabited tenements converted from older homes or abandoned industrial buildings.[7]

Increased housing density in the industrial districts led to unsanitary conditions, which the city did little to alleviate until after the turn of the century. Women at home all day bore the brunt of these conditions, deprived by political decisions of the improvements in municipal technology that made middle-class neighborhoods healthier and pleasanter.

Throughout this discussion, several overall shifts should be borne in mind: the downtown area, the central business district, lost population relative to the rest of the city during the last decades of the nineteenth century. Residential density increased in the Hill District and the industrial mill wards along the rivers and on the South Side. Lastly, as land use shifted from agricultural to domestic in Pittsburgh's eastern suburbs, population density rose. These suburbs remained sparsely inhabited, however, through the beginning of the twentieth century.[8]

Analysis of crowding requires consideration of a number of factors: the number of people living in an area and inhabiting the land available for domestic buildings; the number of dwellings per acre; the number of people per housing unit, and the average size of the home. Each of these factors tells something about housing patterns, but since they are partly independent of each other, one needs to discuss them all in order to obtain a fuller picture of housing and population density. It is then possible to examine the impact of life near the mills on working-class women and their families.

There were significant differences in the overall population density between the industrial and nonindustrial sections of the city and the richer and poorer wards, differences that were exacerbated by Pittsburgh's rapid economic development in the closing decades of the century. The most crowded section of the Hill District, which housed much of Pittsburgh's black population, had a density of 122.5 persons per acre in 1870, rising to 137.3 persons in 1890. Its density was more than triple that of its largely middle- and upper-class neighbor, the Fourth Ward. Outlying sections of the city were less populated; nevertheless the industrial Sixteenth Ward crammed 45 persons to an acre in 1890, quadruple its density in 1870 and twelve times that of pastoral Squirrel Hill, on which fewer than four people sprawled over each acre. Overall population density on the South Side also varied dramatically; remote and hilly Mount Washington housed only five people on each acre, while the neighborhoods closer to the mills jammed eighty-four souls into blocks with no yards or sanitary conveniences.[9]

The number of dwellings per acre provides another measure of residential crowding. By 1890 striking differences existed between the immigrant and black districts and the industrial and elite sections of the city. The Hill District contained nineteen houses per acre, more than four times as many as the fashionable Fourth Ward. Mill wards, represented by the Sixteenth and Twenty-sixth wards, had seven and twelve dwellings per acre, respectively. But the suburban sections of the city, Mount Washington and Squirrel Hill, for example, had fewer than one dwelling to an acre at the turn of the century.[10] Interestingly enough, the average number of persons per dwelling obscures the variation in house size and the number of people per household unit. The seemingly uncrowded Fourth Ward had 7.7 persons per dwelling in 1890, while the teeming Hill District had 7.2. None of the other wards averaged as many people per dwelling. The industrial wards contained approximately 6.6, and the spacious suburbs had but 5.7. Naturally, the houses in the Hill District and the industrial sections were much smaller than those in the upper- and middle-class neighborhoods, which increased the number of people per square foot.[11]

In order to make the variations in housing density meaningful, one must determine the proportion of each occupational class living in dwelling units of different sizes. This avoids problems, not apparent at the ward level, of land use patterns and class distinctions within the wards themselves. One ward of average population density, dwellings per acre, and people per dwelling has been selected for extensive examination here. Pittsburgh's Third Ward housed all occupational groups, immigrants and the natives, blacks and whites. A final, compelling, reason for choosing this ward was its inclusion in the Sanborn *Insurance Map of the Business and Manufacturing Parts of Pittsburgh, West and South Pittsburgh, Allegheny and Birmingham, Pa.*, for 1871 (the only year available). This map contains drawings to scale of each building, the number of stories, and the use.[12] The size of each dwelling was measured and multiplied by the number of occupied floors to obtain the square footage. Each census household was then traced through the city directory to its location on the map. In this manner the size of dwelling could be related to the number of people in the household, their occupational status, and the sex of the head of the household. To simplify analysis, it has been assumed that even though the inhabitants of some houses would have changed in the year

Pittsburgh Ward Map, 1900

ALLEGHENY

PITTSBURGH

OHIO RIVER

ALLEGHENY RIVER

MONONGAHELA RIVER

One Mile

N

between the census and the map's publication, their replacements probably had similar demographic characteristics.

This assumption permits a precise delineation of the extent to which
the various strata of working- and middle-class households experienced
overcrowding, although to a considerable degree the housing stock itself
determined the kind of dwelling each family could occupy. Though it may
have been the middle-class ideal to live in a house of more than 1500
square feet, the shortage of such homes in the ward meant that many
white-collar families had houses similar in size, if not quality, to those of
the laboring class.[13] This also helps to explain some of the push toward
the suburbs and the growing class distinctions in housing at the end of the
century. Figure 2 shows that nearly 60 percent of all houses in the Third
Ward were less than 800 square feet in area; perforce this was the most
common house size. However, the distinctions between classes appear
even within the ward boundaries. Of all unskilled and semiskilled
families, 25 percent had less than 400 square feet of living space or two

Figure 2. Distribution of Housing, Third Ward, 1870

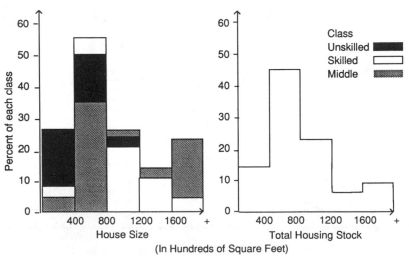

Sources: D. A. Sanborn, *Insurance Map of the Business and Manufacturing Parts of Pittsburgh,
West and South Pittsburgh, Allegheny and Birmingham, Pennsylvania*, 1871; Manuscript
Census, 1870; George Thurston, *Directory of Pittsburgh and Allegheny, 1870–1871* (Pittsburgh,
1871).

small rooms, although only 8 percent of the skilled workers and 5 percent of the middle class lived in such meager accommodation. Whereas 50 percent of the working-class families occupied between 400 and 800 square feet, only 35 percent of the middle class had homes with two to four rooms. The relative poverty and smaller family size of widowed women is reflected in their living quarters in the Third Ward: none had houses with more than four rooms. Nearly 25 percent of the unskilled and semiskilled families occupied 801–1,200 square feet, as did 20 percent of the skilled workers. No laborers lived in the larger houses (six or more rooms or over 1,200 square feet) yet 16 percent of the skilled workers and 35 percent of the white-collar families inhabited such dwellings.

Though the available housing stock forced some middle-class families to live in homes no larger than those of their working-class neighbors, the overall discrepancies between the classes are clear, especially the near monopoly the middle class held on houses containing more than 1,600 square feet. If space is an indicator of status, then the housing patterns clearly demonstrate a middle-class advantage, despite the overlap in smaller homes caused by limited supply.[14] The similarity in area occupied decreased steadily as the middle class moved into larger houses on the outskirts of the city, purchasing space, privacy, verdant vistas, and status, thus increasing the gap in living standards between themselves and millworkers' families.

A small survey conducted among the skilled and semiskilled workers in Pittsburgh by the Bureau of Industrial Statistics in 1882–83 uncovered none living in dwellings of more than six rooms. Indeed, only one puddler reported that his street had any houses of that size. The average house contained between three and four rooms. Given the mixed nature of working-class districts, it can be inferred that some of the smaller houses probably were occupied by laborers' families. The conditions of the houses themselves varied from poor to middling to very good. They were a composite of single-family houses, duplexes, and terraces but tended not to have private yards.[15]

Working-class families and widowed women had smaller, more crowded dwellings than clerks, shopkeepers, managers, or professionals. Although middle-class households were larger than those of the working class, the greater size of the houses themselves meant that each individual had more room and more privacy, which the Victorian middle class valued highly.[16] In 1870 the average white-collar family of 6.5 people had 0.89 persons per room, and the smaller blue-collar family of 5.1 people crowded 1.25 to a room. This ranked Pittsburgh's working class on a par with the densely occupied districts of Baltimore and Chicago, where 1.19 and 1.37 people, respectively, squeezed into each room.[17]

Pittsburgh's housing situation deteriorated as the century progressed. Housing reformers defined slums as dwellings with more than 1.01 persons per room. By the end of the century, many working-class districts in the Pittsburgh region exhibited this degree of residential congestion.[18] Nearly half the steel mill families in Homestead, for example, lived two or more to a room, and recently arrived Southern and Eastern Europeans were most likely to have two or even three persons squeezing into each small room. Housing patterns in Homestead highlighted the disparity between unskilled and skilled steelworkers. Two-thirds of the families with incomes greater than $20.00 per week lived in five- and six-room dwellings, but one-half of the households subsisting on $12.00 per week crowded into one- and two-room apartments, and only one-tenth had five or six rooms.[19] The London Board of Trade investigation into working-class living conditions in U.S. towns cited some horrendous examples of crowding in Pittsburgh's mill neighborhoods in 1909 in the manner common to investigations of the era. A tenement on Manner Street with three rooms ranging from 108 to 210 square feet provided shelter for a Polish couple and their six boarders. In Smallman Street a house of three to five rooms contained eight Croatians sharing two bedrooms; in another a couple with fourteen Slovak lodgers divided eight beds among them; and another contained a Slavic couple with fourteen boarders. In Spruce Alley, where the houses averaged about 500 square feet, the investigators found a couple living with two children and four boarders, another with no children and four boarders, and a third with one child and five boarders.[20] Another investigation into working-class housing in 1914, conducted in the immediate environs of Jones and Laughlin's steel mill in Soho discovered 619 people living in 396 rooms, an average of 1.56 persons per room.[21] Despite some efforts at housing reform and the building of a few model tenements at the turn of the century, working-class homes remained congested until wages rose in the mills, hours of work were shortened, and families succeeded in purchasing homes of their own.[22]

Housing

Letters to the *People's Monthly*, a magazine written for the upper echelons of the working class, complained in the 1870s that the working men of Pittsburgh were "not properly housed and find great difficulty in securing comfortable lodging for themselves and their families."[23] A decade later the Pittsburgh Association for the Improvement of the Poor (PAIP) claimed that it was "difficult to find a room to rent even in the most dilapidated buildings"; houses to rent were in great demand in the mill neighborhoods, "and in some localities, for instance, in the South Side, there is not a small house which can be rented."[24] The crowding and poor sanitation of these districts prompted J. H. Keeley to write a poem for the *National Labor Tribune*, "The Tale of the Tub," which described in verse what social surveys depicted in outraged prose.

> In cellars chill and dingy, oft
> In alleys with foul filthy ground
> Or crowded to a lonely loft
> These toiling ones are mostly found;
> An ancient stove, with sooty scrap
> A box, a bench a broken chair;
> A few patched duds in which to wrap
> Their weary limbs, fed on scant fare.[25]

More prosaically, a 1908 Pittsburgh Board of Health survey discovered over three thousand tenements in the city, half of them "old dwellings built and constructed to accommodate one family, and as a rule without conveniences for the multiple household crowding into them."[26] One such building, "Tammany Hall" in Basin Alley, began life as a planing mill. Subsequently its owner subdivided it into twenty-six rooms, housing twenty-five immigrant families, some having only a skylight or window cut into a passageway for ventilation and light.[27]

Several house types dominated the architecture of mill neighborhoods: brick or frame row houses, of the two-up, two-down variety, in which the stairway to the second floor occupied a narrow hall between the two lower rooms were the most prevalent. Closely set detached houses, two and three stories high, terraced into the hillsides, were also common, their plain fronts providing a sharp contrast to the Victorian propensity for architectural ornamentation exhibited on suburban homes.[28] As well as converting former industrial buildings and cutting up previously middle-class dwellings into smaller units, property owners built "back houses," additions to extant structures, to generate revenue from unoccupied yards.[29] Houses on the streets tended to be more solid and sanitary than the tenements, back houses, and those on the alleys, the last of these frequently accessible only through yards containing privies in close proximity to the kitchen door.[30] Adequate light and ventilation were impossible in such dwellings. An Italian woman inhabiting a ten-by-six cubicle with a two-foot-square window, directly opposite and two feet from the privy's door, told a housing inspector she kept the window shuttered in order to "keep out disease."[31] Other back house dwellers endured the stench for the sake of catching the elusive breezes that might blow through their cramped quarters in the oppressive summer heat.[32]

As the statistical snapshot derived from the 1871 Sanborn *Insurance Map* suggested, laborers and unskilled workers lived in smaller dwellings than either skilled workers or the middle class. According to the grand secretary of the Knights of Labor, Robert Layton, laborers along the Monongahela and Allegheny rivers inhabited row houses, sparsely furnished and without basements, and were no more comfortable than the miners, whom he described in 1883 as living in "absolute distress."[33] The Bureau of Industrial Statistics survey found that the arrangement of the premises did not contribute to tenant comfort. As one nailer noted, the tenement houses in his vicinity "were not so convenient nor as comfortably arranged as they should be for the enormous rents that are charged and I believe it is high time that legislation should be made to compel these cormorants to so arrange these houses that the tenants could receive some equivalent for their money."[34] The *National Labor Tribune* similarly condemned the dwellings in mill neighborhoods as "tumble down houses in rows," merely shelters for the working class but totally lacking in sanitary conveniences. Such houses did not age gracefully; a lack of maintenance as the years progressed aggravated their unsanitary features.[35]

As crowding increased at the century's end, immigrants and blacks encountered worsening housing conditions. The homes of black steel workers were frame buildings on the back streets and alleys; few resided on paved roads.[36] One black remarked that the "only place where there is plenty of room for Negroes is in the alleys."[37] Overcrowding was rife among poor blacks in the Hill District, who had difficulty in finding good, solid homes. Helen Tucker, a former member of the teaching staff at the Hampton Institute, observed that "the interiors of very many of the houses in which the Negroes live were out of repair—paper torn off, plastering coming down, and windows broken." Despite complaints to the landlords, no repairs were made.[38] Black persistence in the Pittsburgh district brought little improvement in their housing conditions in this era.[39]

Immigrants to the Pittsburgh district at the turn of the century also took up residence in the alleys, unable to find affordable housing elsewhere. The protagonists in *Out of This Furnace* lived in two rooms "at the Twelfth Street end of the row, facing the alley, which of course had no sidewalks and was so narrow that Mary could buy from hucksters' wagons without moving off her own doorstep."[40] Others moved into the Soho area near the iron and steel mills, where one-fourth of the rooms were partially or totally below ground level and most families crowded into two- or three-room apartments.[41] Many of the Polish and Italian immigrants in the Strip District lived in homes originally built for the middle class. The proximity of the mills encouraged property owners to adapt nearby buildings to accommodate as many people as possible by turning them into makeshift tenements.[42] Many of the buildings were old, in poor repair, and dingy from smoke, and gave the appearance of being mere "coverings from storm and sunshine."[43]

Regardless of the quality of the dwelling, all those who lived near the mills endured noise, traffic, and occasional explosions. The din pressed in upon the residents from every quarter; the rumble of ponderous machinery and the clatter of iron-laden wagons echoed through the narrow streets. During the summer, residents opening their windows and doors to the air were assaulted by the din of the mills, which forced people to shout in order to be heard and even, according to Robert Layton's testimony before the Senate, drowned out the fiddles at weddings. The high decibel level caused hearing losses among mill families. Many iron- and steel-workers were themselves partially deaf after years of working amid the roaring machines.[44]

The new industrial technology, hazardous to the men in the mills, also endangered the inhabitants near the works. Early in 1885 the careless use of gas caused a series of explosions: the first occurred at a pottery near the Allegheny River when a break in the pipes filled almost every cellar at the Point with gas. An explosion across the Allegheny River in Sharpsburg blew up the aptly named Vesuvius Iron Works. Leaks from street mains to nearby cellars resulted in explosions that demolished three buildings in the Fifteenth Ward and injured twenty-one residents of Lawrenceville. The gas remained trapped until some person went to the cellar on a "household call" with a lit candle and blew the place up. Even after the turn of the century, gas remained a dangerous industrial fuel. Sparks from unguarded machinery ignited gas seeping from a broken pipe in a steel mill, scorching some men and asphyxiating others. Eventually, with the invention of the double iron pipe, gas transportation became safer. Until that time the mills' neighbors suffered mishaps along with the mill workers.[45] The technology of the workplace thus affected not only the men who worked in the mills but all those who lived nearby, deafening them, pouring smoke onto them, and occasionally burning them.

Despite the paucity of adequate working-class housing in the city, most steel mill owners did not provide company residences, although some mills in the outlying towns did so.[46] Pittsburgh's steel magnates did not want to go into the housing business. They claimed to be "manufac-turers, not real estate dealers. We may be forced to build houses in certain new districts in order to attract and hold labor, but in an old settled community, let the laboring man take care of himself. We don't believe in paternalism."[47] The Carnegie Steel Company demonstrated its non-paternalistic posture when it acquired a mill that already had some company houses. It completely renovated the mill but did nothing to improve Painter's Row, leaving five hundred steel mill families to endure back-to-back houses with no through ventilation, cellar kitchens, no drinking water, and privies halfway up a hill, accessible only by steep steps.[48] Pittsburgh's railroad companies also acquired some residential properties along their tracks, not for the purpose of housing workers, but to avoid claims for damage and to provide land for expansion. They neither maintained nor improved the dwellings. Skilled workers avoided these houses altogether. They were inhabited mostly by recent immigrants, who lacked the resources to move elsewhere.[49]

Pittsburgh's skilled workers enjoyed better housing conditions than did their unskilled workmates. Their wages, comparable to those of white-collar workers, albeit less certain, enabled them to have a higher standard of living than the unskilled. Rollers, part of the labor aristocracy, often occupied single-family dwellings. Their houses, along with those of puddlers and heaters, were usually described as being in very good condition; many had their own yards and well-arranged premises. The differences in living standards noted in 1870 persisted through 1907. Few skilled workers' families lived in the smallest houses in 1870, and they, alone among the working class, resided in homes with more than one thousand square feet.[50] Similarly, a 1907 survey showed that no recent immigrants lived in houses having five or six rooms, but three-fifths of the best-paid workmen had homes of this size.[51]

Standard of Living

Margaret Byington's analysis of millworkers' household budgets in 1907 makes it possible to compare the standard of living among skilled and unskilled workers in the steel mill environs. One distinction between Homestead and Pittsburgh after the turn of the century must be drawn: whereas employment had been notoriously unstable in Pittsburgh, the Homestead mill afforded steady jobs, though only to nonunion members. Thus residents of the mill town had more to spend on homes and furnishings than those in the city. Nevertheless, the spending patterns of the unskilled living on less then $12.00 per week and the skilled with an income of more than $20.00 per week demonstrate the distinctions between the strata of the working class itself (see tables 12 and 13). Those at the bottom of the mill hierarchy confined their expenditures to basic items—rent, food, clothing, and fuel—while those at the top had outlays two to three times larger for basic items and spent nearly nine times as much on home furnishings. These expenditure levels confirm the distinctions between skilled and unskilled found in other cost of living studies. Despite the narrowing of differentials in the wages of skilled and unskilled workers that occurred at the beginning of the twentieth century, the gap in living standards between the strata of the working class was still evident at the time of the Pittsburgh Survey. Thus most (84 percent) of the families in Homestead with weekly incomes of over $20.00 per week had water in the house, but only 38 percent of those subsisting on less than $12.00 per week enjoyed this luxury. Homestead's working class was relatively fortunate in this regard: the proportion of laboring families within Pittsburgh proper who had indoor plumbing was much lower.[52]

The contrast in standard of living between the aristocracy of labor and the unskilled immigrants who worked in the mills' labor gangs is strong indeed. William Martin, for eleven years secretary of the AAISW, kept accounts of his family's household purchases. Over a period of two years, the Martin family, who owned their own home, acquired a bedroom suite for $125, a $25 hair mattress, assorted chairs, a sideboard and set of leather-covered chairs for the dining room, and a painting, artist unspecified, which cost $20. They laid forty-seven yards of Brussels

Table 12. Weekly Household Expenditures, Homestead, Pennsylvania, 1907–1908 (In Dollars)

Income	N	Total Expenditure	Rent	Food	Fuel	Clothing	Furniture
Under $12.00	32	9.17	1.88	4.16	0.38	0.94	0.09
$12–19.99	39	15.83	2.55	6.60	0.71	1.88	0.29
Over $20.00	19	25.56	3.73	9.38	0.90	3.36	0.80

Source: Adapted from Margaret Byington, *Homestead: The Household of a Mill Town* (New York, 1910), p.84.

carpet, extravagantly covering the stairs with it. Mr. Martin's scrapbook also contained a receipt for two-and-one-half pairs of lace curtains, for which he paid $16.25, nearly one-and-one-half times the weekly wage of a common laborer in the mills.[53]

Photographs of affluent workers' homes in Pittsburgh show lace curtains, pianos, oak chairs, wallpaper, patterned carpets, and even the occasional parlor organ, the possession of which was a status symbol for nineteenth-century Americans.[54] The secretary of the Knights of Labor testified that if skilled workers "have children that can play a piano or if they have an ear for music they, in many instances, have a piano in the house, and generally enjoy life pretty well."[55] The whatnot collections and drapes over mantlepieces, fire grates, and anything else upon which a cloth could be hung reflected Victorian taste. Skilled workers and their families furbished their homes in a style similar to that of the lower echelons of the middle class.[56]

When they went home at night, the effects of class followed both the owners and nonowners of the means of production.[57] But the gulf also yawned wide between skilled working-class families such as the William Martins and the Smith family, whose house a Humane Society visitor described in 1888 as "the picture of desolation."[58] Mr. Smith could only obtain several days' work each week as a laborer in the steel mills of the Sixteenth Ward. His family's rooms contained few furbelows. The baby lay in a rope sling next to its parents' bed, not in a net-covered crib. In the absence of closets and wardrobes, clothes hung on pegs, over chairs, or on

Table 13. Ratio of Weekly Household Expenditures,
Homestead, Pennsylvania, 1907–1908

Income	Total Expenditure	Rent	Food	Fuel	Clothing	Furniture
Under $12.00	100	100	100	100	100	100
$12–19.99	172	136	159	186	200	327
Over $20.00	278	198	225	237	357	889

Source: Adapted from Margaret Byington, *Homestead: The Household of a Mill Town* (New York, 1910), p.84.

the bed frame. Instead of lace curtains, an odd scrap of cloth was nailed across the window. Some rooms lacked even a small window, receiving their only light through the door. Lacking a dining room, much less a sideboard to put in it, poor housewives such as Mrs. Smith stacked their dishes on a wooden shelf in the kitchen. If the floorboards had any covering at all, it was scuffed linoleum or possibly a rag rug, not the 47 yards of Brussels carpeting that graced the Martin family home.[59] Furniture, linen, and utensils were scarce and well worn among the very poor.[60] Their barren homes contrasted sharply with the lavishly furnished and decorated dwellings of the skilled.

One reason for the minimal nature of the furnishings in the homes of the unskilled was that these families spent a disproportionate amount of their income on housing despite the inadequate nature of the accommodations. Rents in Pittsburgh were almost as high as in New York City.[61] In 1872 the *People's Monthly* claimed that Pittsburgh workers paid exorbitant rents for second- and third-story tenements with no conveniences. John Mason, a laborer, paid 33 percent of his $7.50 weekly wages for rent in 1875.[62] In a survey conducted in 1882–83, the Bureau of Industrial Statistics found that unskilled ironworkers paid anywhere from $10.00 to $15.00 for rent, while rents for semiskilled and skilled workers ranged from $12.00 to $18.00.[63] Several years later the bureau wrote that rents in Pittsburgh, "always exorbitant, have since the introduction of natural gas become more so" and that "the houses of those who are employed in the iron and steel industries rent from $16 to $25."[64] The proportion spent on rent by Homestead's mill families varied inversely with income, so that laborers earning less than $12.00 per week devoted 21 percent of their budget to housing, semiskilled workers earning between $12.00 and $19.99 paid 16 percent, and those with incomes over $20.00 spent 15 percent of their pay packets on rent.[65] Recent immigrants paid relatively more for rent than those who had been in the country longer, a fact that reflected both their need to live close to their employment and fellow countrymen and a certain amount of gouging among Pittsburgh's landlords.[66] Where rent absorbed a disproportionate share of the family income, expenditures for other items had to be pared accordingly, so that in many households the amount spent on food decreased during the week the rent had to be paid.[67]

Boarders and Home Ownership

One strategy working-class families used to increase their income, pay their rents, and save for a home of their own was to take boarders into their household. They exchanged space and women's domestic labor for the cash contributions tenants made.[68] In 1880 approximately one-fourth of all Pittsburgh households had non–family members residing with them, and three-fourths of all lodgers lived with working-class families.[69] Although the proportion of families with boarders was about the same in 1900 as it had been in 1880, certain sections of the Pittsburgh district had much higher concentrations. About one-third of the recent immigrants took in lodgers.[70] Districts near the mills, populated largely by immigrants and millworkers, also had large numbers of subtenants. One-third of the families in the Soho area surrounding Jones and Laughlin's steel works and two-fifths of the Slavic families in Homestead opened their homes to boarders.[71] Taking lodgers was a phase in many families' life cycle, reflecting the wife's other domestic responsibilities and the availability of other wage earners.[72] Childless young marrieds, families with working children, and those whose children had moved away were the most likely to take in boarders. Those with very young children were the least likely to do so, demonstrating that when women's domestic energies were most absorbed in caring for their own families, they were least able to supplement the family income through work at home.[73] Families with young children thus had fewer means of making ends meet than those with older children who might be earning or who themselves needed less attention, so that the mother could devote her attention to boarders.[74]

Contemporary social workers lamented the effects of keeping lodgers on the family, doubted that wise discipline could be maintained by overworked mothers, and worried about the "injury to the moral tone of the Slavic community caused by the crowding together of single men and families."[75] Slavic families, responding to low wages and strong demand from their countrymen for inexpensive housing near the mills, had an average of 3.4 unrelated boarders in each household that took lodgers at all. Italians in 1900 were somewhat less likely to take strangers in (38% did so) but took more of them, averaging 4.4 boarders per family.[76] The average household that took in any lodgers at all housed 1.66, a figure that highlights the extreme overcrowding among these new immigrant groups.[77] Despite the disadvantages, boarders could add 25 percent to the family income. Many working-class families, particularly those newly arrived, calculated that they needed the money more than the space, privacy, or leisure.[78]

Keeping lodgers had a dark side that concerned some members of the working class. As indicated by a rash of announcements published in the *National Labor Tribune*, not all tenants paid their board bills. William B. Smith wrote to that paper warning other boardinghouse keepers near coal mines that Adam Campbell and Lewis Timberly left his house "like thieves in the night," owing him $29.00. Several months later, the same paper published the names of two more workers who "cheated a widow woman out of seventy-five dollars they owed her for boarding" and editorialized that "we regret the necessity of the use of such extreme measures, but a man who will cheat a struggling widow out of board deserves no mercy." Some landladies gave their tenants credit during hard times, so that the accumulated bills might be as large as those incurred but not paid by certain South Side ironworkers for $35.00, $80.00, and $90.00. The notices in the *National Labor Tribune* suggest that some iron- and steelworkers changed their names as they moved about searching for work in order to avoid the obloquy of being labeled boardbill "skippers." For widowed women supporting themselves and their families by taking lodgers, nonpayment might result in their own eviction. Elizabeth Betz, a South Side widow, extended credit to two nail feeders, Frank Baubins, originally from Harrisburg, and William Smith, who had a wife in Wheeling. They skipped out, owing her $55.00 and leaving her unable to pay her own rent. Yet not all men who left without paying their board bills were malicious. James and Felix Donnelly confessed they left an unpaid board bill but, having little work, said they would pay their debts when they could. As they pointed out, "times like these (the depression of the 1870s) will make the best of us fall behind." Unemployment hit hardest at the most marginal members of the community, the widows deprived of their own breadwinners and trying to make ends meet by providing domestic services.[79]

Despite occasional nonpayment of the board bills, taking in lodgers was one way that working-class families saved to buy a home of their own. Perhaps life in a boardinghouse enhanced appreciation of a home of one's own. According to the *People's Monthly:* "No one but he who has been constantly shuffled about from one boarding house to another can truly appreciate the sanctity of a *home:* that blessed feeling of content which comes over one when he feels he has no longer a mere resting place, but a *home,* something he and his family can call their own, which he can improve, and adorn, and beautify, and where all shall belong and minister to the comfort and happiness of himself, his wife, and children, and not to another's."[80] Although the working class idealized home ownership, achieving this goal remained extremely difficult in this era.[81] Twenty-six percent of all Pittsburgh residents owned their own houses at the turn of the century, but the proportion was much lower in the neighborhoods surrounding the mills than it was in the more fashionable districts. About 40 percent of all families living in the suburban East End were owner-occupiers, but less than 15 percent of the residents of the iron and steel mill wards were in 1900. Blacks, recent immigrants, and young household heads had the lowest rates of home ownership; only 7 percent of the black, 5 percent of the Russian, 9 percent of the Italian, and 13 percent of the Polish families in Pittsburgh owned homes, compared with 39 percent of the German and 30 percent of the Irish and British. Native-born white home ownership was lower than that of "old stock" immigrants, 23 percent, but would have included young, second-generation Americans and recent rural migrants to Pittsburgh. Only 7 percent of the families headed by people under 35, 20 percent of the household heads 35–54 years old, and 38 percent of those over 55 had acquired residential property.[82] Many of the recent immigrants came as sojourners rather than permanent residents, but as they relinquished their original idea of returning to the old country with their fortunes, they devoted their energies to acquiring homes. As a result, the home ownership levels among Southern and Eastern European immigrants rose dramatically during the first decades of the twentieth century.[83]

Working-class families needed steady incomes and good money management if they were to buy homes, yet a number of factors already discussed mitigated against widespread home ownership in these decades. High unemployment rates and the devaluation of workers' skills limited the ability of working-class families to save the large cash down payment required, usually half the purchase price, and to repay the balance of the mortgage within a short period, typically five years.[84] The actual burden of buying the home fell most heavily upon the housewife, who managed the family's money, pinching pennies wherever she could to save for the down payment and meet the repayments on the mortgage.[85] Women, then, contributed to home ownership in two ways, by taking in boarders and by careful money management. Immigrant families made great sacrifices to purchase a home of their own. They crowded their dwelling with lodgers, sent their children to work, and relied upon the domestic labor of their women in order to add a few dollars to the family income. Home ownership, in Edith Abbott's analysis of tenement dwellers, was not synonymous with prosperity because it frequently "entailed an effort to secure property and future welfare at the cost of present health, comfort, and decent living."[86] Some working-class families, usually those headed by skilled workers or with multiple breadwinners, succeeded in purchasing homes, but for most this remained an unfulfilled goal through the time of the Pittsburgh Survey. As the new immigrants persisted, their rates of home ownership increased, though those for blacks remained significantly lower than for whites.[87]

Municipal Technology

Though economic and social changes between 1870 and 1907 tended to cause overcrowding and a decline in housing standards among the less affluent members of the working class, certain innovations made domestic life healthier, safer, and more pleasant for some urban families. Sewers, paved roads, streetlights, piped water, garbage incineration, indoor plumbing, natural gas, and electricity all improved the urban standard of living in the last decades of the nineteenth century. Details of the allocation of the new forms of municipal technology, of who benefited from them and who could not afford them, illustrate the relative deprivation of the poorer segments of the working class and the impact that the lack of services had on women.[88] The uneven dispersion of the technological advantages of urbanization reinforced differences in the standard and style of living between the classes already made apparent by industrialization. The middle class in Pittsburgh used their wealth and political influence to obtain better housing and municipal services in the decades after the Civil War, thus attracting a large portion of the city's resources away from the older, industrial districts to the suburbs and the urban fringe.[89] Coupled with worsened conditions in industrial workplaces, narrow opportunities for working-class women, and increased physical separation of the classes, this meant a wider gap between the life-styles and quality of life of the middle and working classes.

At the end of the nineteenth century, city government acted upon the principle that those who benefited from services should pay for them; hence distribution proceeded along class lines and was influenced by political considerations. Since the municipal authorities expected property owners to pay for the services provided to their homes, those who could pay received the new technologies, while those who could not went without them. Although the city treasury (the taxpayers as a whole) paid the operating and maintenance expenses, property owners "abutting and directly affected, to the extent benefited" were assessed the actual cost of improvements.[90] When people could not afford the assessments or their landlords chose not to improve their property, their neighborhoods did not obtain the services or received them later than did the more affluent areas. Conditions were worst in working-class neighborhoods, where the majority of residents were tenants rather than home owners. The general housing shortage meant that landlords did not need to provide services in order to attract tenants, who moved frequently and were reluctant to have the costs passed on to them in the form of higher rents. As a result, working-class districts had fewer amenities than the more established areas and the new suburbs. The lack of services was critical to health and housing in the environs of the mills, because of both the population density and the mills' pollution and traffic.[91]

The steepness of the streets, hillsides, and ravines in working-class districts caused great quantities of gravel, stones, and debris to wash down during rainstorms. The high volume of traffic exacerbated the problem. Heavy trucks traveled to the mills carrying iron castings, machinery, and materials, sometimes drawn by eight or ten pairs of horses. They rapidly wore out the pavements, raising the dust of the streets, adding dirt and droppings to an already unclean atmosphere. The steep hills, unpaved roads, and railroad tracks with frequent freight trains isolated the working class in their own sections of the city. By contrast, the middle and upper classes lived in gently sloping suburban areas, served by streetcars and commuter railroads. The more lightly trafficked streets were wider, cleaner, and altogether more wholesome than those near the mills.[92]

The variations in street paving methods in two sections of the city, the wealthy suburban East End and the impoverished Point, highlight the significance of residential mobility patterns and the political nature of municipal services while demonstrating politically reinforced social distinctions. In 1873 the Pittsburgh Board of Health characterized the Point as "without exception, the filthiest and most disagreeable locality within the limits of the city." The people living in the tenements there were of "the poorer class," renting "the merest apologies for houses." The Board of Health asserted that paving the streets would enhance the general heath of the city, but obdurate landlords insisted that their poor tenants should pay all improvement expenses. Since the tenants moved frequently, they had no stake in the dwellings as such. In any event, they could not afford the cost, so the Board of Health suggested that the city bear it, which the City Council refused to do. These streets remained unpaved through the 1880s, and other working-class neighborhoods still had dirt roads at the time of the Pittsburgh Survey.[93]

Most working-class families could not afford large capital expenditures, as their troubles in purchasing homes indicated. Yet the city required that all improvements be paid for within thirty days of the work's completion. Pittsburgh's City Council held fast to its "pay or do without" dictum at the Point and in other working-class neighborhoods but made exceptions in the East End suburbs. Since improvements were assessed on a per–frontage foot basis, the large estates of Henry Clay Frick and other steel magnates would have been taxed dearly for the roads that facilitated their commuting to work and provided their families with a cleaner atmosphere. The city controller maintained that payment within the specified time limit would seriously burden these property owners. To resolve this predicament a "prominent and public-spirited citizen" of the East End proposed, and the City Council agreed, that the city sell bonds to cover the costs of the street paving. The East End property owners would then reimburse the city in ten equal annual installments rather than the single payment required of inner-city lot owners. When the courts deemed the act unconstitutional, the city assumed the entire cost of paving the suburban roads. It did this during the very same time when it refused to upgrade the streets down at the Point or grant those property owners the right to make their payments on the installment plan. In effect, the City Council relieved the well-to-do of their obligations to pay for urban improvements while rigorously enforcing the rules for the poor.[94]

The working class reacted indignantly to this subsidy of the rich. The great bulk of Pittsburgh's laboring population never saw an avenue from one year to the next, the *National Labor Tribune* thundered, yet they paid the interest on the bonds that built them. Although the working class derived no direct benefit from the new roads, "every poor man's lot and house is taxed to pay this great debt. His labor is taxed. His wages are attached before they are earned and for years to come." Ironically, the rent of the poor paved the streets of the affluent, but not those of their own neighborhoods.[95]

As Pittsburgh's working-class population density increased, families suffered the unsanitary conditions that arose from governmental decisions and overcrowding. Unpaved roads, for example, could not be kept in good order because it was more difficult to sweep or clean them. Horse droppings and human refuse remained there longer, putrefying in Pittsburgh's long, hot summers. Nor did the installation of sewer and water pipes keep pace with urban growth in the areas surrounding the mills. Working-class neighborhoods did not receive sufficient sanitary services, so their growing populations increased the burden on cesspools, privies, and water supplies.[96] These districts had less water and they had it in a less convenient form than middle-class sections. Large water mains and indoor water pipes served the homes of the affluent, but working-class dwellings had smaller water pipes and pumps in the courtyards or down the street. The discrimination in pipe size resulted from an 1872 decision taken by the City Council's Water Commission to let the amount of potential revenue determine the size of the pipe to be laid in each street. Thus the "paying portion of our city" would not be deprived of a "sufficient water supply." This cost-conscious method of allocation ensured that some areas had a lavish supply of water, others had an insufficient one, and some had none at all.[97]

To compound the problem, the city's equipment did not generate sufficient pressure to push water up the steep hills during the summer when the water level in the reservoir was low. As a result poor people living in remote areas reached by small service pipes were subjected in hot weather "when cold water is their greatest boon, to actual suffering for the quantity for which they pay and which is essential to health, cleanliness, and comfort." The city's four-million-dollar waterworks, built in 1877, was of little use to the urban laboring families clinging to the hillsides above the mills who received none of the piped water.[98] Mills and railroads located on the flat land below and among working-class homes placed great demands on the water system, diverting the water before it could reach the small water pipes servicing these families. The Pennsylvania Railroad supplied its locomotives with water from a pipe at the bottom of a hill. In doing so, it decreased the flow from the main pipe to the smaller pipes providing water to the railroad and mill families living near the yards. During the summer many areas of the South Side had no water from seven in the morning until six at night while the mills operated.[99] If South Side women wanted water for their housework or to drink, they hauled it early in the morning before the mills started the day turn. One woman complained that she had to get up at five o'clock in the morning to fill her tubs if she wanted water during the long summer days. The uncertainty of the water supply in the mill environs made women's household chores harder and interrupted their routines. Even the daily newspapers acknowledge that there was "nothing more calculated to disturb the serenity of the household than to have the water supply turned off on wash day." Thus the poor water supply "showed its burden upon womankind."[100]

Pittsburgh's water companies (one public and one private) charged more for indoor plumbing than for a pump in the yard and discriminated against smaller householders by demanding twice as much per room for water in small homes as in larger ones. Since there were no water meters, those with indoor water used it lavishly. In 1879 the water authority complained that "a walk through the wealthy or business portion of the city will show the small regard they have in the use of water or the welfare of others."[101] When water became available at the turn of the tap, usage skyrocketed. Personal hygiene improved as weekly baths became daily, human wastes were removed instantly rather than semiannually, and floor, clothes, and dishes were washed more frequently.[102] Through the first decade of the twentieth century, however, these improvements in hygiene, and therefore in health, were primarily limited to the middle class.[103]

In 1890 the chief of the Department of Public Safety claimed that it was the "custom to have even moderate priced houses fitted with hot and cold water, water closets and bathroom"; however, such amenities were beyond the reach of most iron- and steelworkers' families. They could not pay the rents on houses with indoor water, nor could many afford to install such plumbing even when they owned their own homes.[104] A few labor aristocrats put in their own sewer and water pipes, as did some members of the middle class. In 1887, William Martin hired a plumber to dig a pipe for a toilet. The plumber took three hours to do this, charging Martin $2.75.[105] At the beginning of the twentieth century, Margaret Byington found that almost all the best-paid steel millworkers in Homestead, where houses were newer than in Pittsburgh, had water in the house, but most of the millworkers' homes in Pittsburgh's Sixth and Twelfth wards still had no indoor plumbing as late as 1917.[106] Prescribers of ideal homes told middle-class house buyers that "the various kinds of public service—

water, gas, electricity, telephone and sewer—are of great importance."[107] These luxuries, and the health and convenience they bought, remained too expensive for most laboring families.

Since most working-class women had no indoor water, they carried "every drop of water they would use" into their homes. If they lived on the second or third floor, they brought the water upstairs and back down, disposing of it in a sink in the yard, on the ground, or sometimes out of the window, but always hauling water. Day after day and many times each day, the women residents of mill tenements transported water up and down stairs that their homes and their children "might be kept decent and clean." All laboring women carried water inside for cooking, for cleaning, and for washing dishes and clothes. No matter what the chore, they needed water to do it. Outdoor plumbing complicated housework. "Cleanliness is out of the question when water has to be carried." Heavy particle pollution and the grime and sweat on men's work clothes made washing difficult. The city's decision to provide decent services only to those who could pay for them exacerbated women's problems in keeping their families and their homes clean.[108] Not until 1903 did the state legislature require that new tenements have indoor water and that existing tenements be retrofitted with plumbing on each floor. This law did not apply to the one- and two-family houses that dominated Pittsburgh's working-class neighborhoods (a tenement contained three or more families).[109] As a result, social investigators concluded in 1909 that water taps were to be found only in the kitchens of better houses, but mostly the water supply was a hydrant in the yard.[110]

In addition to the high cost, inconvenience, and scarcity of water, the laboring residents of the South Side suffered from the poor quality of the water itself. The Monongahela Water Company, a private water concern originally established to provide water for the mills and glass houses, provided the only water on the South Side. *Commoner and Glass Worker*, the trade paper of the glassworkers, stated that the Monongahela Water Company drew its water directly from the Monongahela River "just below where the large sewers discharge their filth into the river itself." No pure, swift-flowing stream, the Monongahela was the catch basin for the refuse and sewage of more than sixty thousand people living along it, carrying debris from the mills, glass houses, and slaughterhouses lining its banks.[111] Although the city periodically protested the water's poor quality, it took no steps to improve it. South Side residents complained, but the city solicitor shrugged them off, saying it was "none of his business." Eventually the city ran water pipes to the South Side from the public water company, but these were to protect property in case of fire, not to provide public household supplies. Moreover, the millworkers' on-the-job drinking water came directly from the river without any filtration or purification, the intake pipes being located immediately downstream from the sewage-emptying dump boats. The men in the mills, some of whom drank as many as thirty or thirty-five glasses of water during a shift in order to prevent dehydration from the intense heat, consumed water freshly contaminated by sewage, refuse from other mills, and wastes from the slaughterhouses. Health officials suggested women boil all drinking water to prevent typhoid and cautioned men against drinking directly from the rivers, but to little avail.[112]

The sanitary conditions in working-class neighborhoods improved much more slowly than they did in other sections of the city. These wards suffered from a relative lack of sewers in proportion to their population density. In 1879 the most fashionable parts of Pittsburgh had the most extensive sanitary waste disposal facilities. The central business district and the heavily upper-class Fourth Ward had excellent sewer systems. The Point had no sewers whatsoever, nor did large sections of the laboring wards along both rivers and on the South Side.[113] Ten years later, the chief sanitary inspector described the city as generally well sewered, yet parts of the South Side still had no access to sanitary waste disposal. Several hundred cesspools drained into abandoned coal mines, primarily on the hills above the mills and railroad yards. Since these areas had no paved streets, transporting sewage to a proper dumping ground was expensive. This "led many to resort to the very dangerous practice of drilling their privy wells and cesspools through the comparatively thin crust of earth overlying these coal mines." When these mines caved in, trapping the sewage, it seeped into the wells and contaminated the water upon which some South Siders still relied.[114]

At the turn of the century, less than one-fourth of Pittsburgh's streets had proper sewers. The state legislature outlawed privy vaults themselves in 1901, but not until 1907 did the city, under a new sanitary inspector, proceed against offenders.[115] Nevertheless, some eighteen thousand privy vaults were still in use in Pittsburgh in 1910, many of them "dry closets" that emptied directly onto the ground with no flushing mechanism or possibility of cleaning them. Horrified investigators into working families' housing reported that "some drained down the side of a hill through an open conduit into a neighbor's back yard. One was found emptying at the curb of a busy street into a thickly populated section of the city." Only at that point did it discharge into a public sewer. Creeks also doubled as drains, with water closets built over them or with wooden chutes extending from the privy to the stream. "As a matter of fact excreta were found exposed on the ground at the edge of the run [creek], which was expected to rise and wash the sewage away when the river rose—an uncertain event both as to time and frequency."[116] Despite reformers' efforts, many working-class districts had privies and pumps in the yard rather than indoor plumbing as mandated by law. This situation prevailed in many parts of the city but was at its worst in the crowded immigrant and black sections. On the South Side, Saw Mill Run served as the only "sewer" for some thirty-five thousand people as late as 1914. At the time of the Pittsburgh Renaissance in the 1950s, some families in the predominantly black Hill District still relied upon privies.[117]

These conditions made life in working-class neighborhoods less healthy and more onerous than in the middle- and upper-class sections of Pittsburgh. Laboring women spent their days coping interminably with grime and dirt, trying to compensate for their surroundings. If they were fortunate enough to have a paved yard, they might be seen "at any hour of the day, hard at work with their brooms in an effort to keep the place clean." Where there was no paving, the women themselves spread planks "in an attempt to keep the mud from being tracked into the house." However, water and fecal matter from the privies soaked into the boards, bringing their efforts to naught. William H. Matthews, resident director of the Kingsley House Settlement, believed that "the conditions under which they must live meant constant hardship, sickness, and bitter struggle."[118] The majority of the urban populace crowded into neighborhoods where housing conditions were, in the words of the Pittsburgh Survey, "inimical to public health and private decency," while a minority resided in substantial suburban homes with modern sanitary devices and a cleaner environment.[119]

Public Health and Technological Diffusion

The city authorities were aware of the health problems engendered by overcrowded neighborhoods and inadequate sanitation. As early as 1851, fearing a cholera epidemic, the City Council petitioned the state legislature for a board of health with the power to establish quarantines and remove sanitary nuisances. It grew moribund after the initial scare but was resurrected in 1870. Pittsburgh's Board of Health attacked problems of improper sanitation with vigor but limited resources. Its inspectors toured their districts daily, reporting "tenement houses unfit for occupation or overcrowded, cellars or basements damp or foul or any instance deserving of attention or any defect in any building whatever, as regards light, heat and cleanliness." Most of its activities took place in working-class neighborhoods, where inspectors threatened and cajoled inhabitants into cleaning up alleys, privy vaults, and yards.[120]

The Board of Health's activities expanded during the 1870s and 1880s despite popular and council resistance to its more expensive suggestions. Sanitary inspectors found that the only way to obtain cooperation in tenement house areas was to visit them "almost daily until able to get the tenants to pay some attention to the sanitary regulations." Garbage and ashes were heaped indiscriminately into piles, which were seldom removed except on the urgent prompting of the inspectors.[121] In 1890 the Bureau of Health, reorganized and responsible to the mayor, again claimed it had made progress in educating the working class to meet its standards but admitted that too many still deposited their garbage in "rivers, vacant lots, and other objectionable places." Educational efforts were useless without adequate means of trash disposal. Insufficient means caused overcrowded dwellings, and landlords' desire to maximize profits resulted in minimal or no sanitary conveniences in rental dwellings. Poverty, unsanitary dwellings, and fiscal shortsightedness contributed to working-class noncompliance with emerging sanitary standards. The parsimonious City Council allocated little money for services that did not bring a direct financial return. Not until 1895 did the city contract for systematic garbage collection and disposal. That, rather than educational efforts, alleviated Pittsburgh's garbage problem.[122]

One of the most critical consequences of this uneven distribution of municipal services and technology was a disparity in life chances between the classes. The less densely populated, suburban, and affluent areas had lower death rates than the inner-city industrial wards. A class-based morbidity and mortality differential existed, and many of the advantages from improvements in the urban environment accrued initially to Pittsburgh's more affluent residents. The middle and upper classes took steps that ensured a healthier environment for their own families as much as a matter of convenience and status as for hygienic purposes. Such affordable tokens of affluence as toilets, running water, and iceboxes improved health as they removed the sources of contamination from middle-class homes. Less crowded housing, more municipal improvements, and technological amenities all contributed to the lower sickness and death rates of suburban neighborhoods.[123]

Some historians have questioned the muckrakers' and Progressives' condemnation of the urban industrial milieu, noting that urban health actually improved in the late nineteenth century in the United States as death rates dropped. Writing of the nation as a whole, but focusing on four large cities, Edward Meeker concluded that "the sanitation movement helped to compensate for the adverse effect of urbanization on mortality." His study found little improvement in urban mortality levels before 1880–1885 but a steady decline in death rates from that period onward.[124] This timing would be consistent with the introduction of major innovations in public water supplies and the provision of sanitary waste disposal to at least some sections of large cities. Robert Higgs's study of mortality in large U.S. cities posits that improvements in the urban standard of living, coupled with public health measures introduced between 1880 and 1900, led to declining mortality levels. Urban areas, though somewhat less healthy than rural ones, improved as places to live during the last quarter of the nineteenth century even as, and perhaps because, reformers' efforts to clean them up increased. Thus cities' higher-paying jobs and improving health conditions attracted continued migration from less affluent areas, particularly in Southern and Eastern Europe, where overall mortality levels exceeded those of urban areas of the United States. Despite higher death rates relative to rural areas in the United States, cities offered a healthier environment and greater material rewards than the homelands of many of Pittsburgh's new residents.[125]

In common with those in many other cities, health standards improved in Pittsburgh during the last quarter of the nineteenth century as public health measures and higher standards of living led to declining mortality levels.[126] The crude death rate (deaths per 1,000 of population) declined from 24.1 to 18.8 in large U.S. cities between 1871 and 1900. In Pittsburgh, at least, better health was distributed as unevenly as the sewers. While the crude death rate fell from 27.7 to 19.5 for these years, some groups in the population still suffered far more than others. Working-class death rates, as far as can be determined, were higher than those of the middle class.[127] Although more settled, better paid skilled workers enjoyed higher standards of living and possibly indoor plumbing, the death rates in working-class districts prompted one proletarian author to ask:

But why do I talk of death
That phantom of grisly bone?
I hardly fear his terrible shape
It seems so like my own—
It seems so like my own
Because of the facts I keep;
Oh God!
That bread should be so dear
And flesh and blood so cheap![128]

This writer reminds us that the grim reaper remained a familiar, unwanted caller in laboring households as a consequence of lower standards of living, unsanitary neighborhoods, and dangerous occupations. As was observed in chapter 1, working-class men endured disproportionately high death rates due to industrial accidents. Infant mortality, also skewed by class, will be discussed in chapter 4. The unwillingness of the city fathers to provide adequate services to all parts of the city exacerbated the health problems of overcrowded neighborhoods. Deplorable sanitary conditions, coupled with polluted water supplies in mill districts, led to higher than average death rates from certain infectious and contagious diseases, in particular diphtheria, typhoid, and pneumonia. Poorer Pittsburgh residents suffered grievously from the consequences of an inadequate, unsanitary water supply, as the mortality figures from these diseases demonstrated.[129]

The death rate from infectious diseases was highest on the South Side, where high population densities compounded poor sanitary facilities. In 1877, 44.7 people per 1,000 died from infectious diseases on the South Side; the comparable rate for the East End was 17.7.[130] Some ailments, such as smallpox, became less common because of vaccination programs, whereas others, including diphtheria, reached epidemic proportions. Pittsburgh had the highest diphtheria fatality rate among U.S. cities, followed closely by two other crowded industrial centers, Cincinnati and Cleveland. Diphtheria outbreaks reached their zenith in 1880, when an epidemic in Pittsburgh claimed 206 lives per 100,000 residents; among 1–4-year-olds the fatality rate climbed to 779 per 100,000. The outbreak was worst on the South Side near badly constructed sewers, an indictment of the inadequate sanitation surrounding the mills.[131]

Although oriented toward trade union issues, the popular press recognized the severity of this highly communicable disease characterized by the formation of a false membrane in the throat accompanied by pain, swelling, and, all too frequently, death. During the 1880 outbreak the *National Labor Tribune* published a "cure" that it claimed had been "used with happy effect on the most obstinate cases." Its nostrum consisted of a combination of 10 grains of sulphate of quinia, 90 grains of dilute muriatic (hydrochloric) acid, and 1 drachm of chlorate of potassium with sufficient gum syrup to make a total of two ounces. The poor victim received a teaspoon of this every hour followed by a chaser of good rye whiskey if "the patient needs stimulant." The whiskey might relieve the pain, but the compound could not cure the disease.[132] At the end of the decade, *Commoner and Glass Worker* published another patent remedy of similarly dubious medical validity. Its "surest preventive or its cure" for the "dreaded diphtheria" was to give the victim massive doses of laxatives followed by a teaspoonful of lime water every hour, accompanied by an unspecified but "suitable" tonic.[133] This worthless nostrum did not even offer the patient the benefit of soothing alcoholic oblivion; certainly, purging a sick person would not speed recovery. The diphtheria death rate dropped only with the introduction of a vaccination program by the city in 1897.[134]

Diphtheria affected children primarily, but other causes of death, among them typhoid fever and pneumonia, weighed heavily upon Pittsburgh's laboring men and made widowhood a major feature in the lives of working-class women in the city. In 1900 other large U.S. cities suffered an average of 18 typhoid deaths per 100,000 residents, but Pittsburgh experienced 145. Only Allegheny City exceeded this rate, and Pittsburgh's sister city across the Allegheny River shared its polluted water supply.[135] The trade union correspondents of the *National Labor Tribune* stigmatized typhoid as "that terrible killer." A friend and pallbearer at the funeral of Mr. Reuben L. Martin wrote that the gentleman had been laid to rest in his fifty-first year, "after an illness of ten days, during which time he suffered excruciating pain from typhoid fever."[136] Typhoid affected the working class, particularly on the South Side, more severely than the middle and upper classes because its water came directly from the polluted Monongahela River and millworkers drank so much water to prevent dehydration.

Mr. Martin's death and those of many of his workmates and neighbors could have been prevented through the application of available technology if the city had been willing to use public moneys to install a water filtration system. When the Pittsburgh Survey published the results of its investigation into typhoid fever, it lambasted internecine warfare within the Republican party for delaying the implementation of such a system for twelve years. Although an investigation into the water system began in 1895, the main part of the city received filtered water only at the end of 1907. In 1908 the city acquired the South Side's private and largely inadequate water system, finally delivering pure water to the heavily populated working-class district early in 1909. These delays cost literally thousands of lives. By 1913, Pittsburgh's typhoid fever death rate approximated the national average.[137]

Pneumonia also weighed heavily on Pittsburgh's working class. Only Boston and New York had higher pneumonia fatality rates in 1890. Men, though, were hardest hit: in that year, 208 per 100,000 Pittsburgh women died from pneumonia whereas the rate for men was 279.[138] In 1900 pneumonia struck most severely in the mill districts along the Allegheny River, the South Side, and the black- and immigrant-dominated Hill District. The proportion of pneumonia deaths among unskilled and semiskilled households was twice as high as in middle- and upper-class homes. Particularly for men, pneumonia could result from their working conditions. The disease was a common aftermath of accidents and prolonged stays in bed. Where the accident itself did not kill, the pneumonia that followed it might. Millworkers endured extreme temperature variations, which weakened them and made them susceptible to disease. Particulate matter hung in the air of the steel mills, was inhaled, and irritated the lungs. Men alternated day and night shift every two weeks, losing sleep as they adjusted to the new routine. Moreover, the heat of the mills caused them to sweat freely, drenching their work clothes. The men went home from the heat of the mills in the cold night or morning air during the winter. There was no place to wash other than the "bosh," a water trough for cooling tools. Companies provided no place to change from sweat-soaked clothes into dry ones. All this contributed to the generally weakened physical condition that made men susceptible to viral infections such as pneumonia. As a result, the pneumonia fatality rate was significantly higher for men between the ages of 15 and 54, the primary working years, than for boys or older men.[139] The consequences of millwork were thus higher accidental death rates and a heightened vulnerability to disease.

Through the beginning of the twentieth century, the responsibility for neighborhood cleanliness and family health rested largely upon the individual working-class woman rather than upon the landlords or the city, but personal diligence made little headway against the crowded communities, filthy streets, contaminated water supplies, and inadequate or nonexistent sewers. The middle class escaped these conditions by moving to the urban fringe and purchasing the new technologies. The working class, particularly the newly arrived among them, lived cheek by jowl with the mills, factories, and railroads. They received an inadequate share of municipal resources but bore the full brunt of urbanization and industrialization. The working-class woman carried the major burden of protecting her family through her struggles to keep her home clean. She nursed her family through their illnesses, though not always with success. Her battle for cleanliness made her family's surroundings a bit healthier, despite the crowding and inadequate sanitation of many working-class neighborhoods. Until sanitation and water supplies improved, her struggle was all too often a losing one, particularly for the most vulnerable members of her family, infants and young children.

4 | Childhood and Education

All classes march through the various stages of the life cycle, but those at the bottom moved most precipitately toward adulthood, impelled by economic imperatives to earn their keep at an early age.[1] Reformers, feeling that children's activities were too important to be determined solely by their parents, reacted against working-class child-rearing patterns through the imposition of laws regulating parent-child interaction and the institution of compulsory education for children. External forces, whether poverty or the truant officer, did not operate in a vacuum. Parents and children in this era determined the extent to which children would be educated and when, if at all, they would enter the labor force. Cultural values as well as economic status influenced these crucial decisions but operated within the framework of possibilities and problems posed by the steel mills and other employments in the city. The ability of some parents to afford a more sanitary environment and adequate nutrition for their children and to defer their entry into the labor force enhanced the children's life chances. Cleaner surroundings and more access to education promoted middle-class children's health and well-being. Conversely, the life chances of working-class children, particularly those with unskilled fathers or widowed mothers, were adversely affected by their dirtier neighborhoods and shortened education.

While definitions of childhood and fashions in child rearing have changed over the centuries and between cultures, children's time typically can be divided between play, informal education or training at home, formal education, and work outside the home. The variations between cultures, economic systems, classes, and the sexes at any given historical moment enhance our understanding both of the particular culture and the way in which resources were deployed within it. Historical demographers and family historians have shown that various factors affected the children's lives, roles, and activities, including infant mortality rates, the mode of production, the age at which children could first make labor contributions within or outside the household, the time or monetary cost of training and education, and the prospects for wage labor.[2] High rates of infant mortality, limited employment opportunities, the changing nature of work in the mills, the tenuous financial position of families headed by women or unskilled workers, and an urge to regulate the behavior of the city's inhabitants all molded the early childhood and educational experiences of the working class in Pittsburgh.

Overview of the Life Course

Several factors distinguished the working-class childhood from that of the middle or upper classes. Although overall mortality rates decreased during this era, the working class endured higher death rates among the very young than their more affluent counterparts.[3] For the survivors the typical progression through the life cycle for the working-class child in these years entailed shorter periods of freedom from responsibility and preparation for the future than in the middle or upper classes. The working-class child went to school at the age of 6 and left at or before 14, whereas more affluent children entered school later but stayed longer. By the end of this era, school assumed a more prominent place in many children's lives, but poorer boys still went to work before their middle-class peers. Their sisters either helped out at home or began a brief period of employment, typically as domestic servants, though the range of occupations widened by the turn of the century.

Marriage followed about ten years later. The average age of first marriage was 23 for women and 27 for men. Within several years, most couples had their first child and typically completed their family in ten years. By the time their children had grown up sufficiently to enter the labor force, the father's earning powers would have peaked. By 45 or 50 it was more difficult for the laboring man to keep up the pace demanded by the steel mills, so that income generated by the sons helped support the family until they married or moved from the city in search of work. Although retirement did not exist as a well-defined stage in the working-class life cycle at this time, the steel industry provided few jobs for men past the peak of their physical powers. As a result these men worked either sporadically or at lower-paying jobs. Their daughters typically made either in-kind contributions, by assisting their mothers at home, or smaller cash contributions than their brothers, which reflected the lower wages paid to female domestic servants, factory workers, and (at the end of this era) white-collar workers.

Women's employment patterns were circumscribed by their stage in the life course to a far greater degree than men's. Married women rarely had regular jobs outside the home, though many took in boarders to supplement the family income. If a woman was widowed while her children were young, considerable pressure existed to speed the children's passage through childhood into adolescence and employment. A substantial number of fatherless boys went to work between the ages of 10 and 14, and almost none continued their education past 15. The daughters of widows were also more likely to enter the labor force at an early age than other girls. The timing of important transitions and the quality of life within each stage, then, largely reflected family circumstances and the industrial structure, although cultural differences also existed between different ethnic groups in the working class.[4] The family functioned as an economic unit with members contributing what they could within the socially accepted limits. Especially among poorer working-class families, children were expected to work either inside or outside the home in order to sustain the family unit to an extent to which middle-class children, with their prolonged periods of education, clearly were not.

Infant Mortality

Working-class families suffered a disproportionate share of deaths due to the nature of Pittsburgh's industries and the inadequate servicing of their neighborhoods. Despite an overall decrease of more than one-fifth in the death rate between the 1870s and 1900s (see table 14), mortality levels rose or remained high in proletarian districts. Infant mortality countered the prevailing trend, rising by nearly one-fifth between the 1870s and the 1900s. Unfortunately, the data used to analyze infant mortality preclude

Table 14. Mortality Averages
(Per 1,000)

	Infants	All
1870s	188[a]	26.1[b]
1880s	190	24.4
1890s	199	19.4
1900s	226[c]	20.3[d]

Sources: Executive Departments of the City of Pittsburgh, *Annual Reports for the Year ending January 31, 1911,* vol. 1, pp. 392–93; Frederick L. Hoffman, "The General Death Rate of Large American Cities, 1871–1904," *American Statistical Association,* March 1906, pp. 42–43.
a. 1873–79.
b. 1871–79.
c. 1900–1907.
d. 1900–1904.

precise determination of the class background of all decedents. The fathers of more than one-quarter could not be located in the city directories. Birth certificates are closed to researchers, making it impossible to construct class-specific birth rates and, therefore, death rates. This limits remarks to the somewhat cumbersome measure of percentages of infants dying within each social class as compared with all adults from that class. Despite these caveats, it seems that the children of unskilled workers had disproportionately high levels of infant mortality throughout this era (see table 15). They accounted for at least one-half of the infant mortality where parental class was determinable, though only two-fifths of all men in Pittsburgh were unskilled.[5]

The number of unskilled and middle-class individuals increased at

Table 15. Infant Deaths by Socioeconomic Class

		1880			1900	
	N	% of All Decedents	% Excluding Unknowns	N	% of All Decedents	% Excluding Unknowns
Unskilled	91	37.6	51.7	102	39.4	53.7
Skilled	59	24.4	33.5	55	21.2	28.9
Middle	26	10.7	14.8	33	12.7	17.4
Class unknown	66	27.3	—	69	26.7	—
Total	242	100.0	100.0	259	100.0	100.0

Sources: Pittsburgh death certificates, 1880 and 1900; J. F. Diffenbacher, *Directory of Pittsburgh and Allegheny Cities for 1880* (Pittsburgh, 1880); J. F. Diffenbacher, *Directory of Pittsburgh and Allegheny Cities for 1900* (Pittsburgh, 1900).

the expense of skilled workers both in the population as a whole and in the infant mortality figures. However, middle-class population increases outpaced the rise in middle-class infant mortality. The middle class (as determined by male occupational distribution) increased from 18 to 23 percent of the city's residents between 1870 and 1900. The proportion of infant deaths accounted for by that group rose from 15 to 17 percent. Thus of those infants whose class could be determined, middle-class infants comprised a smaller proportion of the infant death total than of their proportion in the population. Given the large number of infants who could not be traced (presumably mostly of working-class origins), statements apportioning infant mortality within the working class itself must be made cautiously. When one looks only at those children whose class backgrounds could be traced, the overrepresentation of those from unskilled families stands out (see table 16). If infant deaths were proportional to the size of the group in the adult population, the index figure would be 100. Unskilled workers' children, however, greatly exceeded this figure, whereas those in skilled and middle-class families were well below it. This highlights the discrepancies within the working class itself and the extent to which the father's position affected his children's life chances.[6] It also suggests that the onslaughts of the industrial system against skilled

Table 16. Index of Infant Deaths Relative to
Socioeconomic Class

	1880	1900
Unskilled	141	134
Skilled	76	81
Total working class	105	108
Middle class	78	74

Note: Table constructed by comparing proportion of
infant deaths of known class with proportion of adult men
in that class.

workers somewhat weakened their position relative to the middle class by
the turn of the century. Overall, the health of working-class infants, as
indicated by these figures, worsened slightly by 1900, whereas that of the
middle class improved.[7] This trend is confirmed by Children's Bureau
investigations, which indicated that parental poverty was the root cause of
high infant death rates. A study conducted in 1911 in Johnstown, Pa., a
mill town with a population mix similar to Pittsburghs', found a death rate
of 256 per 1,000 among infants whose fathers earned less then $521.
When fathers earned more than $900 a year, the infant mortality rate was
97.[8] In Pittsburgh the overall infant death rate averaged 226 between 1900
and 1904, up significantly from its level of 188–190 for the 1870s and
1880s, and a reflection of the large numbers of impoverished newcomers
in the city. It was significantly higher than the national urban average,
which stood at 162 per 1,000 infants in 1900.[9]

The vagueness of death certificates, particularly in the early years,
hampers any search for the underlying reasons for the increase in infant
mortality and the class biases in the levels. Diarrheal disorders and
nutritional inadequacies—that is, public health and standard of living
factors—both increased, as did neonatal mortality. The main causes of
death for infants can be grouped into six general categories: neonatal
(prematurity, birth defects, the birthing process, and jaundice), respiratory disorders (mainly bronchitis and pneumonia, but including lung
congestion and other symptomatic descriptions), diarrhea (gastroen-

teritis, cholera infantum, teething diarrhea, and summer complaint), nutritional deficiencies (marasmus, inanition, debility, and other vague descriptions of dietary inadequacy), infectious diseases (primarily smallpox, measles, diphtheria, croup, tuberculosis, whooping cough, and scarlet fever), and a residual category for convulsions, fevers, and unexplained or nonspecific causes (see table 17).[10] Though health authorities made some headway in combatting infectious diseases, which, in any event, were not a particularly frequent cause of infant mortality, deaths due to diarrhea and inadequate or inappropriate feeding showed sustained increases. Whatever the actual improvements in urban sanitation and standards of living, these were not translated into lower mortality levels for the very young of the lower classes in this era.[11]

Neonatal deaths, especially premature births, rose dramatically in 1900. The reasons for this sharp increase (from around 2,830 per 100,000 births in the 1890s to 3,986 in 1900) are not entirely clear but may be rooted in several factors, most probably the relationships between the economic cycle, immigration, and childbearing.[12] Following the end of the depression of 1893–1897, many Southern and Eastern European women came to Pittsburgh to marry or join their husbands. Extrapolating from the data developed by Virginia Yans McLaughlin for Buffalo, N.Y., about half these couples were young and without children.[13] Young mothers had higher rates of premature births, as did women of all

Table 17. Infant Death Rates
(Per 100,000 Births)

Cause	1875	1880	1885	1890	1895	1900
Neonatal	2,738	2,607	2,273	2,832	2,828	3,986
Respiratory	2,475	2,691	2,273	2,974	2,592	3,432
Diarrheal	4,503	4,394	5,339	6,693	7,212	6,032
Nutritional	1,947	2,733	2,714	2,832	3,495	3,207
Infectious diseases	2,293	1,779	1,904	2,009	1,184	1,808
Residual	3,124	3,154	2,485	2,231	1,998	1,795
Total	17,080	17,358	16,988	19,571	19,309	20,260

Source: Pittsburgh death certificate sample.

ages having their first child. Thus massive immigration and the early stages of family formation would have resulted in higher rates of prematurity at a time when there were no medical defenses or treatment for the cluster of problems that accompanies a baby's early entrance into the world.[14] Premature infants are vulnerable because their respiratory systems and internal organs are less well developed than those of full-term babies. They have more breathing and feeding difficulties and are more susceptible to cyanosis and jaundice. The death certificates did not specify how prematurely the babies arrived or their birth weights, but the farther from term and the lower the birth weight, the lower the chances of survival.[15]

The Pittsburgh death certificates show that neonatal deaths accounted for a greater proportion of infant deaths among the middle class than among the less affluent, a point confirmed by later studies. When there are few deaths due to, say, diarrheal or nutritional disorders, as was the case for middle-class infants, neonatal problems become relatively more important even though the total death rate for all reasons was lower than for the other classes.[16] The number of deaths due to neonatal problems among the working class may be somewhat understated. Some poor parents declared premature infants who died shortly after birth as stillborn and therefore not requiring either a death certificate or expensive burial. This was more likely to be the case when the births themselves were unattended than when a doctor or trained midwife had been present. Increasingly, middle-class and skilled workers' wives utilized such attendants, but many poor women and recent immigrants relied upon untrained midwives.[17] They had higher stillbirth rates but fewer deaths due to neonatal problems. Prematurity remained a significant cause of infant deaths well into the twentieth century and was one of the major areas where advances in medical technology, rather than improving public health or standards of living, contributed to falling rates.[18]

In Pittsburgh, as in so many cities of this era, diarrheal disorders accounted for more infant deaths than any other group of causes.[19] Babies are extremely vulnerable to sanitary inadequacies. "Infant mortality is the most sensitive index we possess," wrote one leading health reformer, "of social welfare and of sanitary administration, especially under urban conditions."[20] That the actual death rate from diarrheal disorders was more than one-third higher in Pittsburgh than for other cities in 1900 testifies to the inadequacies in standard of living and sanitation that prevailed there. These deaths stemmed from a number of underlying causes including bacterial contamination of food for older infants, bottle feeding using dirty water to make up the feedings, and infections passed between family members. Weaning itself, possibly subjecting the infant digestive system to unsuitable foods, caused many of these deaths, hence the association of teething with diarrhea, since many mothers weaned their babies when their first teeth came through.[21] Impure water supplies, impure milk, and inadequate waste removal all contributed significantly to infantile diarrhea. The overall importance of sanitation and proper food storage can be seen in the increase in infant deaths during the summer months, when the inability of the working class to hold foods at low temperatures resulted in the proliferation of pathogens leading to "summer complaint" (diarrhea that appeared during the summer), cholera infantum, and gastroenteritis. Almost all U.S. cities exhibited increased infant mortality during the hottest months, a pattern that disappeared only when rising standards of living resulted in the widespread ownership of iceboxes, when public health campaigns cleaned up milk and water supplies, and when parents were better educated about the proper way to make up bottle feedings.[22]

The extent to which rapid urbanization augmented infant mortality can be seen in the increase in diarrheal disorders in the last quarter of the nineteenth century in Pittsburgh. About 25 percent of the babies dying between 1870 and 1880 suffered form diarrhea; the figure hovered around 33 percent from 1885 to 1890, peaked at 37 percent in 1895, but fell back to 30 percent in 1900 and stayed at that level through 1910. Urban sanitarians struggled, initially in vain, to protect the public at large, particularly the very young, from the consequences of city life, especially dirty milk and dirty water, which resulted in these high diarrheal mortality levels. The city passed a milk inspection ordinance in 1885, but even the health inspectorate doubted the efficacy of this ordinance, which coincided with the rise in infant diarrheal deaths. The Health Department's meat and milk inspector noted changing distribution patterns that detracted from milk's safety as a beverage for the very young. About seven hundred dairymen living in or near Pittsburgh delivered milk throughout the city from their own wagons. As property values rose on the urban periphery in the 1880s, they could no longer compete with more distant producers, who shipped milk on the railroads and distributed it through retailers. The milk inspector felt that grocers and shopkeepers lacked the proper facilities and knowledge to care for milk, and the increased distance of suppliers from the city and the large number of retail outlets (some twenty-five hundred in 1891) precluded inspection of the milk supplied to Pittsburgh consumers in the late 1880s and 1890s. The milk inspector made recommendations but had no way of knowing if they were carried out.[23]

Although, by 1907, at least some of Pittsburgh's milk was pasteurized, as late as 1913 the Dairy Division of the U.S. Department of Agriculture condemned the railway shipment of milk on the Baltimore and Ohio and Pennsylvania Railroads in unrefrigerated baggage cars. During the summer the temperature of milk not collected immediately from the depots rose to 85 or 95 degrees Fahrenheit, providing an ideal medium for bacterial contamination.[24] Subsequent refrigeration, most likely in middle-class districts, could not compensate for the inadequate protection milk received en route from the dairy. The milk inspector also cited dairies where diphtheria outbreaks occurred that still supplied milk to their customers or sent their cows to other dairies, unwittingly spreading the disease. The state courts hampered the enforcement of quarantines on producers by declaring the milk inspection ordinance unconstitutional in 1894. Effective regulation of the hygiene and temperature of milk production and transportation had to wait until the second decade of the twentieth century.[25]

The quality of milk could be a critical factor in infant mortality, for the tendency toward early weaning grew during these years.[26] Turn-of-the-century physicians blamed mothers for using proprietary milk formulas or untreated cow's milk for feeding babies.[27] This condemnation appears in death certificates filed in Pittsburgh from 1895 onwards where "artificial feeding" is given as the cause of death for a number of babies less than a month old. In some cases doctors blamed bottle feeding even though another cause was listed. A 21-day-old baby's death was attributed to convulsions, but the doctor wrote "raised by bottle" on the certificate. "Hand fed" was noted for an 8-month-old whose death was put down to "gastrointestinal catarrh," and "bronchitis—hand fed" was noted for a 3-month-old. These children came from laboring families, but early weaning was most pronounced among the middle classes and U.S.-born.[28] The Johnstown study found that native-born white mothers introduced formulas, cow's milk, and solid foods more quickly than foreign-born women. Thirty-three percent of the infants of native-born white women had some supplementary feeding by 3 months, compared with 19 percent of those with foreign-born mothers. By 6 months, 59 percent of the children born to native and 45 percent of those born to foreign women were weaned, and by 9 months the proportions were 88 percent and 76 percent, respectively. Thus only a small fraction of infants received complete protection from impure milk throughout their first year.[29] All the rest would have been exposed to the pathogens in milk at an age when diarrhea led quickly to dehydration and death.

One other area of mortality showed a sharp increase during these decades. Deaths due to nutritional deficiencies, marasmus (wasting due to insufficient food or the inability to absorb good food), inanition (lack of food or water), and debility (general weakness) went from 1,947 per 100,000 in 1875 to 2,733 in 1880, peaking at 3,495 in 1895. In 1900, 16 percent of all infant deaths stemmed from these causes. Malnutrition in all its forms was primarily a problem of poverty and inadequate dietary knowledge. Very few middle-class children (3 percent in 1900) died from nutritional deficiencies, but about 16 percent of the unskilled and 24 percent of the skilled worker's children did so.[30] It is unclear why the last group had a higher proportion of deaths from these causes than did those with unskilled parents, who had much higher death rates from diarrhea. It is possible that some of the mortality ascribed to diarrhea among the children of the unskilled was attributed to improper nutrition among the more skilled. Possibly some skilled workers' babies received supposedly "nutritious" supplemental feeding in the form of condensed milks or bottle feedings, both of which were more prevalent in semiskilled and skilled workers' households than in laborers'.[31] Babies whose mothers had been born in Germany and Southern and Eastern Europe had a higher proportion of deaths due to marasmus and inanition (18 percent) than those of native-born whites (13 percent), as table 18 shows. Although foreign-born women breast fed their babies longer than those born in the United States, their demanding schedules may have contributed to inadequate milk supplies before weaning and a lack of nutritional knowledge (certainly not limited to immigrants), but the inability to afford higher-quality foods also figured in these deaths. A machinist's wife fed her 6-month-old baby on soup, milk, coffee, and crackers, adding sauerkraut, cabbage, and pie by 9 months. A steelworker's wife weaned her 4-month-old baby because "her milk left her on account of hard work" and substituted condensed milk.[32] These artificially sweetened concentrated milks were of little nutritional value and lacked vitamins A and D. Children already malnourished or suffering from diarrhea would have been unable to metabolize the di-saccharide sucrose contained in them, and thus their use provoked more diarrhea and slow starvation.[33]

Diarrheal deaths occurred most frequently among unskilled families in Pittsburgh, where 36 percent of the infant mortality in 1900 was attributed to dysentery, gastroenteritis, teething, summer complaint, and cholera infantum, "a term applied indiscriminately to diarrheal condi-

Table 18. Infant Deaths by Parents' Ethnicity, 1900[a]
(In Percentages)

Cause	Native-born White ($N=109$)	German, S. & E. European ($N=84$)	British/ Irish ($N=42$)	Black ($N=11$)	Unknown ($N=13$)
Neonatal	20.2	14.3	23.8	27.3	30.8
Respiratory	16.5	19.0	14.3	18.2	15.4
Diarrheal	29.4	38.0	21.4	18.2	15.4
Nutritional	12.8	17.9	16.7	18.2	23.1
Infectious	10.1	4.8	16.7	—	7.7
Residual	11.0	6.0	7.1	18.2	7.7

Source: Pittsburgh death certificates, 1900.

a. If either parent was foreign-born, that was used as the ethnicity. Not all columns add to 100 percent because of rounding.

tions in infants and young children" (see table 19).[34] By contrast, about 24 percent of the deaths among skilled workers' and middle-class babies were from such disorders. Some of the variance resulted from the inferior water supply in the poorest neighborhoods, the lack of indoor plumbing, and the generally lower standard of living. The number of infant deaths was highest in working-class districts and on the South Side, largely as a result of diarrhea.[35] These high infant mortality rates among the poor alarmed contemporary sanitarians and medical personnel.[36] They perceived that inadequate sanitation led to an appalling waste of human life among the vulnerable, the very young.

Public health campaigns did not lead to lower infant death rates for Pittsburgh babies in this era because they did not conquer the major causes of death—diarrheal disorders due to contaminated food, milk, and water supplies and the nutritional inadequacies of many infant diets. They were more successful, however, in tackling the epidemic diseases that caused

Table 19. Infant Deaths by Parents' Socioeconomic Class[a]
(In Percentages)

Cause	Unskilled		Skilled		Middle		Class Unknown	
	1880 (N=91)	1900 (N=102)	1880 (N=59)	1900 (N=55)	1880 (N=26)	1900 (N=33)	1880 (N=66)	1900 (N=69)
Neonatal	16.4	14.7	13.6	23.6	42.2	24.2	19.7	21.7
Respiratory	15.4	18.6	16.9	12.7	11.5	24.2	15.1	14.5
Diarrheal	24.2	36.3	23.7	23.6	19.2	24.2	18.2	27.5
Nutritional	12.1	15.7	20.3	23.6	7.7	3.0	18.2	15.9
Infectious	17.6	5.9	11.9	12.7	7.7	12.1	12.1	8.7
Residual	14.3	8.8	13.6	3.6	11.5	12.1	16.7	11.6

Sources: Pittsburgh death certificate sample, 1880 and 1900; J. F. Diffenbacher, *Directory of Pittsburgh and Allegheny Cities for 1880* (Pittsburgh, 1880); J. F. Diffenbacher, *Directory of Pittsburgh and Allegheny Cities for 1900* (Pittsburgh, 1900).

a. Given the large numbers of parental occupations that could not be traced, these data should be regarded as suggestive rather than definitive. Not all columns add to 100 percent because of rounding.

many deaths in early childhood (see table 20). The death rate for children ages 1 to 4 inclusive declined from 42 per 1,000 in 1880 to 32 per 1,000 in 1900, in line with the overall improvement in health experienced in the city. Young children still suffered from diarrheal disorders and respiratory infections, but many fewer succumbed to diphtheria and scarlet fever by 1900. As with their baby brothers and sisters, the death rate was highest on the South Side and lowest in the suburban East End.[37]

Paradoxically, although infant and early childhood mortality was commonplace, the popular press rarely published notices of children's deaths except under unusual circumstances. The family of George W. Durbin lost four children within a month when diphtheria struck, and the *National Labor Tribune* sympathized with him in his affliction, as would all who read the notice of his loss. A letter from W. W. Wagner informed his comrades of the death of his eldest daughter at age 13, "making the third one of his family stricken down in three months. His eldest son is lying low with brain fever. This is certainly a sad season for Mr. Wagner, and he has the sympathy of many in this hour of sore distress."[38] The notices tended simply to state the cause of death and extend sympathy on the loss of the daughter or son. Parents might comfort themselves with the thought that the child had ceased suffering. One brief consolatory poem, "'Tis gone," suggested that the child's aura remained:

Table 20. Causes of Death for 1–4-year-olds.
(Per 100,000)

	1880	1890	1900
Diphtheria	779	673	269
Scarlet Fever	740	96	62
Diarrheal	467	385	538
Pneumonia & Bronchitis	448	712	683
Meningitis	224	192	227
Measles	214	481	186

Source: Pittsburgh death certificates, 1880, 1890, 1900.

Perchance to shine in yonder bow
That fronts the sun at fall of day:
Perchance to hang, the brightest gem
In yonder royal diadem.[39]

But poems of children's deaths were a rarity, as were notices of them.

A number of authors have suggested that high infant and childhood mortality rates led parents to be less emotionally involved with their children. In writing of death and the Puritan child, David Stannard posits that parents' restrained affection for their children might have been a response to the probability of premature death and an insulation against it.[40] Ivy Pinchbeck and Margaret Hewitt believed that high mortality rates in England mitigated against the children being the principal objects of parental affection.[41] But even if parents were resigned to these high levels of mortality, they usually grieved heavily at the deaths of their children.[42] It is questionable whether high infant death rates resulted in less emotional or financial investment in the very young or impeded the perception of young children as individuals. Among the working class, they were buried without names, stylized as ''infant'' or ''baby'' in paupers' graves, by parents too poor to memorialize their passing with expensive tombstones and separate grave plots. The lack of individual memorials may be a carryover from preindustrial times. Danial Scott Smith has reported that the utilization of ''necronyms for the successor of a dead sibling'' indicated that '' 'premodern' New Englanders saw children as ultimate adults and not as persons inherently individuated as children.''[43] Some Pittsburgh steelworking families reused the name of a dead child. By calling the new baby after a brother or sister who had died, the family kept the memory of the child alive by retaining the name in the family.[44] The use of a necronym betokened the parents' continuing love for the baby or child who lived for such a brief time. The name acted as a living memorial in place of the cold marble that poor parents could not afford.

Children's obituaries usually referred to the deceased in stylized or conventional ways with little reference to their individual characteristics. Mary and John Douglas's daughter was a ''little cherub . . . a flower springing into light but for a little while." Brother Peter Corrigan suffered the death of his "bright little daughter," and E. H. Davis lost his "very bright intelligent son." In reflection of the gender conventions of the era, girls were frequently described in physical terms, although boys usually were not. When the daughter of Chris Ward, a Pittsburgh printer, died, the obituary described her as his pretty little daughter. Though parents valued children of both sexes for being "bright," girls' epitaphs memorialized their looks, but boys' emphasized intelligence and contributions to the family coffers.[45]

The notices of working-class children in the labor press suggest that their deaths saddened their parents, particularly if the children survived infancy. The notice that Brother Flinn "was presented by his wife with two little Flinns. One died," exacted less sympathy than did the more detailed accounts of the deaths of George Durbin's and W. W. Wagner's older children. Some poor mothers grieved hysterically over the death of their children.[46] Mrs. Rebecca Edwards, a black resident of the Hill District, suffered the loss of her 14-month-old child but, lacking money to buy a coffin or pay for the funeral, kept it with her in her front room, lying in an old baby carriage. Apparently Mrs. Edwards had no friends or relations to help her with the burial expenses, so charity officials laid the baby to rest after a policeman on the beat discovered the mother mourning her dead child alone.[47]

Children usually had less elaborate memorials than adults, a reflection of the large proportion who came from poor families. Approximately three-fifths of those buried in the poor ground at St. Mary's Cemetery, the oldest Catholic cemetery in Pittsburgh, were infants and children under the age of 5. By 1890 the cemetery had a separate section for stillborn infants, although some of the more affluent parents (as indicated by the size of tombstones and purchase of family burial plots) interred their infants with the family. Burial in the poor ground or stillborn sections cost less. The high proportion of the very young in these sections stemmed from the poverty of their parents. Since those buried in the poor ground were permitted no tombstones by the cemetery, these very young children remained anonymous but cherished in their parents memories.[48]

Sex Role Socialization

The training of females for domesticity and males for employment began at an early age. Mothers wanted and needed their daughters' help at home, and they valued their sons' wages and occupational advancement. Advice columns for working-class mothers suggested differential treatment for male and female children that routed girls into domestic chores and boys into more "manly" activities, even at home. Proletarian periodicals urged mothers to encourage their sons' work orientation by paying them for help around the house; the boy who fixed a loose board could justifiably demand "the best wages" obtainable by any good union carpenter. Women were to praise their sons and give them a few pennies or a nickel to demonstrate how valuable the repair work was to the household. Although girls received praise for drying the dishes, scouring the knives and forks, or putting things away, no one suggested they should be paid for the performance of household chores; that was taken for granted for girls as it was for their mothers. The popular press also recommended the utilization of games to inculcate the female role. Making dolls, sewing their clothes, and dressing and undressing them enhanced female domesticity. The *People's Monthly* believed that clothing dolls was "a most pleasant mode of teaching a little girl to work" because it combined play, useful instruction, and training for her future role as mother. The same periodical stressed that training girls in "household duties" made them better wives. Even the design of homes could enhance the socialization process; through careful planning, laboring fathers would save the working-class "wife and daughters a vast amount of toil and trouble." In the performance of their domestic duties, quite young girls could help with the washing by hanging up the clothes, acting as their mothers' assistants in the arduous task of laundering the family's clothes.[49]

Housewifery, domesticity, and marriage were linked in the early training of Pittsburgh females as mothers relied upon daughters' labor and prepared them for the fulfillment of their domestic destiny. If there were preschool siblings or boarders to be cared for, girls were expected to help at home.[50] This troubled some reformers who believed that young girls worked too hard. The Civic Club report on the playgrounds of Pittsburgh noted that working-class girls had a "feverish childlike desire for work" and took their household responsibilities very seriously. "Girls would not come to the playground unless bribed with sewing classes." However, this intense emphasis on female industriousness derived from the parents, who "continually asked that children only six or seven years old be given sewing. They said, 'It is no good to come to play.' " Domestic and familial obligations began early for Pittsburgh's "little sister-mothers," while their brothers did "not reveal such abnormal industriousness." Instead, boys had few household chores until it came time to join the labor force, usually during the early teenage years.[51] Extrafamilial agencies reinforced the role segregation accepted by Pittsburgh parents. For example, boys in charitable institutions learned trades and went to work at age twelve, but orphanage girls learned only the household arts, sewing, and laundry work. Various children's homes retained young women to care for the building and the younger children for an additional five or six years after the boys had been dismissed. Even as youngsters, females provided cheap or free domestic labor while males earned money, freed from institutional constraints at an earlier age. Benevolent agencies instilled rigid sex roles into the orphaned children of the poor: the boys applied themselves to trades while the girls maintained family and household.[52] The stereotypes reflected the external value system and employment realities for both sexes and emulated the training given working-class children by their own families.

Although some historians of childhood characterize nineteenth-century child-rearing practices as the "socialization mode" in which parents viewed their task as training rather than conquering their offspring, physical correction remained a part of the working-class method of parenting. Other scholars posit that heavy drinking among poorer urban dwellers engendered serious child neglect and brutality, so that the force used by fathers had, in Michael Anderson's words, "the effect of increasing affective bonds between children and their mothers."[53] The evidence on parent-child relations in Pittsburgh demonstrates that although women as well as men beat their children, the men were more violent. Of fifty substantiated child abuse cases in the Western Pennsylvania Humane Society's files, 60 percent involved fathers severely chastising their progeny; in 30 percent the mothers had been cruel, and in 10 percent both parents hit their children. The small number of cases involved makes these data suggestive rather then conclusive; nevertheless no one stratum of the working class, no ethnic or racial group refrained from physical correction. Native-born white, black, German, Irish, Italian, and Polish parents all struck their children, as did puddlers, laborers, washerwomen, and glassblowers. Child abusers came from all districts of the city, but almost all were working class. The dearth of middle-class parents in these records may indicate better soundproofing and greater distance from neighbors rather than a more humane approach to child rearing. If the middle class lashed out, they did so in privacy, so that only the family heard or saw.[54]

Alan Dawley suggests that later ages condemn the use of the whip to discipline children, substituting psychological manipulation, suffocating love, and regimentation, which hardly assure individuals of greater freedom.[55] Popular culture among the iron- and steelworkers did not prohibit striking a fractious child, but using a whip or raising welts was considered extreme, and residents of working-class districts invoked the Humane Society to curtail overly abusive behavior. Yet even in the crowded areas behind the steel mills and glass houses, observers might be incorrect in their assessments of family violence. Neighbors invoked the Humane Society's intervention when John Berry, a South Side laborer, chased his 12-year-old son from the house with a broomstick and struck him with it. Apparently the boy had slapped his sister at the dinner table, which justified the father's harshness in the investigator's eyes. No extenuating circumstances, however, could excuse Martha Kinnear's treatment of her little boy. The washerwoman beat her naked son with a strap until welts formed, for which the mayor gave her a choice of a $10.00 fine or thirty days in jail. In both cases members of the community complained about seemingly unwarranted or severe violence against the young.[56]

Frequently, the parents who mistreated their children had been drinking heavily. Anna Schultz, who lived above a saloon, imbibed to excess, then beat her little girl. Another South Side resident, a puddler named Edward Laffy, returned drunk from his shift at Painter's Mill, promptly quarreled with one of his four offspring, and struck his wife when she tried to protect the child. Only the intervention of a neighbor, who hit Laffy over the head with a baseball bat, prevented him from inflicting more harm. As it was, Mrs. Laffy had marks on her head, body, and arms, two children had been knocked down, and one seriously injured. Alcohol, neglect, and abuse were closely coupled in some working-class homes according to the Humane Society investigations. Mary McNulty and her husband Andrew, a glassworker, "both drank and quarreled with one another, the baby often times crying the whole night, and he was heard whipping and cursing it" by neighbors in the South Side alley where the McNultys resided.[57]

Mr. and Mrs. McNulty punished their baby because she cried when they wished to sleep. John Wilson, a white drayman, repeatedly whipped his 15-year-old daughter because she "was inclined to run around at nights." Other parents punished children who did not contribute their earnings or labor to the family. A young domestic servant, the daughter of a German woman, received abuse from her mother "for not giving her every cent she earns." Harry Singleton, a black laborer, beat his step-daughter because she was insolent and stubborn and "would not do anything about the house," according to the girl's mother. In all these cases the parents perceived the children as disobedient, not conforming to their demands, or somehow troublesome, and for this they were beaten. Though there is no way to determine the prevalence of abusive behavior, the neighborly invocation of the Humane Society to protect youngsters from violent parents indicates that the working class did not universally accept strong physical chastisement as a method for controlling children. Direct intervention by neighbors, as with the Laffy family, seems to have been exceptional or passed without public mention. But neighbors sometimes appealed to the Humane Society when community norms had been transgressed. The beating of children may have become less common during the nineteenth century, but parents' own experiences as youngsters influenced their response to their own offspring; many used force because they had themselves been struck as children and knew no other disciplinary methods.[58]

Pittsburgh labor newspapers did not discuss the subject of child abuse directly; instead they encouraged parents to pay attention to their children. Working-class authors cautioned parents against taking their children for granted. Through knowledge born of hindsight, the anonymous author of the poem "Tired Mothers" warned that preoccupation with household chores entailed the neglect of children who might not survive their early years. Given high infant mortality rates among the working class, the author wrote:

> I wonder that some mothers fret
> At their small children clinging to their gown,
> Or that the footprints, when days are wet
> Are ever black enough to make them frown.[59]

Mothers were advised to cherish their offspring, not regard them as nuisances hampering the housework, and yet children soon learned that they were "not to bother mamma when she is busy." The working-class mother might be at home, but she often was too busy to devote much time to her children.[60]

The city's industries impinged upon child rearing by limiting the amount of time a man could spend with his young children. As the hours of work lengthened in the steel mills, father became a distant figure, at work twelve hours out of twenty-four and too worn out to spend time with the children when he was home. In a letter to the *National Labor Tribune*, a miner's wife complained that long working days left her husband too exhausted even to hold the baby. From the woman's point of view, home would be a happier place if husbands worked shorter hours and "would then have time to smile" at their little ones; however, fathers' long hours and debilitating work commonly precluded an active role in child rearing.[61]

In sharp contrast to manual workers, affluent fathers frequently had flexible schedules that enabled them to devote more time to their children. Parenthood so delighted Harry Oliver, an iron mill owner, that he came home for lunch each day to be with his children despite the tedious journey by horsecar.[62] At the beginning of this era, wives or children sometimes carried a hot lunch to the mill, but by the turn of the century, mill owners curtailed this practice. Workers then took their lunch in buckets to eat amid the machines while they worked, never able to come home at midday for the pleasure of their children's company. Thomas Bell painted a clear picture of mill fatherhood. His protagonist received pleasure from his children but encountered "definite limits to the intimacy they permitted." Because he spent so little time with them, the children felt uncomfortable with him and cast him "in the role of Papa, solemn, preoccupied, and not to be lightly bothered." Mihal regretted this, but his attempts to play and joke with the children discomfited them as if he had departed from his appropriate role.[63]

Mill life affected parents and children in another way, through separation. Men left their families as they traveled in search of work. These interruptions strained family ties, made fathers strangers to their children, left the men lonely, and deprived the children even of their father's presence until he returned or sent for them. One disconsolate Slavic millworker, upon seeing a toddler in a railway station in Homestead, coaxed her to come to him in "a voice of heart-breaking loneliness." He explained to the waiting passengers, "Me wife, me babe, Hungar."[64] Children of the working class could grow up without really knowing their fathers, who lived far away, worked long hours, or died young in mill accidents. By commandeering the men, the industrial system reinforced cultural perceptions of women as primary, if not sole, nurturers of the young and men as remote breadwinners. It might be said without exaggeration that the mills socialized both the male and female children, long before the boys ever entered the Vesuvian works, through employment patterns that separated the fathers from their children and placed the burden of raising the young on their mothers.

The demands made on the workers and their wives even shaped the recreational patterns of the very young. Men on the night turn had to sleep during the day and needed quiet in which to recoup their energy. Women preparing meals for husbands, sons, and boarders on different shifts needed to concentrate on their household tasks. But quiet and concentration were difficult commodities to find in homes where the kitchen was the only room without beds in it. Turn-of-the-century reformers noted that "play in a steaming kitchen or a home workshop is difficult, but play in the bedroom of sleeping boarders is impossible."[65] Crowding and the need for quiet in all likelihood led to repeated maternal commands to go outside, so Pittsburgh's children played outdoors in their early years, caring less than some of their elders about smoke in the air, polluted drains, and unpaved streets and courts.[66]

Although children inevitably found places to enjoy themselves outdoors, working-class districts were hazardous. There were no green lawns or white picket fences behind the mills; as Robert Layton testified before the U.S. Senate, "if there is any grass on the South Side of Pittsburgh, it is in a little box sitting on the window-sill" So little girls jumped rope in the alleys and boys and girls alike grazed their knees scrambling over the cinder heaps near the mills. Their play space was the "middle of the street. What little ball playing they indulge in is done on the streets at the risk of breaking windows and being stopped summarily by the police, or run over by a street car or wagon."[67] Lacking private playgrounds, children took their exercise exposed to traffic from which middle-class children were protected by their parents' suburban gardens. As a result, working-class children played among carriages, wagons, and drays, incurring accidents that would have been inconceivable before this era. Prior to 1885 transportation accidents accounted for 7 percent of all accidental deaths, but that proportion doubled by the end of the century. Since the railroad and streetcar lines ran through densely populated working-class neighborhoods and through the hollows behind their homes, children of the laboring classes were frequently their victims. A streetcar knocked down Otto Schultz; a wagon belonging to the Atlantic and Pacific Tea Company ran over a boy named Lyttle; a cart hit David Dreardon; an iron wagon ran over Katie Gallagher, aged 17 months, killing her instantly. Thomas Davis, aged 4 years, died when run into by a sand wagon on its way to a glass factory, and another crushed the foot of Mrs. Smith's 3-year-old daughter. Families received minimal compensation for such incidents. The lawyers of one streetcar company warned the family not to protest a settlement preferred after an inebriated driver knocked down and killed their daughter. They threatened the breadwinner with the loss of his job if he brought suit.[68]

The physical environment of working-class homes and neighborhoods complicated child supervision, but shooing small children outside could have drastic consequences for the children playing outdoors unattended. Maternal inattention (or the carelessness of older brothers and sisters told to keep an eye on junior) occasionally resulted in serious injuries. The records published by the Department of Public Safety of deaths from accidental and violent causes always included children such as 18-month old Joseph Malefski, who tumbled into a tub of wash water and drowned, or little Katie Smith (age unspecified), who fell into a water closet and also perished. Some members of the working class lamented the lack of public play space that resulted in such tragedies. *The People's Monthly* supported a proposed public park in the 1870s, but the city fathers rejected the use of tax money for such a frivolous project. The journal lamented that there was plenty of money to be made in Pittsburgh, but it was rarely enjoyed by the working class. A decade later, *Commoner and Glass Worker* complained that the city built stately prisons, but to "build a public library for the poor, to lay out a plot of ground for a park and a breathing spot for the miasma-stifled children of the back alley and narrow streets . . . that, of course, cannot be done at public expense."[69]

A few parents tried to protect their children from the hazards of the street by creating play environments for them at home. An unemployed Scottish millworker built a playhouse for his two little girls in order to "keep 'em out of the street." Unfortunately it sat against the privy, but given the lack of space in the yard, that could not be helped. Such facilities, while desirable, were most uncommon. One short-lived self-help effort resulted in Little Jim Park on the site of a derelict church near Painter's Row on the South Side. Millworkers cleared the land while they were laid off by United States Steel. The little oasis between Painter's Mill, unimproved tenements, and rank waste ground contained rough benches, flower beds, an iron railing to keep children from dashing out into the path of oncoming trolleys, and its own flagpole. No one gave this park to the people; they took it, cared for it, and even took the geraniums inside their homes during the winter. When United States Steel tore down Painter's Row, it destroyed Little Jim Park as well.[70]

Most of Pittsburgh's working-class districts simply lacked open space in which the children of the iron- and steelworkers could enjoy themselves. The Civic Club described the city's two large parks, both established late in the nineteenth century, as "out of reach of the poor." Highland Park, a barren, treeless hill with a reservoir and a few carriage roads, sat at the easternmost edge of the city, far removed from the mill neighborhoods, and Schenley Park, given to the city in 1889 by Mary E. Schenley of the distillery fortune, lay separated from crowded Oakland by a deep ravine.[71] Children could scramble down the steep slopes to reach Schenley Park's cool woods, but Highland Park and Kenneywood, the amusement ground east of Homestead, were reserved for special occasions since the only access to them was on the streetcar.[72]

Eventually, reformers established supervised recreational facilities for the children of the poor. In 1896 the Civic Club organized several playgrounds in school yards. The first, in a middle-class ward, showed that children would come, but the next two, placed in mill wards, did not flourish immediately. The Civic Club members discovered that "these children did not know how to play" in the accepted middle-class modes and had to be taught to use the sand piles and swings. Whereas the middle-class children were described by Beulah Kennard, chairwoman of the Civic Club's Department of Education, as "active and resourceful," the working-class children who came to the playgrounds were "subnormal and apparently tending to degeneracy because of their unfortunate surroundings." Clearly, reformers such as Ms. Kennard did not recognize the resourcefulness of working-class children, who, despite their tattered clothes, managed to get together bat, ball, and a couple of gloves to make an impromptu baseball game.[73] It became the reformers' first mission to teach these children how to play middle-class games, then to provide "some form of industrial work," information on nutrition, and instruction in manners. By 1914, Pittsburgh had seventeen recreation grounds, mostly in the heavily populated mill districts on the South Side, with a few in the Hill District and outlying areas, and the city had assumed much of the financial burden of maintaining both the playgrounds and the two large and six smaller parks.[74] The reformers' motives might have been ambiguous, a desire to mold a new urban moral order, but at least the new play areas were free from traffic.[75]

Education

Whereas early childhood had been a time of unstructured activity for almost all working-class children, at six they began attending school. The rates of participation varied among the classes, sexes, and ethnic groups, but by midcentury school had become an accepted part of the lives of most Pittsburgh children. Public policy facilitated school attendance in several ways: in 1885 the state permitted school systems to purchase textbooks for their pupils, thus relieving the parents of that burden. Nearly a decade later, in 1893, the legislature required schools to provide free books because certain cities, Pittsburgh among them, had not used tax dollars to buy books for poorer students. In 1895 the state reemphasized the utility of education by making school attendance compulsory for children 8–13 years old. These laws and the growing importance of literacy resulted in slightly increased enrollments in Pittsburgh's schools.[76] In 1880, 63 percent of all children aged 5–14 attended classes in the public and parochial schools; by 1900, 68 percent matriculated.[77]

According to Michael Katz, patterns of school attendance can provide clues to the role of education and children in society and to family strategies for mobility.[78] In Pittsburgh education itself must be viewed in the context of the industries that dominated the city, the employment opportunities available to both sexes, and cultural and class norms. The high proportion of children in school stemmed partially from the city's employment structure. The iron and steel industries did not hire youngsters; in 1870 only 8 percent of the labor force in Pittsburgh's primary products were between the ages of 10 and 15. By the end of the century, the proportion of young iron- and steelworkers had dropped to a mere 1 percent. The employment of children in the glass industry also decreased dramatically in these years. Even so, the proportion of children who worked rose from 13 percent of all those aged 10–15 in 1870 to 18 percent in 1890. Since the gains were in the sweated trades and entry-level white-collar positions, including office boys and clerks, and the losses were in jobs in which fathers might train their sons (skilled iron and glass work) or mothers their daughters (domestic service), increased school attendance indicates an attempt by the working class to ensure upward mobility, or at least employment, through greater reliance upon education to replace skills traditionally passed between generations. A detailed analysis of school attendance patterns demonstrates that certain groups used the school system to prepare their children for white-collar employment. Less fortunately situated families exploited the educational opportunities offered in the Steel City to a lesser extent, and some ethnic groups believed the public schools were culturally inappropriate.[79]

The decision to send a child to school or have one stay there for any length of time reflected the family's current income, its ability to dispense with the child's work or wages, and the employment prospects of the child, so one would expect that poorer families would be less likely to have children in school.[80] Though this proposition holds true within the working class, the children of skilled workers being more likely to attend classes than those of the unskilled or widows, it is not true between the classes because they used the schools differently (see table 21). The working class, particularly the upper reaches, sent their sons to school in large numbers when they were young but withdrew them once they could contribute labor or wages to the family. For the upper classes in 1880, childhood remained a time of play longer. Affluent boys had slightly lower attendance rates than skilled workers' sons in their early years, and middle- and upper-class daughters had lower school attendance rates than their working-class counterparts in the first few years. Although school attendance peaked for all classes between 10 and 14, some working-class sons had entered the labor force and their sisters were staying home to help their mothers. Middle- and upper-class boys and girls, however, were solidly entrenched in their school work. Two-thirds of the upper-class boys aged 15–19 stayed on in school, as did nearly half (45 percent) of their sisters. Middle-class school attendance levels were lower but still exceeded those of the working class. No affluent young women worked, but about one-fifth of those from working-class homes were in the labor force by the age of 15. School attendance levels were about the same for boys and girls of the working class after the age of 15, but boys were much more likely to be employed. Skilled workers' children, both boys and girls, stayed on at school longer than those of the unskilled, reinforcing the distinctions within the working class itself.[81]

Widow's children in 1880 exhibited a variation of the working- class family pattern. Like the children of skilled workers, they had high initial enrollment rates, but their school attendance rate dropped more rapidly than that of unskilled workers' children, particularly as the boys grew old enough to make monetary contributions to the household.[82] Their early withdrawal from school stands as mute testimony to the unmet needs of

Table 21. Work and Education by Socioeconomic Class, 1880
(In Percentages)

	Females, 5–9 Years Old				Males, 5–9 Years Old			
	Home	School	Work	N	Home	School	Work	N
Upper	54	46		52	36	64		63
Middle	50	50		100	49	51		107
Skilled	41	59		189	34	66		249
Unskilled	47	53		384	44	56		360
Widowed	42	58		64	42	58		45

	Females, 10–14 Years Old				Males, 10–14 Years Old			
	Home	School	Work	N	Home	School	Work	N
Upper	14	86		51	9	90	1	70
Middle	22	78		64	22	73	5	76
Skilled	20	78	2	129	9	79	12	187
Unskilled	31	66	3	281	14	71	15	303
Widowed	33	61	6	83	17	44	39	64

	Females, 15–19 Years Old				Males, 15–19 Years Old			
	Home	School	Work	N	Home	School	Work	N
Upper	55	45		49	5	66	29	62
Middle	64	36		47	8	28	64	40
Skilled	54	23	23	121	12	21	67	108
Unskilled	64	16	20	226	15	13	72	227
Widowed	60	13	27	84	4	4	92	90

Source: 1880 census sample. Includes only those individuals living with their families.

widowed women, who could not replace their late husbands' wages through their own efforts. Whatever educational opportunity existed for the rest of the working class was virtually denied widows' children. More than half the widows' sons left school between the ages of 10 and 14, though three-quarters of the working-class boys still attended. Widows' daughters stayed in school longer than their brothers, but they, too, went into the labor force in larger numbers than their friends from two-parent families.

Reform groups, including the PAIP, complained that parents, particularly widowed ones, did not appreciate the value of education. The association's visitors attempted "to impress on the Mothers the necessity of keeping children regularly in attendance at school, a difficult matter to accomplish, as many of the parents are too ignorant and short-sighted to realize its importance."[83] But the school leaving figures suggest that a cruel dilemma trapped many working-class and immigrant parents, including even skilled workers with their frequently unstable incomes and technologically outmoded skills. Although the *National Labor Tribune* asserted that a well-educated child reflected well upon the family but a child brought up in ignorance was "dead weight," many working-class families lacked the financial resources to provide more than a few years of schooling. The official organ of the AAISW estimated that it cost between $2,000 and $3,000 to raise and educate a child; "to bring up a family properly a man must be able to earn enough to keep his children in school."[84] Few laboring fathers and fewer widowed mothers received sufficient wages to educate their children beyond the rudiments in 1880. Of the upper-class 15–19-year-old boys, 66 percent were still in school compared with 21 percent of skilled workers', 13 percent of the unskilled workers', and a meager 4 percent of widows' sons. Parental economic class clearly constrained educational opportunity for Pittsburgh's youth.

Parents from Pittsburgh ethnocultural groups had diverse perspectives on the feasibility and utility of education for their offspring as a reflection partially of economic class but partially also of cultural values. Native-born white children with native-born parents had higher rates of school enrollment than other groups in 1880 and 1900, but by the time a white family had been in the United States for several generations, it seemed to absorb the U.S. emphasis on education. Thus Carolyn Schumacher found in her history of the Pittsburgh schools that poor third-generation teenagers were about as likely as wealthy ones to be in school. First- and second-generation families and blacks used education distinctively depending upon their background and estimation of their progeny's prospects.[85]

German immigrants chose not to send a large proportion of their children to school in such disparate cities as Philadelphia, Milwaukee, and Pittsburgh. In all three cities, the British and Irish were more apt to provide an education for their children than either the Germans or blacks. The trend was particularly pronounced in Pittsburgh in 1880, where working- and middle-class German boys and girls had school attendance rates averaging 5–10 percent lower than other immigrant children from the same economic class. Various hypotheses have been put forward to explain the disinclination of German immigrants to send their children to school. Since many of their fathers were engaged in craft occupations in which the skills of the fathers remained useful, trades or family businesses could be handed directly to sons.[86] But cultural values as well as employment possibilities entered into the German decision to withhold their children from the public schools. According to Schumacher, "school reformers in Pennsylvania had long regarded the cultural conservatism of the Germans as a barrier to assimilation."[87] For the Germans to send their daughters and sons to school meant exposing them to an alien language and an alien religious tradition. While some educated or trained their children at home, others sent their offspring to German Catholic schools run by religious orders staffed by nuns from the old country.

As the decision regarding the child's future occupation approached, the educational gap widened. As table 22 shows, 80 percent of the native-born white and British children aged 10–14 were in school in 1880, along with 72 percent of the Irish and black but only 63 percent of the first- and second-generation Germans. The school attendance levels of all groups declined precipitately in the midteen years, when children either went on to high school and white-collar careers, into the working world, or stayed home to help their mothers. Native-born white children dominated the high school population; about 37 percent were in school between

Table 22. Work and Education by Ethnicity, 1880
(In Percentages)

	Females, 5–9 Years Old				Males 5–9 Years Old			
	Home	School	Work	N	Home	School	Work	N
Native-born white	44	56		257	39	61		254
British	48	52		65	51	49		67
Irish	48	52		210	47	53		204
German	45	55		225	42	58		225
Black	62	39		18	48	52		27

	Females, 10–14 Years Old				Males, 10–14 Years Old			
	Home	School	Work	N	Home	School	Work	N
Native-born white	18	80	2	196	10	80	10	229
British	25	73	2	45	12	81	7	68
Irish	29	68	3	182	12	74	14	175
German	32	66	2	167	17	61	22	223
Black	41	59	a	17	14	86		14

	Females, 15–19 Years Old				Males, 15–19 Years Old			
	Home	School	Work	N	Home	School	Work	N
Native-born white	52	39	9	147	9	35	56	170
British	67	12	21	51	6	15	79	34
Irish	54	20	26	153	13	20	67	149
German	71	9	20	166	7	11	82	170
Black	67	33	a	6	6	13	81	16

Source: 1880 census sample.

a. These data are somewhat misleading since black females who worked did so as domestic servants and lived outside their parents' household. If these young women were included in the table, the data would be:

	Home	School	Work	N
Black females, 10–14	37	53	10	19
Black females, 15–19	33	13	54	15

the ages of 15 and 19. Twenty percent of the Irish, 13 percent of the British and 10 percent of the German children also took advanced instruction. Since so many young black women had left their families to work as domestic servants, a statistical evaluation of the few remaining at home would be misleading. A few older black youths may have continued on in the elementary schools, but apparently no blacks attended high school in Pittsburgh at this time.

By 1900 the attendance levels had risen among all strata of the population as parents recognized the necessity of education for life in the new century. Although native-born whites continued to send their children to school in greater numbers than immigrants, the second-generation pattern resembled that of the native born at the elementary school level. Black children, too, had higher enrollment levels in the city's grammar schools. Children born abroad, mostly Southern and Eastern Europeans by 1900, had the lowest proportion of elementary school attendance, in spite of state laws compelling 8–13 year olds to go to school. Nevertheless, the overall attendance levels continued to rise throughout this era.[88]

Despite rising enrollments, Pittsburgh had one of the lowest high school attendance rates of large U.S. cities. Indeed, the predominantly working-class South Side had no high school of its own until 1898. In 1908, 5.4 percent of all Pittsburgh students were in high school; only Newark, N.J., had a lower proportion. Where the mills and the glass houses provided employment, many children left school as soon as they could (before the legal age in some cases) to make their contribution to the family income. A law enacted in 1905 set 14 as the minimum working age in Pennsylvania, but one study of school attendance in a working-class district showed that the sharpest decrease in attendance occurred at the age of 12, when 21 percent of the students dropped out, the boys primarily to work in the glass houses and the girls to help at home.[89] Many steelworking families, especially the unskilled, regarded academic training for their children as irrelevant. The sons as well as the fathers preferred going to the manly world of the mills to staying on at school or taking white-collar jobs.[90]

Native-born whites continued to dominate Pittsburgh high schools at the turn of the century because few foreign-born or second-generation children went on to get the education that would have prepared them for white-collar jobs. Even had their families been able to dispense with their labor, the chances of an immigrant or immigrant's child being hired in a white-collar position were rather remote. Third-generation and old stock immigrants dominated sales and clerk employment through the first decade of the twentieth century, and high school was a "vocational training institute for white collar office work," from which birth barred the foreign-born, many of the second generation, and virtually all blacks.[91] In 1908 poverty and prospects resulted in 60 percent of the Pittsburgh high school students being native-born whites with native fathers. The next largest contingent came from Great Britain (14 percent) or were Jewish (13 percent). Seven percent of the high school students were of German extraction, and only 2 percent each were black and Southern and Eastern European. The rest came from scattered Northern European countries and Canada.[92]

Mirroring trends among their fellow immigrants in other cities, Pittsburgh's Slavic and Italian settlers at the turn of the century withdrew their children from school earlier than did native-born whites. Polish and Italian parochial schools had much smaller classes in the seventh and eighth grades, for most students dropped out at 12 or 13. An emphasis on property acquisition, women's domestic role, and the unstable and poorly remunerated unskilled jobs of the fathers combined to thrust these children into the adult world earlier than their native counterparts. Their parents stressed the development of skills and early entry into the labor force rather than book learning as the means to individual and familial advancement.[93] There were many girls like Theresa Scorzafava, who stayed home to help her mother care for boarders, and many boys like John V., a 12-year-old Italian, who had been working for a year in a glass house. Ralph and Louis Carracotta's parents believed their sons were unable to learn anything at school, so they sent them to work as "sticking-up" boys in the glass houses at 11 and 12 years of age.[94]

When the children of Southern and Eastern European immigrants did go to school, they frequently attended separate educational establishments. Parochial schools proliferated at the turn of the century because Southern and Eastern European immigrants wanted their children educated in the mother tongue and values of their culture as well as the skills of the new land. In the 1907–1908 school year, 26 percent of all Pittsburgh children attended Catholic schools. "American" or Irish-dominated orders staffed 45 percent of these schools, German nuns ran 38 percent, 14 percent were Polish, and the rest were Lithuanian, Bohemian, and Italian. Educational reformers complained that the parish schools were underfinanced, overcrowded, ill-ventilated, and unsanitary. The Church did not establish standards for either instruction or building maintenance until 1893, when a school board and teacher examination committee were formed. But until 1904, when the diocese appointed a superintendent of schools, the actual supervision of each school fell to the already overworked parish priest. The education given in these schools, then, varied according to the training and inclinations of each ethnic community, their priest, and the nuns and lay teachers who staffed them.[95]

Educational reformers criticized the Catholic schools for their allegiance to the religion and language of the relevant old country and for not being "American" enough. Though education in the public schools of the Pittsburgh district stressed reading, writing, arithmetic, civics, and such American culture as could be imparted through flag salutes and the singing of patriotic songs, many of the Catholic educators were unfamiliar with American customs and the English language; if English was spoken at all, it was by nuns "imperfectly familiar with its meaning."[96] Religious instruction took an hour a day from the curriculum of the parochial schools, leaving little time for instruction in civics, health, or physical education, all important to reformers concerned about the patriotism and health of poor children. Whereas nearly half the Pittsburgh subdistricts offered physical education at the turn of the century, and all did so after the centralization of the school system in 1911, none of the Catholic schools could: either they lacked the equipment and could not afford to buy it, or "the habits of life of the sisters, which unfit them to be leaders in physical exercise," meant there was no interest in teaching games. Many of the nuns, unequipped by education or inclination to be teachers, had been drafted by their orders to staff the diocesan schools. Those in the "American" orders, which included many Irish or Irish-Americans, sometimes took advanced training, but the standards of instruction fell short of those demanded by reformers. The Pittsburgh Survey openly deplored the emphasis on religion as an "academic loss" and the continued instruction in German, Polish, Lithuanian, Italian, and Bohemian as "distinctively non-American."[97] Nevertheless, the education in the parochial schools coincided with the parents' cultural and religious values. Just as importantly, the children of immigrants were not ridiculed in the Catholic schools as they sometimes were in the public schools. Though this might not have induced them to stay in school longer, it did help them keep their self-images intact.[98]

Immigrant responses to social surveyors' questions suggest that they valued education for their daughters less than for their sons. An Italian mother in New York City asked Louise Odencrantz rhetorically why her daughter should go to high school "when she's goin' to be married anyway?" A Slovenian father in Steelton, Pa., told his daughter that she didn't need an American education to put diapers on babies.[99] Yet in Pittsburgh both in 1880 and 1900, the educational rates of boys and girls within each ethnic group usually diverged no more than one or two percentage points. In 1880, British and Irish boys aged 10–14 were more apt than their sisters to be in school, a distinction the British retained through the high school years, whereas the daughters of Irish immigrants were as likely as their brothers to continue their education. The Germans kept their daughters from going to high school in large numbers, fearing that "they wanted to be Americans." By 1900 school attendance rates for the sexes were almost identical, except among blacks and native-born whites, where girls outnumbered boys.[100]

But though the sexes enrolled in the high school in equal numbers, the classes still did not. Middle- and upper-class children made disproportionate use of Pittsburgh's advanced educational facilities throughout the latter half of the nineteenth century. In 1890, about 60 percent of the male enrollees in the academic program came from white-collar, professional, and proprietorial families, as did about 50 percent of the females. Thirty-five percent of the boys and 37 percent of the girls came from skilled workers' families, and a meager 5 percent of the boys and 12 percent of the girls came from unskilled families. Overall, the working class accounted for 46 percent of the students enrolled in the Academic Department of

Pittsburgh's high school. A study of students in the Commercial Department at the turn of the century found that it was more popular with working-class children: 19 percent of its students had unskilled fathers and 35 percent had skilled fathers. Working-class youth thus formed a majority of the students in the Commercial Department, but the unskilled were still drastically underrepresented. Most pupils in the Commercial Department were native-born white; 49 percent had native-born white parents, 42 percent had foreign-born white parents. Only 6 percent of the pupils were foreign-born, and a paltry 3 percent were black.[101] Demand for high school education increased at the turn of the century, but primarily from native-born, skilled families. Poorer Pittsburghers still regarded primary school as sufficient for their needs.[102]

At the beginning of the twentieth century, working-class parents, particularly immigrants, sent their children to school at an early age to have them out of the house, Lila VerPlanck North claimed in her investigation of Pittsburgh's schools. One-fourth of the pupils in Catholic elementary schools but only one-tenth of those in the public elementary schools were enrolled in the first grade. According to North, the excessive number in the first grade was due to the presence of very young children and non–English speaking immigrants. The little ones went to school with their older brothers and sisters so that their mothers might get on with their domestic duties. More affluent native-born whites and members of the middle classes, who had household help and larger homes, had less need to have children out of the house. They could endow their progeny with many advantages at home that working-class and immigrant parents expected the schools to provide.[103]

Urban activists hoped to utilize kindergartens simultaneously to relieve crowding in the lower grades of Pittsburgh's public and parochial schools, wean working-class and immigrant children from the temptations of the street, and make them good U.S. citizens. Although kindergartens began in the United States as institutions for the children of the affluent, they were adopted rapidly by the social welfare movement. The first kindergarten appeared in Massachusetts in the 1870s; Pittsburgh followed in the 1890s. The vice president of the Pittsburgh Kindergarten Association wrote to the local school superintendent in 1894 to justify the work of her organization, then 2 years old. Mrs. William C. Clark claimed that kindergartens provided "moral training for our future voters," the children of the "undesirable thousands pouring in from Europe," and counteracted the "evil influences" that lured young children into unproductive lives.[104] There were five kindergartens in 1894 serving 371 children in Pittsburgh and Allegheny City, almost all of them foreign-born. The number of kindergartens increased rapidly, so that by 1908 there were twenty-three, operating in Pittsburgh's public schools with teachers employed by the Kindergarten Association but paid by the ward school boards from funds raised through private contributions. The 1,380 pupils enrolled in the city's kindergartens in that year represented a small fraction of the city's 4- and 5-year-olds, but a number of area school boards refused to allocate money for this purpose believing that it would only free mothers to "go gadding" or that they had no space in which to accommodate the new programs.[105]

Kindergarteners (the term refers to the teachers, not the students) shared the anti-urban bias of so many reformers. With G. Stanley Hall, president of Clark University and father of the child study movement, they believed that city life was unnatural, "that those who grow up without knowing the country are defrauded of that without which childhood can never be complete or normal."[106] So kindergarteners sought to arouse a love of nature in children from the industrial districts, who, never having seen grass, trees, birds, and flowers, "felt no lack, and found in their cobble-stones ample delight."[107] The kindergarteners educated their young charges in values, not books, and augmented their teaching with missionary visits to the children's homes.[108]

If the purpose of kindergarten was to introduce poor children to the joys of the countryside, then the task of elementary school was to instill such discipline as would enable young people to become cogs in the industrial machinery. A Statement of the Theory of Education in the United States, signed by leading city and state school superintendents and college presidents, stressed punctuality, regularity, attention, and silence "as habits necessary through life for successful combination with one's fellow-men in an industrial and commercial civilization."[109] The superintendent of the Pittsburgh schools believed they should act as a leveling agency in society, raising, in his words, "the valleys to the hill tops."[110] At the very least, the schools should provide "an elementary education" in such subjects as would prepare the children of Pittsburgh's working class for "their chosen work."[111]

Working-class parents wanted the schools to enhance their children's earning power or usefulness at home, and some Pittsburgh schools made tentative steps in this direction in the decades following the Civil War. The Ralston subdistrict, located in the highly industrialized Ninth and Tenth wards, opened an evening mechanical school in 1874 to provide young men with vocational training for the practical duties of life. But despite the Pennsylvania Bureau of Industrial Statistics' claim that children who had a "reasonable amount of labor to perform through the day" were in a better condition to study than those who went to school all day, attendance at evening schools was so irregular that George B. Leakey, the superintendent of schools, believed they accomplished little, if any, good. Even the original evening school in the Ralston subdistrict failed. Some young people came to study, but more stood outside, observed the Kingsley House settlement workers, and "used their utmost efforts to break up the school." Citywide night school enrollments declined steadily from a peak of 4,455 in 37 different ward evening schools in 1876 to about half that level in 1881. They were finally discontinued in 1894.[112]

A segment of the working class wanted mechanical arts and domestic science integrated into the regular school curriculum. In 1886, *Commoner and Glass Worker* criticized Pennsylvania's educational programs as not providing working-class youth with useful skills. According to that newspaper, the state claimed it was "not compatible with our system of education to impart a trade to the public." It further suggested that sewing, knitting, and cooking were appropriate for girls, as were the commonest occupations for boys, including shoemaking, telegraphing, and sign painting, none of which required any capital outlay.[113] Though the choice of occupations may seem unusual in a city known for its heavy industrial capacity, it is significant that iron making was excluded from the list. James J. Davis, trained as an iron puddler in the 1880s, describes the iron-making process as handed down from father to son. "None of us ever went to school, nor learned the chemistry of it from books. We learned the trade by doing it, standing with our faces in the scorching heat while our hands puddled the metal in its glaring bath."[114] But as steel replaced iron and recent Slavic arrivals occupied most laboring jobs in the new mills, there simply were fewer skilled, remunerative places to fill. One Scottish-Irish furnace boss summarized the feelings of many when he declared, "I'm getting along, but I don't want the kids ever to work this way." John Griswold intended to educate his children so they would not have to labor twelve hours a day.[115] Some working-class mothers in particular wanted children to have the advantages of the emerging order, so sons would not stand in the glaring heat of the long turn and daughters would not sleep fretfully, awaiting their husbands' return from the mills. Nevertheless, steelworking families generally rejected the academic training for their children although large numbers of skilled workers' children attended the Commercial Department at the turn of the century.[116]

Even in those instances in which fathers wanted to educate their sons in their trade, changing union regulations, designed to protect the declining number of skilled positions, prevented this. In 1882 the annual meeting of the AAISW declared that nailers could teach their sons the nailing trade, but only after the lad reached 18. Moreover, fathers could teach no more than one son in three years, and no nailer with a son older than 15 could teach any other person. The nailers' protectionist measures forced their sons to seek alternate employments, possibly outside the iron and steel industries altogether.[117]

In view of the declining opportunities among skilled iron- and steelworkers and the increased school enrollments from the immigrants and the working class, various school districts sought to incorporate so-called suitable vocational training into their formerly academic curriculum. A new school erected in Steelton, Pennsylvania, in 1881 "was intended not only to provide a normal education but also to give mechanical and vocational instruction preparing Steelton's youth for work in the mill."[118] A few years earlier, Pittsburgh's high school added industrial education as a separate department, thus providing three tracks within the school itself: academic, commercial, and industrial, the last two being explicitly vocational. Working-class wards instituted special manual training schools in the 1890s in order to provide industrial training geared to employment opportunities in Pittsburgh, but in 1894 the total enrollment in the manual training schools was only three hundred students.[119] The city opened a free evening high school in 1908, the superintendent of schools noting that Pittsburgh had made comparatively little effort to maintain night schools, which had, in fact, been abandoned fourteen years earlier.[120] After the reorganization of the city school system in 1911, special classes were organized for adult immigrants, but the schools continued in the same patterns established earlier.[121] The president of the new school board noted the increased demand for vocational education, manual training, and domestic science and said "the boys have to be taught trades and the girls to cook, bake, and sew."[122] The location of the training had shifted from the home to the school, but for most members of the working class, education remained vocationally orientated or was a brief interlude between play and work.

Childhood amid the steel mills prepared the young for their adult roles, the boys to the mill and the girls to the kitchen. Pittsburgh's working-class children grew up in a sex-segregated environment where men worked outside the home, and almost all women worked within it. Their early experiences taught them as no textbook could that their fathers were distant figures away from home for long periods of time, and that their mothers were in charge of the home and them, but frequently overburdened. Necessity limited childhood to a relatively short span, particularly for the children of the unskilled, widows, and immigrants, whose labor contributions were required to help sustain the family. Although by the beginning of the twentieth century, the state regulated some aspects of child labor and school attendance, it did not seek to prolong childhood beyond the age of 14, when most believed children could make significant labor contributions to their families if so required.[123] The working-class childhood was a short preparatory period for a life of labor in which the values, needs, and resources of the family rather than the dictates of the state determined the extent of a child's education and entrance into the world of useful labor inside or outside the home.

Urbanization and industrialization interacted powerfully to shape children's life chances in Pittsburgh. The deplorable sanitary conditions that prevailed in working-class districts throughout this period, when combined with the poverty of unskilled families, led to very much higher infant death rates for poor children. Mortality levels varied within the working class as well as between it and the middle class. As the new century unfolded, the discrepancy in infant death rates narrowed slightly within the working class itself but widened between skilled and middle-class infants. Even the families of skilled workers could not entirely escape the noisome conditions of poorly serviced proletarian neighborhoods, which middle-class families did by moving to the suburbs. The steadier (and higher) incomes of the middle class meant improved survival rates for their children.

The disparity in standard of living between skilled and unskilled workers' families was great, a fact reflected by their ability and willingness to endow their children with education. Few laborers' sons and daughters learned more than the rudiments. Although the number in high school grew, it remained disproportionately small, as did the participation of the newer immigrant groups and their children. More skilled workers' offspring attended high school, using the Commercial Department as a training mechanism to gain a place in the white-collar occupations that grew in importance at this time. The desperate need of the working-class family to gain additional income combined with the limited opportunities for women in Pittsburgh to constrain some children's education. Economic pressures led unskilled families to remove their young from school as early as possible so that they could earn, however inadequately. Skilled workers increasingly used the school system to help their children avoid the employments of their parents in the mills and in other people's homes. The end of education and beginning of work mirrored the discrepancies between and within the classes, but gender and the structure of Pittsburgh's economy determined the actual occupations undertaken once the child left school.

5 | Women's Work

The extent to which industrialization altered the family economy and women's place within it can be seen by examining the work women did, whether waged or within the home, and the use of children as wage earners. This analysis of women and the family economy is in three parts: women's employment, the entrance of children into the labor market, and women's domestic work. This chapter discusses the family economy as industrialization shifted the locus of work. It places Pittsburgh's employment patterns in national perspective, comparing the Steel City with other large urban areas, and exploring the variation in female employment according to cities' economic, ethnic, and racial composition. Then it investigates women's employment in Pittsburgh, in both old and new occupations. The expansion of women's employment reveals the extent to which considerations of class, race, and ethnicity constrained opportunities for some groups, even as issues of gender restricted opportunities for all women. The next chapter, "Children's Work," investigates the timing of children's movement into the labor force, comparing class, ethnicity, and gender variations in their work rates in order to demonstrate the extent to which the working-class family economy relied upon children to provide the income needed to exist in an industrial society. Chapter 7, "Marriage and Family" examines marital relations in that society, highlighting women's economic contributions outside the realm of paid work.

The Family Economy

Industrialization shifted the location of income earning from inside the home to outside it and limited women's earning potential in the process. It replaced the household with the factory, differentiating sharply between "work" and "life" in E. P. Thompson's description of the new order.[1] This led to a redefinition of tasks into production, which now took place outside the home, and consumption (the purchase and utilization of goods within it). Industrialization thus transformed women's economic contributions. Women in the preindustrial economy produced goods needed by their families, sometimes marketing the surplus. Typically they were involved in whatever work the family sustained itself with.[2] Their labor contributions, according to Joan Scott and Louise Tilly, merged imperceptibly with their household chores, enabling women to be productive while caring for their children and performing a wide range of tasks.[3] But industrialization disturbed this meshing of domestic and productive activities by transplanting work outside the home, thus making it difficult for women to attend to domestic tasks and still earn. Industrial time was less flexible than agricultural time or even that of a small shop or artisan workshop. Larger production units demanded constant attendance and attention from their workers, thus inhibiting married women's combination of family responsibilities with the production of goods.[4] Women now shopped for goods rather than growing and making them.

When work became an extrahousehold activity, the nature of parenting itself changed and, with it, mothers' ability to earn and fathers' to share in child-raising activities. Fathers on farms and in small family-run crafts and shops trained their sons and made use of their labor as soon as the boys were old enough to contribute their efforts.[5] As primary caretakers of young children, mothers had been mostly responsible for the early childhood years and the training of daughters. Industrialization did not lessen maternal responsibilities for child care. Instead, as the locus of work moved outside the home, women remained inside it to care for the children, reinforcing the maternal role. Motherhood became women's major occupation as consumption of store-bought goods displaced household manufacturing and as school and work took older children out of the home. Since fathers increasingly worked away from home as well, the paternal role became primarily that of wage earning outside the household.[6]

The family remained the working unit in a limited number of cases, notably textile production. Some historians believe that the family as a working unit in the textile mills was limited to the first phase of the Industrial Revolution, before the development of highly specialized machinery. But midnineteenth century textile workers in Lancashire were still recruited in family units, and some U.S. textile mills depended upon families to obtain workers through the early twentieth century.[7] In both England and New England, the family's role in labor recruitment increasingly meant that members of a kinship network helped one another find work, not that all family members held jobs. When married women worked in U.S. cities, they usually labored on an irregular and casual basis. Children rather than their mothers became the ancillary workers in the laboring families' battle for bread, as work outside the home was not complementary with women's traditional activities.[8] By the end of the nineteenth century, the family was less likely to work as a unit than at the beginning of the century, but it continued to deploy its resources to maximize family welfare with men and older children in the labor force and married women and younger children at home. There are two important variables to consider in addition to making that general point. First, the economic structure of any city determined the types of jobs available to women and therefore the number who could be in the labor force. Second, ethnocultural values played a part in the willingness of families to permit or require the labor of their female members within various employment environments.[9] One is thus looking at the interaction between economic structure and cultural values when one examines the extent of women's economic activity, but not when one examines men's. Contrary to the situation in Fall River or Lowell, Mass., women rarely came to Pittsburgh in search of work, although they might avail themselves of the limited openings once in the city. Employment opportunities for women did not pervade Pittsburgh's economy; they had to be sought out, and some groups were manifestly less willing than others that their daughters or wives do so.

Women Workers in Large Cities

The contrasts between the experiences of Pittsburgh's women and those in other cities at the end of the nineteenth century place them at the opposite end of the female employment continuum from women in the textile cities. Women's labor force participation in Pittsburgh increased from 16 to 22 percent between 1880 and 1900, which, while representative of heavy industrial cities, lagged behind the national urban average. Twenty-seven percent of the women in cities with more than one-hundred-thousand residents were in the labor force in 1900, significantly more than Pittsburgh's 22 percent. The lack of job opportunities depressed employment levels even for 16–24-year-olds. By 1900, 44 percent of these women in large cities worked, compared with only 35 percent in Pittsburgh. In most cities women dropped out of the labor force after marrying. In 1880, 1 percent of Pittsburgh's married women held jobs; in 1900, 3 percent did so. Nationally, the proportion varied from 2 to 3 percent in centers of heavy industry, around 5 percent in the more heterogeneous economies of Boston, New York, and Philadelphia, to around 20 percent of those in the textile towns and southern cities.[10] Thus the structure of the economy constricted employment for all women in Pittsburgh, whether they were in the groups most or least likely to have jobs in other large cities.

The overall variation in urban economic structures accounts for much of the difference in female employment patterns among U.S. cities. Those devoted to textile milling and fabrication had many single and married workers. In 1900, Lowell and Fall River, Massachusetts, both cotton mill towns, had the highest proportion of women in the labor force in the United States: 45 percent. Unlike Pittsburgh, where most of the women workers were domestic servants, however, between 59 and 73 percent of the textile town women worked in the mills and less than 10 percent were servants. Similar proportions of women mill operatives and servants could be found in the other cotton mill towns, including Manchester, N.H., Lawrence, Mass., and the collar-and-cuff city, Troy, N.Y.[11]

Another group of cities had more than 40 percent of adult women in the labor force, but a very different occupational profile. Atlanta and Savannah, Ga., Charleston, S.C., and Memphis, Tenn., averaged between 41 and 44 percent women wage earners, but textile mills and clothing fabrication played a minor part in their economies. Instead, between 59 and 70 percent of the women workers in these cities were either domestic servants or laundresses in 1900.[12] The ethnic composition of the female labor force and the persistence of wage earning throughout women's lives also differentiated southern cities from northern ones at this time. Native-born and foreign-born white women in the South had considerably lower rates of labor force participation than they did in the northern textile cities. The higher proportion of women in the labor force in southern cities was due to the propensity of black women to work rather than to generally high rates of female employment. About 60 percent of the black women over the age of 16 in these southern cities had jobs, a testimony to the desperate poverty of their families and an economic strategy that relied upon women as supplementary wage earners.[13]

Although black women withdrew from the labor force immediately following the Civil War, their employment rate increased from the 1870s through the early twentieth century. Elizabeth Pleck's research has suggested that black wives' participation in the labor force was much higher than that of Italians, even when incomes were comparable, because blacks and Italians had different approaches to maintaining an acceptable family standard of living, the preparation of children for adulthood, and the utility or desirability of formal education for the young.[14] Virginia Yans McLaughlin, documenting the low employment rate of Italian wives in turn-of-the-century Buffalo, N.Y., emphasized the role of culture as "an interface between the family and the economy, dictating which options were acceptable and which were not."[15] But in Buffalo, as in Pittsburgh, the economy interacted with culture, enhancing the tendency of some groups to deploy children as ancillary wage earners when there were few jobs for women.[16] Thus immigrant families in the textile areas had both more single and more married women workers than they did in the steel centers. Where the economy provided plentiful opportunities, women were more likely to work regardless of cultural backgrould. Conversely, where there were few jobs for women, those groups most resistant to female employment dropped out of the labor market in large numbers.

The difference in persistence rates for women workers in textile cities, southern cities, and those with a heavy industrial base underscores the interaction between economic structure and ethnic values in determining women's labor force participation. Life cycle employment patterns varied with both the economic and the ethnic mix. The textile cities had very high rates of female employment. The overwhelming majority of young women had jobs, as did many older ones. About three-quarters of the 16-to-20-year-olds and two-thirds of the 21-to-24-year-olds in Fall River, Lowell, Lawrence, Massachusetts, and Manchester, New Hampshire were in the labor force in 1900. This fell to under half for the 25-to-34-year-olds, which suggests that women gradually left the labor force after marriage. As Tamara Hareven notes in her study of Manchester, the critical variable was the availability of ancillary wage earners. Mothers worked sporadically in the Amoskeag Company textile mills, if at all, when their children became old enough to enter the mills.[17] As a result, about one-third of the women aged 35–44 worked in the textile factories, but less than one-fifth of those over 45 did so. Women's participation in the labor market in southern cities differed markedly from the textile cities of the north. Slightly more than two-fifths of all women between the ages of 16 and 44 had jobs, the proportion little affected by either marriage or the presence of young children. In 1900 the decline in female employment rates came only after age 45, which suggests that many black women (the majority of women workers in these cities) remained in the labor force while they had young children at home and stayed there until their children were grown. For black women, work outside their own home remained a fact of life through middle age at least. Even when children worked, the families relied upon the mothers' wages for support.[18]

In contrast to both textile and southern cities, centers of heavy industry showed a drastic decline in the number of women working after marriage. About 40 percent of the female population of Pittsburgh, Buffalo, N.Y., Erie, Pa., Elizabeth, N.J., and Toledo, Ohio, were in the labor force at ages 16–20, declining to about 33 percent by ages 21–24, and falling to 20 percent or less at 25–34. By 35–44, between 12 and 15 percent of the women were in the labor force and 10 percent or slightly less worked after age 45. Despite the prevalence of domestic service as an occupation in these cities, the age distribution of the female labor force varied from that of southern cities (also characterized by a concentration in domestic service) largely because of their ethnic composition. Northern industrial cities had small black populations in 1900, so that most of their working women were of European stock or born abroad. Such women eschewed domestic service after marriage and would have avoided it altogether had alternatives existed.[19]

The ethnicity of women workers varied greatly between the different types of city. Blacks formed the majority of the employed female population in the South, but in the northern textile cities between half and three-fifths of the women workers had been born abroad and one-fourth had foreign-born parents. The proportion of foreign-born working women in the centers of heavy industry was much lower, ranging from one-third in Pittsburgh to about two-fifths in Buffalo in 1900, which suggests that these cities were much less attractive to women from abroad who sought employment. Such cities attracted fewer foreign-born women, and those who did come had more domestic expectations or earned money within the home by taking in boarders. The lack of suitable employment combined with the movement of women into the city as brides or to join husbands already there tended to push women out of the labor force after marriage. Since foreign-born women, particularly Italians, tended to marry younger than native-born or black women, this also restricted their wage-earning days.[20]

Even within the heavy industry environment, some groups had higher rates of female participation in the labor force than others. Throughout this era Irish, Germans, and black women in Pittsburgh were more likely to work than native-born white, Italian, or Polish women. Pittsburgh and Buffalo both had low rates of female participation, but that of Italian immigrant women was especially low. Conversely, New York City, with a plethora of light industries and sweated trades, had a higher overall proportion of women workers and a greater proportion of Italian women in the labor force. The garment industry there utilized traditional sewing skills, and more than one-third of the women workers in the clothing industry in 1910 came from southern Italy. The employment base influenced the extent of women's employment before and after marriage. Women of the same ethnic group were more likely to take jobs in cities that offered sweated or textile employments, where women worked in a group at a traditionally female task. When domestic work dominated female employment, as in Pittsburgh or Buffalo, Italian women were less likely to be employed. Although these families previously relied upon the efforts of all members to sustain themselves, the economy did not readily accommodate married women, and the families of single women did not want them to work in isolation as servants.[21] Married black women were unique in their participation rates in the labor force and concentration in domestic service. Such work, however, rarely permitted them to combine caring for their own families with wage earning, for employers demanded that they live in and keep contact with their own families to a minimum.[22]

Women Workers in Pittsburgh

Several important changes occurred in women's employment patterns in Pittsburgh between 1870 and 1900: more women entered the labor force as more white-collar positions became available and fewer joined the ranks of household workers. The expansion of teaching, sales, and clerical work paralleled the decline of domestic service. This, in turn, led to a shift in the composition of the female labor force as white-collar employments attracted young women who heretofore eschewed or were underrepresented in paid work, the daughters of the native-born middle class and skilled workers. Women also had jobs in a few factory occupations in food and tobacco processing and on the fringes of the glass, steel, and metalworking industries. Public opinion and trade unions disapproved of women working in heavy industry.[23]

By 1900 the city began its slow shift out of basic manufacturing and into education, administration, commerce, and service industries. That transition opened a wider range of jobs for women, but still within the confines of a divided work force. Employers at the turn of the century felt that gender characteristics suited women to certain tasks. Women, according to Pennsylvania employers in trade and industry, were content to labor at a limited segment of the job, a low-priced, docile labor force that could be more easily controlled than their male counterparts. It is illuminating that one of the most rapidly expanding sectors of the economy, retail trade, employed women precisely because store and shop owners believed them less expensive, more reliable, and "better adapted" to such work than men. They would work longer hours for low pay without complaining. As Edith Abbott pointed out in her 1909 investigation of female employment, "in recent years the increase in gainful employment among women has not been in the industrial group," but in trade and transportation, into which category both clerical and sales workers were placed.[24]

The proportion of women at work in Pittsburgh remained lower than in other U.S. cities, those with a similar heavy industry base excepted. Nevertheless, the jobs performed by women in Pittsburgh reflected national trends as domestic service declined and white-collar jobs proliferated locally and nationally. In 1870, 8 percent of Pittsburgh's working women wore white blouses to work; by 1900, the comparable figure was 28 percent. Some white-collar posts—those of typist, stenographer, and telephone operator, for example—had not existed in 1870, and others, including teaching and sales, expanded greatly (see table 23).

Having examined the questions of which women worked and the

Table 23. Female Occupations

	Profes-sional		Domestic and Personal		Clerical and Sales		Manufac-turing		Working Women	Women as Proportion of Total Labor Force
	N	%	N	%	N	%	N	%	N	%
1870	165	4	2,935	69	181	4	977	23	4,248	14
1900	1,862	8	11,722	50	4,889	20	5,138	22	23,618	18

Sources: U.S. Census, Ninth Census, 1870, vol. 1, *Population,* p. 795; Twelfth Census 1900, vol. 2, *Population,* pt. 2, pp. 682–83.

forces that propelled them into the labor force, this chapter continues with an exploration of the actual nature of women's jobs in this era. The employments focused on here were selected either because they were prevalent (domestic service, for example), because they demonstrated what women's work was becoming in the dawning commercial age (teaching and sales work), or because they typified the range of jobs available to women (canneries, cigar rolling, and prostitution.) Each employment is examined to see how it changed over time, how easy it was to enter, and which groups undertook it. The other reason for the selection of employments for detailed consideration is to correct the impression given by the Pittsburgh Survey that Pittsburgh's female labor force was an industrial one.

The Pittsburgh Survey's *Women and the Trades,* Pittsburgh 1907–1908, written by Elizabeth Butler, gives a somewhat misleading impression of women's work in Pittsburgh at the time of the Survey by simply ignoring that half of the female working population which toiled in domestic, personal, and professional service.[25] A handful of women in the city did work inside Pittsburgh's main industries, but most did not. Butler wrote that "from a national standpoint, the trades of far-reaching significance are those in which we find women molding metals, shaping lamps and making glass. Here women's work has reached the midst of the mechanical industries upon which is founded the city's wealth."[26] Butler's investigation concentrated primarily on factory trades, in which she believed that women were "extending the boundaries of their industrial activities." Nevertheless, women were peripheral to those industries. They comprised a minute proportion of the total iron and steel labor force, and the few women who held such jobs were only a small segment of the female labor force during this era. Using Butler's figures for 1907–1908, with the 1910 census as the base for employed women, yields 3.8 percent of the women workers in the metal trades and less than 1 percent of all metalworkers being female, roughly the same proportion as twenty or thirty years earlier.[27] The major change in the female labor force came not in Pittsburgh's primary industries but in the retail and white-collar sectors, where appearance, the ability to speak English, and a reasonable level of education helped a young woman gain access to a job. Such employments thus remained out of the reach of foreign-born and black women but went to native-born whites, the daughters of skilled workers and the middle class.[28]

Men and women occupied segregated labor markets. Employment for Pittsburgh's men was primarily in manufacturing, mostly heavy industry, but *Women and the Trades* notwithstanding, few women penetrated this sector of the economy. By 1880, two-thirds of the city's manufacturing capital was tied up in iron, steel, and glass. Three-fifths of all men worked in manufacturing during these decades, but not many women. A few women had jobs as cutters, solderers, stampers, and wrappers in the tinware industry, and a small number worked packing, sorting, and inspecting nails and screws in the 1880s. Indeed, manufacturing employment for women may have contracted during the century. In the middle of the nineteenth century, there had been five large and several small cotton mills in Pittsburgh and Allegheny City. The Civil War starved these mills of their raw materials, so that by 1870 no cotton mills remained in Pittsburgh and few women crossed the river to work in those left in Allegheny City. Nearly one-quarter of all Pittsburgh's working women labored in "manufacturing and mechanical" pursuits, mostly (four-fifths) as dressmakers and seamstresses. At the beginning of the twentieth century, the proportion of Pittsburgh's women working in manufacturing remained about the same, still heavily concentrated in the clothing industry: two-thirds of this group were dressmakers, seamstresses, milliners, and the like. There had been a handful of women tobacco, cigar, and cigarette workers in 1880, but by 1900, one-tenth of the women in manufacturing were in this category.[29]

The contrast between men as workers in heavy industry and women as domestic servants or workers in traditionally female manufacturing and light industry remained strong at the beginning of the twentieth century. In 1870, 69 percent of Pittsburgh's women were domestic servants, a figure that fell to 50 percent in 1900. In 1880 about 8 percent of the glassworkers were female, as were about 1 percent of those in the metal trades. By 1900 the number of women glassworkers had fallen and the proportion of women in the metal trades remained about the same. Work for women in Pittsburgh continued to be primarily domestic, but the proportion of women in trade rose fivefold in these decades (from 4 percent in 1870 to 20 percent in 1900) and reflected a shift in Pittsburgh's economy away from manufacturing to administration and service. This introduced a further divergence of male and female employment patterns because work for Pittsburgh's working-class men remained the physical world of the mills while for their daughters and sisters it increasingly became that of the shop and the office.[30] The decline in the proportion of domestic servants among economically active women indicated both a preference to move out of the kitchen and the opportunity to work in more socially acceptable and less isolated environments.

A number of factors besides location differentiated male and female jobs in this era, including the possibility for upward mobility, the range of remuneration, and the degree of freedom accorded to the workers.[31] Almost no women's jobs held out any prospects for career advancement. Women in Pittsburgh worked at dead-end jobs with virtually no opportunity to move into more skilled or supervisory work. Few women made anything approaching a wage on which they could be self-supporting, and the actual variation between lowest and highest paid was much narrower than for men. Lastly, many women's jobs limited their autonomy. Domestic service was notorious for attempts by the employer to control the servant's every waking hour, meager time-off, and circumscribed social life. No male occupation suffered the same constraints. Women preferred cleaner, safer, more genteel employments to rougher ones, even when the latter paid more. The emphasis on gentility had two consequences. Employers in favored occupations could and did restrict access by race and ethnicity, and a highly stratified labor force resulted. The high demand for such places also led to low wages, so that *genteel* did not necessarily mean "well paying." The lack of employments open to women who wanted or needed to work depressed wages for all women workers.[32]

Teaching demonstrates how these processes worked at the upper echelon of the female employment spectrum. Pittsburgh's small female professional class consisted mostly of teachers in schools and professors in colleges. The expansion in numbers at the end of the nineteenth century did not lead to any diversification in the type of women who obtained such positions, however. They were almost all single (96 percent), born in the United States (92 percent), and white (99.5 percent). They differed from other groups of working women in being more likely to be independent, self-supporting and career-oriented. About 30 percent were heads of families or boarded with nonrelatives, although only 18 percent of all Pittsburgh women workers (apart from domestic servants) lived on their own in 1900. Teachers in large cities tended to be older than those in small towns or rural districts, where "a pupil of one year may be the teacher of next," since urban teachers had more training than rural ones.[33]

Indeed, Pittsburgh's teachers were older than other women workers in the city. More than three-fifths were over 25, compared with about two-fifths of the total female labor force. Although teachers tended to be older than other women workers and to live apart from their families, they did not have complete autonomy. School boards felt they could regulate the personal lives of their teachers. Even so, teachers enjoyed higher status than women in other occupations, both because the job embodied what many saw as the feminine, nurturant role and because lower overall female educational levels and ethnic prejudice restricted access to the profession at this time.[34] The number of women seeking entrance into the teaching profession outnumbered the available positions. This depressed salary levels and led to higher unemployment rates for teachers than other women workers at the turn of the century.[35]

Employees in the other rapidly expanding sector of the female labor force, sales and clerical work, had shared one attribute with the teachers; almost all were born in the United States and came principally from Irish, British, and German stock.[36] However, they exhibited little of the career-orientedness and independence of the teachers. White-collar workers in Pittsburgh's offices and shops tended to be younger than their sisters in the classroom (63 percent were under 25), and most lived with their parents.[37] An 1894 Pennsylvania Bureau of Industrial Statistics survey found that only 14 percent of the city's saleswomen lived with strangers; 11 percent lived with relatives (mostly sisters), and the rest lived with their parents, a portrait confirmed by the 1900 census. This survey also highlighted the limited duration of their stay in the labor force. Most of the women were working at their first or second or, at most, third job. By contrast women in less favored jobs changed them more frequently.[38]

The paucity of genteel employment for women led them to hold onto whatever position they found. Dr. Annie MacLean wrote in 1910 that "the life of a 'saleslady' seems most alluring to many young girls. They see only the delight of being more or less dressed up, on exhibition in fact, all the time."[39] Indeed, the department store owners expected their sales force to dress well. One cash girl recalled that she had one big hair ribbon and one shirtwaist, "which she washed and ironed every night" in order to be presentable. The women had to dress well lest they lose their places. This entailed real sacrifices on their parts; frequently they stinted on food in order to dress stylishly and thus maintain their positions. Clerical workers were also expected to dress appropriately, wearing hats to work and business suits, the cost of which could absorb a large part of their wages.[40]

Many of the women in Pittsburgh's stores began work as cash girls at the age of 14 or younger, contributing to the expansion of employment of young workers at the turn of the century. The cash girl's job was to run the money from the sales personnel to the cashier and return with a receipt. Other positions included wrappers, whose skill in wrapping parcels might gain customers. According to Elizabeth Butler's survey of working women in the Pittsburgh district, the better stores maintained their "exclusiveness by distinctive paper and seal, and even a more plebeian store gains many a customer by the care and attractiveness with which its parcels are wrapped."[41] As they became familiar with the store, cash girls might hope to advance to a position in the sales force, but they rarely moved farther up the store hierarchy. A few exceptional women moved beyond the rank of saleslady, but retail work, like other female employments at this time, furnished little scope for a career, as opposed to a job.

Department stores provided one of the few environments where women in Pittsburgh worked in large groups, offering some of the comraderie found in industrial employments but in a more socially acceptable environment.[42] Nationally, sales jobs ranked eighth in non-domestic occupational importance for women in 1900; in Pittsburgh, they ranked third, closely behind domestic service and sewing. Contemporary analysts believed that sales work was less exhausting and the conditions, being cleaner and more sanitary, more attractive than those to be found in a factory. The women themselves preferred sales jobs to factory or domestic work, regarding them as more genteel. Employers restricted sales jobs, insofar as possible, to native-born white women. Thus prejudice and self-selection resulted in a labor force dominated by native-born white women; both nationally and in Pittsburgh, 88 percent of the women in sales positions were born in the United States of native-born, British, Irish or German parentage. Both in 1890 and 1900, about 35 percent of all women in the retail trades in Pittsburgh were the daughters of native-born white men, and more than 50 percent were second-generation Americans. The stores were able to maintain this high proportion of native-born white workers because they had more applicants than positions.[43]

Despite the desirability of department store employment, the working conditions left a great deal to be desired. The women worked long hours; ten-hour days were common, and two or three nights a week the stores remained open until 9 or 10 P.M. Saleswomen remained on their feet for the entire time. An 1877 Pennsylvania statute required storekeepers to provide seats for "lady clerks," but apparently few did so. At the time of their investigation in 1888 the Anti-Cruelty Society discovered that most stores had no seats on which the clerks might rest. Sales women responding to inquiries by the Bureau of Industrial Statistics felt that their hours were too long and that seats should be provided. In 1905 the state legislature again demanded that stores furnish clerks with suitable seats and permit their use "when the employees are not necessarily engaged in active duties."[44] Yet a survey conducted in 1907 uncovered flagrant abuses among the better department stores. One contained 19 seats for 500 employees on its main selling floor; another had 16 for 400. In fact, a tacit understanding existed in most stores: a clerk had to stand if she wanted to remain employed. Even with all these disadvantages, department store work carried more prestige than domestic or factory work, so that once a woman had such a job, she made sacrifices to keep her place, accepting low wages and long hours on her feet in order not to lose caste by falling back into the ranks of factory or household workers.[45]

Industry

Women in various industrial pursuits enjoyed less prestigious places in the occupational hierarchy than teachers or saleswomen. They came from more varied ethnic backgrounds and had less education than the white-collar group. The Pittsburgh Survey found Jewish women from Poland and Russia in the stogy and garment factories, Slavic women in the canneries, laundries, and metal trades, and Irish and German women sewing jeans and railroad jumpers in the hills around the outlying coal mines. Although the number of women in heavy industry never grew beyond a handful and was not increasing proportionately to other female jobs, women did comprise about one-half of the work force in the food processing and cigar industries. There were two general divisions of labor in these industries: by ethnicity and by sex. Native-born white women held the more desirable positions and toiled in the better workplaces, while the foreign-born were relegated to the most unpleasant jobs. Slavic women, for example, had the disagreeable task of filling the cans in a molasses plant by placing them under a continuous flow of sticky stuff, ending each day covered in molasses splashes. Native-born white and German-American women in these establishments had the cleaner tasks of cutting tin and soldering the cans.[46]

The sexual division of labor transcended ethnicity, so that even when women and men worked in the same plants, virtually all male jobs paid better than any female ones, regardless of the women's background. Wages in the food industry were lower than in other trades, but women earned less than men in such enterprises.[47] Men did all the responsible work in the canneries: they cooked and preserved the fruit, pickled the cucumbers, and baked the beans. Women's tasks were ancillary and mechanical. Women washed and filled bottles, scrubbed floors, sorted and prepared the raw materials. They had always held these subordinate positions. As early as 1869 and 1870, women in the canneries were the packers, bottlers, corkers, and laborers.[48] Butler's investigation of women and the trades declared that "when cooking is for a critical public, and not for an indulgent home, some rule of survival selects the undomestic sex to do the work." Men presided over Pittsburgh's confectionery factories, melting the chocolate, baking the peanuts, combining green, white, and red sugared slabs into candy canes, ships' anchors, and candy kisses. Men reigned as confectionery artists; women wrapped the sweets, covered cooked centers with chocolate, bagged and boxed them.[49] Prevailing notions of male and female employment resulted in a sexual division of labor in these industries, as elsewhere, where men held the skilled, better-paying jobs, while women were segregated in the repetitive, low-paying positions.[50]

Cigar making was the largest factory pursuit for women in Pittsburgh at the turn of the century and increased in importance as the workingman's use of tobacco burgeoned. Pittsburgh was noted for its manufacture of rough, cheaply made cigars, referred to as stogies, which enjoyed a local following.[51] In 1880 cigar making had been skilled work undertaken mostly by men; a mere fifteen women worked in the trade in that year, packing and labeling the finished product. By 1900 women accounted for 47 percent of the cigar makers but differed from their male counterparts in a number of ways.[52] They entered this trade earlier than men, stayed for a few years, then left as they married. Ninety-one percent of the female stogy workers were under 25, and 23 percent were between 10 and 15 years old, making this trade a disproportionately large employer of very young women. Men remained as tobacco workers longer: only 45 percent were under 25, and 7 percent were under 15.[53] Thus they accumulated skills denied to women. Most female cigar makers performed repetitive tasks in subdivisions of the trade, stripping the stems from the leaves, tending the bunching and rolling machines, and packing the cigars into boxes. They either were machine operators or prepared the tobacco for further processing. Men did the skilled work, although the use of machines operated by women increasingly displaced male artisan hand stogy makers with female mold stogy makers.[54]

In contrast to the women who wore white blouses to work, stogy makers were overwhelmingly foreign-born or had foreign-born parents, primarily Russian- and Polish-born Jews. Most worked in small tenement factories in the Hill District characterized by poor lighting, overcrowding, and unsanitary conditions. The factories were generally poorly ventilated. Contemporary analysts did not believe there was conclusive evidence to prove that working with tobacco caused disease, but they felt that the long hours sitting in one position at the rolling bench, with the tobacco dust heavy in the stagnant air, resulted in lung and throat diseases, especially tuberculosis.[55] Employers in the larger factories controlled by the Union American Cigar Company drove their young immigrant work force hard, firing those who fell below a specified output and fining the least productive. The smaller tenement factories did not push their workers as ruthlessly but did have irregular hours and more overtime work. Few of Pittsburgh's women stogy makers belonged to a union. The constitution of the National Stogy Makers excluded them, and the family shops resisted organizing efforts. Male cigar workers viewed the young female workers with suspicion, blaming them for accepting low wages and being the tool used by employers to drive skilled workers from the trade through mechanization.[56] The employers hired more women, believing along with retail store owners that they were more easily controlled, less liable to smoke, more reliable, and better adapted to the work.[57] Women and men in the cigar trade worked under different conditions to produce a different grade of product. The women were young, a temporary work force, performing unskilled and semiskilled operations. Employers excluded women from the skilled tasks in the industry, using them to keep wages down and productivity up.

Women's work in heavy industry, limited though it was, bore some resemblance to that of the stogy makers. The workers were young immigrants or had immigrant parents; two-thirds were Polish, Hungarian, or Croatian. These women undertook unskilled or semiskilled tasks, where machines helped them do what had previously been the province of skilled workers. They were confined to peripheral jobs, small-scale, lighter, or simplified versions of the work done by men.[58] In some cases the working conditions were awful. The women in the South Side nut-and-bolt factories stood throughout ten- or twelve-hour stints, hands wrapped in rags, screwing the nuts onto the bolts under a continuous drip of fish oil. By the end of the day, oil spattered everywhere, covering them in a film of smelly grease. As with women in the tobacco industry, women coremakers' tasks differed fundamentally from men's. The few women coremakers made simple stock shapes, working only on the lighter cores.

The oven-baked sand forms were set into molds over which molders poured hot metal. Only men made the heavy, intricate cores, which took great skill and training. Women workers in heavy industry, such as the bolt threaders and coremakers, held positions that provided little scope for acquiring a broad range of skills on the job. They rarely had the satisfaction of seeing a job through from inception to completion. Most performed highly repetitive tasks such as feeding six or seven thousand bolts into a threading machine or threading four thousand nuts onto bolts in a day.[59]

Their male co-workers did not accept women's place in the skilled, better-paid segments of industry and feared that they would be used to debase the work itself and lower the wages.[60] Seeing the trend in other industries, glassworkers worried that their employers would replace skilled men with unskilled women machine operators.[61] Although Pittsburgh's glass industry declined in size between 1880 and 1900, the number of women remained constant. The introduction of machinery and the division of work into its component processes opened the way for the substitution of unskilled women and boys for skilled men.[62] At the turn of the century, women in the glass houses primarily performed mundane tasks, cleaning, washing, and packing glass. A small group worked on various finishing processes, cutting off, grinding, and setting the tumblers on a tray to be passed under a flame that melted and smoothed the surface. Women also worked as decorators, stamping designs on the glass, preparing glasses for etching, and—the most highly skilled work that glass house women did—hand decorating with liquid gold and ruby paint. They did not blow glass. An ethnic division of labor existed even within this limited range of female occupations. After 1900, Eastern European women began moving into glass work, replacing those of German stock. Native-born white women did the decorating and Polish and Croatians the unskilled and semiskilled jobs. Unionized plants managed to keep the women out altogether, and women's work in the nonunion plants was strictly confined to finishing tasks rather than glass making.[63]

The city's trade unionists understood why women worked but wished their efforts to be confined to the domestic sphere. The *National Labor Tribune* opposed women's work outside the home if it transgressed the traditional sexual boundaries. In a properly ordered universe, men earned the bread, and women baked it. Females should not compete for male jobs. In 1885 the paper heartily supported a proposed law forbidding the employment of females in coal mines, coke works, and iron and steel mills. It was acceptable for women to toil in the textile factories in the eastern part of the state, but the presence of Hungarian women in the Connellsville coke works closer to home constituted a "beastly invasion" that could not be tolerated lest it unsex American women and interfere with the employment of men. Though these women were apparently so degraded as to want to work in men's jobs, they set a bad precedent, and the power of the state was summoned to banish them from the mines and mills.[64]

Ten years later the Monongahela Tin Plate Works began employing women, which enraged "Populist," a pseudonymous correspondent of the *National Labor Tribune*, whose sense of decency and morality was offended. Employment amid the smoke, gas, and profanity violated the purity of glorious womanhood, as did working under the same roof as the men. Unless employment at the tin works was confined to men, domestic and social relations would be affected, and men would suffer in their wages. Working men, particularly trade unionists, roundly condemned the threat to the accepted order heralded by the employment of women at the tin works.[65]

Cigar rollers, coremakers, and glassworkers, among others, resisted the unionization of women in their trades. Iron- and steel-workers protested the employment of women in factories and foundries, where they might compete with men for jobs or be used by employers to lower wages. Cigar makers complained about the number of women and children entering their trade and opposed the use of machinery, which they operated.[66] The 1900 International Convention of Coremakers believed foundry work not suitable for the "gentler sex" since it (somehow) made them unfit for married life. But if women had to work, the convention resolved, they should receive the same pay as men so as not to lower the wage scale generally. Coremakers, a minority among organized labor, wanted the women to "organize and demand equal pay for equal work."[67] Nevertheless, they quickly reversed their support for women in their trade. By 1910 they advocated protective legislation to limit the size and weight of cores made by women and to prohibit them from working in the same room as the ovens, in effect excluding them from the foundries.[68] Glassworkers did not want women in their organizations; they believed that if women left the factories to men, everyone would be better off: factory wages would increase, and the female sex, through confinement to the domestic sphere, would "elevate itself to a higher plane."[69] These trade unionists wanted a family wage, which would enable them to support their families without help from women.

Domestic Service

Pittsburgh's trade unionists preferred women to be domestic servants or to labor in other nonfactory jobs where they could not be used to debase men's work by operating machines that deprived male workers of their skilled positions. *Commoner and Glassworker* counseled that domestic service prepared females for their primary roles in life, housewifery and motherhood, which the demoralizing influence of the workshop did not. Despite the ability of better-educated women to obtain jobs outside the domestic sphere, household service remained the single largest employer of women in Pittsburgh through the 1930s, although it became a residual occupation—one that women undertook when they could get no other.[70] It is perhaps indicative of the low esteem in which so many regarded housework that the one volume of the Pittsburgh Survey that analyzed women's employments in the Pittsburgh region completely ignored domestic service, which even in 1909 gave employment to most of the women and girls who toiled in the city. *Women and the Trades* examines the labors of women in cigar rolling, food processing, mechanized laundries, hand sewing, and mercantile establishments, but not of those who worked in private kitchens or took in washing.[71] The reasons for the disdain of domestic service are complex but may be rooted in the association of domestic work with "women's work" and its private, nonmodern nature. The problems of the women factory and sweatshop workers were far more visible than those of the private household worker, which had been chronicled by Lucy M. Salmon in *Domestic Service*, published in 1901.[72]

The employment shifts in Pittsburgh paralleled those in other industrial areas, where education and new opportunities in industry and commerce gave young women the option to do something besides housework, whether paid in someone else's home or unpaid in their own or their parents'.[73] By the end of the century, most American women regarded domestic service as something one did only if one had no education and there were no other jobs available. Most believed that housework was a dead-end occupation with numerous social disadvantages including little freedom, social stigma, loneliness, and removal from one's own family.[74] As more opportunities opened in other fields, those who could left domestic service, so that a shift in the ethnic composition of Pittsburgh's servants accompanied their declining share of the labor force.

In 1880, as table 24 shows, 64 percent of all servants in Pittsburgh came from either Irish or German backgrounds. Twenty years later this proportion had fallen to 52 percent as Irish-American women rejected live-in domestic service as a relic of feudalism. The *Irish Pennsylvanian* remarked in 1889 that "no one asks male workers to live in these days."[75] Housework performed by outsiders still required subservience in the form of uniforms, constant availability to the employers' demands, and submissive behavior. As Irish-Americans obtained more education, they were less constrained in their choices of occupation and so left service.[76]

Table 24. Ethnicity of Servants by Father's Nativity
(In Percentages)

	Native-born White	British	Irish	German	S. & E. European	Black	Total	N
1880	19	8	38	26	1	8	100	606
1900	19	8	29	23	8	13	100	8,368

Sources: 1880 census sample; U.S. Census, Twelfth Census 1900, vol. 2, *Population*, pt. 2, pp. 682–83.

Black women moving north in greater numbers at the turn of the century found fewer outlets for their talents. In 1880 blacks comprised 8 percent of Pittsburgh's servants, a figure that rose to 13 percent by 1900, even though they formed only 7 percent of the female labor force by that time. Despite expanding opportunities for women generally, few black women obtained nonservice jobs in Pittsburgh through the beginning of the twentieth century. No hospitals trained them as nurses, no department stores hired them except as maids, nor did they find work in industry. A few black female clerks and stenographers worked in the stores and offices of black men, but whites employed black women only in menial positions. There were a handful of black professional men in Pittsburgh at the turn of the century, but the local schools virtually refused to hire black women to teach. This closed one avenue of employment mobility to aspiring black women and reinforced their concentration in domestic and personal service.[77]

Moreover, domestic service for black women had different characteristics than it did for whites, both in its pervasiveness as an occupation for women (95 percent of the unmarried black women workers in the 1880 census sample and 90 percent in 1900 were servants or laundresses) and in the role it played in black women's life cycle. Very few black women lived their teenage years with their parents. In the 1880 census sample, the number of black females living with their parents declined by two-thirds among 15–19-year-olds, although the number of males remained stable. These young women did not disappear from the city; they joined the ranks of household workers. In doing so, they left their families of origin to join households with a very different class and ethnic background. Most servants (four-fifths) lived with their employers, so that although the proportion of black women who lived in was lower than it was for the group as a whole (about three-fourths resided in their employers' households), the very commonness of the occupation among black women meant that as a group they were particularly distant from their own families. There are several probable reasons for the somewhat lower proportion of blacks living in: these include racism on the part of employers, the greater likelihood that the servant herself would be married and therefore insist upon living out, and the overall transition beginning to occur in the nature of service itself as it moved from a residential to daily occupation, something that occurred first among black women.[78]

The other hallmark of black women's work was that they remained employed over a longer period than did white women. In 1900 nearly one-fourth of the black female labor force was married, and about one-half of these women worked as domestic servants. This contrasts sharply with the experience of white women: very few worked after marriage, and fewer still were servants. Service was a transitional period for white women, a bridge between their parents' home and a home of their own. Whites entered service, stayed a few years (longer among the Polish and the Irish than among German and native-born whites), then left service and the labor force simultaneously when they married. Black women began work at a younger age, had fewer options as to their employment, and remained in the labor force longer, primarily as domestics.[79]

The poverty of the new immigrants also led them into service. By 1900, 8 percent of Pittsburgh's domestic servants came from Southern and Eastern Europe (see table 24). Once again, Pittsburgh's lopsided employment opportunities shaped the work women did. Nationally, only 21 percent of all Russian and Polish and 12 percent of all Italian working women were servants. In the Steel City the proportions were 45 percent and 26 percent, respectively. For the restricted labor market for foreign-born females left them few alternatives for employment, a situation that suggests how strongly the nature of the local economy influenced women's work patterns. Even though Italian women in Pittsburgh had low rates of employment, 25 percent of those who worked did so in other women's kitchens.[81]

Domestic service provided an indirect subsidy to the families of the servants themselves: when daughters lived out, employers bore the cost of room and board, but parents still expected the young women to contribute to the family coffers.[81] Most young household workers came from poor families living in small homes. Employment of their daughters meant that the middle and upper classes carried some of the costs of raising them, but the price of the subsidy was almost total subjugation to the mistress's demands and isolation from one's family. Particularly as the physical distance and gap in standards of living widened between working- and middle-class at the end of the nineteenth and beginning of the twentieth centuries, service provided one of the few points of contact between the classes and ethnic groups. Glimpses of middle-class life-styles made working-class folk more aware of the poverty and poor surroundings in which they grew up and could expect to live after marriage. Domestic service might indicate "how one could be proud of one's possessions, the way one lived," but it did not necessarily provide good training for life on $1.65 per day.[82] Lucy M. Salmon believed that domestic service gave servants a knowledge of household affairs, for which every woman, "whatever her station in life," had a most pressing need.[83] Servants in wealthy homes might learn extravagance instead of frugal home management and a narrow range of skills unsuited to the tiny homes and diverse duties of the working-class housewife. Their work could vary from that of the overburdened maid-of-all-work (literally) to that of a household assistant who worked alongside her employer. Few households in Pittsburgh employed more than one servant, so all the tasks the employer did not care to undertake herself were delegated to hired help.[84]

Domestic service declined in importance during these years as many women left the world of the servant for that of the shop or factory. Blacks and foreign-born women encountered more constraints on their employment than white native-born women and so remained longer in the residential service category. Such women constituted a highly mobile group within the black population, changing jobs frequently, typically leaving one place for another with no real improvement in working conditions or wages. As this suggests, not all servants were young women; in 1880, 68 percent of the women workers under 30 but 83 percent of those over 30 were domestics. Many of these older women took in washing, traveling from house to house, washing clothes at each stop or collecting and delivering them. Though these women did not endure the constraints placed upon live-in servants, theirs could be a hard life. They frequently traveled long distances to reach their clients. They were liable to rheumatism. The constant immersion in hot water reddened and chapped hands and arms. It was nevertheless one of the few occupations open to older women.[85]

Prostitution

Washerwomen tended to be older women, frequently widows, foreign-born, or black. Prostitutes shared few of these characteristics. Pittsburgh's male-dominated occupational structure made prostitution a choice, if perhaps a desperate one, for young women in search of work.[86] The large number of men separated from their families and the taxing nature of men's jobs all encouraged iron- and steelworkers, among others, to have a fling after payday, drinking and perhaps patronizing prostitutes.[87] Two cameo views of prostitution in the Steel City, one drawn from the 1880 manuscript census and the other from the reports of the Pittsburgh Survey in 1907 and the Morals Efficiency Commission of 1913, illustrate who practiced this occupation in Pittsburgh.[88]

Black and foreign-born women were underrepresented in the ranks of Pittsburgh prostitutes in 1880. Virtually all prostitutes listed in the 1880 manuscript census had been born in the United States, about half in Pennsylvania.[89] Black women, designated as servants or cooks, also lived in brothels, an apparently common practice in northern cities.[90] It is unclear whether these women engaged in prostitution.[91] In Pittsburgh, according to social surveyors, the black women servants "generally became corrupted," and their employment in brothels "was not the least source of Negro prostitution in the North."[92] Employment agencies also sent blacks to houses of prostitution, the women being indebted to the agencies for their fare north and unable to reclaim their belongings until they paid off their debt.[93]

About 12 percent of the unmarried native-born white working women were designated as "sporting women" in the 1880 census sample, making 3 percent of all working women prostitutes. Since the census takers designated no foreign-born women as streetwalkers or prostitutes, the actual proportion of prostitutes among Pittsburgh's working women may have been somewhat higher. During the 1880s a number of sporting women lived in or above "cigar stores," which fronted for houses of assignation. In 1888 the chief of public safety attempted to close cigar stores run by women lest they undermine male morals. He said that "a cigar store attended by women in a place of this kind is a trap for young men and boys."[94] There were twenty such cigar store front–brothel back combinations down at the Point, which served as one locus for disreputable activities at this time. During a drive spearheaded by the Law and Order Society to rid Pittsburgh of prostitutes in 1887, some moved to Allegheny City, where they rented rooms, sometimes with private families, according to an article in *Commoner and Glass Worker,* and received "their company very quietly."[95] The reform efforts shifted but clearly did not eliminate prostitution.

Even more than most women's work in the Steel City, prostitution was a young woman's occupation. A mere 4 percent of Pittsburgh's prostitutes were over 30, although 25 percent of all working women were. It was also an unmarried woman's occupation in 1880, but some of the cigar store proprietors listed their marital status as widow, and a few women with children turned to prostitution to support themselves. Outraged welfare agencies attempted to take children away from such mothers, and it was a criminal offense to keep a minor in a brothel.[96]

Prostitution expanded among immigrant women during the first decades of the twentieth century.[97] The Morals Efficiency Commission survey of 1913 determined that prostitutes came from a more varied background than those of 1880. There were blacks as well as whites, and one-fifth came from foreign lands, primarily Austria, Russia, and Germany. They were working women from working-class families. The single largest group, over one-third, had previously been domestic servants. Waitresses, factory hands, and clerks each comprised about one-tenth of the 506 prostitutes questioned. Others had been telephone operators, seamstresses, laundresses, milliners, and cashiers, but nearly one-fourth had come directly from home without having held other jobs, though very few had white-collar fathers. In the commission's view, the low wages of men contributed as much to the making of prostitutes as those paid to women, for they produced "an unattractive home life, parental neglect, a taste for cheap amusements and strong stimulants, and similar elements in the psychology of poverty."[98] Though this does not explain why some women turned to prostitution and others did not, it does suggest the close link between the sporting life and the poverty and lack of remunerative employment for women.

Despite a greater age range, most prostitutes in 1913 were young women. About four-fifths were under 30, and only a handful were over 40. Most had never been married, but one-fifth were divorced or separated, and one-seventh were widows. Nevertheless, few women made careers of prostitution; three-quarters stayed in the sporting life for less than five years.[99] Prostitution, like other women's employments, then, was a phase of the woman's life, although the commission report did not indicate what happened once they left the life.

Some of Pittsburgh's brothels served the well-to-do, but most had a working-class clientele. Though a few fancy houses catered to businessmen, the majority were one- and two-dollar houses that served clerks, mechanics, and railroad men and fifty-cent houses with an immigrant and unskilled clientele. Pittsburgh was a center of prostitution, according to reformers, for the surrounding mill and mining towns; "hundreds of footloose wage-earners from all parts of the industrial district look to the city when bent on having a good time."[100] Working-class men and boys could be seen lining up waiting to enter the brothels scattered throughout the city, which led one reformer to call upon the unions to educate their members with a class consciousness that would preclude "the daughters of working people soliciting debauch at the hands of youths of their class."[101] According to Beatrice Webb, fifty-cent prostitution also abounded in the noisome mill wards of nearby Homestead and Munhall.[102]

Both James Forbes and Elizabeth Butler, investigators into "The Reverse Side" and women's work, respectively, called for higher wages as a preventive measure against prostitution, since low wages made the working-class home unpleasant and led the young to accept more readily the bright lights and glitter of the underworld. "As long as the merchants and manufacturers of the country pay many girls wages which are not enough for subsistence, much less for normal amusements," they would be tempted to augment their meager income with casual or full-time prostitution.[103] *Women and the Trades* contains several accounts of young women who turned from paths of virtue to the sporting life in order to make ends meet. "Vera . . . is twenty years old. Four years ago she was employed as a salesgirl at $3.50 a week. After a year she left for another store where she was employed as a cashier at a salary of $10 a week, for making concessions to her employer. After two years she left the store for a house of prostitution."[104] Vera and countless others entered the sporting life because it paid more than domestic service or the coveted white-collar positions. Some cash girls made as little as $1.75 a week, and nearly three-quarters of the department store workers made between $3.00 and $6.00 per week in 1907.[105] One clerk got to the heart of the matter when she wrote the Bureau of Industrial Statistics that she did not understand why women did not receive as much pay as men for the same kind of work. "It is no excuse for proprietors of stores to say that men have to support families; so do a great many of the women."[106] The myth that women worked for pin money, the pernicious greed of employers, and the lack of alternate employments all contributed to women's low wages.[107]

Wages and Hours

Women's work generally paid poorly. Except for prostitutes and teachers, women rarely received wages on which they could be self-supporting. Few women, regardless of experience or skill, earned more than half what an unskilled male laborer made in his first week in the steel mill. Women and men existed in segregated labor markets, but where they did similar or the same work, as in the cigar-making industry, women earned about half as much as men.[108] Even teachers, the best-paid of women workers, had lower earning potentials than all but the least-skilled men. Teachers' salaries averaged about $545 per year in 1889, about the same as those of semiskilled millworkers.[109] The feminization of the teaching profession occurred because women would accept lower pay for the same work as men. Since employers would not hire women at the same pay as men, if women wanted to work they had to accept lower wages. Women teachers were concentrated in the elementary grades, where the wages were lower than in high schools, and they rarely reached supervisory positions. Teaching did have one advantage over other female employments: the working day and week were shorter than factory, clerical, and especially domestic work.[110]

Domestic servants had the lowest wages and longest hours of all women workers. They rose before their employers in order to make up the fires, get breakfast, and bring in water. For many their day ended only after their employers went to bed. According to the Pennsylvania Bureau of Industrial Statistics they earned between $2.00 and $4.00 a week, but adolescents were paid only $0.50. They did receive their room and board as well.[111] These wages appear to have remained fairly static through the end of the nineteenth century.[112] The Civic Club of Philadelphia recommended $3.00–$3.50 as the appropriate wage for chambermaids, children's nurses, and waitresses in 1895. Seamstresses, laundresses, and cooks were to receive $3.50–$4.00. Such a recommendation, incorporated into Lucy Salmon's pioneering investigation into domestic service two years later, suggests that domestic wages did not rise appreciably until the twentieth century, although as late as 1935 black women received $3.00 for a week's cleaning. Black women's wages, even in domestic service, were lower than those of white women.[113]

Although domestic service paid poorly in absolute terms, social surveyors viewed the provision of room and board as a substantial subsidy to the young woman and her family. But the valuation placed upon the in-kind component of servants' wages varied according to one's perspective. Salmon believed the servant's keep to be worth about $5.00 per week, far more than the average domestic wage. She calculated this upon the costs a woman would incur at a boardinghouse where each woman had her own room.[114] Yet most working women in Pittsburgh did not live in boardinghouses but with their families. In addition the live-in servant herself performed the work that would have been done for her had she lived in a lodging house. She cooked the meals, cleaned up, and did the washing. When she lived at home, she helped her mother after her working hours with the washing and tidying, but she had a larger absolute wage to contribute to her family than most servants did. The family lost the labor contribution of a daughter who went out to service, whatever she may have given back to her parents in wages. Thus the value of in-kind wages has been overstated. Servant's cash wages were about one-half to two-thirds those paid in trade and manufacturing.

Some employments with more prestige paid poorly, in part because they were more genteel and women would accept lower wages in order to work in them. White-collar work sometimes was less remunerative than domestic service but, as Alice Kessler-Harris noted, among the Jewish immigrants in New York City much more socially acceptable than manual labor of any variety.[115] Three-quarters of the women in Pittsburgh's retail establishments earned less than $7.00 per week at the turn of the century. A survey conducted by the Pennsylvania Bureau of Industrial Statistics found $6.00 per week to be the most common wage, but many received less than this.[116] Thirteen-year-old Emma B. went to work as a cash girl in a Pittsburgh department store at $2.25 per week, but after the deduction of carfare and lunch money, there was nothing left of her wages. Avoiding domestic service altogether, her mother "overcame the pride" that had kept the girl out of the factory, and Emma started work at the cork factory, which paid her $4.00 per week for a ten-hour day. Although her pay was the same as a servant's, her hours were shorter. She also avoided the lower status and restricted freedom that accompanied household labor.[117]

The wages paid to women in manufacturing were somewhat higher than those in the retail sector and domestic service. In 1907 about 55 percent of all female manufacturing workers in the Pittsburgh district earned between $3.00 and $7.00 per week; the comparable figure for trade was 73 percent, indicating an overwhelming concentration among the lowest paid. A few skilled occupations offered higher wages to women but still held women's wages lower than men's. Women telegraphists, for example, all earned between $8.00 and $10.00 per week in 1907. That was half the male wage since women were permitted to work only on the lighter wires, which attracted lower recompense. At the other extreme, laundry workers who shook out heavy, wet sheets averaged about $4.00 or $5.00 a week. The majority of women glassworkers earned about $6.00 weekly. Unlike the glassworkers, who toiled in the factories, many Pittsburgh seamstresses worked at home and in effect subsidized employers by paying their own overhead costs, heating and lighting their rooms in "back alleys, dark cellars, and dingy garrets." Seamstresses made as little as $0.06 a piece for vests, $1.35 per dozen for men's pants, $0.15–0.20 for children's dresses, and $0.35 for cutting and sewing a woman's wrapper. The United Garment Workers organized the factories in 1900, which had the effect of raising wages both in the factories and in the outlying districts where families sewed jeans. The relatively few women garment workers in factories did rather better than other industrial workers: more than half earned between $8.00 and $10.00 per week in 1907.[118]

Low pay accompanied direct transfers of "housewifely" jobs into the paid sector of the economy. In 1880 laundresses comprised 3 percent of the female labor force but 33 percent of the clientele of the PAIP. Most washerwomen traveled the city picking up clothes, taking them home to wash, and returning them to their owner. For this they might receive as little as $0.75 per load of clothes.[119] When this work was mechanized in the 1880s, it still paid poorly despite the long hours. According to one laundress at one of the new steam laundries, they came

> on duty at 7.00 A.M. and during Monday, Tuesday and Wednesday of the week, laundry workers worked until 9.00, 10.00, and sometimes until 2.00 and 3.00 o'clock in the morning and on Friday, though we started to work at the usual hour, we were compelled to work until 3.00, 4.00 and as late as 6.00 o'clock Saturday morning. On Saturday we had to go to work again to clean up and get out job lots, and I want to impress on you that we never got a cent for the extra time worked.[120]

In 1890, one plant owner paid his "best girl in the laundry" no more than $6.00–7.00 per week, while inexperienced hands made about $2.50. At this time common laborers in the mills made $1.75 per day or $10.50 per week. Inexperienced laundry workers earned the same as servants, but without either room and board or the constraints domestic service placed upon the workers.[121]

Reacting to the low wages and deplorable working conditions that characterized steam laundries, some of the laundresses organized under the auspices of the Knights of Labor in 1887. The Brace Brothers' laundry fired the organizers; Mr. Brace arrogantly said, "I will run my own business; I will hire whom I please, pay them what I please, and make them work as long as I please." The "laundry girls" appealed to the organized workingmen of Allegheny County not to patronize the establishment, saying "Those who wish to call it a boycott or a 'girlcott' may do so." A judge issued an injunction against the boycott, and Brace sued the leaders of the strike for $10,000. Although the workers received support from the trade unions of Pittsburgh, the strike failed. Brace Brothers and the other steam laundries remained nonunionized.[122] Employment of women in the laundries increased during this period since the owners believed them to be better adapted to laundry work and more reliable than men.[123]

Steam laundries, however, were dangerous workplaces. The women might work as many as fourteen to eighteen hours a day in hot, steamy workrooms among unguarded equipment. Automatic mangles, introduced in the early 1880s, ironed sheets, tablecloths, and other large flat goods. A woman stood at one end of the mangle and pushed the material to be ironed until it caught between the rollers. These rollers also caught the fingers, hands, and arms of the operatives, crushing them as "flat as the cloth that they had been guiding, for there is no halting in the perfect mechanism of the mangle, no stopping place before the length of the rolls is reached unless the belt is shifted and the machine thrown out of gear." Although the work was dangerous, it was not as frequently fatal as that in the steel mills. Nevertheless, an accident impaired earning capacity, if it did not end the woman's work outside the home altogether.[124]

The laundries and other new employments for women little altered the basic composition of Pittsburgh's labor force, which remained overwhelmingly male through the beginning of the twentieth century. Education was critical to the new occupations, and thus white-collar employment was restricted primarily to the daughters of skilled workers and the middle class, native white or Northern European in origin. At the same time the separation of women and men, of the female and male experience, was reinforced by their divergent work and home experiences. Even though more occupations opened to women at the beginning of the twentieth century, the domestic sphere encompassed the lives of most. Almost all young women regarded marriage and family as preferable to ill-paid lifelong economic activity. Those for whom education and ethnicity opened white-collar jobs decisively rejected domestic service as an employment only to accept it, after a brief period in the labor force, as their vocation.

Children's Work

Pittsburgh's working class used the labor of their children to advance the family's well-being. The average industrial family required work contributions from more than one member if it was to do more than barely survive in the uncertain economic climate of the late nineteenth and early twentieth centuries.[1] Unskilled laborers rarely earned enough to support and house their families unaided, which led some segments of the working class at this time to agitate for a family wage, which would enable men to be the sole support of their wives and young children.[2] The Pennsylvania Bureau of Industrial Statistics found that the head of a family of five with an income of less than $600 invariably got into debt, which meant that most unskilled families in the last quarter of the nineteenth century could not survive on the father's income alone. Indeed, children in Pennsylvania contributed 25 percent of the earnings of all families and 40 percent of the earnings of unskilled families at this time. Few migrants to American cities expected to make the Horatio Alger-like transition from rags to riches, but many hoped to buy a home of their own, send money back to relatives in the old country or subsidize their passage and reunite the family.[3] The vehicle through which they achieved these ends was the family economy, one which had changed from preindustrial times, to be sure, but which nevertheless enabled working-class families to survive and sometimes to conquer the industrial world in their own way and with their own goals in mind.

The new industrial order led to a redefinition of the relationship between parents and children, replacing the training of children by their parents with school-based education. Schools withdrew children from their families, placing them in the alien world of letters and numbers, disciplined by the clock and extrafamilial authority. The content of their training became a matter of public policy rather than parental discretion, although clear class variations in attendance levels highlight the extent to which families perceived education as either relevant or affordable. The debates over child labor reflected tensions over the disposition of children's time and the determination of their best interests.[4] A detailed analysis of the labor force participation of Pittsburgh's young people shows how some families needed them as ancillary wage earners. It illustrates the ways that different ethnic and class groups utilized the labor of their children to sustain the family, sometimes putting the needs of the family before those of the individual, and treating their sons and daughters differently.

Entrance into Pittsburgh's Labor Force

Despite rising female employment, the decision to send a child into the labor force remained a complex one and shows that parents perceived the utility of their sons' and daughters' labor contributions quite differently. In 1880, 4 percent of the girls and 14 percent of the boys aged 10–14 were in Pittsburgh's labor force.[5] Changes in the census categories make it difficult to make exact comparisons for 1900, but the proportion of young workers rose to about 8 percent of the girls and 21 percent of the boys aged 10–15. The city's closed occupational structure led to a family economy in which males continued to hold primary responsibility for wage earning. Young as well as older women's lower participation rates in the labor force reinforced trade unionists' beliefs that women should work only when men were not paid enough to support the family.[6] Of the 15–19-year-old girls, 20 percent worked in 1880, compared with 69 percent of the boys in that age group. Among the entire 16–24-year-old group, only 39 percent of the females and 89 percent of the males had jobs in 1900. Within each age, cultural, and class group, far more boys worked than girls. Employment had not yet become the norm for most young women, although some groups had many more working daughters than others.

There were sizable discrepancies among ethnic groups in the timing and extent to which they sent their daughters and, to some degree, their sons into the labor force. As table 22, above, showed, the proportion of 10–14-year-old girls in the labor force was about the same for all whites (between 2 and 3 percent in 1880) but much higher (about 10 percent) for blacks. The rates varied more for 15–19-year-olds, among whom labor force participation of German, Irish, and British women in 1880 was about twice as high as that of those with native-born white parents. It was highest for the Irish (26 percent worked) among the whites but was dwarfed by that of the blacks, 54 percent of whom had jobs. Many more boys entered the labor force, though again the proportions varied; Germans in the younger group had the highest proportion (22 percent), more than twice that of native white lads. At 15, German and black youths had the highest rates of employment, followed by the British and Irish, and trailed by those with native-born white parents.

Among the older group, boys and girls in each ethnic group had approximately the same level of school attendance despite the wide variation among the cultures. Nevertheless, boys had higher rates of labor participation because many parents chose to keep their daughters at home rather than send them into a labor market that offered little besides domestic service, especially at the beginning of the age of steel. This pattern was less prevalent among young blacks and Irish-Americans, who had the highest rates of participation precisely because so many became servants. The relatively low utilization of young women's labor parallels the pattern in Essex County, Mass., and Philadelphia but diverges from that of textile centers such as Manchester, N.H., where the mills offered acceptable employment to foreign-born and native women.[7]

The divergence between young men's, and young women's economic activity continued into the twentieth century. In 1900 women born abroad had the lowest rates of participation in the labor force of any group of women in the city, a fact that reflected that many of them came to the country as wives or brides. One-fourth the native-born women of foreign (principally German, Irish, and British) parentage worked, as did more than one-fifth of those with native-born white parents, but one-sixth of those born abroad did so. At the other extreme, almost one-third of all black women over the age of 15 had jobs. Few Italian women and rather more Poles worked in Pittsburgh's trades. A social investigator observed that "ties of tradition that keep the Italian girl to her house and to early marriage are too strong for more than a few to break, and Pittsburgh offers small opportunity for them at once to preserve their self-respect and to earn money by sewing at home." The smoky air precluded the delicate hand embroidery at which many of their countrywomen earned money in the New York tenements. Only 5 percent of Pittsburgh's Italian women held jobs in 1900.[8] Their families relied heavily upon the labor of sons and married women taking in boarders to sustain themselves. Particularly where the families had many boarders, daughters eased the extra burdens they imposed by helping their mothers at home with the additional cooking, cleaning, and washing, as well as caring for younger siblings. They helped their mothers earn money but were not enumerated as part of the labor force. These women worked but were not counted.

Pittsburgh's labor market was not particularly hospitable to young workers, although it became more open with the expansion of trade and administration at the beginning of the twentieth century. In the 1870s the Bureau of Industrial Statistics pointed out that there was only 1 male minor employed for every 25 men in manufacturing and mechanical pursuits in the state, but 1 minor for every 4 adults in cotton and wool manufacturing. Boys might work in the rolling mills as helpers, catchers, and laborers, but usually not until they were 14 or 15.[9] They were more likely to be employed in the glass houses, in which physical strength was less important than in the iron and steel industries.[10] Few girls in Pittsburgh held industrial jobs; when they entered the labor force at an early age it was as domestic servants. This pattern altered in the new century; by 1900 some found work in the downtown shops and in the sweated trades. Families living in outlying sections of the city or in steel mill districts where there were few opportunities for young workers kept both sons and daughters at home longer.[11]

Although familial poverty sometimes demanded that a child be sent to work at an early age, necessity did not make this desirable. A survey of five hundred workingmen conducted by the Pennsylvania Bureau of Industrial Statistics in 1889 indicated an ambivalent reaction to the question regarding child labor. The survey asked if parents should put their children to work when "dire want dictates." About two-fifths of the laboring men responded that they should not, and almost as many thought poor children should work only under certain conditions. Many felt the state should provide aid until the children reached the age of 14 or 15 because "children who are left orphans should not, by their misfortune, be handicapped in the battle of life." Most regarded 14 or 15 as the right age for a child to enter the labor force; nevertheless, some felt forced to send their children to work at a younger age. One worker wrote, "An unskilled laborer cannot, on his own individual earnings, afford to occupy a suitable house and rear his family and live as an American citizen should live."[12] In such households working children made a significant contribution to familial well-being. The glassworkers' newspaper praised the young woman who went to work to help her family. Her hand might be stained with printers' ink or factory grease, but it was an honest and helping hand. "It stays misfortune from many homes, it is the one shield that protects many a forlorn little family from the almshouse and asylum—brave, polite, refined, ambitious."[13] Children who supported their families were the real treasures in the working-class household, particularly if they had widowed mothers. Yet when the state labor bureau asked if widow's children should work, two-fifths of the respondents still said no. Almost as many believed such children might seek employment as a last resort.[14] In Pittsburgh, where almost no jobs existed for women with children, widowed mothers had little choice but to send their offspring to work. Even though little Johnny Dobrejcak made only pennies collecting bottles, bones, rags, and old iron for the junk man, his contributions to the family helped sustain his widowed mother and the three younger children.[15]

Boys and Young Men

Two interrelated factors influenced the age at which a young man sought employment and his subsequent occupational level. Parents' socioeconomic status had a considerable impact on the timing of a boy's entrance into the labor force. As table 25 shows, a mere handful of middle- and upper-class boys began their life's work between the ages of 10 and 14, but 14 percent of the working-class boys and 39 percent of those with widowed mothers did so in 1880. The proportion of boys in the labor force rose dramatically in the 15–19 age bracket for middle- and working-class boys, 64–72 percent of whom worked. Nearly all widow's sons had jobs by this time, but only 29 percent of the upper-class boys began to earn their keep. Virtually all widows' and working-class sons had jobs by their early twenties, but about 20 percent of the middle- and upper-class youth still depended upon their families for support. After the age of 25, those sons still at home were all in the labor market.

Ethnicity also played a significant role in determining the entrance of younger boys into the labor force. Twenty-two percent of the 10–14-year-old sons of German immigrants were working in 1880, 14 percent of the Irish, 10 percent of the native-born white, and 7 percent of the British (see table 22, p. 130). No black youths this age had jobs, perhaps because opportunities were very limited for them. There were no craft or shop openings for young blacks, as there were for white lads their age. Nor were they yet able to compete for laboring jobs, at which most young workers toiled. This delayed their entrance into the labor force. The experience of older native white boys set them apart from second-

Table 25. Sons Living at Home and Participating in Labor Force, 1880
(In Percentages)

Parents	Age of Son							
	10–14		15–19		20–24		25+	
	N	%	N	%	N	%	N	%
Unskilled	303	15	227	72	144	94	47	100
Skilled	187	12	108	67	71	97	29	100
Middle	76	5	40	64	32	78	12	100
Upper	70	1	62	29	32	81	22	100
Widow	64	39	90	92	97	97	69	100

Source: 1880 census sample.

generation whites and from blacks in 1880. Over 80 percent of the German and black 15–19-year-olds, 67–79 percent of the Irish and British, but only 56 percent of the native-born whites were in the labor force. In 1900 all but a handful (93 percent) of foreign-born youth over 14 were at work, and there were nearly as many black youths (88 percent) at work. The proportion of working white youths with foreign-born parents (83 percent of those 15–19) was somewhat lower than for blacks and immigrants and only 73 percent of those with native-born white parents had joined the working world.[16] At the turn of the century, then, native-born white youths were particularly advantaged over their immigrant and black counterparts, but a gap still existed between those with foreign-born parents and the native-born sons of native-born white parents.

Boys' initial occupational levels in 1880 depended heavily on the age at which they entered the labor force—which reflected parental standing and ethnicity. Of the 10–14-year-olds in the labor market 86 percent had unskilled jobs. This declined to 70 percent for 15–19-year-olds and to 58 percent for men over 20 who still lived at home. As table 26 highlights, young lads rarely had artisan or white-collar jobs, but 15–19-year-olds moved into these positions (14 and 16 percent). Those 20 years and older were somewhat more likely to do skilled work (23 percent) than white-collar (19 percent). Though these data do not show whether early entrance into the labor force precluded moving up the job hierarchy, the experience of boys with unskilled fathers or widowed mothers suggests that it did. Almost all boys who lived in laboring households had similar jobs (see table 27). Eighty-four percent of the sons from unskilled families had

Table 26. Occupational Level of Sons by Age, 1880
(In Percentages)

Age	Unskilled	Skilled	White-collar	N
10–14	86	8	6	97
15–19	70	14	16	361
20+	58	23	19	529

Source: 1880 census sample.

unskilled jobs, the remainder being divided almost evenly between skilled and white-collar positions in 1880.

Widows' sons, forced into the labor force prematurely, apparently had neither the contacts nor the education to gain access to the world of middle-class or skilled work. More than two-thirds held laboring jobs in 1880, and less than one-fifth were skilled workers.[17] Although the proportion of skilled workers and white-collar workers was higher than among the sons of Pittsburgh's laborers, the more varied paternal occupational background of the widows' sons must be taken into account to understand the magnitude of the sliding involved. Some came from families in which the father had himself been an upper-echelon millworker or had worn a white collar; nevertheless, the father's demise usually resulted in his son's employment as an unskilled worker.[18] Higher rates of white-collar employment notwithstanding, these lads closely resembled laborers' sons in their expectations. Their father's death propelled them quickly into the labor force, usually at the bottom of the heap.

Upper-class boys made their first foray into the working world with their white collars firmly in place, as sheltered from manual toil as unskilled boys were exposed to it. Eighty-four percent had white-collar positions. Middle-class parents were somewhat less successful than upper-class ones in passing on occupational advancements, but 48 percent

Table 27. Sons' Occupational Level by Parents' Socioeconomic Class, 1880 (In Percentages)

	Sons' Occupation			
Parents	Unskilled	Skilled	White-collar	N
Unskilled	84	9	7	391
Skilled	52	40	8	192
Middle	37	15	48	67
Upper	9	7	84	67
Widow	69	18	13	270
Average	65	18	17	

Source: 1880 census sample.

secured their sons a place in the white-collar world through education or connections. As table 27 shows, 37 percent of these boys held unskilled jobs while still living with their parents, but whether this indicates occupational sliding or starting out at the proverbial bottom of daddy's business is unclear. Whereas 52 percent of the sons of skilled workers held unskilled jobs, 40 percent followed their fathers into various craft jobs in the mills and shops. Their success rate in obtaining such coveted positions was twice that of any other group. The boys got their jobs through their fathers or other male relatives. In the 1870s and 1880s skilled fathers still passed on their positions and skills, training the sons in their own work. As these higher-echelon jobs themselves became rarer in the 1890s and 1900s, technology substituted for skill and training in the steel industry. This meant that direct parental control over the sons' work also became less common in the twentieth century.

The close relationship between class and ethnicity is highlighted by table 28, which shows how sons' occupations varied according to their racial or ethnic background. Four-fifths of all black youths living at home in 1880 had unskilled jobs, as did about two-thirds of the second-generation Irish, Germans, and British. The British were comparatively successful in passing skilled status on to their sons, as were the Germans, Irish, and native-born whites, to a lesser extent. Black men rarely had

Table 28. Sons' Occupational Level by Parents' Ethnicity, 1880
(In Percentages)

	Sons' Occupation			
Parents' Ethnicity	Unskilled	Skilled	White-collar	N
Native-born white	53	15	32	258
British	65	24	11	72
Irish	66	18	16	257
German	70	20	10	375
Black	80	4	16	25
Average	65	18	17	

Source: 1880 census sample.

such status, and neither did their sons. At the other end of the ethnic hierarchy, nearly one-third of the sons of the native-born white men wore white collars to work, whereas one-half were laborers. About one-sixth of the Irish sons had office, shop, and professional employments, as did a like proportion of blacks. However, the number of black youths in the 1880 census sample was too small for this figure to be anything more than suggestive.

These rather low proportions of intergenerational mobility, even though taken at one point in time rather than over time, support the general findings of other investigators for Boston, Poughkeepsie, N.Y., Steelton, Pa., Waltham, Mass., Warren, Pa., and elsewhere.[19] Men might rise through the occupational ranks, but slowly, sometimes as a result of their own aptitude, diligence, or luck, but usually through the parental endowment of education through the high school level. Carolyn Schumacher's study of high school graduates in Pittsburgh demonstrates the latter proposition; by the end of the nineteenth century, few high school boys had blue-collar jobs; although two-fifths of the high school entrants came from working-class families, only one-eighth had unskilled or skilled employment five years after they had entered the ninth grade. By contrast, in 1855 nearly one-half of the high school class came from working-class backgrounds and less than one-half had middle-class employment five years later. By the turn of the century, many skilled workers' sons took the high school's commercial course and moved into lower-echelon white-collar work.[20]

Despite variations in occupational categories between 1870 and 1900, certain trends are clear: the proportion of employed children actually rose as the new immigrant families sent their offspring into the labor force to compensate for their fathers' wages.[21] Fewer young boys labored in the iron and steel industry than earlier in the century, but the glass houses continued to be one of the major employers of young children, particularly boys.[22] Most glass house boys worked as blowers' assistants, standing close to the furnaces, holding the molds open and closing them after the blower inserted the started bottle; others reheated the bottle necks for finishing. "Carrying-in" boys transferred trays of bottles from the finishers and were constantly on their feet.[23] Technological innovations made the work more arduous. Night work began in Pennsylvania glass factories in 1888 when a Jeannette, Pennsylvania, producer replaced the pot system of heating glass with a continuous tank. Work no longer had to be stopped each day in order to warm the materials for the next day's production. Glass houses then emulated the steel works and required their employees, irrespective of age, to work day and night turns on alternate weeks.[24] The conditions in the industry deteriorated to the point where one glassblower remarked, "I would rather send my boys straight to hell than send them by way of the glass house." As a result, most of the glass house boys were recruited from the ranks of the orphaned and half-orphaned or from the poorest strata of the working class, whereas the sons of skilled glassblowers stayed on at school or looked elsewhere for employment.[25]

An investigation into the conditions of child labor in Pittsburgh in 1888 included a tour of the glass houses on the South Side and found boys of 9 and 10 acting as tenders and gatherers in most of them. The manager of one glass factory stated that any boys under the age of 12 were there as an act of charity because they were either motherless or, more commonly, fatherless and had to make their own living. But employing young boys in the dusty atmosphere where boys and men alike suffered eye trouble from the intense glare and cuts from the broken glass hardly constituted an act of charity, for it served the manufacturers' interest to have a cheap labor force. Glass makers paid the boys half as much as unskilled workers, and opportunities for advancement were limited.[26]

Responding to the increased number of young workers at the beginning of the twentieth century, particularly in the sweated trades, reformers attempted to prolong education and limit children's employment. There was no effective regulation of child labor in Pennsylvania during this era despite Progressive pressure and the example of other industrial states. New York adopted 14 as the minimum working age in 1887, and Massachusetts followed suit in 1894. Glass house owners and other employers of young children consistently opposed similar laws in Pennsylvania, claiming that they could not operate their factories profitably without young employees. Most boys in the glass houses were the children of recent immigrants who, employers claimed, would not benefit from an

American education. Their parents believed they needed and had a right to children's cash contributions in order to sustain the families.[27] Recent immigrants differed in this from more affluent working-class parents such as Lou R. Thomas of the Patternmakers Union who wanted a "rigid child labor law that will protect the children so that they are not sent into the factories at an early age and have their minds and bodies stunted by toiling in the mills and in factories."[28]

The Civic Club and other women's groups spearheaded a successful campaign for a child labor law in 1905. The governor signed it, complaining nevertheless that it violated the private rights of citizens. The new law forbade children's employment in stores and factories but required a parent's affidavit attesting to the age of a child. It also prohibited the employment of illiterate children, but most notaries or aldermen did not give literacy tests or merely required the child's signature before granting the affidavit. The courts deemed unconstitutional the requirement of documentary proof of age rather than parental testimony. Opponents of child labor advocated documents rather than the parents' word in the belief, probably correct, that a parent who needed to send a child into the glass house at the age of 9 would be prepared to lie. In 1909 the state courts finally accepted a law setting educational, hour, and age standards.[29]

Yet the child labor legislation as written, enforced, and interpreted, little protected young workers. The Pittsburgh Survey complained that an "absence of zeal" characterized the enforcement of the 1905 protective legislation. The law virtually excused glass houses from compliance with the provisions limiting hours of work.[30] Boys under 16 and girls under 18 were prohibited from working more than ten hours a day and between the hours of 9 P.M. and 6 A.M., except where the factories usually ran continuously. Then boys over 14 could be employed for not more than nine hours out of twenty-four, an exemption intended specifically for the glass houses.[31] Sweatshops also received lenient treatment. The so-called Delaney Amendment, named for Pennsylvania's chief factory inspector, who proposed it in 1909, stated that no minors under 16 could be employed in tobacco establishments "unless it is proved to the satisfaction of the Department that the danger to the health of the child has been removed." The Survey believed such provisions opened the doors for blackmail and defeated the spirit of the law. It uncovered instances of water boys in the steel mills working a full long turn (day and night shifts consecutively) once a fortnight alongside grown men. The glass house boys kept the same hours as the men they worked with, and the 1910 Census reported 227 girls aged 10–15 working in cigar and tobacco factories.[32] Although reformers at the state level obtained laws that seemingly negated the collusion between parents and employers over the early entry of poor children into the labor force, parents' need and employers' greed combined with ineffective enforcement to vitiate legislation.[33]

At the other end of the employment spectrum from the glass houses, a slightly larger proportion of young workers obtained entry-level jobs in offices and shops than previously. In 1880 youths 10–15 held about 3 percent of these jobs; by 1900 this had risen slightly to about 6 percent. Despite the expansion of this sector of the economy, few new immigrants or their young children worked in it. Most white-collar workers were native-born whites of either the second or third generation. Eighty-seven percent of the office boys were U.S.-born, and a mere handful came from Italy, Russia, and Poland in 1900. During the early years of the twentieth century, a high school education opened the doors of the city's offices, so that those families who relied upon their children's labor from a young age foreclosed this work to them.[34]

Girls and Young Women

The employment pattern of girls and young women contrasted sharply with that of their brothers in type and in duration. Many fewer worked, and, as shown in chapter 5, almost none found jobs in the iron and steel industries that dominated the city's economy; instead, most labored in other people's homes as domestic servants and lived away from their families.[35] For boys and men work was a facet of their lives from leaving school until old age, but for girls and women employment, if it occurred at all, was a phase in the life cycle, a hiatus between school and marriage. Though this was true of women's work in many cities, Pittsburgh represented an extreme version of the pattern: most women workers were young and worked for only a few years. Particularly in the beginning of this era, employed young women in Pittsburgh tended to come from the lower end of the economic spectrum. Pittsburgh women entered the labor force in 1880 if their fathers' wages were low. Thus young women's employment, but not men's, correlated with poverty, although for both sexes very early entry into the labor force indicated extreme poverty. Daughters' presence in the work world reflected both the family's need for money and the decreased productivity of households that no longer manufactured almost all they used.[36]

Given the low status of the most available female employment in the Steel City and the increasing emphasis on education, early participation in the labor force indicated acute family need: the lower the family income, the earlier girls went to work. In 1880, 6 percent of the 10–14-year-old widows' daughters joined the labor force, impelled by the same stark need as their brothers. Three percent of the daughters of the unskilled and 2 percent of the skilled labored outside the home, but none of the middle- or upper-class girls did. The disparity in levels of employment between widows' and other working-class daughters continued as the girls got older. About 21 percent of the skilled and unskilled workers' daughters between the ages of 15 and 19 worked, but 27 percent of the widows' daughters had jobs. As table 29 shows, no daughters of the affluent classes worked until they reached the age of 20 and had received the

Table 29. Daughters Living at Home and Participating in the Labor Force, 1880 (In Percentages)

| | Age of Daughter | | | | | | | |
| | 10–14 | | 15–19 | | 20–24 | | 25+ | |
Parents	N	%	N	%	N	%	N	%
Unskilled	281	3	226	20	95	32	30	30
Skilled	129	2	121	23	48	33	17	35
Middle	64	—	47	—	29	24	7	43
Upper	51	—	49	—	42	7	26	8
Widow	83	6	84	27	65	37	53	57

Source: 1880 census sample.

education that enabled them to undertake genteel employment appropriate to their backgrounds.[37] Even then, a greater proportion of working-class daughters had jobs: 32 percent of those still living at home worked, as did 37 percent of the widow's daughters. Middle-class women entered the labor force at this point, but the number still living at home was rather small. These women were dedicated to their careers (primarily teaching), pursuing their vocation. Although few daughters in their midtwenties still lived with their parents, those who did tended to work for their keep.

Detailing the experience of young women living at home highlights the influence of class on female employment patterns, but it excludes the many women servants who lived in their employers' households. Table 30 shows dramatic class differences in women's occupations. The occupational level of employed daughters reflected that of their parents, even allowing for the omission of many servants from the data. Thirty-three percent of the working daughters of unskilled workers residing with their parents were servants, compared with 21 percent of the widows' working daughters, but only 15 percent of the young women from skilled families. Middle- and upper-class daughters avoided domestic service altogether. All but a few of the small number who worked had white-collar jobs. The

Table 30. Daughters' Occupational Level by Parents' Socioeconomic Class, 1880 (In Percentages)

| Parents | Daughters' Occupation | | | |
	Domestic[a]	Manual[b]	White-collar[c]	N
Unskilled	33	63	4	95
Skilled	15	72	13	54
Middle	—	20	80	10
Upper	—	—	100	5
Widow	21	61	18	82
Average	23	61	16	

Source: 1880 census sample.

a. Household servants, washerwomen, hotel and restaurant employees.

b. Seamstresses, factory workers, dressmakers.

c. Teachers, proprietors, clerks.

daughters of skilled workers preferred sewing or factory work to domestic service in 1880. Although very few unskilled daughters penetrated the ranks of white-collar workers, 13 percent of the skilled daughters did so, demonstrating that they benefited from their parents' ability to endow them with some high school education even before the surge in attendance levels at the turn of the century. Widows' daughters had higher levels of white-collar employment than skilled workers' daughters in 1880, but both had a higher proportion of white-collar jobs than their male counterparts.[38]

One very important caveat must be included here about the occupational distribution of Pittsburgh's women as discussed so far: since these figures included only those daughters living at home, they significantly underrepresent the number of servants coming from Pittsburgh's working class. At this time most domestic servants lived in their employers' households. Groups who numbered many domestic servants among their women typically had few teenage daughters living at home. None of the teenage black women living at home in the census sample worked. Of all black women, however, 10 percent of those aged 10–14 and 54 percent of those aged 15–19 lived in white people's homes as servants. Since the number of widows' sons at home exceeded that of their daughters, it may be that the daughters were living out as domestic servants, reducing the size of the mother's household and contributing money to it simultaneously. It is also probable that the occupational distribution of daughters of unskilled workers underrepresents the proportion of domestic servants for the same reason.[39]

Early employment patterns were harbingers of occupations to come for the daughters of the working class, who, even as they grew older, toiled on the bottom rungs of the labor ladder.[40] Of the youngest female workers 76 percent were domestic servants in 1880, and the rest held various manual jobs. Few of their sisters in the poorest Pittsburgh families ever located anything but unskilled employment. Over 70 percent of working women over the age of 14 who lived at home were servants, seamstresses, and factory workers. If one looks at all young women workers whether residing with their parents, with employers, or in boarding houses, the concentration in domestic service and manual occupations stands out starkly. Table 31 analyzes the occupational structure of women workers aged 10–29. Seventy-one percent of this group were domestic servants, compared with 23 percent of the daughters living with their parents (compare table 30); 22 percent were seamstresses and factory workers (61 percent of the home-based women were so employed). Seven percent wore white blouses to work (16 percent of the women living at home did). By 1900 about 40 percent of the youngest workers were servants, which reflects the expansion in the range of jobs open to young women, both in sweated industries and in shops. Affluent working-class parents sent their daughters to high school in larger numbers, enabling them to obtain white-collar jobs. Early entrance into the labor force and a lack of schooling precluded middle-class jobs for almost all women from unskilled families. Domestic service continued to dominate their employment opportunities well into the twentieth century.[41]

In 1880 the daughters of native-born white families were the least likely to work, followed by the British, Irish, German, and black. As women grew older and remained unmarried, they were more apt to join the labor force: 36 percent of all unmarried 15–19-year-olds worked, but 53 percent of the unmarried 20–24-year-old women held jobs. Of course the actual number of older women in the labor force was small, as many married and left the ranks of the employed altogether. Participation in the labor force varied greatly among ethnic groups: native-born white, German, and British women of this age group had lower rates of participation

Table 31. Occupational Level of Unmarried Women Aged 10–29, 1880[a] (In Percentages)

Age	Domestic	Manual	White-collar	N
10–14	76	24	—	33
15–19	71	26	3	265
20–24	73	17	10	262
25–29	67	24	9	116
Average	71	22	7	

Source: 1880 census sample.

a. Excludes prostitutes in order to be comparable with table 30.

than the Irish or black women (see figure 3). Whereas 44 percent of the third-generation unmarried white women ages 20–24 held jobs, 91 percent of their black contemporaries did. The proportion of unmarried women who worked climbed steeply amongst British and Irish-American women over 25 but not for German or native-born white women. Older unmarried black women sustained the near total labor force participation rates of their younger sisters at this time.

Because so many women worked as domestics, it is useful to consider the range of jobs for all women whether living at home, with

Figure 3. Participation of Unmarried Women in the Labor Force,
by Age and Father's Ethnicity, 1880

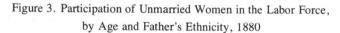
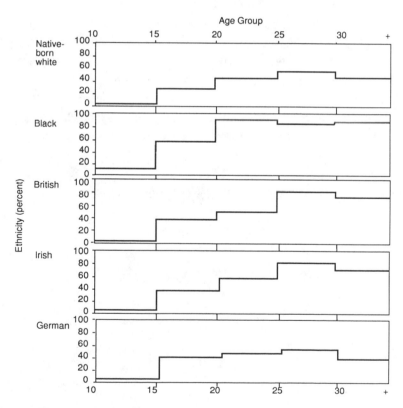

Source: 1880 census sample.

employers, or in boarding houses. The ethnic distribution of occupations for all women emphasized how work experience differed between groups of women. Almost all black women workers in 1880 were servants, as were about 75 percent of the Irish and German daughters who held jobs. Table 32 shows that fewer British daughters worked as domestics, but more worked at other manual tasks including sewing and factory work. Between 4 and 5 percent of these second-generation women held white-collar jobs. Native-born white women had the highest proportion of white-collar workers, (more than twice that of their counterparts with foreign-born fathers), about the same level of manual jobs, but a much lower level of domestic servants than other women workers. The census indicated that a sizable minority, about 12 percent, of native-born white women workers were prostitutes.

The 1900 data (see table 33) reveal a similar ethnic structure to the female labor force. Native-born white women with native-born parents still had the lowest rates of participation among women in the prime working ages (under 25). About 33 percent worked, but the proportion trailed away rapidly after marriage. Native-born women with foreign parents had a higher proportion at work in the 16–24-year-old group, 42 percent. They, too, withdrew from the labor force in large numbers after

Table 32. Occupation of All Unmarried Women by Ethnicity, 1880
(In Percentages)

Ethnicity	Occupation				
	Domestic	Manual	White-collar	Prostitute	N
Native-born white	48	19	9	12	210
British	68	28	4		71
Irish	76	19	5		299
German	75	21	4		195
Black	96	2	2		57
Average	71	20	6	3	

Source: 1880 census sample.

the age of 25. Foreign-born women exhibited an extreme variation of this pattern; they had the greatest proportion of employed 16–20-year-olds, which dropped dramatically by the age of 25. Only 15 percent of the 25–34-year-old women born abroad were in the labor force compared with 21 percent of the native-born whites. Black women had a somewhat different pattern. Their labor force participation rates for the under-25-year-olds approximated those of women with foreign-born parents. However, they sustained a very high employment rate among the older women: over 25 percent of all the black women over the age of 25 were in the labor force.[42]

Class, race, and ethnicity all shaped participation in the labor force in these decades. Women's work outside the home indicated family need. Black women had the highest overall rate of economic activity of all ethnic groups, but the narrowest range of occupations.[43] As the new century unfolded, parental poverty and widowhood still propelled young women precipitately into employment at the bottom of the labor hierarchy. A study conducted in Sharpsburg, just across the Allegheny River from Pittsburgh, found that one-fourth of the working children came from households without a father and in more than half the fathers were common laborers.[44] Because the occupational choices were so limited, women's work outside the home continued to be associated with dire poverty for the youngest workers, but, as will be discussed below, the

Table 33. Age, Race, and Nativity of Women Workers, 1900
(In Percentages)

	Age				
	16–20	21–24	25–34	35–44	45+
Native-born white					
Native parents	31	33	21	16	9
Foreign parents	42	38	22	14	10
Foreign-born white	53	36	15	9	7
Black	41	37	28	26	25

Source: U.S. Twelfth Census, 1900, *Statistics of Women at Work*, pp. 148–51.

range of occupations expanded for those whose families could afford to educate them past the rudiments.

If one views the family economy from the standpoint of children's contributions to it, one sees that native-born whites and the middle and upper classes required less work outside the home from their children, particularly their daughters, than did immigrants, blacks, and the parents of sons. Many parents preferred to utilize the labor of their daughters within the household; thus the majority of all 15–19-year-old girls in 1880, irrespective of class, race, or ethnicity, were described by the census as being "at home," rather than in school or at work. Margaret Byington found that the English-speaking families of Homestead assumed it was their daughters' place to be at home assisting their mothers while the boys went into the mill. In effect, the boys assisted their fathers in the male's primary role as provider for the family, while the girls helped their mothers to fulfill their domestic duties. The rising proportion of working daughters does suggest, however, that there was less need for their labor within the home as the century ended. Ethnicity and class combined to propel some young women into the labor force in large numbers. Slavic families were eager for their daughters to work, and black families throughout this era accepted the necessity of their daughters working away from home as domestic servants.[45]

So far this discussion has focused on whether children worked and under what circumstances. But the mere presence of children in the labor force might not bring cash back into the household, although many working-class daughters regarded work as an extension of their domestic obligations and turned their entire wage packet over to their parents.[46] There were ethnic variations in the extent to which children used their wages to augment family income. Black children tended to retain their earnings, their families having adopted a different route to survival than those of immigrants. In the latter, working children contributed most or all of their wages to their families, and the mothers stayed at home, possibly taking in boarders. Among black families, children and many mothers worked, but young people retained their earnings or gave only a portion of them to their parents. This seemed to be the case in a number of cities. Mary White Ovington wrote that the young black woman servant in New

York City brought no pay envelope home to her mother but kept her pay herself and allocated her money as she saw fit.[47] A study of black migrants in Pittsburgh concluded that fewer than half gave money to relatives.[48] Oral histories confirm this pattern, concluding that "out of a deep concern for their children, black parents were nurturing attitudes of self-sufficiency because they were unable to offer material resources or social connections to assist their children's survival in adult life."[49]

Possibly the type of work available to black youngsters reinforced their tendency to retain their wages. Domestic servants frequently lived far from their families and may have felt less of an obligation to them. Several employers complained to the Humane Society that their servants' parents tried to take some or all of the daughters' wages. A German woman went to her daughter's employer's house demanding her entire earnings to help support the other children. When the girl demurred, her employer reported the incident to the society, which worked out a solution whereby she gave her mother $1.00 a week and kept the rest. The wife of an Irish laborer tried to collect her daughter's wages, complaining that the girl had not been home for six weeks and should have brought her wages home.[50] These young women living away from their families and not responsible to them for their keep perceived less obligation to them than those who lived at home. Many children residing with their parents turned over their entire wage packet, small as it was.[51] But servants' room and board was provided not by their own families but by their employers. Their lower wages reflected this in-kind component and clearly led some servants to retain the entire amount.[52]

The roles of women and children in the family economy altered somewhat during these years as children's labor power was increasingly deployed outside the home and the domestic role devolved upon their mothers. The withdrawal of children from the home had two aspects. State-mandated education took them away from the household just at the age when they could be useful watching younger children, helping about the house, and doing chores. The tendency of the working class, even at the poorest extreme, to keep daughters home when they might otherwise have gone into the labor force suggests the need families perceived for their labor, but as opportunities expanded so did their employment levels.

Nevertheless, the lack of alternative employment reinforced domesticity for women, before and after marriage.

As more socially acceptable jobs became available, the upper echelons of the working class sent their daughters into the labor force to teach, clerk in department stores, and take office jobs. This lessened the concentration upon domesticity for younger women but reinforced it for older ones, who in effect traded their daughters' assistance in the home for the pittance they could contribute to the family funds. The family's need for money meant sons and, increasingly, daughters went to work, while their mothers managed the household in growing isolation with less help from other family members. The extent to which different ethnic groups followed this pattern varied somewhat, but in Pittsburgh only black families used married women as additional wage earners at this time. With this exception, Pittsburgh's working class sustained itself through the wage labor of men, boys, and to some extent, teenage daughters, while married women had the responsibility for the housework and cooking associated with family life with less assistance from other members of the family. The jobs done by women outside the home expanded in this era, but the structure of Pittsburgh's economy kept the number who worked outside the home lower than in other cities. Women's work experience in Pittsburgh exemplified that of their counterparts in heavy industry cities in the middle Atlantic and midwestern states but varied markedly from those with a textile or mixed economy. For almost all women in this era, marriage ended their employment outside the home, but not their economic contributions to their family.

Pittsburgh, c. 1870. *Carnegie Library, Pittsburgh*

Pittsburgh Industry, c. 1870. *Carnegie Library, Pittsburgh*

Pittsburgh, c. 1890, View Across the South Side to the Point.
Carnegie Library, Pittsburgh

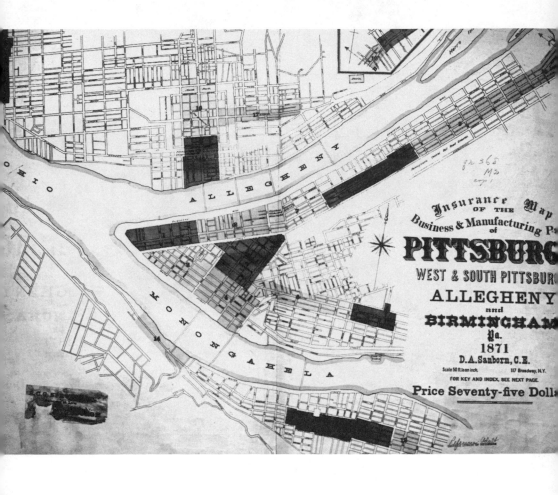

Sanborn Insurance Map, 1871. *Carnegie Library, Pittsburgh*

Homes with Privies Above the Railroad Tracks, Sylvan Avenue, Hazelwood, February 1907. *Carnegie Library, Pittsburgh*

Privies and Kitchens, c 1900. *Carnegie Library, Pittsburgh*

Housing Near the Mills, c. 1900. *Carnegie Library, Pittsburgh*

Kitchen with Laundry Equipment. *Author's collection*

Working-Class Kitchen, c. 1890. *Author's collection*

Infant in a Cradle, 1915. *Carnegie Library, Pittsburgh*

The Ball Team. *Carnegie Library, Pittsburgh*

Relaxing by the Stove. *Author's collection*

The Charity Laundry of the Pittsburgh Association for the Improvement of the Poor.
Pittsburgh Association for the Improvement of the Poor

Working-Class Kitchen, c. 1900. *Author's collection*

7 | Marriage and Family

The Industrial Revolution had profound consequences for familial relations and sex roles, separating home and workplace, family life and sustaining labor.[1] Nowhere was this more apparent than in Pittsburgh, where industrial patterns channeled women's and men's lives into totally different spheres. The Pittsburgh pattern was an extreme variation of the basic pattern of family relationships repeated in other heavy industry and mining centers, where married women were excluded from the labor force and men spent long hours away from their families in order to earn the cash income that made life possible in the industrial setting.[2] In other cities, "the sexes came into new relations as women left the hearthside to take jobs outside the home," Alan Dawley wrote of Lynn, Mass.[3] But the limited duration of female economic activity reinforced patriarchy in Pittsburgh. The popular press captured the fundamental relationship between the sexes in the emerging industrial world of the nineteenth century as it emphasized dominant masculinity and a happy hearthside attended by an "esteemable wife" who devoted herself to caring for her husband and their children.[4] Though in no way repeating the sex role differences of preindustrial times or other economic settings, Pittsburgh's industrial structure influenced the development of a gender-segregated world with little or no overlap between women's and men's efforts.

Joan Scott and Louise Tilly describe the preindustrial family as an economic partnership to which both wife and husband contributed, with household and workplace typically coterminous. The traditional division of labor endowed men with legal power, whereas "the wives' power in the household stemmed from the fact that they managed household expenditures for food."[5] As industrialization shifted much of the fabrication of basic necessities outside the home, cash wages isolated the tasks women performed within the household from "work", which now meant paid participation in the labor force. At the same time, and in reaction to the movement of men outside the household, Catherine Beecher and others propounded a cult of domesticity, which emphasized women's tasks within the home, focused on women's role in caring for their children, and placed a positive value on women's efforts.[6]

The experiences of working- and middle-class women diverged as the production of household goods moved into the factory. Middle-class women gained leisure time, some of which they devoted to their children, and some to social and reform activities. In contrast working-class women purchased basic materials and continued baking their own bread and sewing their families' clothes. They did all their cleaning, washing, and ironing without benefit of either the new technologies that became available toward the end of the nineteenth century or the servants who eased the workload of the more affluent women.[7] More daughters moved into the labor force, but, except among blacks, their mothers did not. Employers demanded full-time workers who concentrated entirely upon production rather than combining work with family-orientated tasks. The home did not move into the factory when the locus of work shifted, since women continued to have domestic responsibilities, especially the care of small children. Employment outside the home was difficult, if not impossible unless other members of the family could be relied upon to watch the little ones. This resulted in a much sharper differentiation between single and married women's work than in the preindustrial world. Ironically, the view of a woman's place within the home developed at the time when female employment was increasing, and it ignored this discrepancy between single and married women's roles.[8]

Unless women earned, they depended upon men for support, and the nature of the partnership between the sexes altered as women became more closely identified with domesticity and child rearing. Female dependency upon male breadwinners replaced the mutual dependence of preindustrial and subsistence economies. Among the American middle class these changes resulted in the twin cults of true womanhood and domesticity, but the working-class experience varied according to the jobs available in the community.[9] The number of employed women was far higher in textile centers than in steel mill towns. This economic independence led women to delay marriage, preserving their social autonomy. Even in light industry, once married, women tended to be a reserve labor force, at work when the family needed additional income rather than permanently employed, as were their husbands.[10]

The Asymmetric Family

Women in Pittsburgh lived in the nonindustrial world of the home, while their husbands, laboring in the iron and steel mills, had industrial occupations and moved to an industrial rhythm.[11] The industrial world penetrated the household and structured women's tasks around men's employment, but the women's environment was emphatically non-modern. New household and municipal technologies barely reached working-class women in the late nineteenth century. Home, family, neighborhood, and church, if any, encompassed these women's lives. Women and men had little understanding of each other's world and had separate existences conjoined by bed and board, with domestic services provided by the wife and financial ones by the husband.

It was in this context that the asymmetrical family emerged.[12] Sociologists have described this family type as characterized by a strict division of labor where the woman had little idea of how much the man earned. She relied upon him for support, but he kept some of his weekly pay packet for himself. Spouses had segregated leisure time activities except when festivities with relatives brought the entire family together. There was little or no sharing of tasks; men and women inhabited distinct and unequal worlds where wages were the measure of the man but the women could only wait for their husbands to bring home the money that they then managed.[13]

If asymmetry typified gender relations in industrial cities, it developed in an extreme form in Pittsburgh. Thomas Bell's perceptive and sympathetic novel of life among the steelworkers at the turn of the century depicted the separateness of women's and men's lives. One Hungarian immigrant complained about his wife, and another suggested he put himself in her place. "How would you like to live her life, eh? But that was beyond Kracha's imagining and he had brushed it aside as nonsense. As well ask Elena how she would like to take his place in the gang. Since it was impossible there was no point in suggesting it."[14] Nor did women seem to understand men's work very well. A Slavic woman reminisced about the work her husband did at Crucible Steel after World War I. "One day I went up to the mill to take him his lunch," recalled Mrs. Cubelic. "I didn't know him, all wrapped up [in wet rags to pull ingots out of the open hearth furnace]. I cried when I got home, knowing what my husband was doing for a living."[15] They lived together, but their lives were worlds apart, hers in the home and his in the mill. Her world had a narrower scope than his, rooted in family and domestic cares while his was largely extrahousehold, encompassing the mill, the tavern, and recreation in which his family did not participate.[16]

The popular press reflected and reinforced the distinct roles of women and men. *The People's Monthly* lauded the workingman's wife for bearing and nursing his children; her existence was "eminently a home life."[17] When women did the work that God intended, house and child care, asserted the *National Labor Tribune*, there ensued "less crime and vice, less ruined characters and stained consciences, less misery and wretchedness, more Godliness, more happiness." When women recognized their place in the home, "more of all that tends to make life worth living" resulted.[18] But if they moved into other realms, social chaos and misery followed. For *Commoner and Glass Worker* the only appropriate work for young women was domestic service, which qualified "women for all the future duties of a wife and mother." If they took other jobs, men could not "maintain their homes and provide their wives and daughters with a sufficient supply of food and clothing" nor a comfortable house.[19] Female transgression of their domestic roles led to the degradation of the human race. Male transgressions, including infidelity and drunkenness, were to be understood and forgiven, but not condemned out of hand.

Given the paucity of manuscript evidence from working-class women, it is difficult to know how they themselves regarded their roles, but letters published in the *National Labor Tribune* suggest a diffident and defensive posture toward the external, nonhousehold world. Obviously interested in their husbands' jobs, working conditions, and labor disputes, they rarely stated their opinions in public. When women did so, they begged leave to express themselves in areas of men's concerns. A miner's wife prefaced her remarks on wages and working conditions by saying, "I am but a woman, but. . . ."[20] Another woman married to a coal miner was encouraged to write after seeing a letter from a woman in a labor paper that had given her great pleasure. She asked for a small space in the paper although "some may think that being a woman that I had no right to take part in such matters." This woman, who identified herself solely as a coal digger's wife, rationalized her boldness by saying that she was a wife and the mother of seven children. She relied upon her husband's wages to put bread on the table as they moved frequently from coal town to coal town around Pittsburgh so that he might find work.[21] In order to legitimate her opinion, she phrased it in terms of what concerned her most, her household and family. Yet another workingman's wife stated that "some people say a woman has no right to meddle in men's affairs, but I contend that whatever is serious enough to affect my husband concerns me."[22] A dilemma trapped these women: their culture maintained that a woman's place was in the home, but the external world dictated the internal one of the home. Therefore they explained whatever interest they had in nonhousehold affairs by reference to the affairs of the household itself and women's job(s) within it.

The concentration of working-class women in domestic employment before marriage and inability to obtain work afterward circumscribed their world to the household itself. They would be men's equals only when they "achieved a practical equality with men in wage earning," asserted the author of the *Irish Pennsylvanian's* "Women and Home" page. Amid recipes, advice on the renovation of old chairs and the disposal of household slops, this woman explained to the Irish women of Pittsburgh that it was futile to discuss "sanctity of motherhood and the dignity of wifehood while the reality of unloved wives and doomed

children is heartbreaking."[23] She believed that women's low status derived from their exclusion from remunerative employment on an equal
basis with men. This woman expressed an exceptional viewpoint, for few
people publicly acknowledged the difficulties women encountered either
in employment or after marriage. Women of Irish ancestry were well
represented in the labor force and by the end of it were moving up the
female occupational hierarchy. Nevertheless, most wed and eschewed
wage labor after marriage, as did all but a few Pittsburgh wives. Yet
marriage did not resolve all women's problems, according to the *Irish
Pennsylvanian* columnist.

Marriage

Marriage and family created different realities for each sex, ending
female wage labor while reinforcing the male role of breadwinner. The
timing of individual marriages, and therefore the length of time any
individual spent as part of a couple, having and caring for children, varied
by ethnic group. It was partially structured by demographic factors (that
is, the availability of suitable partners) as well as cultural values.
Pittsburgh had a preponderance of males, although some segments of the
population had particularly lopsided sex ratios. Since most marriages
were endogamous, the presence of many more men could result in either
delayed marriage or the importation of brides from the old home.
Pittsburgh's new residents rarely availed themselves of a third option,
marriage outside the group, although this had been a popular practice
among the more easily assimilable British immigrants earlier in the
century.

The transition from the single to the married state occurred between
the ages of 20 and 35 in Pittsburgh, the average age of marriage being 27
for men and 23 for women in 1886. Women in Pittsburgh married
somewhat earlier than did those living in the textile cities, where their
work outside the home was the basis of the economy.[24] The tendency of
the new immigrants, especially the Italians, to import young women as
brides reinforced the early marriage pattern at the turn of the century. In
1900, 39 percent of all 20–24-year-old women in Pittsburgh were married

compared with 34 percent in the textile center of Manchester, N.H. By 35 a similar proportion of women in both cities had married (about 70 percent). The proportion of Pittsburgh men marrying early (between 20 and 24) was much lower than in Manchester. The Steel City attracted a large number of young men seeking work and not ready or able to settle down as quickly as in the textile town. Only 16 percent of the 20–24-year-old men in Pittsburgh were married compared with 28 percent of those in Manchester in 1900. By the age of 35, 67 percent of Pittsburgh's men and 80 percent of those in Manchester had married.[25] Thus men in Pittsburgh existed for a longer period outside the marital context and without family responsibilities than did men in other cities, whereas for women the reverse was true. Some men, of course, were sons in their parents' households helping support their family of origin, but many lived in boardinghouses.

In reflection of the number of available marital partners, great variation existed in the tendency of Pittsburgh's ethnic and racial groups to marry. In 1880, 27 percent of the British and 22 percent of the native white, Irish, and black men over 25 had not married, but only 16 percent of the German men were without wives. The range among the women demonstrated that even in a city with an overall surplus of males, some could not find mates or delayed their entrance into the connubial state. Black women suffered the least favorable sex ratio in 1880. They tended to stay in the labor force longer than whites and had the highest proportion of unmarried: 34 percent, followed by 23 percent of the Irish women, who also worked longer than other white women and postponed marriage. In contrast 11 percent of the native-born white and British and 13 percent of the German women over 25 had not married.[26] Marriage enabled working-class women to leave the labor force and the limited jobs open to them in this era. There is little qualitative evidence available bearing on this issue of choice. Did black and Irish women remain in the labor force because they preferred working, did not want to marry, or could not find partners? Certainly, a few middle-class women chose the single state in order to continue working in their professions, but they were exceptional.[27]

The average age of marriage remained unchanged in 1900. The

foreign-born as a group had the lowest proportion of single women and men. Ninety-one percent of the women over 25 who had been born abroad were married, as were 80 percent of the men. The very high proportion among the women reflects the favorable sex ratio within the Southern and Eastern European population in the city and the circumstances under which many came to Pittsburgh: as wives or brides-to-be of men who had come to the city a few years earlier. Blacks also had a very high proportion of married women, in contrast to the experience of the previous generation. In 1900, 86 percent of those over 25 had husbands. As the sex ratio among blacks in Pittsburgh changed, so too did the proportions of women who married, for only 65 percent of those over 25 in 1880 were or had been married. Black men were less likely to marry; in 1900, only 71 percent had married. Native-born white women with native parents and those with foreign parents were more likely to stay single. About 76 percent of the women over 25 and men over 30 had married. Where there were more women than men, as among native-born whites both with native and foreign-born parents, the proportion of women who found marital partners was lower.[28] This group also had the most occupational choices and may have delayed marriage for a few years in favor of interesting employment.

Matrimony stated personal choices within carefully defined social and economic limits. Endogamy prevailed in this era, increasing as the population diversified. People chose partners from within their group, whether defined by ethnic, racial, or economic factors. In 1880, three-fourths of all marriage partners were both from the same ethnic group. The marriage dockets filed in 1900 indicate that spouse selection became somewhat more endogamous as time progressed; more than four-fifths of all people married in that year chose partners of the same ethnic group. This suggests that Pittsburgh was no melting pot at the turn of the century for new immigrant groups. Many of the seemingly exogamous marriages occurred between second-generation women and male immigrants of the same ethnicity.[29]

But though Italians, Poles, Austrians, Hungarians, and Russians married countrymen and women in 1900, old stock immigrants ranged more widely in their choice of partners.[30] In 1880 the Irish, British, and

German communities in Pittsburgh had more adult men than women. Thus some men sought wives outside the ethnic community, mostly among the ranks of native-born white women. Lacking partners from within their own group, native-born white women were receptive to proposals from foreign-born men; about 27 percent married first- or second-generation men. Fewer Irish and German men married endogamously than did their sisters; 78 percent had partners of the same ethnicity. In contrast, 82 percent of the Irish women and 94 percent of the German women took spouses from their own ethnic groups, but only 60 percent of British men and women did so. Native-born white men also married endogamously: only 13 percent had first- or second-generation spouses. By 1900 the proportion of native-born whites of either sex with foreign-born partners was 15 percent, but among old stock immigrants intermarriage ranged from 29 percent for Irish-American men to 75 percent for the British-American men. In many cases, particularly among the Germans, the native-born partner had a name indicative of membership in the ethnic group of the foreign-born spouse, indicating that ethnicity remained an important factor in spouse selection. Nevertheless, the exogamy of old stock immigrants suggests greater social acceptance than earlier in the century.[31]

A shortage of partners did not result in the marriage of black women to white men in 1880, although a smattering of black men had white wives. In terms of spouse selection, Pittsburgh blacks resembled those in Philadelphia, among whom W. E. B. Dubois found little intermarriage. Of the 33 interracial couples in Philadelphia's Seventh Ward in 1898, 29 consisted of white women with black husbands and 4 of white men with black wives. Speculating that more separations occurred in mixed marriages, DuBois cautioned that these marriages had to endure "not simply the social ostracism of the whites but of the blacks also."[32] Blacks in other cities, with the exception of Boston, also had low rates of intermarriage, which suggests how far apart they stood from other Americans in this era.[33]

Economic class also influenced spouse selection in the Steel City, but to a lesser extent than ethnicity. In 1880, 25 percent of the married couples contained women and men from different races or ethnic groups, but in 1886, 48 percent of the marriages took place between individuals with different class backgrounds.[34] Endogamy was most pronounced among the unskilled and decreased as the partners' economic class increased. Most cross-class weddings allied people from adjoining classes, although 15 percent of the laborers and 7 percent of their sisters married into the middle class. Among skilled workers the pattern reversed: more men took wives with unskilled fathers.[35] When fathers maintained their status into middle age, they passed certain advantages to their daughters, endowing them with the attributes needed to marry well. The seeming downward marital mobility of skilled workers themselves could be more apparent than real, for their partners' fathers may have been skilled workers who lost their positions in the mills as they aged and were less able to keep up the pace required of skilled industrial labor.[36] The marriage dockets for 1900 indicate that a greater percentage of couples (70 percent) married within the same economic class. It is likely that the great concentration of unskilled Southern and Eastern Europeans in the sample (27 percent), all of whom married within their own ethnic and class groups, tended to emphasize homogeneous marriage patterns.[37]

The weddings themselves occasioned family and community gatherings with celebration, good food, and extensive drinking. Slavic families hired musicians, fiddles emblazoned with ribbons, to play for the guests.[38] Some working-class men felt diffident and overwhelmed by the ceremony and merriment; weddings were really women's affairs. "There was a profusion of orange blossoms, tucks, frills, and flounces, blue satin and white Swiss embroidery, and other such feminine fixings as a glass blower, used rather to swinging a pipe than a pen, finds it hard to enumerate, " an anonymous correspondent of *Commoner and Glass Worker* wrote in 1886.[39] In distinction to working-class weddings in London at the turn of the century, which one observer described as "almost unnoticed," occurring at the weekend and attended only by "a small circle of lady friends," those of the steel- and glassworkers and recent immigrants were festive holidays from the cares of work and household.[40]

After marriage, most women settled into a domestic pattern, contributing to the family economy through having and raising children, managing the family finances, and, among the very poor, taking in boarders. Few white wives, however, worked outside the home.[41] Some coal miners' wives sewed jeans by hand and poor steelworkers' wives took in washing, but neither group considered themselves employed because they worked irregularly.[42] Despite a small increase, married women's participation in the labor force in Pittsburgh remained lower than in all other U.S. cities except Scranton and Milwaukee. Some of the increase can be attributed to the growing number of black women in the city who continued their work as domestic servants after marriage.[43] Most European stock women, Margaret Byington observed in Homestead, "apparently think it wiser to save money by good housekeeping than to earn a little more and neglect the home." This rational decision had three components: the lack of nonhousehold employments for women, the need to look after their young children, and the incredible burden placed upon housekeepers by the schedules their men worked.[44]

Childbearing

Childbearing occupied most of these women's married lives. The average Pittsburgh woman married at 23, had her last child about nine or ten years later, and would be in her mid-fifties by the time her youngest set up housekeeping.[45] Almost all families contained children. During these years few couples remained childless voluntarily. In 1880 a mere 10 percent of all households in Pittsburgh consisted of childless couples, some of whom were at the beginning or end of their marital careers. Excluding institutions, about 74 percent of all households were headed by couples with children present and 11 percent by widows with children. Five percent contained single people (primarily older women), groups of siblings, or unrelated individuals.[46]

Family sizes contracted between 1880 and 1910. Completed families averaged 5.4 children for white urban Pennsylvanians in 1880 and 4.5 children in 1910. The comparable figures for black women were 5.9 and 4.3, respectively, showing slightly larger families earlier and a greater decline in family size.[47] Despite the decrease in family size in these years, most women in Pittsburgh had between 3 and 6 children to care for. About one-half of all children living with their parents were under the age of 10 and one-fourth were under the age of 5. They thus required close supervision. Southern and Eastern European immigrants tended to have larger families than native-born whites, which meant that women from these groups spent a greater proportion of their lives looking after children.[48] Moreover, most women had little help with their family responsibilities. Older daughters could be and were detailed to care for their younger siblings, but as more of them went to school for longer periods and undertook paid employment, they were less available to deputize for their mothers.[49] Some middle-class women had domestic servants who might combine child care with housework. About one–tenth of all Pittsburgh's families in 1880 and 1900 employed domestic servants, but except in a few of the very large boardinghouses working-class families did not hire help. Thus virtually all working-class women spent the majority of their adult lives caring for their children, trying to combine nurturance with housework.[50]

Almost all immigrant women and most of those born in the United States carried on with their household duties until the day the baby came. The children themselves were delivered by a midwife who, in addition to helping the mother to have the child, performed many little household services that physicians considered beneath their dignity. The midwife might make a pot of soup, bring the mother cups of tea, or stay with the family until called to the next birth. Yet more affluent women, even among the working class, were increasingly likely to have a physician in attendance. Poorer families and most immigrants still relied upon a midwife or occasionally had no attendant at all at the birth.[51] Midwives received between $3.00 and $5.00 for their services, and that sometimes in installments. Neighbor women and relatives might visit after the birth, relegating the new father to the background, but mothers quickly picked up the reins of the household.[52] The discrepancy between native and foreign-born mothers on this point was quite marked. Nearly two-thirds of the immigrant mothers, primarily Polish, Slovak, Serbo-Croatian, and Italian, were back at their daily chores by the time the baby was a week old. Only a handful of the native-born women were. A Johnstown, Pa., study concluded that foreign mothers, ''with less education, more numerous and arduous tasks, less opportunity for leisure, and smaller incomes,'' began their housework sooner than native-born white mothers.[53] Many of these women also had lodgers, a situation that increased the pressure on them to get out of bed to cook, clean, and wash clothes. The financial need to devote time to these lodgers adversely affected the mother's health and was a factor in the higher rates of infant mortality experienced by the babies.[54]

Housework

For the wives of the steelworkers, home was a workplace whose activities revolved around the coming and goings of men in the mill. Shift work determined all household activities. If several men in the household (whether husband, sons, or boarders) toiled in the mills, they might all have different schedules. Some mills had ten-hour day and fourteen-hour night turns; others worked the men eleven and thirteen hours, or in two twelve-hour shifts. Puddlers began work anywhere from 2 to 4 A.M.; other men reported in at 6 or 7 A.M. for their ten-, eleven-, or twelve-hour turns. Meals had to be cooked almost around the clock, for a woman might easily be feeding men and children on three or four different schedules, cooking meals for different day and night turns.[55] After a year spent talking with steelworkers and their families, John Fitch concluded that "the wife of the steel worker, too, has a hard day and an even longer one than her husband's."[56] In order to cook for all these shifts, the millworker's wife rose at 5 or 6 A.M. to prepare breakfast. She continued cooking throughout the day, as men returned from the mills, children came home from school, and lunch buckets had to be prepared. Each man expected a hot dinner when he returned home. Children were fed in between the men's comings and goings.[57]

The typical round of chores for the working-class housewife was time-consuming and arduous, though neither as heavy nor as dangerous as her husband's. Some evidence indicates that women felt their husbands did not appreciate their efforts. Working-class newspapers felt it necessary to remind men of the work that their wives performed. The *National Labor Tribune* published the folk lament "A Housekeeper's Tragedy" several times during the last decades of the century, detailing the drudgery and seeming futility of so-called women's work.

> Oh, Life is a toil and love is a trouble
>> And beauty will fade and riches will flee
> And Pleasures they dwindle and prices they double
>> And nothing is what I could wish it to be.
>
> There's too much of worriment goes to a bonnet
>> There's too much ironing goes to a shirt
> There's nothing that pays for the time wasted on it
>> There's nothing that lasts but trouble and dirt.
>
> It's sweeping at six and dusting at seven
>> It's victuals at eight and dishes at nine
> It's potting and panning from ten to eleven
>> We scarce break our fast ere we plan how to dine
>
> With grease and with litter from outside to enter
>> Forever at war and forever alert
> For no rest for a day lest the enemy enter
>> I spend my whole time in a struggle with dirt.[58]

Eventually the poor housekeeper simply laid down her broom and was buried in dirt. As the song indicated, a woman's life entailed endless cleaning and cooking.

Working-class men expected their wives to work willingly in the home. They took this household labor for granted, sometimes to the detriment of their wives' happiness, if not their marriages. Just as the popular press found it necessary to remind men of their women's efforts, it also encouraged men to be grateful to their wives for the work carried on at home. "Praise your wife, man; for pity's sake give her a little encouragement; it won't hurt her."[59] Since it was the woman who made the home comfortable and the food agreeable, she deserved some recognition from her family.[60] Many women thirsted for a few words of praise, itself "the language of encouragement, through summer's heat, through winter's toil, they have drudged uncomplainingly, and so accustomed have their fathers, brothers, and husbands become to their monotonous labors that they look for and upon them as they do the daily rising of the sun." The *National Labor Tribune* reminded its readers that the clean shirt in the drawer got there only because somebody's fingers "have ached in the toil of making it so fresh and agreeable, so smooth and lustrous."[61]

The popular press advised working-class women to finish all the chores before the husband arrived home from his hard day's work in the mill, mine, glass house or railroad yard. Her work should be completed so that he would have a pleasant environment and a well-ordered household to which to return.[62] Insofar as the woman completed her tasks before "the mister" came home, it is understandable that he rarely or never noticed her labors and took them for granted.[63] It was both part of the segregation of sex roles and the way in which a conscientious woman accomplished her work.

Working-class women had no mechanical contrivances to help in their struggle to keep their neighborhoods and homes clean and sanitary. Although domestic technology revolutionized housework and increased creature comforts in the early twentieth century, only the middle classes and the very upper reaches of the working class could afford washing machines, central heating, indoor plumbing, telephones, iceboxes, gas, or electricity.[64] Middle-class women used a variety of mechanical devices to conserve their own energy. The telephone enabled them to call shop-keepers and arrange for the delivery of goods. Pittsburgh's first telephone directory lists a handful of private subscribers, five manufacturers, a metal merchant, and an undertaker. By 1886, 11 percent of the city's telephones were in homes, all in the hands of merchants, professional manufacturers, undertakers, and their wives. No artisans had home phones, although a few had them in their shops.[65] New machines and fuel sources made middle-class homes healthier, safer, and more comfortable but did not ease the domestic burden of working-class women. Although the city became dirtier, less sanitary, and more crowded through increased industrialization and urbanization, these women still did housework in much the same manner as their mothers had. Cleanliness became more difficult to obtain at the very time when it became more important for the family's health. Women's efforts in their own homes enabled proletarian families to manage on inadequate and uncertain wages at the same time as

Pittsburgh devoted resources to bettering conditions in middle-class neighborhoods. Their domestic labors made bearable their husband's low wages and absorbed the financial impact of whatever drinking, smoking, or spending habits their husbands might have indulged.[66]

Two factors kept working-class women tied to older, more laborious methods of housework when other women began to substitute machine for human power. The first and more significant was the scarcity, irregularity, and low level of wages. The new household technology required a larger capital investment than most working-class families could afford. Even "the decision to buy a new piece of furniture" was "a matter for grave consideration" in poorer families. In a period of economic unrest, working-class families kept expenditure to a minimum. Though the expensive items eased women's work load and enhanced self esteem, they were not necessary for family survival. Although "housework might be materially lightened by the use of gas instead of coal, " it was too expensive for working-class families.[67] Instead, these women carried heavy scuttles full of coal in and ashes out. With older children at school and husbands toiling intolerably long hours in the mills, these women were deprived of ancillary workers in the home and did more of this work themselves. They became primarily if not entirely responsible for domestic order.[68]

A second factor kept working-class women from acquiring consumer durables. Their husbands did not appreciate the amount of work they actually performed: since men considered it natural for women to do housework, they did not see the need to replace their wives' physical efforts with machine power.[69] They lived in a sex-stratified society in which women's work in the home seemed natural precisely because there was no other place for them to work.[70] When money was scarce, working-class women continued to do housework in the old way. Replacing their labor with machines did not have a high priority in family budgets geared to survival and saving sufficient sums to move from rented to owned accommodation.[71]

Thorstein Veblen described middle-class women as the medium through which their husbands displayed affluence.[72] However, working-class women, whose labor made the tenements and mill apartments habitable, still brought water in from the pump in buckets to heat on a coal or wood stove. The stoves themselves needed tending; lamps had to be kept trim and clean. Ammonia, cleanser, soap and water, rags, dusters, and the all-important elbow grease were the only tools working-class women had to combat the grit, dust, and dirt from the mills. Middle-class women had indoor hot and cold running water, gas stoves, lights, heat, washing machines, telephones, and, frequently, servants to do the heaviest work.[73]

The new household appliances substituted mechanical for human energy. Housework became less arduous, and those who could afford the innovations gained some respite from physical drudgery. The forced hot air furnace provided even, dust-and-dirt-free heat to the entire house. It was a great advance over the fireplace, which needed frequent tending and did not heat an entire room, and the closed stove, which heated a room but needed to be fired up, fed, and cleaned. Furnaces cost anywhere from $75 to $3000, while closed stoves cost $10 or $11. The majority of working-class homes had such stoves, although some still relied upon fireplaces. The high cost of owning and operating even one stove meant that most working-class homes had heat only in the kitchen. Photographs of turn-of-the-century working-class dwellings show a single chimney in the rear of the house over the kitchen. In contrast, middle-class homes had chimneys front and back and on both sides. These homes had clean gas heat rather than the coal and wood common to the homes of skilled and unskilled workers.[74]

As with heating, gas replaced wood and coal as a cooking and lighting fuel in middle-class homes. The gas stove was cleaner, cooked evenly, and, most marvelous of all, did not heat the entire kitchen to insufferable temperatures during the summer. The fancier ones contained ovens that baked and roasted at an even heat. Kitchen ranges with "water backs" (hot water heaters) became popular among the middle and upper classes. Although expensive to purchase and requiring indoor plumbing, they made it possible to have a supply of hot water always available.[75]

Good lighting also facilitated housework. In 1870 some working-class homes were still lit with candles. For example, a policeman investigating the murder of Isabella Campbell, wife of an express wagon driver, described her kitchen as being very dark, lit only by a candle in a wall holder.[76] Most working-class families, however, had kerosene or oil lamps. The lamps needed to be kept clean and fitted with the proper size of wick lest they explode. Middle-class homes now relied on gas lighting. By 1870 advertisements for "desirable city property" touted gas and water fixtures. The wealthy and upper middle classes considered gas lighting a necessity by 1880. Kerosene remained the major light source used by "the vast majority of dwellings among the common people" through the end of the century.[77]

In 1888 and 1889, *Commoner and Glass Worker* carried a column called "The Working Man's Wife," which contained a scrap pile of information "gathered solely for her instruction, amusement and education." It stressed "facts for women folks to read." The author, a "lady reader" and model housekeeper, spoke from practical experience when she reflected the never ending struggle with dirt among the working class. This working-class Catherine Beecher wanted her readers to organize their chores so that they could be performed efficiently.[78]

The orderly housewife devoted each day to a separate facet of housework performed in addition to the tasks done daily. Monday, of course, was laundry day. Actually, the tidy working-class woman began her washday preparations on Sunday night, when she gathered and sorted the clothes and positioned her tubs, washboard and washboiler. She did as much as possible the night before since the washing process took up so much time.[79] Virtually all working-class women washed their family's clothes themselves, possibly with some help from an older daughter. The steam laundries that appeared in Pittsburgh during the 1880s catered for the affluent and some single men. Laboring families sent their soiled clothes out only if the wife was sick and no daughter, relative, or neighbor could wash for her. Nor did many women have washing machines to assist them, although the first mechanical washers appeared in Pittsburgh in 1870. Only middle-class women owned the Dexter Washing Machine. An advertisement for this machine listed thirty-eight women as references: all but four lived in the fashionable wards. Their husbands were businessmen, grocers, professionals, gentlemen, and bankers. Of the remaining four, two ran boardinghouses, one was married to a carpenter, and the other to an alderman. These machines were advertised as "cheap, simple, durable, effective," and capable of doing "the ordinary washing of a family in *only* one or two hours." The makers claimed they saved soap and required no boiling of clothes.[80] Since such machines cost $15.00 even after the turn of the century only the aristocracy of iron, glass, and steel families with larger incomes purchased the patented washing machines.[81]

Working-class women did laundry the old-fashioned way. They brought water in from the pump, heated it on a coal or wood stove, emptied it into a washtub, and scrubbed the clothes as they bent over the "back-breaking washboard." They carried the soapy water outside, brought clean water in, heated it again, and rinsed the clothes. Especially sweaty or dirty clothes, those worn by men in the mills or children's play clothes and soiled infant wear, were soaped and rinsed again, then wrung out and hung out to dry in the courtyard, alleyway, or kitchen. In winter women did laundry in the kitchen. During warm weather, they washed on the back porch, if the family had one, in the courtyard or alley, or in the overheated kitchen.[82] The author of "The Workingman's Wife" advised against soaking soiled clothes in anything except cold water because the commercial washing fluids available actually harmed fabrics. Old-fashioned elbow grease remained the best laundry aid available to the readers of this column.[83]

Wash day completely disrupted the household routine. It took all day, since work clothes, flannels, whites, and cotton prints all had to be laundered separately. Each had to be put through two sudsings and rinses, the whites blued, and the flannels accorded special care to keep them from shrinking or getting as hard as a board. Water slopped everywhere as women carried it about in buckets. Clothes were wrung out and hung to dry either outside or in lines strung across the kitchen. Although household advisers thought it preferable to have a separate area for washing clothes in order to contain the mess and chaos, few nineteenth-century working-class homes actually did.[84]

After the working-class woman cleared away tubs and buckets, she took down the clothes to set aside for ironing. The model housekeeper suggested that she next wash and dress the children so that they would be "nice and neat when papa comes home." Then she was to fix herself up and put on "her smiling face" so that her husband would not think her tired when he came home from work; yet she still had supper to prepare.[85] How difficult it must have been to put aside her weariness so that her husband might relax with his paper while she cooked. No wonder the model working-class husband was one who would eat a cold dinner on wash day without grumbling.[86] Since the stove was used for heating the wash water and boiling the clothes, a quick or a cold supper was in fact all that might be available. Whereas the middle class had hot water heaters that freed the stove for cooking, the working class devoted their stoves each Monday to washing clothes.

Tuesday was ironing day, which meant more hard work, albeit less disorder. The good housewife rose before her children and her husband so that she could finish at least " a nice line or horse full of clothes" before her family demanded breakfast. It took all morning to do the "fine and most particular" pieces. These were done first, before she got too tired, so that they would not be scorched with a carelessly applied iron. The coarse clothes, which needed less attention, were ironed after lunch. The working-class woman was advised against stopping for a big meal. Rather, she should eat quickly and return to her ironing so that she would have time to fold and put away the clothes before preparing a good supper and tidying up the house, the children, and herself. The ironing itself took place in the kitchen near the stove on which she heated the iron, exhausting the housewife in Pittsburgh's sticky summers.[87]

At midweek the working-class housewife restored order to her home. She swept, washed the oil cloth on the kitchen table, polished the stove, and dusted amid interruptions from the children, errands, and running to the store. Sewing, mending, and visiting were done on Thursdays, according to the lady correspondent of the glassworkers' paper. A really conscientious housekeeper could always be relied upon to help a neighbor in sickness or trouble but did not spend her time in idle gossip.[88]

The working-class woman baked on Fridays. She made enough breads, pies, and cakes to feed her family of six or seven people and whatever boarders she might have. This was a full day's work in itself, but, according to the household adviser, she should also scrub and shine the pantry, clean the bedrooms, and "rub" some of the windows. After washing the children, cooking dinner, and tidying herself, the working-class woman soon found Friday to be "one of the busiest days of the week." Despite that, she was advised to let the children into the parlor to play with their toys, even if it made a mess.[89] Though child rearing might have become an important task for middle-class women, working-class mothers seemed not to focus their attention upon their children because of the pressures of housework and the need to keep order in cramped dwellings.[90]

Since the men received their pay on Friday, working-class women did their major shopping on Saturday. Marketing took the entire morning, although some women postponed it until their husbands returned from work in the evening.[91] Then the entire family might visit butchers, grocers, and other merchants, or take a streetcar downtown to browse in the shops and patronize retailers who styled themselves as friends of the workingman and sometimes offered reductions to union members.[92] A large range of enterprises advertised in the labor press offering groceries, dress goods, and furnishings available on "easy payments" or with a "discount for cash." Some concerns arranged special Saturday hours to attract working-class money. The Iron and Glass Dollar Savings Bank on Carson Street on the South Side opened from 6 to 8 P.M. on Saturdays so that men might deposit a portion of their pay.[93] Those who shopped at neighborhood stores paid higher prices, but small grocers offered credit whereas the chain stores demanded cash. Immigrant women tended to patronize shopkeepers of their own nationality, who spoke their language and stocked familiar items.[94]

Although refrigerated railroad cars and canned foods meant more variety in the diet, packaged foods had higher prices. William Haslage and Son sold stringless beans for $0.15 per can, and tomatoes were 3 cans for $0.25 on special.[95] For laboring families living on $1.50 or $2.00 per day, these items were expensive luxuries. A barrel of flour that lasted the average family six weeks took nearly a week's wages to purchase. Since provisions in Pittsburgh cost more than in other cities of comparable size, women tended to make their purchases in smaller, less economical quantities. Small homes, lacking storage space and iceboxes for perishables, meant frequent trips to the store by millworkers' wives.[96]

The diet of Pittsburgh's working class varied with their income. More affluent workers' wives included more meat, fresh vegetables, and fruit in their families' fare, but recent immigrants pared food costs as low as possible by eating more potatoes and less fresh fruit and vegetables. They ate starchy foods and cheap cuts of beef and pork.[97] Since the men needed protein, the typical breakfast would include fried pork chops or steak, with the pan drippings poured onto the meat or over mashed potatoes.[98] The American-born daughter of Polish immigrants remembered that during hard times people would buy plate meat for $0.05, add bones, and make soup. "We made soup from everything . . . we had tripe soup, barley soup, red beet soup . . . anything that would stick to the ribs. We ate a lot of potato pancakes, too."[99] As with rent, the poorer the family, the greater its proportionate expenditure for food. Those earning less than $600 per year (unskilled workers) spent about 46–48 percent of their income on food, and for those with incomes over $1,000, 36–38 percent went for groceries.[100] The settlement houses tried to educate the immigrants about nutritious and economical foods, emphasizing the utilization of cornmeal, potatoes, and cheaper cuts of meat that the poor could afford.[101]

Withal, working-class women's daily routines revolved around household chores and the creation of a suitable environment for their children and husband. As the emphasis on having the household put back together by the time the husband returned home from work demonstrates, he was the center around whom other family members' activities turned. If a man came home late, the good wife had his dinner waiting, saw to it that his wants were supplied, and sat down with him while he "satisfied the inner man." Should she return late from an extended shopping tour, however, no one had supper waiting for her. Instead, she shifted for herself and got what satisfaction she could from "cold potatoes and a bone that was once the centre of some toothsome sirloin steak, but which then appeared to be useful only as a bracelet."[102]

Husbands

Some husbands harangued or abused wives who failed to perform their household duties; they took it for granted that the women would cook, clean, and wash for them.[103] The *People's Monthly* stated that "men seldom appreciate the worth of a devoted wife and look upon her many kind acts as a matter of duty."[104] If she was remiss in her service to her husband, he reacted, sometimes violently. A blacksmith came home from work and, finding supper not ready, beat his wife. In a similar situation, a laborer arrived home drunk and "compelled his wife to get out of her sick bed and get him something to eat as late as 12 o'clock at night."[105] Other cases brought before the aldermen's courts and the Humane Society illustrated a tendency for some husbands to behave violently when their expectations were not met and their needs not served by their wives. Some women then protested harsh treatment from their husbands, but others accepted a measure of abuse as part of the relations between the sexes. One woman responded to an investigator's query, "Does your husband beat you?" by quoting a Russian proverb, "Doesn't beat, doesn't love."[106] Though this is not systematic evidence, it does imply that a certain amount of rough treatment was to be expected from husbands.

The husband's duty included providing an income and place for his wife and family to live. Men who did not work or refused to give their wives a portion of their earnings violated their assigned roles. There were many women in the same situation as the wife of Michael Doran, a laborer, who was "almost continually drunk, gave her no money and a shameful beating," thus echoing the reformers' contention that alcoholic excesses led to family violence.[107] Lizzie Cress complained to the alderman that her husband had been drunk for three weeks and did not provide for her.[108] In addition to wives' complaints of nonsupport, neighbors sometimes took husbands to task for shirking their duty. The residents of Gist Street tired of seeing Richard Brennen, a puddler, take "the part of the woman in the house" by not working, compelling his wife to take in washing to earn the family's living, so they registered a protest with the

Humane Society. Sometimes the husband could not get work in his field, as happened with Hugh Malone, another puddler. As fewer mills made iron, Malone found himself with infrequent work over a nine-month period. Although his neighbors presumably understood the problems of skilled ironworkers whose skills had been made obsolete, someone complained nevertheless that he had not met his obligations to his family.[109]

Legally and socially, a man's responsibility was to support his family, and though many women suffered along, eking out a living on what their husbands gave, subsisting, as one did, on stale bread and beef tea (a broth made by boiling a beef bone in water to extract as much flavor and nutrition as possible), others appealed to the Poor Board for assistance or prosecuted their husbands for nonsupport. Such suits could be counterproductive, for a husband in the workhouse could not contribute to his family's sustenance. He might, however, mend his ways and not commit the same crime again. Alternatively, he might leave the city altogether after serving his sentence or when threatened with the alderman's constable.[110] Since formal divorce proceedings were costly, some working-class men solved their domestic problems by leaving the neighborhood or city completely.[111] Such action prompted some women to publish notices of their husband's desertion or nonsupport in the labor newspapers. A typical notice stated that Mrs. Mitchell, the wife of a boiler, suffered great distress due to her husband's unexplained absence. "Let him at once go home if he sees this. Men who have no more heart for a wife than to leave her penniless among strangers and not say a word, ought to be made an example of. Such men do not deserve loving wives."[112] Unfortunately, the newspapers never indicated whether husbands returned to their families or sent them money.

Wives

Though the responsible working-class husband earned the wages that supported his family, his wife actually managed the money. This does not imply necessarily that she had a significant control over the family finances.[113] Female management might entail making do on the sums doled out by the husbands. Testimony given in family quarrels before the aldermen, social survey data, and accounts in the labor newspapers showed that husbands gave their wives a certain amount for the housekeeping and expected them to get by on it.[114] Women frequently did not know how much money their husbands earned and hesitated to ask. Typically, a man took a portion of his pay for beer, tobacco, and other personal expenditure and only then turned over the remainder to his wife for the household expenses. A husband who drank heavily on payday or allocated his family only a fraction of his pay packet strained family finances.[115]

The popular press lauded women who managed creatively within limited resources through a lack of selfishness and a willingness to place others before themselves when it came to spending or not spending the family's money. A good woman had "only the interests of her family at heart." She understood the family's needs better than her husband. She was, moreover, "more unselfish and less liable to self-indulgences and a more skillful purveyor."[116] Domestic frugality extracted full value from a limited pay packet. "A few dollars backed by a tasty wife will surround a snug little home with such an air of grace, comfort, and beauty and heartsomeness that it will excite admiration and may be the envy of all passers-by."[117] The good woman, of course, spent the carefully managed money on her home and family rather than on herself.

During the depressions and periods of unemployment or underemployment, women economized drastically to make ends meet on the reduced family income. They had the responsibility of seeing the family through the financial crisis when their husbands worked less or looked for work elsewhere. Some managed, as did one miner's wife, by "boiling the soup bone as long as she smelt beef on the water."[118] Others took in washing or returned to their parents' homes. Many got through hard times by taking in boarders, although this added still more work to a busy day and more people to a crowded household.[119] Taking strangers into the home was more than giving a home to a workmate or a compatriot. It was a business in which poor women used their domestic talents to augment their husband's meager wages without joining the labor force.[120] It could add as much as one-fourth of an unskilled worker's wage to the household funds.[121] Women tended to take in subtenants when there were no ancillary wage earners in the family.[122]

Lodgers increased the workload for the housewife since she had responsibility for their care. These hardworking women did the extra shopping and cooking, accommodated themselves to the various shifts and schedules, and kept the children quiet. They struggled to do all the additional cleaning and mending that resulted from having three or four single men in their homes. Those who took in boarders found themselves sorely burdened by the sheer quantity of washing, for they had the men's under and outer clothes and bedclothes to cope with. Some found it impossible to keep the house clean and care for their families at the same time. Life for them became a continual treadmill of carrying water, cooking, cleaning, and washing.[123] As a result, they had even fewer opportunities for relaxation than other working-class women. "Sometimes they gossip around the pump or at the butcher's, but washing, ironing, cleaning, sewing, and cooking for the boarders leave little time for visiting."[124] Older women counseled those taking in lodgers for the first time to keep additional workload to a minimum by doing the plainest cooking possible. The novelist Thomas Bell succinctly described laboring wives' lives: "with six boarders, three children and a husband to look after, meals to cook, clothes to wash [the immigrant boardinghouse woman's] hours were from 4.30 in the morning to 9.00 at night, seven days a week."[125] Keeping lodgers meant extra money for the household and cheap living accommodation for compatriots trying to save money to bring over their own families or return to the homeland with a nest-egg. These benefits came at the direct expense of whatever relaxation the working-class woman might have and reinforced the domestic constraints of her life.[126]

The woman who did all her housework and reared her children wisely was said to have accomplished as much as her husband laboring industriously at his job, but she nevertheless remained subordinate to him. Short stories and advice in the proletarian press told women to establish the tone of the household, not to dominate it. Instead they should be humble and modest before their husbands. They were helpmates who should not express themselves freely. The household adviser of *Commoner and Glass Worker* went so far as to suggest that "a bit of necessary wearing apparel for the homemaker is a bridle for the tongue." A woman should not make cross or irritating remarks lest she open up a "vein of resentment and anger."[127] It was her job to make the home a pleasant place, although her husband shared this obligation, particularly when it came to setting an example for the children. Nevertheless, marital discord resulted from female irritability. The appropriate attitude for a wife was one of helpfulness and obedience. She should be a "meet helper," contented, gentle, reasonable, humble, obedient, useful, and observant. A prayer published in the *National Labor Tribune* suggested that she play Ruth to her husband's Naomi; in other words, she should be a loyal follower. The working-class woman should be content and refrain from unreasonableness of passion and humor.[128]

The working class valued manliness, which, as David Montgomery points out, included a belief in patriarchal supremacy.[129] Many of the heroes in proletarian short stories and melodramas were skilled workers who triumphed over attempts to subordinate body and soul to external processes.[130] They did this in the workplace by resisting efforts to undermine their autonomy on the job and in the home by dominating their wives, like the machinist's apprentice who "conquered his wife . . . won her esteem and compelled her to acknowledge a physical strength and moral purpose greater than her own," namely, his.[131] Proletarian authors believed unhappy marriages were largely the woman's fault and stemmed from her violation of the supportive, submissive female role. A woman who wanted her husband's love forever learned to be "forgiving, gentle, and considerate." In an article entitled "A Woman's Duty to Her Husband," the author considered the wife's responsibility if her man was shiftless or a poor provider. "Did it ever dawn on you that where there was one shiftless man there were about a hundred shiftless women, who made untidy homes, who raised careless children, and whose life was metaphorically speaking spent in a wrapper and curl papers, yet men have patience with these women?"[132] The author equated the female gender role violation of sloppy housekeeping with the male violation of nonsupport of the family. Somehow women's messiness justified or explained men's shiftlessness, even though the nonproviding male might, in fact, have a tidy, neat wife.

In any event, it was the wife's job to redeem the husband when he violated working-class norms. The drunkard, after all, was nothing but a sick man, and no wife would refuse to nurse her husband through an illness. The good wife ought to do anything to save her man, to pick him up from the gutter if need be, to restore his self-respect rather than let him lie there and drag her down with him. She was to forgive him everything but unfaithfulness. Yet even when a man committed adultery, his wife's conduct required examination. Had she done her duty so entirely "that her husband was strong enough to withstand temptation?"[133]

In the urban industrial family, the man earned the money and the wife kept the family together. The working-class wife contended with overworked and irascible husbands, irregular housekeeping money, cramped quarters, and never ending dirt. It is no wonder that the *Irish Pennsylvanian* tried to persuade its readers that "home is not a battlefield, nor is life one long, unending row. The trick of always seeing the bright side, of shining up the dark one is a very important faculty, one of the things no woman should be without."[134] Women had little choice but to endure; it was more difficult for them to leave their work behind through drink or leisure time activities. Women had always cared for their children and the household, but with industrialization men worked definite, if very long hours. Women, expected to service their husband's needs and those of children and boarders, labored ceaselessly as they tended hearth and home.

Leisure

With several significant exceptions, women and men were as segregated in their recreational activities as at their respective occupations.[135] Many of the man's nonworking hours were spent at the tavern, which led *People's Monthly* to advise women that a pleasant, well-kept house was an important means of luring husbands away from the saloon.[136] The men believed a glass of beer and a shot of whiskey settled their stomachs after drinking enormous quantities of water on the job, that whiskey cleared the dust from their throats, and that it overcame exhaustion.[137] Joseph Bishop, when president of the AAISW, said the men used alcohol as a *"stimulant* to revive exhausted nature, and as we all know, this relief is too often found in *saloons.*"[138] Union officials attacked the taverns as luring men to intemperance and profligacy. John Jarrett, former AAISW president, warned good union men that their ten cents spent in the saloon bought them only two cents' worth of whiskey or less than a penny's worth of ale.[139] President Bishop claimed that frequent visits to the dram shop, as he called it, kept the men in a "poverty stricken state" and prevented their preparations for a rainy day, by which he meant strikes or unemployment.[140]

Even sympathetic observers of immigrant life criticized the heavy drinking that took place in the saloons. Margaret Byington wrote of the Slavic residents of Homestead, many of whom lived in boardinghouses, that, "as in all barracks life, drunkenness and immorality are common."[141] But for the tired millhands and glassblowers whose days and nights were spent amid intolerable dust and heat, the saloon was an oasis, and alcohol gave momentary relief from unrelenting toil. The tavern was an extension of the man's world of the mills, where sociability could be had in more comfortable surroundings than their cramped homes furnished.[142] It gave surcease from the demands of both work and family, so the men lined up, foot on the rail, to have a beer and a shot of whiskey, perhaps another beer and another shot, then home to dinner or breakfast, sleep, and another day in the mills. The foreign-born spent proportionately more on alcohol than native-born whites, who had more diversified leisure activities including the music hall and nickelodeon. Immigrants unfamiliar with English eschewed these amusements, although the nickelodeon certainly was popular with their children.[143]

Most women accepted this pattern of separate male drinking, though some tried to lure the men home, either by following the *People's Monthly's* advice and providing a cozy house, or by providing amusements at home.[144] One Homestead woman counteracted the festivity of the saloon by encouraging her husband and his cronies to play cards in the house rather than in the tavern's back room.[145] A Polish woman reminisced about the parties the immigrants had at home where someone played the accordian and everyone danced. The houses were so small, however, that they had to move the furniture out to the yard to make room for the guests.[146] Weddings, christenings, and funerals also provided opportunities to gather, to celebrate, and to be convivial.[147] Ethnic societies sponsored a panoply of entertainments: balls, picnics, parades, and songfests were common. The Greek Catholic Union had an annual picnic. The Irish celebrated St. Patrick's Day with lectures, songs, declamations, and drinking. The Italian Mutual Benefit Society held balls. Parades, bands, and sermons in German and English accompanied the opening of the new Catholic College in 1885. Churches themselves provided a major social center for many. Attendance was predominately female despite male membership in church-sponsored lodges.[148]

The unions provided another source of recreation and entertainment for working-class families. Attendance at a performance of "Octoroon" raised money for striking puddlers and helpers in 1875, while it provided pleasure to the theatergoers. The annual reunions of the AAISW conducted union business but also beguiled the crowd with various diversions. The second annual reunion featured refreshments, baby doll stands, shooting galleries, a half-mile race, an Irish jig, a hobnail clog, and a plain clog dance. Of the 6,000 union members and their wives making the excursion to Beaver, Pennsylvania, 1,620 came from Pittsburgh. The fifth convention chartered a special train to convey the members, "the wives and fair daughters of some of the delegates and their friends" to 48th Street, whence they marched to Arsenal Park on 43rd and were entertained and led by the lodges of the Pittsburgh District. They enjoyed a sumptuous spread and songs by the Malichi's Quartet Club. In 1890 the Knights of Labor Brass Band and the Cathedral Band enlivened the proceedings. Though these social affairs integrated the union into the lives of working-class families, most union gatherings were for men only.[149] These entertainments, moreover, appealed primarily to union members and had little attraction for the large number of unskilled immigrant workers in the mills who neither belonged to the Amalgamated nor spoke English. The recreation of the Southern and Eastern Europeans focused on lodge dances, church, and drinking. Attendance at balls was a rare treat for the newcomers to the industrial city, made possible by frugality and the extra income brought in by caring for boarders.[150]

There was conflict in the city over how laboring families enjoyed their leisure hours. Steel mill owners complained of "Saturday night debauches and Sunday carousals" among their workers, and it is true the Saturday night held a special place in the working-class family week.[151] It was the time for relaxation and celebration at the end of the week. The working-class housewife gave everything "an extra rub or shine for Sunday" and tried to finish all her chores in order to have the evening free and to make Sunday as much a day of rest as possible.[152] Since Sunday was the one day of the week when everyone in the family could gather together, unless the man was on the long turn, women tried to clean for Sunday on Saturday. Sabbatarians and Prohibitionists made strenuous efforts to curtail public recreations on Sundays, asserting their cultural hegemony over the immigrant working class and curtailing their enjoyments by prohibiting Sunday baseball and other fee-paying leisure time activities.[153]

Only two formal holidays were recognized by the mill owners: Christmas and the Fourth of July. A few millworkers missed even these holidays; for example, blast furnace workers had none at all. For most, these days were great occasions, times when the entire family could be together with no one leaving for the next shift. This differentiated the holidays from Sundays, when special pains were taken with the meal but some of the men had to work.[154] Christmas and the Fourth of July, and Sundays to a lesser extent, occasioned family get-togethers. Married sons and daughters returned to their parents' house to celebrate. Particularly at Christmas, the women cooked and baked more than usual to celebrate the respite from work (for men), the holiday, and the family gathering. The holiday was a holiday for men but entailed additional work as well as a break from routine for women. It was joyous, but hard work. As the immigrants' stay in Pittsburgh lengthened, if work were steady and the boarders paid their bills, families, like those of the more skilled second- and third-generation millworkers, would have extra food at Christmas, a gaily decorated tree, and presents to put under it.[155] Unfortunately, not all families could afford the lavish meals and gifts warranted by these occasions. One elderly Slovak woman reminisced that the only way she knew a holiday from an ordinary day as a child in the early years of this century was that her mother managed to trade a few eggs for a cake of yeast so that she could make white bread instead of the hard cornbread that was their normal fare.[156]

Except for these family gatherings on holidays, millworkers and their wives tended to spend the men's leisure hours separately at the turn of the century. Louise Odencrantz, writing of Italian immigrants in Manhattan at that time, observed that "the mother had no recreation and the father took his alone."[157] In Pittsburgh families did not participate in the holidays organized by workingmen. Some mill and glass house workers enjoyed their leisure time in fishing clubs, which provided a vacation in the country during the glass industry's annual summer closing. The glass houses shut down in late June or early July, and for "two weeks after that every man fortunate enough to belong to a fishing club would be in camp."[158] Other workers envied the glass house men their guaranteed vacation even though it meant no wages for several weeks. The *Commoner and Glass Worker* lauded the "needful rest during the extremely hot weather" and pointed out that all work and no play made "Jack a dull boy." According to the paper, this rest period made for steadier employment, did not injure the trade, and refreshed and invigorated the workers for the months of labor to come.[159]

Whether the glass house worker received a vacation or the steelworkers simply took a week or two off without pay to go fishing in the summer or hunting in the autumn, the clubs belonged to men alone. When the men went out to "sport, frolic, and recuperate," their wives and children remained at home in the sticky Pittsburgh heat.[160] The PAIP attempted to send women and children to the country for a week or two but encountered initial resistance from the objects of their intended benevolence. Women dependent upon their own labors for support feared leaving their jobs for a week; the husbands of others would not let them go, since "they would be unable to get breakfast or supper with the wives away."[161] At the end of the century, the Kingsley House Settlement Association sponsored more successful outings for mothers and children. These trips provided the only rest some working-class women ever got other than confinements and illnesses. One mother, the Kingsley House *Annual Report* noted, "had not been out of Pittsburgh for seventeen years. Can you wonder that she said she would never forget this special week and that it was the happiest of her life?"[162] Occasionally women domestic workers accompanied their employers on vacation, still at work, but enjoying a change of scenery and cool ocean or mountain breezes.[163]

The circumscribed domesticity of most working-class women's lives limited them to a small radius around their homes, frequently no farther than church, shops, and fraternal organizations. Immigrant women, joining their husbands already at work in the Steel City, remained within the ethnic community and might be uncomfortable outside it, further narrowing their world. Vincenzo Scotti, who came to Pittsburgh in 1903, married an Italian immigrant woman, who, like many, had trouble adjusting to life in the city. "When I came home from work, I'd find her crying behind the door. The first few years were hard for everyone who came. She spent so much time in the Italian neighborhood she had a hard time learning English. I learned it right away, working."[164] It is unlikely that Mrs. Scotti would have been comfortable on a Kingsley House outing unless other Italian women went also.[165] She and thousands like her brought their children up in the language of the mother country, not the new one; the language of their streets was Italian or Polish or Slovak, not English. They felt uneasy in the world beyond their ethnic community and rarely went beyond its borders without their husbands or an English-speaking child to interpret.[166]

Although primarily oriented toward the world of home, working-class women were not necessarily isolated from all companionship. Michael Anderson had demonstrated that the proletarian women of Preston, England, maintained the family assistance networks.[167] In Pittsburgh, where immigrants might have no coresident kin, the women shared their resources among neighbors, though perhaps to a lesser extent than among relatives. Lodges and their visiting committees substituted for family in times of crisis in the Slavic community. The helping and neighborly behavior, which will be described below, had its specifically female component.[168] Women shared the tenement courts in which they scrubbed their laundry at the same time as their neighbors. They gathered at the pump or while shopping for a few minutes' gossip. They helped one another during confinements and emergencies.[169] The midwife herself was a neighbor who cooked for the family and stayed with the mother through delivery and afterward.[170] For women who did not speak the language of their new country, such contacts were especially significant, for it would have been very difficult for them to seek aid outside the boundaries of their family and neighborhood.

Working-class men no less than working-class women labored under stereotyped roles. In fact, the degree of domestic violence and disruptions suggests that the burdens of the male role exacted a toll. It was particularly difficult to support a family without ancillary workers in times of industrial depressions and high accident rates.[171] The external or nonhousehold perspective of the male meant that he spent little time at home because of the onerous hours of work and the location of much of the male social life in the tavern and fishing club.[172] Many men were devoted fathers and loving husbands. The extreme segregation of male and female roles and the physical exhaustion engendered by work in the mills placed added hurdles in the way of male participation in family life. Just as working-class women knew mostly the world of the household and rarely ventured outside it, so working-class men knew primarily the world of work and had a limited understanding of the world of the household itself.

Ironically, women's endeavors within the home enabled men to work long hours in the industries that gave Pittsburgh its identity. The entire society either ignored women's services, took them for granted, or glorified them beyond recognition. Working-class women's contributions were defined as a labor of love rather than as the productive work they actually were.[173] Any suggestion that they might move into paid employment, as some married women did in other cities, or might participate in voluntary activities outside the home met with the response that to do so would destroy the family. For women, marriage and family meant a round of chores and restricted horizons. For men, they meant wage labor under brutal conditions at hazardous jobs. These roles complemented each other; both partners were necessary to the family economy. Given the rigid segregation of their roles and the arduous nature of household work at this time, the family needed women's domestic services as much as it required men's wages. Pittsburgh's modern industrial economy rested as much upon these unpaid services as it did upon the work of the men in the mills.

8 | The Final Stages of the Life Cycle: Aging, Widowhood, and Death

Most women devoted their adult lives to caring for their families, raising their children, and making their homes as comfortable as possible within the constraints of the urban, industrial environment. Men's role was to earn the money needed to support their families, assisted by older sons and, increasingly, daughters. As the entire family aged, if the husband died, the children left home, or an elderly parent moved into a grown child's household, these roles could alter radically. Indeed, any change in the composition of the family forced the remaining members to accommodate their behavior to the new reality. Widowed women needed to earn money to support themselves and their families. Their children had adult responsibilities thrust upon them prematurely. Older men found their skills outmoded by rapid changes in industry and their strength insufficient to their tasks. Daughters and daughters-in-law were expected to house and care for aged parents (usually mothers). Aged women with children married and husbands dead needed to support themselves and fill their days. Many lived out their lives in contentment, nurtured and loved, but some were less fortunate. This chapter explores the images and realities of family breakdown through aging and death, how Pittsburgh residents cared for the widowed and elderly and buried the dead.

Essentially, Frederick Winslow Taylor supplanted Benjamin Franklin in the American pantheon. Those who could not produce were rapidly set aside for younger, more agile workers. These changes occurred

231

nationally and were most apparent in industrial towns such as Pittsburgh, where new processes in the steel mills quickly superseded traditional skills. College-trained engineers in white shirts supplanted numerous skilled iron- and steelworkers; mill laborers burned out young, and many mills banned older workers or relegated them to peripheral positions. As in so many aspects of society colored by the mills, the industrial economy left its sooty imprint on older women's lives. Widowhood was a common occurrence in the steel mill districts, and these women experienced great difficulty in supporting themselves in a city that had so few occupations open to females.[1]

Nevertheless, technological and organizational changes account for only a portion of the shift in the perceptions of the elderly and the way they lived out their senescence. As urbanization progressed, cities left behind their older population. Younger couples with families moved to the new sections of the city, whether suburban homes of the middle and upper classes or industrial suburbs of the working class, while older Pittsburghers remained concentrated in the original districts.[2] This increased residential segregation reflected the physical immobility of older people, itself a reflection of their roots in older occupations and their relative poverty. The physical separation of young and old, like that of the working and middle classes, gave rise to institutions and agencies that cared for some small portion of the population left behind by urban expansion. The new institutions attested to the poverty endured by many in their old age, particularly women, and the difficulty experienced by informal and familial networks in coping with the problems of aging and the elderly in an urban, industrial society with a high degree of population mobility. They suggest that society no longer perceived the aged as making valuable contributions and so forced them to one side.

Images of the Aged

Historians of old age maintain that attitudes toward the elderly became more negative during the nineteenth century, although the precise timing of this decline in esteem varies. David Hackett Fischer places it between 1770 and 1820, whereas W. Andrew Achenbaum locates it between the Civil War and World War I. Carole Haber believes both these historians neglect the negative valuation of certain members of society, typically those who were propertyless or without family who would protect and care for them. William Graebner's study of retirement finds that by the beginning of the twentieth century, Americans began to perceive aging as a matter for social concern.[3] Without becoming enmeshed in the debate over whether there ever was a "Golden Age" for the elderly in North America or trying to find a precise turning point for older Americans, an examination of the changing nature of the economy and some critical shifts within the family economy help one to understand why old age came to be seen as a problem rather than merely another stage in the life cycle by the late nineteenth century.

The mobility inherent in the U.S. economy, with people moving frequently in search of work, with new types of work outmoding older skills, and with a growing emphasis on wringing the last drop of effort from employees tied to the pace of tireless machines, all served to isolate and segregate older people from those still in the labor force. As family size declined, parents were also cut adrift from the economic support that nearly grown children could provide, and population mobility might mean they lived distant from their kin. As late as 1850 large families and foreshortened life spans meant that parents rarely survived the marriage of their last-born children by more than a few years. By 1890 the average father experienced a seven-year gap between these events, and for mothers the empty-nest period lasted for about fifteen years.[4]

Many trends coalesced in the decades between the Civil War and World War I. As Achenbaum suggests, the advice of scientists and professionals replaced the wisdom of experience in an increasingly technological and bureaucratic society. Advancing medical knowledge and the development of the helping professions generally led the Progressives to categorize older people as in need of aid precisely because of their advanced years. This, coupled with employers' desire to introduce new labor techniques and speed up their machines, led to a view of the elderly as slow and irrelevant. After the turn of the century, pensions served to tie workers to their employers and to retire them when they were no longer considered able to keep up. In their own defense, some older workers tried to hide their age from their employers in order to keep their jobs from being given to younger men.[5]

Susan Tamke's insightful study of attitudes toward the elderly points to three models of older people in the didactic literature of the Victorian nursery. There were wise and moral old people, who were essentially passive; foolish or malevolent elderly, whose conduct was inappropriate to their years; and old people who had no behavior at all, who were neither good or bad, merely old and typically the target of abuse or ridicule from younger members of their society.[6] A similarly tripartite image of aging appeared in the proletarian press of Pittsburgh during these years: the aged as lonely and poor; those who felt content and had pleasant reminiscences (this corresponds to Tamke's first category); and lastly, the old who needed assistance and received it from within their own community or family. Each depiction of the aged conformed to various working-class experiences in the Steel City but could be found in other cities as well.[7]

The first and most tragic theme characterized old age as a time of poverty, physical disability, and loneliness. Entitled "Poor and Forsaken," the following poem portrayed the so-called golden years in negative terms for older women who struggled in isolated pauperism with no family to care for or to comfort them.

> Only a woman, shrivel'd and old
>> The prey of the winds, and the prey of the Cold
>> Cheeks that are sunken
>> Lips that were never o'er bold:
> Only a woman, forsaken and poor
>> Asking an alms at the bronze church door.
>
> . . . .
>
> Only a woman—waiting alone
>> Icily cold on an ice cold throne
>> What do they care for her
>> Mumbling a prayer for her
>> Giving not bread but a stone
> Under the gold laces their haughty hearts beat
>> Mocking the woes of their kin in the street.[8]

The old woman's age and poverty made her an object of pity for the laboring readers of the *National Labor Tribune*, a point enhanced by the reference to the haughty hearts of the gold lace set, for by implication the working man or woman would have dropped a few pennies in her cup.

The image of old age as a time of contentment and pleasant reminiscences applied to couples rather than to widowed women. Alice Cary's poem "Old Folks" counseled acceptance of aging, as the husband addressed his wife:

> We are old folks now, my darling
>> Our heads they are growing grey;
> But taking the year all round my dear,
>> You will always find the May.
>
> We had our May, my darling,
>> And our roses, long ago
> And the time of year is coming, my dear
>> For the silent night and the snow.[9]

The wise older person accepted aging as an inevitable part of life, senescence.

But whereas earlier Americans might have venerated the elderly, by the late nineteenth century they were seen as dependents, and dutiful children returned the care that good parents had lavished on them while young.[10] Mary E. Lambert's poem "Rewarded" contained a clear message for young and old alike: if you would have a comfortable old age, provide one for your own parents. In this poem a 5-year-old notices her mother's hands are wrinkled, to which her mother responds:

> "Yes, child" I answered "I am growing old,"
>> And then I lifted her upon my knee,
> And asked "my darling, in the years to come,
>> When I am helpless, who will care for me?"
>
> "Why, Mamma dear, you care for Grandma now;
>> When you're real old, I'll tell you what I'll do—
> I'll be a woman, you can live with me,
>> And Mamma darling, I'll take care of you."[11]

Such poetic sentiments depicted the elderly as dependents not capable of managing for themselves, but they also showed how important the family was in providing for the elderly, a point that will be enlarged upon later.

Even the activities of the elderly in their last years reflected a need to be cared for: a considerate family placed tongs near grandfather's chair so that he might stir the fire with ease. Grandmother sat in her high-backed chair on the other side of the fireplace, knitting,

> And Nellie takes up the stitches dropped
>   For grandmother's eyes are dim.
> Their children came and read the news
>   To pass the time of day.[12]

The infirmities of the aged couple necessitated assistance from the young. The author enjoined readers:

> Be kind unto the old, my friend;
>   They're worn by their world's strife,
> Though bravely once perchance they fought
>   The stern fierce battle of life.
> They taught our youthful feet to climb
>   Upward life's rugged step;
> Then let us lead them gently down
>   To where the weary sleep.[13]

These authors depicted old age as a time of physical debility, but the more fortunate among the elderly had family who guided them through the last years, sheltered and eased them gently to their reward. How well did the poems mirror the life experience of Pittsburgh's elderly population? The portrayal of the solitary poor old age, the pleasant contentment by the hearthside of the couple who accepted their years, and the comfortable old age surrounded by loving, caring family, reflected the diversity of the experience of aging, as molded by industry and city.

Aging and the Mills

The iron and steel industries required strong workers and made brutal demands on their bodies. Although some industrial jobs required skill and training, most also required sheer physical strength, and as a result older workers experienced downward mobility. As their strength gave out, older men left their skilled and better-paying jobs to return to the ranks of the unskilled, where many had begun work forty or fifty years earlier. In both 1880 and 1900 nearly two-thirds of the men over 60 held unskilled laboring and industrial positions while less than one-half of the 20–59-year-olds did so. Despite this occupational sliding, most older men remained in the labor force in their advanced years. Three-fifths of all men over 65 held jobs in 1900, but the percentage of older men among the iron- and steelworkers declined from 1.4 percent (over 60) in 1880 to 0.7 percent (over 65) in 1900.[14]

Abraham Epstein, who investigated the conditions of black steel-workers for the Pittsburgh Survey and later conducted the fieldwork that formed the 1919 Pennsylvania Commission Report on Old Age Pensions, wrote that "advancing age is looked upon with great apprehension and dread even by many who are engaged in the skilled trades." Epstein concluded, perhaps melodramatically, that the thought of helplessness gradually filled workers with fear as the prospect of the poorhouse, so detestable to the honest wage earner, haunted him like a dark shadow and sapped his vitality.[15] Even skilled older workers were forced down the occupational hierarchy into the ranks of common laborers, lowering their incomes at precisely the same time as their children started their own families and thus curtailed their contributions to their parents' house-hold.[16]

The men who worked in the mills felt the debilitating nature of their employment and the toll it took as they grew older. John A. Fitch, investigating the lives of steelworkers at the turn of the century, wrote that he was often "told by workmen of forty and forty-five that they had been at their best at thirty years of age, and that at thirty-five they had begun to feel a perceptible decline in strength."[17] Thomas Bell's novelistic treat-ment of steelworkers observed that "there were men, young and lusty, who could go swinging home at the end of the long turn but after a man passed thirty he plodded like the oldest, shoulders slumped, legs heavy, bloodshot eyes burning in a blackened face." Years of work in the mills, where temperatures regularly exceeded 100 degrees Fahrenheit, where the air was thick with dust, and where accidents maimed if they did not kill, meant that a man's strength went with his youth. Their lives were foreshortened by a routine of twelve-hour shifts and the fortnightly long turn, a routine of work, meals, and a 9 P.M. bedtime in order to get them through the next day's work.[18]

The prevailing attitude in large firms during the nineteenth century was that workers were dispensable commodities, to be used up, then tossed out. In 1874, "A Toiler" wrote "God Bless the Workingman" to lament the common practice of keeping men on the job only as long as they had the strength of youth.

> And often, when a man grows old,
>   And cannot work so hard—
> They give to him, in accents cold,
>   A very strange reward:
> "We've kept thee, now," to him they say,
>   "As long as e'er we can—
> Therefore we must send thee away,
>   And find a younger man."[19]

As a result of employers' attitudes, older laboring men experienced higher rates of unemployment than other Pittsburgh workers, for once fired they had difficulty locating new jobs.[20] Some firms consciously excluded older workers: men who could not keep pace with the machines were a liability in efficiency-conscious Pittsburgh, and the steel companies discharged them. In 1904 the Carnegie Steel Company codified informal policy by refusing to hire men over 40 and employing men over 35 only in certain departments of the mill. Another large steel producer, the American Steel and Wire Company, refused to hire inexperienced hands over 35 or experienced ones over 45.[21] Clearly, the mill owners valued their workers for their brawn and ability to toil alongside the relentless furnaces as skill and accumulated wisdom became steadily less important to the industry. Through the end of the century, workers retired by company policy received no pension benefits and had only their savings or private pensions to sustain them through old age. The American Steel and Wire Company gave pensions in 1902, as did Andrew Carnegie through his relief fund for "long and faithful service," with somewhat limited coverage.[22]

Though the employment picture looked bleak for older laborers and skilled workers at the turn of the century, it was less so for businessmen, white-collar workers, and professionals (see table 34). They continued working after manual workers had left the labor force. Clergymen remained active in their profession longer than most: 8 percent of Pittsburgh ministers were over 65 in 1900, although the proportion of older clergy was lower there than elsewhere in the nation.[23] Merchants also continued working in their later years, but blue-collar workers were, on the whole, younger than the white-collar strata. Those who had a craft at their command, such as carpenters, remained longer in the labor force than those who offered only their physical prowess, such as laborers. The majority of older men in the labor force held unskilled jobs.

Excluded by company policy, few iron- and steelworkers remained on the job past their sixty-fifth birthday, and, in fact, relatively few were employed past the age of 45. Steel mill rules, however, did not require the firing of their white-collar employees in their middle years or even at 65. The men in the offices were kept on long past the age at which manual workers were fired. The mill owners suspended the rules against hiring those over 45 "in the case of 'special' or professional services, which indicated an expectation of physical deterioration on the part of mill workers at an age when professional men were still deemed capable of discharging their duties," John Fitch noted.[24] Employment prospects for white-collar and professional workers, then, remained good as they aged, but they were bleak for manual workers who no longer had the physical strength or agility required by the mill owners.[25]

Table 34. Age Distribution of Selected Occupations of Men, 1900
(In Percentages)

	10–24	25–44	45–64	65+	N
Clergymen	2.6	51.5	37.9	8.0	390
Merchants	8.4	59.0	28.2	4.4	3,791
Carpenters	12.4	54.0	30.1	3.5	2,628
Laborers	28.4	52.8	17.0	1.8	23,430
Iron- and steelworkers	27.7	54.3	17.3	.7	9,641

Source: U.S. Census, Twelfth Census 1900, vol. 2, Population, pt. 2, pp. 679–81.

In this era, working-class men rarely retired voluntarily; usually an accident, declining health, or the employer's policy forced them out of the mills. They did not retire voluntarily because they could not afford to be without an income. Many suffered reduced income due to accidents. By the age of 50, more than one-half of the steelworkers had either stopped work altogether or worked less than full time because of injuries and illnesses.[26] Low wages and unsteady employment prevented these workers from making adequate provision for their old age. About four-fifths of the iron- and steelworkers in 1891 earned less than the $600 per year that authorities believed necessary to support a family of five. Such families relied upon multiple wage earners to sustain themselves. Expenses decreased as the children left home to establish their own households, but income fell faster, leaving many older couples in dire financial straits.[27] Most working-class men stayed in the labor force, even if they only worked sporadically, because they could not afford to leave the workaday world behind.

Widowhood

In contrast it took a crisis, the death of the breadwinner, to force older women into the labor force. Both in 1880 and in 1900, about 12 percent of the female population in Pittsburgh were widows, a figure that approximated the national average despite the city's relatively young population base. Many widows were poorer women whose husbands had worked in the dangerous trades and who endured lower standards of living. In 1880 more than one-fifth of the households in the neighborhoods surrounding the mills were headed by widowed women, compared with only one-tenth of those in the more affluent suburban wards. In 1900, 9 percent of the native-born white women 20 years old or older had lost their spouses, whereas 15 percent of the black women and 16 percent of the foreign-born women were widows.[28]

While the disruption of the family unit through the death of a partner could happen through the death of either spouse and to any ethnic group or class, it mostly resulted from the husband's early demise, particularly among the working class. Of all people widowed in Pittsburgh 73 percent were women, many of them with young families. As table 35 shows, in 1880, 19 percent of the women 20–39-years-old and in 1900, 28 percent of those aged 20–44 were widows. Since these women found it difficult to remarry (the marriage certificates both in 1885–86 and in 1900 contained many more widowers than widows), they had the problem of supporting themselves and their children in Pittsburgh's economy. Widows in the middle years usually had nearly grown children upon whom to rely for support, but those with young children had few resources other than their own labor. For many, then, their bereavement precipitated entrance into the labor force; about 10 percent of Pittsburgh's working women in 1900 had been widowed, and 21 percent of all widowed women worked, a figure that contrasted sharply with the proportion of married women in the labor force, which was less than 3 percent.[29]

For women, widowhood rather than aging per se represented the sharpest discontinuity with earlier years since a woman's social and economic status both came from her marriage. She lost these with the death of her husband. Helen Znaniecki Lopata notes in her sociological analysis of widowhood that the widow's "status is not as high as that of the wife, since women have traditionally derived most of their social position from that of their husband."[30] Widowhood left women bereft of mate, income, and place in society simultaneously; in a culture where daily life revolved around the man's coming and going, the husband's death deprived the woman of the linchpin of her existence. His death

Table 35. Age Distribution of Widows
(In Percentages)

	20–29	30–39	40–49	50–59	60+	
1880 (N = 326)	4	15	30	26	25	
	Under 25	25–34	35–44	45–54	55–64	65+
1900 (N = 10,821)	1	9	18	22	24	26

Sources: 1880 census sample; U.S. Census, Twelfth Census, 1900, vol. 2, Population, pt. 2, p. 338

could be an incalculable emotional loss with drastic economic and social consequences, for even when the man carried insurance, it rarely paid for more than the funeral, with perhaps enough left over for several months' maintenance.[31]

The laboring community responded with sympathy and support for widowed women. Raffles, collections, and contributions all helped those left without a breadwinner. Widows and orphans sold chances on the late breadwinner's possessions, hoping that the sympathy of his former colleagues would prompt them to purchase tickets for the watch, gun, cane, or, less commonly, piano or organ. The death of a puddler, Peter W. Miller, left his wife, Rose, in destitute circumstances and delicate health, so she raffled his silver watch. The union newspaper supported her cause, editorializing that "she is deserving of help and we hope all friends will give her assistance." Apparently they did so, for a letter from Mrs. Miller expressed "her heartfelt thanks to James Carey and the puddlers of McKnights' Rolling Mill and of Lew, Oliver, and Phillips Rolling Mill for their generous subscription" to her and her family.[32] Another raffle in May 1890 helped the widow of John J. Morgan, who died suddenly in February of that year, to pay the mortgage on the family home. The interval between his death and her appeal suggests that first she exhausted savings and spontaneous donations, then turned to a broader pool of contributors.[33] The *National Labor Tribune* offered a sewing machine to the group or individual who obtained sixty paid subscriptions, with the suggestion that the machine might be donated to a widow. "Is there not, depending upon your society," the newspaper inquired, "some poor widow to whom a sewing machine would be for years to come a blessing . . . a most valuable present for some needy family?"[34] The more fortunately situated responded to the obligation to assist needy widows and older women.

Yet widows could not rely upon the sustained support of the community, for despite the widespread sympathy to the plight of the widow and her orphaned children, working-class families had little enough to share during these economically troubled decades. A widow of one generation counseled a younger one in *Out of This Furnace* that others would forget her trouble long before she did. "For a few days everybody is sorry for you; after that you're just another widow. And a widow—there are a hundred widows. Widows are nothing."[35] Indeed, widows were commonplace in Pittsburgh, and though not all were old, they shared a common problem with elderly women: that of support. As Michael Anderson's investigation of life among the textile workers of Lancashire during the 1850s demonstrates, widows' families led a precarious, poverty-stricken existence, living on inadequate diets, and though "they seldom actually died from starvation," they suffered the consequences of malnutrition, including lessened resistance to disease.[36] The charity authorities in Pittsburgh discovered similar cases. Ellen Silefsky, whose husband died in 1900, subsisted alone with her three children on the charity of neighbors. The "Polish priest" helped her pay the rent until the Department of Charities sent her to the poor farm and gave her children into the keeping of the Humane Society. She was, according to the Department of Charities, probably demented from malnutrition and beat her children when they cried for food.[37]

The Mrs. Silefskys of Pittsburgh with their small children had few choices open to them. They could try to locate work that would not take them away from home, subsist on charity, or have someone care for the children while they worked. Once again, the economic structure of the city limited the employment available. Since Pittsburgh's principal industries excluded women, there were few nondomestic opportunities. Even in good times, "when work for laboring men is comparatively easily obtained, the women who battle for bread do not share equally this prosperity." As a result, about three-quarters of the clientele of the PAIP were widows with young children trying to maintain their families through domestic service and washing clothes. Anderson found that no widows with children in Preston, England, entered household service, but in Pittsburgh some did.[38] As table 36 shows, domestic service was the most common employment for widowed and elderly women, followed for widows by sewing, washing, taking in boarders, and owning a small shop, and for the elderly by shopkeeping, sewing, midwifery, and taking boarders.

A study of widows partially supported by the Charity Organization Societies in nine U.S. cities discovered that although even widows with the home or took in laundry, sewing, or boarders.[39] Domestic service, as was noted in chapter 5, required the servant to live with her employers, but few middle-class families wanted to house the young children of their servants, nor did many women who had run their own homes wish to be relegated to the rank of servant and subordinate in someone else's. These factors help to explain why the proportion of widowed and elderly women who undertook domestic work was lower than that of women workers generally. In 1900 29 percent of all widows but 53 percent of all employed women held such positions, though there was a great deal of variation between ethnic groups. Black widows had the greatest concentration in domestic service (45 percent), trailed distantly by foreign-born widows (27 percent) and native-born whites (24 percent). Similar discrepancies

Table 36. Occupation of Widows and Elderly Women, 1900
(In Percentages)

	Widows ($N=2,246$)	Elderly Women (65+ Years, $N=164$)
Domestic Servant[a]	29.3	27.4
Sewing worker[b]	13.4	11.6
Laundress	12.4	3.1
Boardinghouse keeper	10.1	5.5
Merchant/Dealer	9.9	18.3
White collar[c]	4.6	1.8
Nurse/Midwife	4.1	6.7
Janitor/Sexton	2.9	1.2
Teacher	2.2	3.7
Miscellaneous manufacturing workers[d]	1.7	3.7
Proportion of female workers accounted for	90.6	83.0

Source: U.S. Census, Twelfth Census, 1900, vol. 2, Population, pt. 2, p. 682–83.

a. Includes housekeepers, stewardesses, servants, and waitresses.

b. Includes dressmakers, milliners, seamstresses, and tailoresses.

c. Includes agents, bookkeepers, clerks, messengers, errand and office girls, packers and shippers, saleswomen, stenographers, typewriters, telephone and telegraph operators.

d. Includes bakers, bookbinders, boxmakers, confectioners, glassworkers, iron- and steelworkers, printers, and tobacco and cigar operators.

among ethnic groups existed in the proportion who lived with employers rather than in their own homes or those of relatives: 29 percent of all widowed women lived in, compared with 43 percent of all single women workers. The proportion of widows living in varied from 27 percent among white working widows to 39 percent of comparable black women.[40] As table 37 shows, widowed women workers were far more likely than others to be heads of households, rather than living in employers' households or with parents or other relatives.

The unwillingness of employers to house their servants' children meant that women who turned to domestic service for sustenance needed alternate shelter for their children. The Western Pennsylvania Humane Society furnished many widowed women with positions as servants and housekeepers and facilitated the placement of their children in orphanages. Mrs. Wright appealed to the society to place her son in the Newsboys' Home in 1889; she had no way to earn a living except by household service, but she did not want to lose the boy permanently. Mrs. Bingham placed her three daughters in the Children's Temporary Home. Another widow placed her 5-year-old son at the Gusky Orphanage in the hope that she might be able to support herself and an older daughter.[41] In each instance the widowed mother believed she had no option but to break up her home in order to find employment.

The Pittsburgh Survey investigated the problems of half-orphanage

Table 37. Marital Status and Residence of Working Women, 1900
(In Percentages)

| | Residence | | | |
	At Home as Head of Family	With Parent(s)	With Other Relative[a]	Boarded by Employer
Single (N = 18,300)	3	45	9	43
Married (N = 1,532)	20	10	40	30
Widowed/Divorced (N = 2,373)	57	7	7	29

Source: U.S. Census, Twelfth Census, 1900, Special Report: Statistics of Women at Work, p. 287
a. Includes husband.

through an examination of children's institutions in the city. Although widowers comprised a far smaller proportion of the population than widows, they were more likely to institutionalize their children. One-quarter of the children's home residents were fatherless, but one-third were motherless. The Survey explained that when faced with the loss of the breadwinner, mothers turned to institutions as "isles of safety" for their children.[42] Yet it was fathers, at work all day and possibly lacking a daughter old enough to undertake the mother's role, who depended upon these homes. The Humane Society advised a South Side laborer, Mr. Kunbe, to place his children in St. Joseph's Orphan Asylum after finding that he made "very small wages, consequently the children are neglected." He consented readily since their mother was dead. While Mr. Kunbe, Mrs. Wright, and Mrs. Bingham were relieved to find shelter for their children, some widows rejected friendly visitors' advice to place offspring in orphanages. Mrs. Burns supported her family with the help of her laborer son and domestic servant daughter. She went out washing and cleaning every day she got work, leaving her three youngest children in charge of the older daughter, who mostly lived out. When she was not home, the oldest little girl looked after the baby. Mrs. Burns was most exercised over complaints about her behavior, stating that some of the missionary women wanted her to place the children in a home.[43]

Other women with young children took in washing to make ends meet. About 12 percent of all working widows took in laundry, and these lived in their own homes. From the prevalence of washerwomen in the charitable agency caseloads, laundry work seems to have been an occupational last resort for older women or widows with children they did not wish to institutionalize and with strength but few marketable skills. About one-third of the caseload of the PAIP washed clothes for a living. The supply of washerwomen exceeded the demand, and so wages were low. Since many of the families who had their washing done for them left the city in the summer, year-round unemployment was uncertain.[44]

Washing clothes was heavy physical labor requiring the carrying of buckets of water and the wringing out of heavy wet clothes and bed linen. This explains why so few old women (3 percent) took in laundry (see table 36).[45] Taking in washing had other disadvantages for the washerwomen had to travel throughout the city either laundering in other people's homes or picking up the clothes, which they carried home to wash. Mrs. Wurl, a widowed German immigrant who spoke little English, left her 7- and 11-year-old daughters alone for long periods during the day while she picked up and delivered the washing, as did Mrs. Burns, whose three little children were under the casual supervision of her oldest daughter. Mrs. Smith, living on the South Side, went out washing, relying on neighbors to look in on her two sons. Informal community support from a neighbor or relative who might keep an eye on the children enabled many women to support themselves and their families until an older child could share the burden.[46] The precarious living they made kept away the "gaunt wolf of starvation" while more fortunate women helped by turning a neighborly eye on the children at home.[47]

In recognition of the significance of washing to widowed women seeking to support themselves, the PAIP opened a charity laundry in 1898, which the association claimed "made it possible for widows to keep their homes with their children under their own care." The laundry furnished work to "thousands" and arranged its hours so that mothers could work while the children attended school. It actually trained the women in "high class laundry work," then recommended them to outsiders. The wages paid in the laundry indicate that the price of charity was low indeed; in 1914, the "Improvement Laundry" paid its employees $329 for working a 49-hour week, 302 days a year. The widows earned little more than a dollar a day, about 60 percent of the wages paid to common laborers.[48]

Most of the women over 65 and widows whom the census listed as "merchants, dealers, and peddlers" owned small shops, frequently in their own front rooms or inherited from their late husbands. They came into their own as businesswomen late in life, and many of the enterprises were quite marginal. In 1887 the Law and Order Society campaigned to close small shops on Sunday in order that the Sabbath might be observed with decorum, although there was never any mention of closing the mills. *Commoner and Glass Worker* reacted to the puritanical blue laws by suggesting that they injured the poor most severely. "There is a poor old widow women away down in Mansfield who keeps a little cigar store.

Her son and her only support was killed on the railroad less than a year ago. It has been reported that this old lady has committed the terrible crime of selling on Sunday. Arrest her quick in the interest of public peace and morality and add another to the list of persecuted cripples and orphans."[49] The poor widow in Mansfield may not have been arrested, but the Allegheny City magistrates' dockets show that other women were, including the one who ostensibly sold liquor without a license in her cigar store. The store consisted of a room in her house where a German singing society also met on Saturday evenings. Another woman arrested for selling liquor without a license in a little store near the mills on 2nd Avenue had three small children to support.[50] Such small shops enabled mothers to care for their children and make a living at the same time, but they depended upon an initial capital investment that women from the poorest stratum of the working class could not make.[51]

Once the widow's children were old enough to leave school, they contributed their share to the family earnings, and the mother may then have retired from the labor force. As was shown in chapters 4 and 6, widows' children, particularly the sons, began work earlier than other young people. They also continued to reside with their mothers long after their peers from two-parent families had left the nest. Eighteen percent of all widows' sons and 14 percent of their daughters living at home were over the age of 25 (see table 38). Only 3 percent of all working- and

Table 38. Children Living at Home Over the Age of 25, by Socioeconomic Class of Parent, 1880

| | Class of Parent | | | | | | | | | |
| | Working[a] | | Middle | | Upper | | Widow | | Average | |
	N	%	N	%	N	%	N	%	N	%
Male	76	3	12	3	22	7	69	18	179	5
Female	47	2	7	2	26	10	53	14	133	4

Source: 1880 census sample.

a. There was no difference in the proportion of unskilled and skilled workers' children living at home.

middle-class boys and 2 percent of their sisters still at home were in that age group. This highlights the extent to which widows depended upon their children for support. Widows' sons and daughters shouldered this burden even though it meant delaying the start of their own families.

The instances of children not supporting aged or widowed parents in the reports of the Humane Society and in the newspapers give the impression that sons were more likely to shirk this responsibility than daughters. Whether young women had greater sympathy for their mothers' plight, or sons' movement about the city in search of work caused them to feel less duty toward their mothers is unclear.[52] In light of the larger number of sons living at home after the age of 25, such cases may reflect greater obligations placed upon male offspring for financial aid. The few scattered cases of neglect recorded in newspapers and welfare organization records provide no evidence that relatives were more apt to care for elderly of the same sex.[53] John Rogan, aged 63, had no occupation and said he had no home. He did have two sons connected with the Fire Department in Pittsburgh who declined to support their father. When the old man took ill in public, one son told the police to "dispose of him as they saw fit," and the other acquiesced, so the father went to Marshalsea, the city poor farm.[54] Other men treated their older relatives more sympathetically, as a short article in *Commoner and Glass Worker* indicated. Peter Shields, a staunch Knights of Labor member, "lost his best friend this week by the death of his grandmother, Mrs. Ann Shields. She was 73 years old and made her home with Peter."[55]

Rogan's sons refused to succor their father during his last years, though Shields cared for his grandmother until her death. Shields's actions were more acceptable in the working-class milieu, as a short story in the *National Labor Tribune* illustrated. An aged widow supports herself selling apples on the wharf because her son does not help her. The young man gets engaged, but upon discovering his neglect, his intended breaks the engagement. The selfish son would not make a kindly husband. He is subsequently injured in a train accident, and his mother nobly cares for him. In a romantic ending, the young people marry and the mother lives with them, supported by son and cherished daughter-in-law.[56] Some sons grew into a sense of responsibility for their aged parents, but others, like the Rogans, never did. Their callousness left their aged parents dependent upon the city's reluctant largesse.

Residential Patterns

Few older people of either sex actually lived by themselves. Some widowed women became heads of household following the death of their husbands, keeping unmarried children or boarders with them, but others rented a room in another person's home or lived with their children. Older men experienced less household restructuring than women, for they typically lived with their wives in their own homes until they died. In 1880, 25 percent of Pittsburgh's older women resided with their children, while 7 percent of the older men did. At this time, all ethnic groups equally accepted the obligation to care for aged parents: 14 percent of the German, 15 percent of the native-born white, and 17 percent of the Irish elderly lived with their children.[57] The pattern in Pittsburgh followed that of other cities, where less than 10 percent of the men but substantially more aged women lived with relatives, typically their children.[58] Although coresident parents contributed their labor to the household, few of the men and none of the women who lived with their children were in the labor force, and this implies that parents moved in with their grown children only if they could no longer support themselves without assistance.[59]

Wealth data from the 1860 census for Pittsburgh reinforce the notion that poverty of the parents led to coresidence. In 1860, 90 percent of the older women sampled owned no property, whereas that owned by the rest had a value of between $1 and $100. For men, old age could be a time of extremes: more old men were propertyless than any other group of men over 35, but those who did own property tended to be somewhat wealthier than the younger men.[60] A national study of old age dependency in the United States conducted after the turn of the century showed that individual nondependent aged women had an income of $4.50 a week, more than half of which came from relatives, while that of aged men was $7.32, with one-third coming from relatives.[61] These data cannot be applied directly to Pittsburgh, but they do suggest the precarious position of older people, particularly women. Living with daughters or sons enabled widowed women and unemployed men to avoid the utter destitution that might otherwise have been their fate.[62]

Coresidence was not a panacea, however, for some sons and daughters accepted their parents' presence but did not treat them kindly. One aged mother in a short story in the *National Labor Tribune* was passed from child to child after she had grown "too old to be useful in their houses."[63] This story reflected nonfiction reality to some aged Pittsburghers. Peter Kinsley, a laborer, abused his mother so violently that the PAIP requested Humane Society intervention. Kinsley mistreated his mother physically, kicked her, and evicted her from the home they shared. Her only recourse was to institute a suit against him for assault and battery, which she was reluctant to do because he was her sole means of support.[64] James Madison also attacked his widowed mother, who lived with him and his sister. In this case the sister intervened by having her brother arrested and undertaking her mother's maintenance.[65]

Relatives were the primary caretakers of the aged. Few children who had the resources refused to assist an elderly parent, but social surveyors concluded that the older persons suffered because they lost their independence and became burdensome to their children. In turn, the children might lose respect for the parents, while the third generation also suffered as resources and parents' energies were diverted away from them to care for their grandparents.[66] Supporting an aged parent might entail genuine hardship for the working-class son or daughter who undertook the task, for it could stretch limited resources to the breaking point. Jesse Fritz, who was old and blind, lived with his son and daughter-in-law and their several children. Although the daughter-in-law took in washing, they still could not make ends meet. According to the agent of the Humane Society, "the old man was a great charge on this poor woman." She could not care for her own family, do the extra washing, and care for her invalid father-in-law all at the same time. The family's effort to maintain Mr. Fritz at home reflected the strength of kinship ties and the horror that hung over many at the thought of ending their days at the county poor farm or of consigning an aged relative there.[67]

Most older people, of course, did not reside with their children. In some cases pride combined with a lack of resources resulted in the elderly enduring appalling conditions. A few older couples were like Mrs. Zella and her husband, who lived in two rooms of an old farmhouse surrounded by ill-fed cats and dogs. She was a "decrepit little woman," and he was old, feeble, and "very sick, unable to move about." They could not care for themselves. The man was willing to go to one of the charity hospitals, but the woman refused to go to the poor farm. Ultimately, her husband went to the hospital, the cats and dogs went to the rendering plant, and the woman moved to another dwelling after the Board of Health condemned her home.[68]

Senescence and the Social Services

Conditions such as these prompted Pittsburgh's middle class to establish a wide variety of social service institutions as the nineteenth century progressed. These institutions filled some of the gaps in services provided by individuals, families, and working-class organizations and expanded services beyond the limitations of public generosity and the public purse. The primary public welfare agency, the Board of Guardians of the Poor (after 1887, the Department of Charities), preferred institutionalization of those who sought assistance to outdoor relief (aid given to people in their own homes), which reflected national trends in the care of the less fortunate.

The City Poor Home sheltered approximately three hundred persons, some old, some destitute, and some in poor health. According to a state investigation conducted in 1876, the City Home was carefully managed. The numerous inmates were "judiciously distributed, if not in accordance with the strictest rules of classification in all cases so desirable, yet with so great a regard for their comfort as unfavorable circumstances will admit of." But the home was too small to contain all those who needed its services. Although the city built a separate insane asylum in 1873 and a new City Home in 1893, not everyone who sought admittance could be accommodated.[69] Some elderly went from one agency to another until they were finally admitted or gave up trying. The following example comes from the records of the Western Pennsylvania

Humane Society, whose jurisdiction the state limited to children and animals but which sometimes became involved with other needy souls. It could as easily have come from the records of the PAIP or any other of the agencies that did outreach work in working-class neighborhoods. "An old German lady, Louisa Matkofsky, was sent to the office for me to get her admitted to the City Farm. I took her up to the Office of Public Charities and learned that she had been there twice before but was refused. After I had talked to them for some time they finally gave her a permit and sent her up on the 11 o'clock train."[70]

Since the City Home was crowded and the poor numerous, there was considerable sentiment against young, fertile couples cohabiting there. The state viewed this as being "of very questionable propriety" because it tended to increase the pauper population. There were, however, no similar scruples or anxieties about older couples living together at the city's expense. "That the aged husband and wife should cohabit together in these poor homes is entirely clear and freely admitted." Although there are no records to indicate whether aged couples actually shared rooms in the Pittsburgh City Home, at least the Board of Commissioners of Public Charities of the State of Pennsylvania, which set general policy, felt that personal contact among elderly couples was acceptable and to be encouraged by institutional arrangements.[71] Other almhouses kept the sexes segregated in separate buildings.[72]

The City Home could not serve all who needed its facilities, nor did all the indigent, regardless of age, wish to be uprooted from friends, family, and familiar surroundings. Outdoor relief (coal, shoes, and groceries given to people who lived in their own homes rather than institutions) was not obtained easily, particularly for the older person with impaired mobility. The Guardians of the Poor and their successors designed application procedures to weed out all but the most deserving, or perhaps the most persistent, thus reducing the charitable burden upon the taxpayers. Applicants had to appear at the City Office to present an account of their circumstances. In a period of poor and relatively expensive public transportation, this presented an obstacle to relief for the weak and ailing. If applicants convinced the clerk of their need, an investigator visited them in their homes to establish the legitimacy of their claims; only then was relief given. Only coal was actually delivered to the home; groceries, shoes, and clothes had to be picked up at the City Office by the needy person.[73] This system was intended to protect the city from potential welfare abuses. Nevertheless, the humiliation involved in proving destitution inhibited many needy elderly from making an application. Others found it physically impossible to make the long trip to the Guardians' offices. The public charity system excluded many indigent through its application procedures and worked particular hardships on the elderly and infirm.

The general intransigence of the public relief agency led to the establishment of private welfare organizations by concerned, comfortably situated women. Though the elderly were not the first concern of these philanthropies, as distance between older and younger Pittsburgh residents grew, so did separate institutions and organizations for their care. The first such institution for the aged was the Home for Aged Protestant Women established in 1869. The rules for entrance to the home indicated that the managers, like the Guardians of the Poor, believed it necessary to regulate and control the recipients of their largesse. Women over 60 gained admission after a thorough investigation into their circumstances and character.[74] The applicants, as in many such homes, came from the middle rank of society.[75] The Home for Aged Protestant Women was by no means a home for the transient poor. The women must have resided in Pittsburgh for at least ten years prior to admission and needed "satisfactory testimonials of the respectability of their character and propriety of their conduct." The home charged an admission fee of $150, "except where otherwise ordered." It offered a haven for genteel older women, not the indigent or improvident.[76] Ten years after opening, the home had sixty-four residents, of whom 25 percent never had been married. The rules implied that the inmate had no family who would care for her or be interested in her circumstances. Several references were made to friends of the inmates, but none at all to their families. This emphasizes a point made by other students of the aged: those who required aid tended to be bereft of kin. As families were completed earlier and mobility severed communications between family members, the problems of the aged in urban settings became more acute.[77]

The home had strict rules of conduct for their aged Protestant women and dismissed at least one for "persistent disobedience". In effect, the home reduced its residents to the status of children, who were "to treat the Managers and the Matron with deference and respect and pay strict attention to all rules and regulations for the government of the Institution." The managers enforced certain behavioral norms, perhaps to separate their establishment from the City Home and other institutions for the destitute. The Home for Aged Protestant Women required its inmates "to endeavor by a quiet, gentle, and lady-like deportment, to diffuse an air of cheerfulness and good feeling through the whole establishment." They were expected to behave with compassion toward others and through "acts of kindness and forbearance to gain the esteem and promote the comfort and happiness of each other."[78]

The home was a way of life, a surrogate family, with the matron and the Board of Visitors taking the place of parents. Rules preserved "order and harmony in the family." Aged Protestant women were expected "punctually to attend family prayers," notice of which was given by the ringing of a bell. The Board of Managers expected the residents to be active in the domestic affairs of the home, to keep their beds made and rooms swept and assist those physically unable to do so. The rules enjoined the women to "sew, knit, assist in domestic duties, and generally render all the service they can for the benefit of the Institution." This expectation reflected a general attitude that women in institutions were to perform household chores because they were women, although establishments for men hired others, almost always women, to do this work.[79]

As in many institutions, contact with the outside world was limited. An inmate who wanted to visit friends obtained permission from the Visiting Committee, "the time of making visits as well as their frequency" being at the committee's discretion. Friends of the inmates might visit on Wednesday afternoons between the hours of 2 and 5 P.M.[80] Residents led genteel, ordered, domestic lives somewhat removed from the general hurly-burly of the city. Women of some means retired to the home when they felt they could no longer manage urban life but did not wish to reside with their families or had none to take them in.

The home established a familial atmosphere for older women who presumably had no close kin. Other religious and social groups began similar institutions specifically to care for the elderly of their own group. By the end of the century, there were two Roman Catholic homes for the aged poor, which housed approximately three hundred persons. The Episcopal home provided shelter for aged Anglicans; a home for aged Protestant men and aged couples housed other denominations. The black community supported a small Home for Aged and Infirm Colored Women through fund raising. These divisions mirrored those found among orphan asylums, where blacks and whites and Protestants and Catholics lived in separate and generally segregated institutions.[81]

The development of these old age homes in the last quarter of the nineteenth century suggests a pervasive perception of the senescent as a "problem" for which institutionalization rather than outdoor relief or pensions was the short-term solution, particularly for women. As long as a ready supply of inexpensive labor existed through overseas immigration, steel company officials had little interest in using pensions as a lure to tie workers to their plants.[82] Although David Brody maintains in his masterful *Steelworkers in America* that "the promise of old-age assistance was in every case a powerful incentive toward company loyalty," few steelworkers in the decades between the beginning of the pension schemes and the closing of the gates to immigration actually received occupational pensions.[83] In 1919 the United States Steel Corporation and its subsidiaries had several hundred thousand employees but only 2,436 pensioners. Half the industrial firms in Pennsylvania with more than 500 workers had no pension system in operation as late as 1918. Less than one-tenth had a regular pension scheme, but one-fourth tried to give older employees lighter work.[84] The lack of such pensions and the difficulty of saving for old age led some older residents to seek shelter in denominational or secular residences for the elderly or, as a last resort, the city poor farm.

Though the Home for Aged Protestant Women was built on the edge of the city, some institutions for the aged sought to keep them in the community rather than removing them from it. The Widows' Home and Tenement House provided rooms at "moderate cost to widows with little children and to aged women."[85] In so doing it enabled them to live in the city, within reach of family and friends rather than removed from it and them. It recognized, as did the Widows' Home of Allegheny County, that most of Pittsburgh's widowed women had real problems making ends meet. These homes were designed as a refuge for "breadwinners who, unwilling to ask for alms or receive them, were wearing out their lives in miserable cellars or crowded houses striving to maintain their families, dreading the landlord's monthly claims which they felt to be their heaviest burden."[86] The homes for widowed women subsidized their residents, but at most, could accommodate approximately one hundred women and their dependent children. Their significance lay not in the number of residents but in their aim, which was to provide housing at a reduced cost and to enable older and widowed women to remain a part of their communities.

Indeed, most of the homes for the aged and widowed were quite small and provided shelter for a tiny portion of Pittsburgh's elderly and widowed population. Eighteen people lived in the German Protestant Home for the Aged. In 1895 the Home for Aged and Infirm Colored Women housed 14 women, and 17 resided in the home for the aged sponsored by the United Presbyterian Church's Women's Association.[87] Approximately 500 widowed and elderly lived in all the various homes at the turn of the century, but there were 3,370 men and 4,244 women over 65 and 10,846 widows in the Steel City in 1900.[88] Thus, about 3 percent of all the widowed and elderly population lived in public and private institutions as the twentieth century began.[89] The rest worked at unskilled jobs, turned to kin, particularly children, for support, or eked out a bare subsistence with some aid from charitable associations.[90]

For most older Pittsburgh residents, their last years were not the golden autumn of their days but rather a period of want and anxiety. Few men and fewer women had any income or savings; in some instances families could not provide for their parents' last years, and a few unfeeling children refused to aid their parents.[91] Many men were physically unable to work in Pittsburgh's strenuous industries where accumulated wisdom had little value because technological processes changed radically from the time when they first entered the mills. Job opportunities for older women remained severely constricted; hence few worked outside the home, but many resided with their children, or turned to charitable agencies.

Sex role stereotypes also played a part in shaping the experience of the elderly. Women with no trade but domesticity found it difficult to support themselves if widowed. If widowed while relatively young, they found it difficult to accumulate savings for old age.[92] Working-class men had greater access to jobs but still had trouble keeping up with the pace of the machines and the new skills introduced. Since men died younger than women, they were more likely to experience a comfortable old age, tended by wives who grew old in the service of the families, but who frequently had no means of support once their husbands died.

While old age could be a time of warmth and comfort by the fireside, it was not so for many working-class women and some men. The new institutions recognized the differences in the experience of old age for women and men when they concentrated their charity on aged women. Since their society valued production and older men were less productive than younger ones, they suffered some loss of status, but older women, particularly those with their children gone and their husbands dead, experienced a total loss of function. When they no longer had a family around whom to orient their activities, their old age became in many instances a time to wait for death.

Responses to Death

Popular attitudes toward death ironically reflected the social realities.[93] Even in death, working-class women received little recognition for their contribution to the industrial family economy. In Pittsburgh the incidence of infant and early childhood mortality far exceeded that of adult males, but the popular press chose to emphasize the deaths of men, particularly traumatic accident fatalities, virtually excluding children's and giving only passing mention to women's mortality. The reasons for this are rooted in the male-centeredness of Pittsburgh's working-class culture: life revolved around men, their work in the mills, and the income they brought home from them. In the asymmetrical family that developed in the Steel City, women and children were, to some extent, replaceable, but men were not. Families could and did have other children (although that does not mean they did not grieve for those who died). The marriage certificates filed in the city provide a clue to the ability of women and men to replace their partners. About 10 percent of the men but only 2 percent of the women married for the second time, so that although there were many more widows than widowers, few of them found another person willing to help them shoulder the burden of caring for and supporting their families.[94]

Bereaved parents turned to their older children for help if they did not remarry. In particular widow's sons entered the labor force earlier than their counterparts in two-parent families in an effort to help sustain their mothers and siblings. The late mother's responsibilities devolved upon the oldest female child. Friends told the daughter of Welsh immigrants that it was her job to rear her younger brothers and sisters, to bring them to Jesus and to train them for heaven following her mother's death. She did this with the help of her "sober, kind, and indulgent father."[95] She became mother as well as sister to her siblings and, it might be added, her father's housekeeper. One function she could not replace was that of nursing an infant. If the mother died in childbirth or as a result of it, the baby's health might suffer given the inadequacy of artificial formulas at this time.

Ann Douglas's analysis of consolation literature notes that "liberal clergymen and devout women were the principal authors of the mourner's manuals, lachrymose verse, obituary fiction, and necrophiliac biographies" of the mid–nineteenth century, so the characteristics of this literature can be taken to reflect "clerical and feminine ambitions."[96] The consolation literature, obituaries, and memorials of Pittsburgh's working class, however, were largely male in authorship and mirrored the attitudes and anxieties of working-class men in their own lives. Indeed, the obituaries of adult women in the proletarian press tended toward the formulaic and stressed their motherly qualities, wifely virtues, neighborliness, and Christian charity. For example, many families would miss the "kind and encouraging words and Christian-like acts" of Mrs. Cox, the deceased wife of a coal miner. Mrs. Hannah Hammet, the mother of several glassworkers, "had many friends in life." Oft recurring motifs succinctly expressed the ideal values of the workers who composed the obituaries. Many working-class women went to their reward namelessly, as did the "esteemed" but anonymous wife of Fred Herbster of Pittsburgh's Thirty-first Ward. Despite cheerful maternal attributes, women's memorials placed them in relation to their husbands and sons. Just as they had lived in the context of family and neighborhood, so they died, remembered as "estimable" wives with "motherly qualities" but without a record of their names or separate identities.[97]

Working-class men were described in more varied terms than their wives and mothers; their obituaries displayed their greater permissable range of jobs and behavior. With the exception of older men, retired from the labor force and occasionally eulogized as someone's father, men were rarely subsumed into their wives' or children's identities. In interchangeable formulae, men's obituaries spoke of them as "kind husbands and loving fathers" or "loving husbands and kind fathers." Their eulogies went beyond these phrases to emphasize their work, union activities, dispositions, and diligence. Reuben L. Martin's obituary epitomized the stylized memorials of the late nineteenth-century working-class male. He was a "first class" workman, a faithful member of the AAISW, and a "manly, upright, honest man."[98] Such tributes spoke well of the dead, fitting them into the male roles of good workers, good comrades, good union and family members, manly men all. They went to their reward as esteemed and respected citizens, with hosts of friends and genial dispositions. The death notices channeled grief, gave vent to it in socially provided modes, and reflected and encouraged an outpouring of solidarity within the working-class community.

The working class seldom spoke ill of their own dead. Indeed, the average obituary notice was "notoriously an inexact reflection of the estimation of the dead."[99] Courtesy toward the departed extended to the friends of the working class, including sympathetic mill managers, superintendents, and some owners, but excluded those who kept their wealth to themselves. Thus "Vanderbilt is dead, and so far as we now remember a most uncompromising and thoroughly selfish life has passed away" both stigmatized Cornelius Vanderbilt and highlighted the emphasis on generosity and neighborliness in other obituaries: the working class valued those who lent a hand at work, at home, or in the community. Obituaries attributed to the dead of both sexes the virtues desired in life.[100]

Death was a community affair in which family members were the chief mourners, although neighbors, workmates, and fellow trade unionists also participated. Relatives received their acquaintances' condolences and the community's "heartfelt sympathy" in their "sad bereavement" and "sore distress." People mourned the family's loss as well as the dead person's memory. Resolutions of condolence went to kin with advice to trust in God and accept the actions of Divine Providence. The working-class community expected the family to be bereft and acted accordingly. This communal aspect of funerals extended past the nuclear and into the extended family. In fact, the family reunion gave some funerals an almost festive atmosphere, according to the reminiscences of the director of the Allegheny County Funeral Directors' Association.[101]

By contrast, the family who did not rally around the dying or dead was treated with contempt. The employees of the Tyler Tube and Pipe Company, south of Pittsburgh, sneered at the father of one employee who refused to help his dying son. The father neither went for the body nor attended the funeral; instead he telegraphed the terse message, "Bury him there." The employees memorialized the father's unconcern on a tombstone inscribed "Buried by the employees of the Tyler Tube and Pipe Company. We take care of our sick and bury our dead." Since the father had shirked his obligations to his son, the ironworkers felt that "such treatment will surely get its just reward." The father's callousness violated working-class conventions and brought public shame through denunciation in the labor press.[102]

Funeral Customs

The working class shared some of the values epitomized by the middle-class rural cemetery movement. They wanted their dead to have picturesque graves like those of the worker's son buried "on a gentle slope overlooking the valley below where the first rays of the morning sun fall." But whereas the middle class bought family plots, laboring families purchased individual lots as the need arose. Cemeteries gave discounts to those who paid cash for large plots but charged interest to those who could not afford the full price and had to buy on the installment plan. They also discriminated against these single purchases by placing the "singles" sections off to the side, near fences, without views. Cemetery associations kept careful records of the location of plots or multiple interments but not of the single graves, in the apparent belief that those who could not afford a family plot were not entitled to the same detailed services as the more affluent. Cemeteries in working-class districts had more single interments than those in wealthier neighborhoods, and since single plots were less desirable (the family could not be buried together), a large number of these indicated relative poverty.[103]

The city buried those who could not afford private funerals in unmarked graves, but interment in the potter's field, or common unmarked grave, was anathema to the working class as disrespectful. The authorities put an unfortunate tramp in a coal mining town to rest in an unmarked grave "like a beast—without washing, and with his hat beneath his head in the coffin for a pillow." A widow in a short story published in Commoner and Glass Worker expressed the feeling of many when she said of her late husband, "I won't have him put in the potter's field if it kills me."[104] But many had no choice: 14 percent of those buried in St. Mary's Cemetery lay in pauper's graves without tombstones to mark their final resting place. The poor did not have what one rural cemetery advocate termed "hallowed and beautiful places of repose."[105] Instead, they lay crowded in unmarked graves, anonymous in death as in life. Rural cemeteries demonstrated that the survivors cared about their departed kin. A pauper's grave deprived the working-class dead of that symbolic devotion, so they sacrificed mightily to bury their dead with respect and dignity.[106]

At the beginning of the century, a suitable funeral with cemetery plot, Masses for the dead, and a handsome tombstone cost $500, more than most laborers made in a year, while a very basic funeral cost about $75–$100. Burial and insurance societies prominently advertised the payment of funeral costs—testimony to the importance of a decent burial and the inability of many working-class families to afford one. Workers passed the hat to pay funeral expenses; many belonged to ethnic, fraternal, veterans', or benevolent associations, which defrayed part or all of the costs, and the rapid formation of ethnic associations among Southern and Eastern Europeans, most of which began as death benefit societies, attests to their poverty and high death rate. The more affluent members of the AAISW rejected death benefit and burial fund proposals from 1878 until 1904, when the union finally established a death benefit fund.[107] By that time, however, the AAISW had ceased to be a force in the Pittsburgh district.

Most working-class folk rested under plain grave markers with only the names and dates of birth and death inscribed upon them. Ethnic variations in the tombstones resulted from retention of traditions brought from the old country. Frequently, Italian grave markers in Pittsburgh contained a picture of the dead person covered by purple glass, and the inscriptions on the tombstones of other recent immigrants were composed in their native language. The maker of the headstone rather than the family usually composed the inscription, so these tended to be stylized. Mausoleums and ornate markers with poems or accounts of the deceased person's life appeared only in the expensive sections of the cemetery. The tombstones in the cheaper sections were smaller and plainer, and those in the singles section were plainest of all, sometimes no more than a simple iron cross.[108] In fact, cemeteries reflected and perpetuated class differences by relegating the poor to the periphery of the burial grounds and by denying paupers the right to a memorial of their final resting place.

Disrespect toward poor people's remains offended the working class, as did proposals for cremating the dead. Individuals concerned about the health problems posed by large numbers of dead interred several feet below ground in heavily populated districts led the cremation movement. But efficient burial held no appeal to steelworkers and their families. Cremation reduced the body to a shovelful of ashes, complained the *National Labor Tribune*, but the contract for burning the dead belonged to the Devil, a "responsible party who possessed all the facilities and appliances, and has an excellent reputation for doing his work in a workmanlike manner." Since cremation violated traditional notions of respect for the dead and the practices of some churches, the working class rejected it.[109]

Funeral customs showed respect for the dead and provided comfort for the living. The care of the dead began with laying out the body, usually at home, arranging the clothes, and combing the hair. These offices might be performed by a family member, but in contrast to earlier times and traditions, undertakers were frequently employed. Unless the body had been mutilated in an accident, the coffin remained open, but even when dismemberment or disfigurement had occurred, the undertaker made every effort to hide the unpleasant sight so that the body might be viewed. It was customary among Pittsburgh's Slavic community to say that the dead person looked like he or she was asleep, making death a peaceful process despite the violence that might have caused it.[110]

The viewing period itself lasted three or four days, and someone remained with the corpse at all times. Many families held open house at this time with unlimited hours for visiting. The Irish wake has been described by one observer as "anything but a lonely vigil" accompanied by heavy drinking. The men who kept watch at Slavic wakes also drank heavily and played cards to pass the time. If women kept the vigil, male relatives insisted that they leave the body and rest, but other mourners replaced them so that the dead person was never left alone. Funeral services might take place in the home, or the undertaker's hearse would take the body to the church for a funeral service or Mass or directly to the cemetery for graveside services.[111]

Large funeral processions, ornate floral tributes, and many mourners indicated class solidarity and the popularity and worthiness of the deceased and the family. The death of William R. Reese "cast a gloom over" the mill where he worked. The members of Allegheny and Bishop lodges, AAISW, "turned out and walked up to the suspension bridge to meet his remains coming over from Pittsburgh, where he has lived the past three years and a half, and escorted them to Bellevue Cemetery. The services at the grave were conducted by Gomer Lodge, No. 64 IOOF of which he was a member for a number of years. The Association has lost a good member and a good friend."[112] Following the accidental death of John Joyce and T.Kearns at Olivers' South Side mill, the mill closed down; five hundred fellow members of the Amalgamated and Joyce's lodge brothers marched behind the coffins to the cemetery. The imposing and solemn procession honored the deceased loyal union members.[113]

Friends, neighbors, and fellow workers as well as family members attended the obsequies. Funeral accounts frequently specified how many people attended and their relationship to the deceased. The workmates of a spouse or parent showed respect for the bereaved family, although they may not have known the dead person. The funeral of Mrs. Emma Pemberton, wife of a window glassblower "was very largely attended by his fellow workmen and friends." Mill men, neighbors, the Junior Temple of Honor, and the Improved Order of Red Men all attended the services for a young iron worker. A good turnout at the funeral, moreover, demonstrated solidarity as well as respect. The parents of a boy crushed in the Loyal Hanna Coal Mine near Latrobe, Pennsylvania, requested that his friends and workmates attend the burial. When they did so, the pit boss discharged them, either for missing work or for their sympathy with the poor boy's parents. The miners accused the boss of grinding his employees into the dirt at every opportunity and prayed "that the earth may refuse a grave to such a villain." Bosses who gave permission for workers to attend funerals or who went themselves were, in contrast, well regarded by the workers and their families. One of the largest funeral processions in Pittsburgh was for Thomas A. Armstrong, editor of the *National Labor Tribune*. A committee of veterans, newspapermen, small shopkeepers, Knights of Labor, and AAISW planned the funeral, which included a parade through downtown Pittsburgh.[114]

Music accompanied many of the funeral processions. The Cathedral Band marched with Joyce's and Kearn's remains, playing dirges and forming a "most solemn" procession. The West End Cornet Band piped an ironworker to his last resting place. But not all agreed that music belonged at a funeral. The organizers of one worker's funeral prevented the St. Mary's Cornet Band from playing in the procession, disagreeing with the notion that there was nothing more solemn than a "dead march."

Nevertheless, church, fraternal, and mill bands, or at least a choir at the church accompanied many working-class women and men to their final reward.[115]

Flowers, too, were an essential part of the working-class funeral, although some religious authorities opposed them as wasteful and pagan. The wreaths had formal names: "Gates Ajar" was a favorite, named after Elizabeth Stuart Phelps's famous mourning manual. Particularly large funerals had flower bearers who carried the wreaths as well as pallbearers for the coffin.[116] The infant's coffin of Slovak immigrants had a small floral offering adorning it, with its significance indicated by inclusion in the family funeral portrait. This group believed that the dead returned after the burial to cleanse their souls. Following the funeral, a family member would place a full glass of water on a table with a towel next to it, so that the dead person could return the evening after the funeral to wash his or her soul. This cleansing of the soul was a folk custom that existed separately from the formal church rituals.[117]

The emphasis on the men's deaths in Pittsburgh's popular press directly expressed working-class values. As breadwinners in an economy that provided few employments for women, men were publicly depicted as more important than their wives. Just as women served their families during their lives, so their representations in death reflected a domestic identity. Just as men's careers were acted out in the public sphere, so their deaths received more publicity. The descriptions of funeral customs in the proletarian papers reflected the concerns and priorities of Pittsburgh's working people, caught as they were by grinding poverty, grotesque accidents, and a troubled future for survivors.

The communal solidarity expressed in the observance of funerals and the support given to parents, widows, and orphans eased some of the pain and also pointed to a principal aspect of working-class life, namely, that assistance from within the family and the community was often the sole resource available to troubled souls. It is hardly surprising that working-class culture valued this social cohesiveness. The primary hope for the workers and widows of Pittsburgh lay in their ability to find strength in one another, since on their own they encountered a harsh and alien world. Solidarity in death as in life blunted this harshness, easing the transition between stages of the life cycle. Ultimately the working-class family was alone with its grief, and each had to find its own solutions to the problems left in death's grim wake. Where these solutions were insufficient, survivors turned to the wider community for assistance. This community assistance took varied forms, spontaneous or systematic, but reflected the stresses that urban industrial life placed upon members of the working class.

9 The Response to Urban Industrial Life: Mutual Assistance and Social Services

Personal and familial resources could be insufficient bulwarks against the onslaughts of the urban industrial economy upon working-class women and their families. As long as the family economy remained intact, if the wife took in boarders or the older children worked, even unskilled families could make ends meet. They had little margin of safety in case of emergencies, however, unlike skilled workers' families, whose incomes were usually large enough to enable them to set money aside for a rainy day. The death of the breadwinner, an industrial accident, or failing strength could all result in impoverishment. Although the working class attempted through collective actions to staunch the wounds inflicted by the mills and the general maldistribution of wealth and services, it was largely beyond its capacity to bring order and equity to Pittsburgh. Middle-class charitable groups cared for the poor, widowed, and orphaned throughout the nineteenth century, joined towards the end of the century by societies that sought to reform the behavior of the poor. They responded to the distress of less fortunate urban dwellers, but they also sought to alter the activities of the poor, the foreign-born, and non-Protestant.[1]

These groups became part of the urban environment for the laboring class and were especially important for women and children, who were their primary clientele. They supplanted informal and community-based mechanisms for coping with the strains of crowded urban conditions and

268

family tensions. Developments in Pittsburgh during these years support the contention that reformers justified their intervention into working-class family life by disparaging it, in Paul Boyer's analysis, as a flawed institution that could be "thrust aside in new instrumentalities of moral nature."[2] Reformers in Pittsburgh, as elsewhere, condemned laboring families as inadequate in order to justify their social engineering. No account of urban working-class family life would be complete without an analysis of these interventions into their family relationships.[3] The transition in social services detailed here paralleled those that occurred at work. The family lost some of its autonomy when confronted with outside experts, as did skilled millworkers when new methods of making steel were introduced. Scientific management and engineers replaced workers' judgment. Welfare agencies and systematic philanthropy replaced informal assistance and parental wisdom in the home. In both cases, the goal was efficiency and a better product, whether steel or children. In the mill or in the home, laudable goals might lead pioneers of new management techniques to ignore the human consequences of their actions.

There were three major types of charity and social welfare in this era—self-help, private philanthropy, and public assistance—but the balance between them shifted as the city grew more complex. Mutual assistance included family and neighborly mutual support, sickness, death, ethnic, and religious benefit societies, spontaneous collections, raffles, balls, and picnics, and various insurance schemes. Private charity provided cash assistance, clothes, shoes, food, and coal, homes for the aged, orphaned, and widowed, day schools for the children of working mothers, and hospitals. Private welfare organizations instigated investigations into child abuse, maltreatment of women, and conditions of housing in the closing decades of the century. They received delegated powers from the city and state to enforce recommendations regarding the removal of children from their parents' homes. Services provided by the city itself included the organs of security and justice, that is, nightwatchmen, police, aldermen, courts, the fire service, sanitation, garbage collection, public baths, insane asylum, and the city poor farm.[4] The aldermen deserve detailed attention here as elected, frequently working-class officials who resolved domestic and local disputes and attempted to rectify the suffering arising from neglect or wrong doing. They illustrate how working-class women sometimes used formal means to correct problems in their own families and neighborhoods.

This chapter focuses on working-class perceptions of the problems faced by families in the industrial city and on their solutions. It also examines middle-class attempts to ameliorate the worst conditions and establish rules for family behavior. It is beyond the scope of this work to detail the development of public charity.[5] In any event the reaction of the city government to the distress of impoverished women and children was minimal. The city was the provider of last resort, but this meant institutionalization under distressing conditions rather than outdoor or noninstitutional relief. Charity, except for the hospitalization of the indigent insane and housing of resident paupers, was left to private philanthropy in order to keep taxes down. Services not directly translatable into public safety remained the province of private initiative throughout this era. In 1897, at the end of five-year depression, Pittsburgh's mayor felt that all noninstitutional relief should be given by private charities. Sixteen years later a report by a Progressive firm of efficiency engineers reiterated the mayor's beliefs. The Emerson Company's *Report on the Department of Charities* advised the abolition of public outdoor relief because private agencies could do it better. At no point did the city provide much aid to the impoverished. In 1895, at the depths of the depression, it spent a meager $4,000 on cash relief. In 1908 the budget of the Department of Charities totaled $313,014, about 18 percent of the estimated expenditure on charity and welfare in that year. With the exception of the Juvenile Court appropriation, the rest came from private funds. Equally significant is the small proportion of all these moneys spent on direct aid to the poor. Most of the money was devoted to the salaries of friendly visitors, doctors, nurses and the costs of running buildings and acquiring property.[6]

The Evolution of Welfare

Mutual Assistance and Private Insurance

Some of Pittsburgh's social and welfare services in these years were carryovers from an earlier, more informal era or represented the attempts of various ethnic and occupational groups to help one another. The very nature of mutual and informal assistance patterns makes it elusive to the historian, since daily kindnesses were rarely recorded. Some analysts have suggested that the working class relied upon relatives rather than neighbors for help because people moved so frequently that aid to a neighbor might never be returned. Families were small enough to impose sanctions upon members who took but never gave.[7] Scattered evidence for Pittsburgh and environs indicates that relatives did assist one another. Where family members lived nearby, some certainly helped one another in time of crisis, although many immigrants and migrants resided far from their kin. Despite small homes working-class parents might take in married sons and daughters if there were financial difficulties or trouble between spouses. For example, the wife of Michael Doran, a laborer, sought refuge with her two children in her father's house following severe physical abuse from her husband. Harry and Alice Thackeray moved in with her mother in order to economize. Families cared for children, nieces, nephews, and grandchildren and were the first recourse for many in times of domestic and financial crisis.[8]

Among the highly mobile iron- and steelworkers, however, relatives could not always furnish assistance in hard or troubled times. Sometimes they were too distant, had no money or room, or simply refused to help. Parents abandoned children, and children refused to look after aged parents; so it fell to individuals and organizations outside the family circle to share the task of caring for those in need. Women in particular, as tenders of the domestic fires, were expected to succor their neighbors and kin.[9] The *National Labor Tribune* wrote of Alice Lloyd, daughter and wife of South Side steelworkers, that "she was highly esteemed by all who knew her as a friend and neighbor in time of need."[10] Innumerable acts of benevolence passed between the residents of the rows and tenements, observed mostly by the people involved and rarely remarked upon except for their absence. Settlement house workers such as the authors of the Kingsley House Association *Annual Report* noted the pervasiveness of daily charity; "the spirit of helpfulness toward each other is very marked" among the working class. Neighborly sympathy manifested itself during sickness as the "mustard jar and liniment bottle at once become the property of an entire row." Men as well as women lent a helping hand, according to Kingsley House residents, for the "grimy hand of the mill worker can carry to his neighbor 'the cold cup of water' with the gentleness of a woman."[11] Many people looked in on one another, lent small sums to buy medicine, and nursed the sick. Yet familial and neighborly assistance had limitations. Most importantly, lengthy depressions, unemployment, and underemployment strained the ability of iron and steel families to render aid. Some crises, notably the death of a breadwinner, disrupted the social unit and frequently led to dependence upon more sustained assistance from outside sources.

A number of working-class and ethnic organizations with benevolent goals emerged during the last decades of the century. The sick, benefit, funeral aid, death benefit, and other kindred societies were largely "confined to those who are in the humbler walks of life," the *National Labor Tribune* wrote of this proliferation of organizations in Pittsburgh, claiming that "the good they have done is incalculable, carrying substantial aid to thousands of stricken families and inspiring those who are fortunate enough in being members with a courage which might not exist in their lives without them."[12] The largest of these organizations was the AAISW which, although a trade union concerned with wages and hours, also provided assistance in times of crisis and sustenance in dark hours to members and their relatives.

Paradoxically, the Amalgamated recognized the problems of industrial poverty, the distress that followed the death of a member, and the inability of families to support themselves in steel mill towns when the husband and father was too sick to work, but it refused to establish regular sickness or death benefits during its first quarter-century. Pittsburgh lodges periodically proposed the adoption of a national benefit system. In 1879, Eureka Lodge 43 recommended that subordinate lodge constitutions include a sick and relief committee that would visit each ill or disabled member, serve as a "watch committee" for a brother needing attendance during the night, and report if sick brothers needed financial aid. The annual convention defeated this proposal and that of the Soho Lodge in 1886 to make the association beneficial in case of death or permanent disablement. The Amalgamated established a protective fund to assist members but turned a deaf ear to a suggested relief society into which each member would contribute a dollar following the death of one of their number to support his widow, fifty cents for each injured member out of work for more than two weeks, and twenty-five cents for each disabled helper.[13] A few Pittsburgh unions furnished death benefits in the mid-1880s. Following the example of the Brotherhood of Railroad Brakemen, which paid $1,000 in case of death or total disability, the Carpenters' Union had a $500 death and sick benefit, and the Painters' Union paid $100 in 1887 but hoped to increase the amount when their organization grew in strength.[14]

Despite the unwillingness of the Amalgamated to sponsor national benefit programs, many of its members were charitably disposed toward one another and distressed families. There were spontaneous collections in the mill or at the gates on almost every payday. The workers and their families shared what they had, aware that they, too, might suffer a similar tragedy. The collective culture enshrined generosity and reinforced it through appeals in the labor press "to do the handsome thing" for disabled comrades. It was the trade unionists' duty to do everything in their power to make philanthropic gestures "a grand success financially."[15]

The majority of benefit balls, picnics, and concerts had disabled workmen as the objects of their charity, but money for widows and orphans typically was raised through appeals in the newspapers, solicitations at the workplace, or raffles. Benefit balls aided, among a host of others, Brother Alfred L. Stevens, a disabled puddler's helper, George Boyd, sick for several months and unable to work, and John Davis, a puddler thrown out of work by an errant hot cinder that burned his eye, who had a wife and five children. Not all balls and raffles raised sufficient funds. One held on behalf of John Durkin failed, for the subordinate lodges of the Amalgamated were "backward in showing their sympathy to this worthy object."[16] Moreover, the raffles, balls, picnics, concerts, and plays were short-term solutions that usually benefited union men or their families. Most iron- and steelworkers did not belong to the union. The Southern and Eastern European immigrants who filled the laboring positions in the steel mills were not part of the Amalgamated. Separated by language, custom, and religion, they were not easily integrated into the older millworkers' culture of which the benefits were a part. This led the newcomers to develop fraternal insurance and benefit societies, which, neither new in Pittsburgh nor unique to the new immigrants, burgeoned with their arrival.

Except for German branches of the Masons, Odd Fellows, and American Order of United Workmen, Pittsburgh's city directories listed few ethnic societies in the 1870s, although Germans had their own churches, singing societies, orphanages, and schools.[17] As in Milwaukee earlier in the century, there were fewer Irish organizations than German. By 1880 the Emerald Beneficial Association had twelve chapters in Pittsburgh; it claimed nearly four hundred paid-up members in 1885 but disappeared from the city by 1890. In its place emerged a network of thirty-seven Catholic Mutual Benefit associations and twenty Ladies' Catholic Benevolent associations, mostly in the Irish Catholic parishes. Four of the German Catholic churches had male benevolent societies and five had branches of the women's group.[18] None of the Polish, Lithuanian, or Italian Catholic churches participated in the Catholic Mutual Benefit or Ladies' Catholic Benevolent Associations, although several Polish parishes had been formed by 1885, including St. Stanislaus in the Strip District, and St. Adalbert's on the South Side. The Slovak and Polish parishes in Pittsburgh established their own beneficial societies at the turn of the century, including the National Slavonic Society, the First Catholic Slovak Union, the Polish National Alliance, the Polish Women's Alliance, the Polish Roman Catholic Union, and St. Joseph's Union. When they developed secular societies, they emulated the example of the German Beneficial Union, which had seventeen branches in Pittsburgh in 1895 including one "Ladies' District" division, which met in the German Library Association Hall in the Third Ward. By 1895 the Italians and Hungarians had also formed secular beneficial societies.[19]

The new immigrant societies did not necessarily hark back to a history of collective action in the old country, but were a response to the new urban, industrial environment. They helped in sickness and death at a time when few members of the ethnic group had sufficient resources to meet traditional charitable obligations. Typically, they provided life insurance, cared for sick members, and aided the poor. The Pittsburgh and Allegheny Schwabian Benevolent Union, founded in 1885, was a life insurance association that admitted men of good health and character to membership. Younger applicants paid lower fees than older ones, presumably because they would contribute to the fund over a longer time. Although a few men described themselves as *arbeiter* (laborer), most members were skilled workers, petty proprietors, and clerks. Initially all had been born in Germany, but after the turn of the century, some second-generation men joined.[20]

Representative of the immigrant organizations, the Greek Catholic Union of Russian Brotherhoods of the United States of America, founded in 1893, rendered aid to persons of good moral character of Slavic Russian birth or descent in times of death, sickness, and distress through its network of lodges, schools, and churches. It promised to pay benefits upon death, disablement, or sickness of its members to the proper beneficiaries and levied dues of fifty cents per month to provide funds for its activities. The Greek Catholic Union had parallel groups for women and men. Although its women's groups were founded later and there were fewer of them, they participated in both the benevolent and social activities of organization.[21]

Immigrants used the lodges as protection and a source of sociability for both the women and men of the family, although there were fewer all-female lodges. An interpreter's account of the participation of a Slavic family in Homestead succinctly described the benefits brought by membership. The man belonged to St. Stephen's Lodge and the woman to St. Catherine's, both church lodges. They attended one meeting every month unless something happened to prevent their going, in which case they sent in their dues. The lodge granted the man $5.00 weekly sick benefits and a promised $1,000 death benefit, for which he paid $2.00 monthly in 1907. Even when the mills provided accident benefits, coverage was not comprehensive and families needed their own insurance. The sick benefit would have helped out after the accident this man had in the mills, for which the Carnegie Relief Fund gave no aid. For $1.00 monthly dues, this Slavic family would receive $700 if the woman died. She was not covered in case of illness, and the family would have to turn to neighbors and the older children to do her work at home. The wife belonged to this lodge so that her family might have benefits paid by the lodge in case of her death, recognizing the role women's labor played in maintaining the family. These lodges also held regular entertainments, to which the couple went, for every member was expected to buy tickets.[22] St. Catherine's and St. Stephen's lodges, and countless others like them, thus fulfilled both the social and beneficial needs of Pittsburgh's new arrivals.

Some immigrant beneficial societies began on a very marginal basis. The Croatian Fraternal Union of America started in a rented hall, had fewer than three hundred members and $42.52 in its treasury during the first year. Although it grew to be "one of the giants in the fraternal field of insurance" by its own assessment, a special subscription had to be levied in 1894 to pay the first death claim. The impetus for organization came from the publisher and editor of a Croatian-language newspaper who observed the difficulty his countrymen encountered in securing life insurance. Zdrauko Muzina was a charter member of the Croatian singing society, and presumably the membership of the two organizations overlapped. Most of the fraternal union's members were "hardy toilers"; one owned a dry goods store, another was a butcher, and the rest could not be found in the city directories but were probably laborers.[23] They needed protection from the misfortunes of life in the industrial city; many had no relatives in Pittsburgh on whom to rely, or their kin were, like themselves, newcomers without a sound financial footing in the Steel City, so they spread their burdens by pooling their resources.

As was discussed above, the iron and steel companies accepted little responsibility for industrial accidents until the turn of the century. This led workers to carry insurance policies through private carriers or beneficial associations to protect their families in the event of their death or disability.[24] Workmen in the mills tried to keep their insurance in good order. William Martin, AAISW secretary, carried a $2,000 life insurance policy, for which he paid a $2.00 membership fee and $2.48 seven times a year. But Martin's policy was an unusually large one, befitting his status as a skilled worker and union officer.[25] Most families carried smaller policies, even if they had to borrow money from the butcher or a neighbor to pay the assessments. Life insurance, either fraternal or commercial, served as a hedge against an uncertain future. If employment was stable, anxiety focused "on the possible sickness or death of the breadwinner,"

Margaret Byington wrote of Homestead steel families. "The usual way in which working people prepare for these two emergencies is by insurance."[26] The limitation of the few employer insurance schemes at the turn of the century is suggested by the large proportion of workers who paid for their own. In Homestead, where Carnegie's Homestead Works did provide accident benefits, 86 percent of the survey families carried insurance, 58 percent in lodges and fraternal orders, the rest with commercial carriers. In a survey made in the Strip District in Pittsburgh in 1915, Metropolitan Life Insurance Company canvassers discovered that only 49 percent of the millworkers had life insurance, the lowest proportion of any group residing there. Since employers had begun to provide death and accident coverage in imitation of the Carnegie Relief Fund, perhaps the Strip District steelworkers felt less urgency about maintaining their own, or their more unstable employment made them less able to do so. Individual policies, typically for $100, $500, or $1,000, paid for the funeral and perhaps tided the widow over for a few months, but they did not assure her of a financially secure future.[27] In fact, neither informal self-help nor formal union, ethnic, and fraternal organizations insured Pittsburgh's iron and steel families against the long-term effects of industrial disasters.

The Aldermen and the Humane Society

The self-help organizations gave financial help where they could, providing a measure of security, and strengthening social coherence. At the same time neighbors established codes of behavior for the treatment of children and women and reciprocal relations between neighbors themselves. These conventions could not cope with extreme infringements, and it was in this province that the aldermen were so important. As the city's population expanded and grew more turbulent, the efficacy of the aldermen declined, and their activities were supplemented by those of the Western Pennsylvania Humane Society and the police.[28] The aldermen represented an older method of resolving familial and neighborhood problems whereas the Humane Society, founded in 1874, was part of the scientific philanthropy movement, the precursor of the social work profession.

From Pittsburgh's earliest days, aldermen had a unique social role as working-class dispensers of social justice. It is not clear to what extent this system was paralleled in other cities. They were not members of the City Council, as in other cities, but squires, or justices of the peace. They handled virtually all minor civil litigation and maintained jurisdiction over all preliminary proceedings connected with criminal prosecutions. They acted upon complaints, issued warrants, held hearings, granted bail, and passed sentences. Each ward elected one alderman and one constable. Since they received their incomes from litigation fees, it was to their financial advantage to entertain even minor civil suits.[29]

As long as the wards remained small, aldermen were a part of their community and responsible to it, as were any locally elected officials. They came from the ranks of the working class and petty proprietors. Of a sample group of aldermen, 44 percent had been skilled workers before election, 12 percent had been unskilled or semiskilled workers, 31 percent had been proprietors, mainly of small stores and saloons, and 13 percent had been clerks or notaries. Significantly, most squires were longtime residents of the wards that elected them. Of this same group, 71 percent had lived in the same ward for at least ten years, 20 percent lived in the same ward five years earlier, and only 9 percent had moved into their ward within the last five years. This is not to say that these people never moved; 50 percent had changed houses within their ward, usually moving a few blocks away.[30] They were the stable people in the constantly shifting populations of their communities. A contemporary described one alderman as "a familiar acquaintance with every man, woman, and child within the limits of his baliwick." They were identifiable figures, known as the person to whom one took problems of family and neighborhood.[31]

The Pittsburgh newspapers of this era carried a local news column with items about judicial activities. Of the cases mentioned, the aldermen saw about one-half of those involving women. The mayor saw one-quarter of such cases, and all other courts saw the rest. The squires' and the mayor's courts worked on different bases. The mayor's police looked for culprits, but aldermen acted upon complaints brought to them. Thus the cases before the aldermen were matters about which people chose to register formal complaints rather than instances of being "caught in the act," which was typical of cases tried by the mayor. Squires saw proportionately more cases involving assault (spouse beating, assault and battery, rape, and murder), immorality (keeping a brothel, fornication, seduction, and bastardy), and family abuse (cruelty to children, nonsupport, desertion, and neglect). The mayor saw proportionately more cases of neighborhood disturbance (theft, receipt and sale of stolen goods, and arson), and violations of city ordinances (loitering and vagrancy).[32]

As far as can be determined, the aldermen were used primarily by the working classes. Higher up the judicial scale culprits and accusers tended to be middle class. The aldermen's courts were working-class institutions, and their role is of special interest to historians concerned with the relationship of the working-class family to the city. The aldermen's ability to enforce community standards typically supported women in disputes against their husbands. It provided a forum for women's complaints about home and neighborhood relations and utilized legal sanctions as a counterbalance to physical strength. Working-class women sought justice or at least retribution on a voluntary basis at the local, that is, aldermanic level. The very informality and neighborhood base of the courts made them accessible to women in need.[33]

In one-third of the aldermen's court cases involving women the accuser and the accused were related, typically as wife to husband, Wives brought their husbands before the aldermen to have physically abusive behavior stopped. The aldermen settled the "family dispute in a legal way," made the deserting husband promise to treat his wife better, or gave him a "good reprimand" for beating his wife and children. Not all cases were settled to the mutual satisfaction of the parties involved; habitual offenders received sentences of one to six months in the workhouse. One murder trial made it clear that the alderman was regarded as the person to whom family problems were taken but that his services did not always have the desired effect. In the testimony, the alderman stated that a woman charged her husband with assault and battery. He appeared to dispute her contention, claiming that she had been criminally intimate with another man. She returned later the same day to press charges again. On the following day, the husband killed her. Such dramatic cases notwithstanding, the aldermen's courts provided some relief for abused women.[34]

Records show that spouse abuse occurred because wives or husbands allegedly did not meet their spouses' expectations. Husbands physically abused their wives for having sexual relations with other men or because they suspected that such relations occurred. They also abused them for not fulfilling their domestic roles, for example, not having meals ready on time. Wives were more likely to take their husbands to task in the aldermen's courts than vice versa because husbands had more power within the family: they were stronger and earned money. Husbands used violence against their wives and families to get their way or to express their frustrations. When the abuse grew too severe, some wives complained formally to the aldermen about nonsupport, physical harassment, and desertion. In some unknown and unknowable proportion of the time, they complained informally to their relatives and neighbors. The few instances of women attacking their husbands appeared to be of the "last straw" variety. For example, one woman hit her husband with the flat of an ax because he came home drunk, threw water into the flour barrel, ruined its contents, and refused to give her the money to buy more.[35] Husbands' public complaints about their wives behavior usually occurred at the nonaldermanic level as divorce suits.[36]

Neighbors also used the aldermen's courts to intervene in community problems. They asked the squires to resolve minor disputes that had their origins in the crowded conditions of the working-class environs. When one woman tore down and destroyed another's clothesline valued at forty cents, the alderman tried to act as peacemaker, but he failed and was "compelled to hold the neighborly ladies to bail for court." The lack of sanitary facilities in working-class households was another source of tension. Women threw slops out of the window rather than carry them down two or three flights of stairs. When passersby were hit, they sometimes brought suit in the squires' courts. Methods of relieving neighborhood tension also brought people into court. If the name calling grew too obnoxious, the alderman was requested to intervene. When disputes went beyond the name-calling stage, his services were sought as well. When a delicate 6-year-old boy was whipped by a neighbor man, his mother called upon the alderman, who worked out a compromise. After a fight in which one woman got the worse of the scratching, biting, and hair-pulling, she brought charges before the alderman in order to get even.[37] Aldermen adjudicated tensions originating in the congested working-class neighborhoods as well as those stemming from overburdened families.

At the beginning of the twentieth century, the Pittsburgh Survey accused aldermen of being corrupt and ignorant of the law. The Survey also claimed that they took advantage of immigrants who knew neither the language nor the customs of their new country. The aldermen were not educated, urbane judges but ward officials, elected by their neighbors, and not all, to be sure, were wisely chosen. One district elected Samuel Frankel, who charged the county more questionable fees than any other alderman and at one point was indicted for leasing bawdy houses. Other aldermen had been convicted of crimes while in office. Some of their cases had to be retried at higher levels of the judiciary because the squire was ignorant of some finer point of law. Insofar as they were unaware of the law, venal, or corrupt, the Pittsburgh Survey correctly condemned the aldermen; but not all were. Many served a vital function in working-class neighborhoods through these crucial decades of change.[38]

The Survey's case against aldermen reflected both their strengths and their weaknesses. The aldermen's usefulness stemmed precisely from their local orientation, with all the potential problems that entailed. The cases they saw, by their nature, were not dignified examples of the art of justice, nor were they conducive to the development of sophisticated legal knowledge among the aldermen themselves. Though the complaints and fees involved seemed petty to crusading Progressives concerned with abstract notions of efficiency, the aldermen's courts nevertheless provided a much needed forum for the community to air specific grievances, frequently against their nearest or dearest. They applied local standards to neighborhood complaints, providing an immediacy swept away by more complex legal systems. Mazella Cox complained to the local squire after some boys hurled racial epithets at her and bricks through her window. It was unlikely that Mrs. Cox would have taken the time or felt comfortable and competent to go downtown to complain to the mayor.[39] Yet many of the complaints brought before the aldermen were of this nature: important to the individual, although efficiency might dictate that they should not be brought at all. The crowded conditions under which the working class lived made it imperative that there be someone to sort out the frictions inherent in densely populated urban areas. Name calling, striking a neighbor's child for throwing stones, or pulling down a wash line blocking the passage across an alley were significant to the people involved, though perhaps trivial from a metropolitan perspective.

As the city's population increased in density and complexity, it grew beyond the informal aldermanic approach. During the last quarter of the century, the police supplanted the aldermen and their constables as the judicial agents of the city. New courts at the turn of century were established to hear civil complaints involving amounts up to $1,500 and cases of desertion and nonsupport. The police took over the criminal side of the aldermen's caseload. These reforms made justice more uniform by removing it from the local level and transferring it to citywide jurisdiction. In effect, they were part of the Progressive impulse to rationalize government into larger administrative units, but they also made it more remote from the clientele served by the aldermen.[40]

The Humane Society

At the same time as a uniformed police undertook the criminal side of the aldermen's work, the state vested social welfare functions in the hands of private agencies that responded to urban disorder from a moral, reformist perspective.[41] The Western Pennsylvania Humane Society at first coexisted with the aldermen, then largely replaced their social welfare functions. The Humane Society, like other urban agencies for the prevention of cruelty to children, actively sought to intervene in family relationships and to remove children from the family unit if the agent thought it in their best interests. Proponents of scientific philanthropy, these societies stressed investigation into individual cases as they grappled with the difficult issue of child abuse. Earlier notions that children were miniature adults to be subdued gave way to a more enlightened attitude, namely, that they were innocent creatures with special needs for gentle nurturance and guidance.[42]

The new attitude extended to the regulation of children's behavior and substituted the judgment of the child savers for those of the parents and youth themselves. In order to justify intervention into other families' affairs, reform organizations stigmatized impoverished and immigrant families as economically and morally inadequate, to be manipulated in order to achieve the new urban morality. They utilized the police power of the state to enforce their standards. In 1877 the Pennsylvania legislature gave the Western Pennsylvania Humane Society the power to remove children from unsuitable homes, to punish brutal parents, and to make arrests. All cases of child abuse were referred to the Humane Society for action, as were many cases of general family abuse. Poor families feared the reformers' power to take children from their homes not only for physical mistreatment but also for nonconformity to emerging norms, including regular school attendance. The middle class and skilled workers were able to invest in their children's education but unskilled workers and recent immigrants needed their labor to help support the family as soon as they could be economically useful.[43] The problems perceived by these agencies troubled many members of the working-class community, who sometimes invoked them in cases of abuse. However, excessive zeal could lead reformers to interfere with an unduly heavy hand.

The Western Pennsylvania Humane Society (founded in Pittsburgh in 1874) and the Anti-Cruelty Society (established in 1885) reflected at the local level the national reformist emphases on child welfare and willingness to intervene in the child-rearing practices of individual families. The board of directors, along with those of other social welfare agencies such as the PAIP (founded in 1875), came from the industrial, mercantile, and professional elites of Pittsburgh and Allegheny cities. They lived primarily in the upper-class sections of the city at a distance from the working class and the mills, participating in civic affairs without direct contact with the recipients of their largesse.[44] Unlike earlier philanthropically minded women, the social housekeepers of this era did not go among the poor themselves.[45] Their societies hired agents to investigate, the boards established policies and raised funds. The aldermen came from the same neighborhoods and economic backgrounds as many of their clientele. The "friendly" visitors of the Humane Society and the PAIP did not, and they could be unsympathetic to the pressures under which the poor labored. Although the aldermen still adjudicated cases of cruelty, the Humane

Society's agents both brought the cases and served as expert witnesses. Since poor families rarely had access to legal advice and the aldermen had no legal training, the Humane Society's agents and lawyers held sway on points of law and interpretation. Their expertise dominated the proceedings.

The Humane Society and the aldermen had approaches to the problems of the working class as divergent as their backgrounds.[46] The aldermen waited for people to come to them; the Humane Society searched for clients. Squires tried to settle disputes to the satisfaction of all parties; the Humane Society sought to enforce its abstract standards of right and wrong. As members of the working class and neighborhood residents, the aldermen knew the constraints and tensions under which their clientele lived, in complete contrast to the outside agents of the Humane Society. Humane Society agents actively sought cases of family and child abuse, neglect, and improper behavior and encouraged neighbors to inform upon one another. They condemned the drinking habits of the poor, assuming, as did many reformers of this era, that alcohol, rather than poverty, was the root of working-class problems. Since many of the reformers belonged to Protestant churches opposed to alcohol consumption and many of their clients came from ethnic backgrounds that accepted drinking, the Humane Society used its position to promote cultural values at variance with those of the poor.[47]

One of the most sensitive areas in which the new social service agencies involved themselves was the relationship of parents to children. The agencies intervened in the child-raising practices of individual families to dictate correct modes of behavior and explain parental responsibilities. The PAIP reported that the daily papers were full of accounts of deaths and accidents where mothers and older members of the family went out to work, ''entrusting infants to the care of children whose tender years render them unfit to assume the responsibilities placed upon them.''[48] Unfortunately, few institutions provided daily places, and mothers resisted attempts to separate them from their children. Some working mothers relied upon neighbors or relatives to look in; others left their children at home alone while they worked or picked up and delivered washing and ironing. These women were occasionally charged with neglecting their children. The Children's Temporary Home and similar ventures filled the need "long felt by many poor and worthy women" of the Pittsburgh community for a comfortable spot to leave small children at a minimal charge, but it could provide for only a handful. The Children's Temporary Home sheltered eighty-five children, of whom only fifteen were cared for in the day nursery.[49] Whereas older residential institutions such as orphanages had waited until death severed family ties or parents recognized that they could not support their children, these new societies sought out children who needed such facilities or whose parents were, in their eyes, incompetent or unable to support them, and thus they broke the family apart despite its efforts to remain intact.

By placing her children in such a home, the working mother avoided their potentially permanent removal by the Humane Society or the Anti-Cruelty Society. The Humane Society agents lectured parents on how to care for their children and where they should be placed. It was improper, for example, to board children in a saloon, or leave them all day even if they had plenty to eat and neighbors looked in on them. Such children should be boarded in orphanages. The child-saving societies placed a handful of children in the Children's Temporary Home, several dozen each were placed there by the home's own visitors or parents and friends. The PAIP placed a similar number of children in sectarian orphanages and sent many more (317 in 1890) to the County Home.[50]

Once in an orphanage, children remained there until they were reclaimed by their parents or friends, were too old to require custodial care, or were placed in such jobs as could be found for them. The Pittsburgh and Allegheny Home for the Friendless undertook to provide food, clothing, and schooling for neglected or deserted children until suitable places could be found for them, "with the understanding that in all cases they shall conform strictly to the rules of the house, accept cheerfully such situations or service places as may be deemed suitable, and endeavor to acquit themselves creditably." When the Humane Society sheltered children in an orphanage as a result of their parents' cruelty or neglect, it retained custody over them. Pittsburgh's Poor Board had the legal power to declare as abandoned those children resident in an orphan asylum for more than one year without payment for board and lodging.

The child could then be indentured to the asylum, which could, in turn, indenture the child to an employer. Unless the Poor Board or the Orphans' Court could be persuaded to act, these children existed in a legal limbo. The managers of St. Paul's Orphan Asylum approached the Humane Society in 1890 over a number of children who had been there since 1885, abandoned by their parents. The managers wanted legal possession of the children to indenture them out. They petitioned the Orphans' Court through the Humane Society and were thus able to indenture them.[51]

Women who were not respectable in the eyes of the child savers risked having their children taken from them. Mr. O'Brien, an agent of the Humane Society, had Mrs. De Roll arrested for keeping her children in a brothel. After paying her fine, she promised to place them in an orphanage and so retained custody of them. A year later he sued to have them removed from her custody because her house had been raided again. Her attorney had the case postponed so that he could obtain witnesses to prove Mrs. De Roll a reputable woman. Although the court remarked that the lawyer "had a great deal to overcome," it granted the request. Since no one would testify to her character, the children were placed in an orphan asylum, and the mother lost her rights over them.[52]

Though some of the cases involved physical abuse, such as that against a washerwoman who beat her son with strap until she raised welts, others had their roots in the inability of the impoverished to obtain decent quarters. The Humane Society agent visited a laborer's family living in a cellar, where the sunlight never penetrated, and informed the husband that if he did not find more suitable accommodation very soon, he would bring suit against him and remove the children. In another case the Humane Society investigated complaints against a ragpicker who lived with his spouse and three children in a shanty boat on the river. The boat contained "two rooms and miserable looking at that." In the agent's opinion the ragpicker was a big, strong man who should get his wife and children off the boat and keep them properly or he would remove the children. In response to these threats the man promised he would rent a house. On investigating a complaint made by a skilled worker against a laborer, the agent found a widowed black man living with his four children in a small building, half of which was a stable. The boys, 16 and 14 hauled ashes, and the girls, 12 and 10, kept house. According to the agent, the father did nothing but drink and live off his children. He was told to get more suitable quarters, his current residence being no better than the stable to which it was joined. He should get a job to support the family and hire a woman to come in once or twice a week to do the heavy cleaning. If better quarters were not secured quickly, charges would be brought against him for neglect. "Although the girls were comfortably clad, they were undoubtedly neglected." The girls had not been ill-treated; nor were they hungry or dressed in rags. The agent did not approve of the way the family lived, even though they managed to stay together, with the members contributing what they could, and no one in the family complained.[53] Though the family's quarters were, no doubt, deplorable, the original accusation may have been motivated by racial prejudice. The Humane Society agent exhibited little understanding of the problems of poverty and the difficulties blacks had in finding adequate work or decent living quarters. This family also demonstrated how necessary children's labor could be for the sustenance of poor families.

The Humane Society agents made explicit threats. One, named Collins, told a man whose job brought in very little money that "if he did not mend his ways and help to keep the family, Collins would see that he did not live off them," and if there were another complaint of his profanity and abuse to his family, he would be sent to the workhouse. The agents acted on anonymous complaints, frequently investigating the situation without telling anyone who they were or what they were doing. They used the threat of the workhouse as a club. It was not unusual in these circumstances for a wife to defend her husband to the Humane Society in order to keep the family intact. She worried about having the breadwinner jailed and thus losing her only, albeit inadequate, support. The police arrested Charles Engle, a laborer, for beating and abusing his wife and two children. The wife pleaded that he not be put in the workhouse. He was let off with a reprimand after paying court costs and promising to do better in future. A South Side puddler's wife defended him from her sickbed. He could not get much work, so she went out washing "til she broke down from being overworked and took sick." The agent "read the riot act" to the husband and told him what authorities expected of him.[54] It is important to separate the issues of abuse and neglect here: in the Engles' case, the husband was physically violent. The South Side puddler, for whatever reasons, was an inadequate provider. In both cases the approach of the Humane Society was to intervene directly, to remove the "offender" from the family, but it is difficult to see how placing an inadequate provider in the workhouse would help his family.

Whatever the actual circumstances behind the puddler's unemployment, whether short time in the mill, ill health, or laziness, many of these cases hinged upon the economic inadequacy of the parents. The impoverished family could be broken up precisely because its domestic arrangements did not conform to prevailing middle-class norms. The complaints came from outside the family itself, and the underlying problem was the inability to find work, not abuse or neglect. In 40 percent of the cases handled by the Humane Society in 1889, legal proceedings were begun, the offending parent or parents jailed, fined, or sent to the workhouse, or the child removed from the care of its parents. Although the numbers involved were not large (about two hundred cases per annum in the surviving Humane Society Record Book and some six to eight hundred annually for the Anti-Cruelty Society), the fear of having one's family separated by the actions of outsiders such as the Humane Society and other welfare groups intimidated poor parents.[55]

The Humane Society agents were aware of the power they had to inspire fear. In a complicated case the bookkeeper at the Isabella Iron Works complained about the abusive treatment meted out to a 14-year-old girl by a millworker uncle who boarded with her parents. The parents begged the agent not to cause them any trouble. He asked the neighbors if they had seen the girl knocked down and kicked, but they were "drunk as oysters." Mr. O'Brien then returned to the Humane Society office to discuss the case, which did not properly come under his jurisdiction because the abuse had not been committed by the parents and they refused to bring charges against the wife's brother. The agent could prosecute the uncle for assault and battery, but under the circumstances it would be difficult to get witnesses. His employers at the Humane Society were well pleased with what he had done because "it would have a good affect through the whole row." In the course of investigating allegations of neglect against a widow supporting two infant children by keeping a small shop, the agent made his presence known. After he told Mrs. O'Connors who he was, "she became badly frightened." He made inquiries among the neighbors and told her that if she did not take better care of the children and stop drinking, he would "feel obliged to take the children from her."[56] In both instances the Humane Society investigators paraded the troubles of the families before the neighbors, using their power to bring charges of abuse and neglect to obtain the desired behavior and to warn other families of the consequences of transgressing the society's norms. The society quite correctly tried to curtail abusive behavior, but sometimes it exhibited misplaced zeal in its methods.

The descriptions of proceedings begun by the Humane Society suggest a class bias in its evaluations; neglect and cruelty against children appear as working-class phenomena in its records. The middle class conducted its family affairs privately behind heavily curtained windows with little direct observation. Those of the working class could be heard through the thin walls and spilled out into the street and alley for all to see. When the general manager of the Heard Cracker Factory complained that the parents of Maggie Clark took her away from her job and abused her shamefully, it was the neighbors who testified that they heard her shriek and cry. Neighbors saw John Berry strike his 12-year-old son with a broom stick in the yard, complained that Peter Baccigalupo ill-treated a girl, and witnessed Frank Kaski turning his wife and children out of doors. Without condoning such behavior, it is possible to see how the cramped quarters of the working class made family problems apparent to the neighborhood. There were few accusations against middle-class parents, and these tended not to be pursued with much vigor. Mr. Collins dropped his investigation against an Oakland man alleged to have abused his 9-year-old son because the man was "very respectable" and no witnesses could be found. In many of the cases reviewed here, neglect betokened an inability to provide a sufficient standard of living, an endemic problem in Pittsburgh's fluctuating economic climate and among new immigrants who had not yet secured a foothold in the marketplace.[57]

Drinking also constituted a black mark against mothers and fathers. The accusations brought against a Mr. and Mrs. Smith suggest that the Humane Society saw alcohol as the problem whereas the family believed underemployment was to blame. Father, mother, children, and house were all the picture of desolation. When asked why, Mr. Smith replied that he worked in the mill and did not make more than half time. The agent said he had been informed that Smith and his wife "drank up all his earnings which was the cause of his house and children being in such a condition." If the parents did not take better care of the children, the Humane Society threatened to remove them. Missionaries complained to the Humane Society about a mother of four children who bought alcohol and drank it. The agent found no signs of drink on her when he visited and noted he would have to get some proof before he could prosecute.[58] The Humane Society warned such parents that if they did not curb their drinking, legal action would be taken against them to remove the children.

Where the parents did not conform to the image of child rearing desired by the welfare societies, these organizations attempted to substitute their wisdom for the parents' or to place the children in institutions, thus removing them from the parents' control. Though some child savers may have attacked or doubted the long-term value of institutionalization of children, those in Pittsburgh favored the use of orphanages as a means of protecting the young from the harmful behavior of their parents and the direct consequences of poverty.[59] They did not perceive any adverse effects, or if they did, they considered that the benefits outweighed them.

While the Western Pennsylvania Humane Society investigated instances of cruelty to children and neglected wives throughout this period, day nurseries and the courts provided other mechanisms for dealing with distressed families and children. The Pittsburgh Survey lauded the creation of the Juvenile Court in 1901 as "the most thought-provoking step in behalf of children taken in the District." The court's regularized procedures and secretive sessions were more intimidating to poor parents and a far cry from the public and informal aldermen's courts.[60] The more formal mechanisms for resolving family and community conflict lessened working-class control over their own lives and substituted urbane expertise for the sometimes rough and ready justice of the aldermen.

The Evolution of Private Philanthropy:
Ephemeral to Permanent

In the same years when private agencies undertook welfare services, supplanting informal advice and public officials (the aldermen), the provision of charity shifted away from the city government to private agencies. The development of permanent, citywide philanthropic societies mirrored national trends toward the systematization of giving while reflecting Pittsburgh's unwillingness to provide for the poor from the municipal purse. The reluctance of the city's public charitable organizations (the Board of Guardians of the Poor, later the Department of Charities) to give outdoor relief and middle-class women's search for respectable activities outside their homes stimulated the growth of private charities in Pittsburgh.[61]

Private philanthropy blossomed during the 1873–79 depression as individual and municipal relief efforts proved ineffective in face of massive unemployment and distress.[62] Joseph Bishop, president of the AAISW said that the stoppage of the mills, some for as long as two years, had forced iron and steel families into poverty. By 1878 they were "out of work, out of money and well nigh out of hope. . . . Distress, misery, want and destitution stare them in the face and for the first time they have known what it was to want bread for themselves, their wives and little ones."[63] Impoverished workers besieged genteel folk, many still resident in the downtown wards, with pleas for assistance during the harsh winter of 1875, when the city did little to relieve distress. Louise Herron, founder of the PAIP believed it necessary to investigate the circumstances of "those who might be innocent sufferers or to deal harshly with impostors."[64] A series of meetings in fashionable Fourth Ward parlors produced the association, many of whose members also belonged to other charitable and welfare organizations in Pittsburgh and Allegheny City.[65]

In order to systematize charitable giving, the association established a cumbersome system designed to prevent ne'er-do-wells from receiving assistance and eliminate multiple donations to the needy. Businessmen and householders received tickets for distribution to street and house beggars, who were to apply to the association for aid, ticket in hand. A paid friendly visitor then determined the individual's eligibility. The system worked well from the standpoint of the organization: in 1879, one-third of the two thousand applications for assistance were denied because investigators considered them undeserving. The association wished to develop "an authorised system to seek out and ascertain the worthy and deserving poor of the City of Pittsburgh; to relieve their material want and minister to their spiritual welfare, thereby shielding them against the injustices which they suffer through imposters and professional beggers of all kinds, and affording the charitably inclined an opportunity to dispense liberality without fear of conferring unmeritted aid."[66]

It accomplished these objects through the use of paid female missionaries or visitors who were pious, prudent, intelligent, sympathetic, and possessed of common sense, according to a PAIP description. The association assured donors that the visitors were "always ready to make careful investigation into every case referred to them and report the results to those interested." The paid female missionaries made house-to-house visits in search of families in need of assistance. This differentiated the new charities from the old, which had waited for people to come to them, and paralleled the welfare societies' active search for clientele. The association sought mothers who could not support their children, children left alone all day, and individuals in need of medical attention. Although the organization hoped to prevent people from receiving more aid than they needed, the visitors also wanted to ensure that the deserving poor obtained sufficient assistance. By hiring professionals to investigate conditions in the poorer districts of the city, it determined the precise circumstances of the impoverished but eliminated the need for donors to come into direct contact with the needy or their surroundings. The use of paid visitors distanced the recipients of benevolence and the providers of it. This reflected the growing physical and financial separation between the classes and the professionalization of philanthropy itself.[67]

The PAIP was the largest and longest-lived of the charitable societies (its telephones were still answered one hundred years after its founding with the ringing phrase "Improvement of the Poor"). In 1875 it stood alone as a secular outdoor relief agency amid the Home for the

Friendless, the Sheltering Arms, the Episcopal Church Home, and other orphanages and temporary shelters, providing more aid to the poor than the city authorities. Many of the early charitable ventures provided relief to members of a particular ethnic or religious group. This prompted other groups to institute similar parochial facilities for themselves, so that by the turn of the century there were Protestant, Catholic, Black, Jewish, and German orphanages. By 1900 the Women's Christian Association, Hebrew Benevolent Association, Fruit and Flower Mission, and Children's Aid Society had joined the PAIP but the emphasis on private institutional charity in Pittsburgh continued as secular and church homes for the aged, orphaned, infirm, and working girls and boys opened.[68] Reformers responded to the problems of the impoverished from a limited pool of ideas for their improvement, and many Pittsburgh agencies emulated examples set in larger cities. Sometimes this imitation was conscious; in 1899 the founders of Pittsburgh's Legal Aid Society modeled their organization after the one established in New York City in 1870. The PAIP borrowed its name from New York's Association for Improving the Condition of the Poor, founded in 1843, and the Western Pennsylvania Humane Society was established at the behest of the state organization.[69] Pittsburgh's charities were not unique, but the large number of homes for widowed and destitute women and orphans does suggest that such institutions had particular utility in a city where dangerous industries made widows of many women and orphans of their children.[70]

The PAIP's records show that most of its clientele were widows and orphans, although high rates of unemployment during depressions increased the number of men it served. In 1885, 1,147 of the 1,881 families aided (61 percent) were headed by widowed or deserted women or supported by women and children, but only 18 percent were in need of aid because of "scarcity of work," a category used in the "Causes of Want" tabulation furnished by the association's annual report. In 1895, at the height of the depression, 4,336 families received assistance, 1,440 because they lacked a male breadwinner and 1,745 because work was hard to find.[71] In 1915 the PAIP published a pamphlet entitled "Solving the Problem," in which it stated that "families in which the mother is the bread winner have always comprised a large percentage of those aided by the Association.'"[72] The difficulties women experienced simultaneously working and raising a family left them dependent upon external agencies for support.

The new charitable associations' reliance upon professional investigators resulted in a biased distribution of aid, with English-speaking families benefiting more than recent immigrants. Between 1880 and 1900 the PAIP caseload contained few Southern and Eastern Europeans, underrepresented Germans, and concentrated on native-born whites, Irish and British immigrants, and blacks. In 1880, 2 percent of its clientele were Polish, Italian, Russian, or Austro-Hungarian: despite the tremendous increase in immigration from those countries to Pittsburgh at the turn of the century and the poverty of the new immigrants, only 3 percent of the organizations caseload were from Southern or Eastern Europe then.[73] It would seem that poverty alone did not qualify one for aid, but a combination of poverty and the ability to speak English did. This lack of assistance from Pittsburgh's largest charitable society helps explain the reliance of the Germans and Southern and Eastern Europeans upon fraternal and beneficial organizations. Communication barriers prevented their turning to external agencies for aid and kept the charitably minded from helping them.[74] Since between 25 and 50 percent of all relief recipients belonged to no church, according to the PAIP records, presumably they had no denominational source of aid. Many new immigrants had strong church ties or actively sought to create mutual benefit and ethnoreligious organizations. They turned inward for assistance to people who shared their language and their values.[75] The PAIP helped those outside the purview of laboring organizations: unskilled workers, domestic servants, widows, and orphans, but few new immigrants.

Some of the new social service agencies attempted to overcome the barriers between the foreign-born, non–English speaking immigrants and the dispensers of charity by moving into the immigrant neighborhoods. Pittsburgh's first settlement house, Kingsley House, grew along the same lines as other middle-class residential "spearheads for reform" in working-class districts.[76] The settlement house idea came to the United States through Stanton Coit, a native of Columbus, Ohio, and an Amherst College graduate who received a Ph.D. from the University of Berlin.

Coit's concern for the social and moral welfare of the poor led him to Toynbee Hall, the pioneering London settlement, where he became one of the first American residents. After a brief stay, Coit journeyed to New York City, where he founded the Neighborhood Guild in 1886. Coit returned to London in 1887 to work among the East End poor and preach the gospel of Ethical Humanism. The early Progressive impulse to improve conditions in the industrial city as exemplified by Vida Scudder's College Settlement in New York City and Jane Addams's Hull House in Chicago led to the establishment of similar institutions in many cities including Pittsburgh.[77]

As with other settlements, the Kingsley House ideal was that of "a cultured home in a crowded quarter of the city" that would adapt "itself to the life and needs of its own neighborhood." Settlement houses hoped to transmit middle-class social values to their working-class, foreign-born neighbors by "living in the midst of those they sought to improve," thus avoiding the problem other philanthropists encountered, namely, that "the people do not care to come to them through misconception of their intentions."[78] Kingsley House residents initially focused on activities for children. Within a few years, the board of directors sought increased outreach to men and boys, firing the first two women head residents and replacing them with William Matthews of the Union Settlement Boys' Club in New York. Henry Clay Frick provided the funds to purchase and remodel Montooth Mansion, a structure large enough to house a gymnasium and a swimming pool, both of which were to lure laboring men into the Americanizing premises of the settlement house. Matthews and his successors sought to improve the tone of the settlement neighborhood, inveighing against corrupt aldermen, saloons, and prostitutes, but not querying the fundamental structure of Pittsburgh's economy: the low wages and frequent unemployment of many Kingsley House neighbors. Throughout its early years, the settlement preferred the worthy poor to the destitute; it wanted to uplift, not give alms. It selected its clientele in accordance with the prejudices of its Protestant residents and board of directors, urging Jewish neighbors to attend the Jewish Irene Kaufmann Settlement and barring its portals to blacks.[79] At no time did Kingsley House cooperate with local ethnic organizations or encourage laboring people to organize to improve their position relative to that of capital, although the Irene Kaufmann Settlement did.[80]

Settlement houses prided themselves on providing mental and moral improvement, not charity. The Kingsley House charter lists its goals as the provision "of social intercourse, mutual helpfulness, mental and moral improvement and rational and healthful recreation."[81] Even the charities of this era stressed advice, not aid. The Associated Charities of Pittsburgh, founded in 1908 as part of the Charity Organization Societies movement then sweeping large U.S. cities, believed that "the principal need of the poor is not alms, but friends" who would investigate the needs of their clientele and "kindly enter into their problems." It rationalized aid by registering the poor and sharing information about applicants among its members, following in the footsteps of the PAIP in the 1870s. The aim was to provide systematic, efficient aid, directing benevolent effort in a constructive way.[82] Such privately financed alternatives muted the consequences of industrial poverty and women's inability to support themselves in Pittsburgh's economy while simultaneously keeping property taxes low and urging conformity to the moral values of the urban industrial elite.

Regardless of the intentions of Kingsley House, the PAIP and other worthy ventures, they could only investigate and ameliorate the worst housing, health, and social conditions. They implicitly accepted the distribution of wealth while hoping to relieve the "material wants and minister to the spiritual welfare" of the deserving poor, those impoverished through misfortune, not malfeasance.[83] Though William Matthews tried to find work for the worthy poor, he wasted no time on the vagrant or loafer.[84] Such reformers proposed no changes in the basic distribution of resources in society because they themselves derived from the comfortable classes and benefited from the existing socioeconomic order. Money for Kingsley House came from Pittsburgh's leading bankers and industrialists, the Mellons, Fricks, and Carnegies.[85] The boards of managers of the PAIP, the Women's Christian Association agencies, and the Pittsburgh and Allegheny Home for the Friendless (among the largest agencies in Pittsburgh that left written accounts of their activities) came from the entrepreneurial and professional classes of the two cities.

Of those board members who could be positively identified, twenty-three were the wives of merchants, seventeen of professional men, and sixteen of manufacturers; none were employed outside the home themselves. They resided in the Fourth Ward, the upper-class section of the downtown area, in the then fashionable suburban sections of Oakland, East Liberty, and Squirrel Hill, and across the river in Allegheny City. Many of the suburban residents had husbands who commuted to work in the city.[86] As such, they had an interest in the affairs of the city even though they lived outside it.[87]

Those who gave their own and their husband's money used it to modify the behavior of the recipients. Although the PAIP claimed that it accepted the poor as it found them, "whether made so by their sins or by their misfortunes," its purpose was to elevate their morals and improve their sanitary habits, to "lift up the lowly and instruct them in such principles as will, if followed out, lead to lives of industry and competence." The paid female missionaries taught "the poor sound morals," leading them to industrious and frugal lives with sewing classes and household and personal advice. Children were to go to Sunday school and parents to abstain from alcohol. The Gilmore Mission and Industrial School, which gave sewing lessons to two hundred "mission children" every Saturday from November to April, hoped to use the little ones as a means of reaching their parents and thus exert a far-reaching influence for good among the "neglected masses."[88] Progressive reformers expanded upon the earlier exertions of the Sunday schools and missions to acculturate the young. Their efforts to uplift the masses included the supervision of playgrounds designed to cultivate the moral nature of children, the promotion of civic unity, and the provision of social training and discipline.[89]

At least some of these neglected masses perceived the irony of these ventures: the same people who underpaid their workers subsidized good works among their families. *Commoner and Glassworker* railed against the Phipps Cooking School held at the Grant Street Public School. Mr. Phipps, partner of Andrew Carnegie, paid all the expenses of the school including the salary of the "cultured Boston lady" who taught the art. The glassworkers' newspaper editorialized in 1888 that the two thousand "idle workmen of Carnegie, Phipps, and Company at Braddock don't care much how the cooking is done, but they are greatly interested in knowing where the food to be cooked for them is to come from."[90] Working-class women felt the cooking schools were rather far removed from their own daily routine and a usurpation of their traditional skills. Homestead housewives of 1907 scorned the theoretical aspects of the problem as taught in the cooking classes of the Schwab Manual Training School, given to the town by Charles M. Schwab, onetime superintendent of the Homestead Works. They felt that practical experience was of more value than any theory.[91] These schools, with their emphasis on fine cooking, properly set tables, and theories of balanced diets, hoped to impart a glimpse of the middle-class mores to the daughters of steelworkers and, through them, their parents.[92] Such schools made no allowances for the validity of working-class or immigrant culture and were implicitly intolerant of their values.

The working class itself understood these charitable exercises as a mixed blessing at best.[93] They recognized the need for assistance in hard times and for the families of disabled or dead workers, but they resented accompanying attempts to control behavior, an attitude expressed most clearly during strikes and other class conflicts. One women's relief association refused assistance to millworkers' families when the Boilers' Union went on strike in 1875. Out for thirteen weeks, the puddlers and boilers exhausted their resources. The charitable organizations maintained that aiding the strikers' families would be a form of intervention in the strike itself on behalf of labor. By denying benefits, the philanthropists in effect helped the manufacturers break the strike. According to the *National Labor Tribune*, these actions were but a "cudgel to hammer the Puddlers into work" and a direct support of the mill owners. The AAISW newspaper was particularly incensed because union funds had helped nonunion strikers, but the relief association turned down requests from all unemployed puddlers regardless of union affiliation or participation in the strike.[94]

During another prolonged labor struggle in 1879, the "charitable ladies" of the Pittsburgh region, led by a prominent minister and abetted by the manufacturers, again declined support to those thrown out of work by an industrial dispute, this time a strike at the Clark Mills. The relief association maintained that work was available; to which the unions responded that the only employment was at the struck mill, so a return to work would "defeat the workingmen and give victory to the manufacturers." In this way, charity became a tool of class warfare. The city tendered very limited noninstitutional assistance, and the private philanthropists gave aid on their own terms and in their class interests. Such benevolence covered "a multitude of sins, but charity of the quality above mentioned is wickedness and sin in itself."[95] The price of relief was acceptance of the assumptions of those whose wage and work policies made aid necessary in the first place. The *Irish Pennsylvanian* asserted that "if all were just charity would be unnecessary." Those who prided themselves on what they did for the poor really received charity from them in the form of "unearned luxuries" but returned very little to the producing classes.[96]

Working-class families suspected that upper-and middle-class benevolence masked hidden motives. Andrew Carnegie gave millions to establish libraries and other cultural institutions. The daily press lauded him, told how much Carnegie did for the working-class family and, in the sarcastic words of *Commoner and Glassworker*, "they ought to fall down and worship his body for it." Workers on strike at one of Carnegie's mills viewed his philanthropy in a different light: he never gave a nickel for charity, public purposes, or anything else for that matter, "except he calculated fully the notoriety it would return him."[97] Millworkers believed his altruism was a public relations gesture to maintain popular support for his management policies. Men who worked long days and nights in the mills preferred higher wages and more leisure in which to enjoy them to buildings they were too tired to use. Steelworkers told the Pittsburgh Survey, "We'd rather they hadn't cut our wages and let us spend the money for ourselves. What use has a man who works twelve hours a day for a library, anyway?"[98] Contributions from Pittsburgh's "broadcloth and lace society" eased the guilty consciences of the donors but did nothing to improve the conditions under which working-class families labored and lived. Tenement dwellers accepted "real charity" from those who toiled before the hot furnaces as a form of social insurance against disaster. They knew it would not be turned against them or used as a tool to force striking men back to work, unlike assistance that came from the women and men of the upper orders. It had no ''means test'' attached to it, nor did it depend upon conformity to external notions of propriety.[99]

Members of the working class perceived the rhetoric of reformers in Pittsburgh, as in other cities, as that of social control. The new institutional ventures also eschewed interference in labor relations. The Kingsley House settlement, financially dependent upon the industrial elite, did not open its doors to unions although its head resident later investigated working conditions in the mills at the request of United States Steel stockholders. Such private agencies worked not at the clients' behest but according to standards that came from their own citywide organizations and were enforced by professional charity and social service workers who neither resided in working-class communities nor lived working-class lives and who frequently had little sympathy with the problems poverty engendered.[100]

The Emerging Balance

In these years the number and types of social service agencies proliferated. The working class developed its own insurance and relief systems, but for most these were insufficient protection from the uncertainties of urban industrial life. Even in 1908 fraternal organizations spent only $5,700 on aid. Private and public philanthropic agencies changed from sporadic responses to specific problems to institutional care, actively provided. Charity became the work of professionals paid to interact with the working class. Though the elite still provided the financial wherewithal, having moved from the central business district, they had no direct contact with the poor either in their daily lives or their philanthropy. Moreover, the basis of social services had changed. Citywide organizations supplanted local officials with an intimate knowledge of their people and their circumstances, although the change was by no means total and complete. But agencies such as the Humane Society, the PAIP, and the Associated Charities of Pittsburgh, with their metropolitan, interurban approach, reliance upon paid workers, the emphasis on investigation and the worthy poor, were part of the new approach to urban problems that emerged during the Progressive era.[101]

The removal of welfare services from local control and direct contact to citywide control and minimal contact meant that the primary recipients of these services, women and children, increasingly were considered not as people with particular problems but as part of the total problem of urban poverty. The working class who received such services had no control over them, as they had with their own Mutual assistance, fraternal, and beneficial societies. The "help" was more frequently unsolicited than in the aldermanic cases. If an alderman was unpopular, he could be unseated at the next election. If the Board of Guardians of the Poor was unresponsive, people complained to their city councilmen. But the new, private agencies were not elected; they did not receive their funds from the public purse. Since the money came from private contributions—frequently the industrial, banking, and commercial interests—the agencies distributed largesse in accordance with the values of their sponsors. They were private groups with public functions, trying to impose their own sense of order upon a heterogeneous working class whose interests differed radically from those of their benefactors and their agents.[102]

The working class actively used the aldermen's courts to resolve domestic conflicts, whereas child-saving societies attempted to impose solutions externally. Mutual assistance organizations such as fraternal societies and those sponsored by the immigrants' churches were part of the millworkers' cultural world. They understood the values and problems faced by the newly urbanized and industrialized millworkers and their kin on construction sites, in factories, in glass houses, and in sweatshops. The reforming societies never penetrated to the roots of their clients' problems: an economy in which the profits of industry rested on treating labor as a commodity and in which the family unit could be sustained only through the work of both parents and older children. Families broken by the premature death of the mother or father, particularly if there were young children to be cared for, found it very difficult to function in the absence of external support. Fluctuations in the business cycle engendered frequent bouts of unemployment and impoverished families. The capitalists who underwrote the charities also underpaid their employees, who, in turn, became the charities' clients.

The decades of Pittsburgh's greatest industrial growth witnessed several fundamental shifts in the provision of human services in accordance with national trends toward the professionalization of these services and the attempted imposition of external moralities and deferential behavior upon the poor. Private organizations and citywide bureaucracies pushed informal welfare and charity ventures to one side as the massive influx of people placed intolerable stress on the social fabric. Reformers such as the PAIP, the Western Pennsylvania Humane Society, and the settlement house residents sought to ameliorate the worst side effects of the industrial city while regulating the behavior of the working class. The Pittsburgh Survey condemned the somewhat rough and inelegant justice aldermen tendered to their clients, but the unceremonious nature of the squires' courts made them accessible to working-class women in a way in which the Humane Society with its threats and penalties was not. The child savers, friendly visitors, and social reformers demanded an acceptance of external norms, at no time challenging the maldistribution of wealth and resources consequent upon rapid urbanization and industrialization. The comfortable classes kept their taxes low by limiting the public provision of assistance, preferring to give when it suited them and on their own terms, so government's responsibilities did not keep pace with urban distress. It is significant that immigrants developed their own insurance and welfare organizations, providing admittedly limited assistance from within the ethnic communities and in accordance with their own norms. Although these efforts were dwarfed by the large-scale private philanthropies, they suggest that the new residents of the city did not passively endorse the welfare solutions proposed by the more affluent.

Conclusion

10

The major changes that occurred in Pittsburgh between 1870 and 1907 resulted in a more stratified, segregated society. Without positing some mythical golden age in the past, it is still possible to see how industrialization, urbanization, and bureaucratization had negative consequences for Pittsburgh's working class that were not shared by the middle class. Irregular employment, a deteriorating urban environment, increased bureaucratic intervention in family matters, and rising infant mortality and industrial accident rates were ill winds blowing through the daily life of the working class, chilling and challenging their families, but leaving those of the middle class relatively unscathed. Survival in the city required the unremitting effort of all proletarian family members, but gender considerations controlled each individual's contributions. A number of indicators of the quality and quantity of urban life have been examined in this book that demonstrate these widening gaps between the working and middle classes and between women and men.

The substitution of steel for iron as the mainstay of Pittsburgh's economy and the increased mechanization of production processes generally led to an expansion of the unskilled labor force at the expense of skilled workers, longer working days, and higher accident rates. Because employers viewed the work force as transitory, there was little or no attempt in this era to improve the conditions of labor. Labor became a disposable "raw" material rather than an investment. It could be hired or fired as dictated by orders for goods. The steel mill owners had little incentive to keep older workers on since accumulated wisdom no longer compensated for declining strength, as it had done in the iron mills.

The experience of workers in the mills led to a collective approach to family welfare.[1] The transition from iron to steel brought in the gang labor system, lengthened the working day, and used a mainly immigrant, unskilled labor force. Individual efforts rarely resulted in overall improvement of one's situation. They could not lower the number of hours worked in the week nor lead to movement up a job hierarchy that had a declining number of skilled positions. In this era, three changes impeded the working-class search for an adequate standard of living: the continual threat to skilled workers' jobs from new technology; the elimination of the unions as a bargaining force for skilled workers; and the ethnic stratification of the labor force. The extent to which men actually achieved autonomy in the workplace or perceived that they were losing some of their control over the productive process has been amply documented elsewhere.[2] The application of new technologies in such disparate industries as glass and cigar making fragmented production into unskilled tasks. The elimination of unions in the steel mills of the Pittsburgh district after the Homestead debacle of 1892 reduced skilled men's ability to improve conditions through collective actions at the workplace in this era. The introduction of large numbers of unskilled workers from Southern and Eastern Europe stratified the labor force by ethnicity as well as skill level and created a large pool of cheap labor.

Thus, to survive in the steel mill districts, workers had to enlist the aid of their entire family, or as many as could find work. Particularly for the unskilled, whom employers viewed as a cheap, replaceable factor of production, rising above subsistence levels required putting more members of the family into the labor force and crowding one's home with lodgers. The higher incomes of skilled workers made their children's early entry into the labor force less necessary, although many still relied upon their sons' income to boost the family standard of living. Middle- and upper-class families alone could live comfortably on one income. Incomplete families, whether broken by the death of the husband or the wife, were at a real disadvantage in Pittsburgh. They lacked either income or domestic services, both of which were necessary for family survival.[3]

The increase in industrial accidents highlights the divergent experiences of the classes. Few middle-class men died as a result of accidents, rather more skilled workers did so, but laborers had the highest death rates due to accidental and violent causes. The accidental mortality rate rose in these years since steel making was more hazardous than iron making, relying as it did on inexperienced men. Unskilled workers were frequently new immigrants who had only just entered the mills. Their families, if resident in the United States, received minimal compensation; if still overseas, they received none at all. Since unskilled workers had limited abilities to save, the death of the breadwinner was a financial as well as an emotional disaster, felt by all family members.

The ability to educate one's children and keep them out of the labor force indicated disparate life chances between unskilled and skilled workers' children, those whose mothers were widows, and those from the middle and upper classes. Unskilled workers lived on a subsistence margin that precluded much expenditure on education. These families could not forgo adolescent contributions to their finances. Children's early entrance into the labor force augmented low paternal wages, served as a hedge against the uncertainties of the father's employment, and meant that mothers did not need to seek employment. For immigrants at the bottom of the occupational hierarchy of the steel mills, family objectives took precedence over individual goals.[4] Only where the family standard of living was above the subsistence margin, as for skilled workers, could resources be used to promote individual advancement through schooling. It became more difficult in this era for skilled workers to pass on their trades to their sons, although their comparatively higher standard of living enabled some to go on to high school. Skilled workers' children could use the new high schools in order to achieve middle-class occupations, and middle- and upper-class youngsters attended school longer still. Widows' children, reflecting the dire poverty of women without partners in a city that offered few nondomestic employments, left school earlier than other youngsters. Their employment mitigated their mothers' poverty, hence they continued living at home longer than other children. Their father's death ended childhood and heightened their family responsibilities.

The need to make ends meet helps explain both the rising rates of employment among young people in Pittsburgh and the increase in female participation in the labor force at the turn of the century. Smaller family sizes and the purchase rather than manufacture of many domestic items reduced the overall level of work within the home and partially explain the willingness of mothers to let their daughters take jobs. The growing availability of socially acceptable white-collar employments in stores, offices, and schools also contributed to the expansion of young women's work outside the home. The female labor force became more differentiated in these decades as the daughters of skilled workers and the middle class used their education to avoid domestic service and move into white-collar occupations.[5] Few young women from unskilled families stayed in school long enough to qualify for teaching, clerical, or sales jobs. Their parents needed their labor contributions either in the home or as wage earners too desperately to permit many to acquire more than the rudiments of education. Both the rate and type of female employment thus reflected the discrepancies between the middle and working classes and within the working class itself.

The overall impact of urban growth prompted by industrial expansion was to increase the physical and psychological distance between the working and middle classes. New laws were enacted to control what seemed to the middle class, increasingly resident on the periphery, to be the chaotic consequences of city growth and resulting deterioration of the urban environment. As the compact walking city gave way to the sprawling industrial city, the middle classes took advantage of new forms of transportation to leave the urban core. Thus the population became more and more segregated, with unskilled labor concentrated around the mills and ethnic enclaves developing around preferred employment locations. Older people were also left in the city center while the middle and upper classes moved to the edges. This segregation contributed to many of the social attitudes of the era, particularly the attempt to impose a plethora of unfamiliar practices upon newcomers and the poor.

The suburbanization of the middle and upper classes had serious consequences for the physical environment and health of the less affluent. The cost-conscious city fathers viewed it as logical to improve services, drainage, water supply, and street lighting in those areas that could pay for them, increasing the differentiation in standard of living between the classes. With the institution of the twelve-hour day and fortnightly long turn in the mid-1880s and the need for multiple wage earners, mill families could not take advantage of the new transportation systems to leave their crowded neighborhoods behind. They needed to live close to the mill gates, which led to high population densities in the neighborhoods surrounding the works. The poverty of newcomers, when combined with a desire to live near people who shared their language and values, also increased crowding in some nonmill areas, notably the Hill District. These residential areas were characterized by old housing stock, high population densities, and poor sanitary services, which led to high mortality levels from infectious diseases. The suburbs, in contrast, had new houses, lower populations densities, paved streets, sewers, piped water, and lower death rates.

The reliance upon market forces to distribute municipal improvements worked to the severe detriment of the poor. Given the demand for housing, private landlords had little incentive to install proper facilities for the working class. Tenants who changed homes frequently in their search for work had no reason to improve their landlords' property. As a result, only public recognition that the state must make such facilities mandatory led to their installation in poorer neighborhoods. Progressive reformers, such as the members of the Pittsburgh Survey, pressured city and state governments to pay for water filtration and sewer systems from the public purse and to require private landlords to install indoor plumbing in existing dwellings. These improvements occurred largely at the end of or after the era examined in this book. The combination of heavy industry, polluted water supplies, and municipal slackness in pursuit of improvements exaggerated the negative consequences of urbanization in Pittsburgh.[6]

The incidence of mortality mirrored the differences between the classes. Working class death rates exceeded those of the middle and upper classes. Here distinctions should be drawn between the strata of the working class itself. Infant mortality levels were far higher among un-skilled families than among the skilled, and the gap between skilled workers' children and those of the middle class grew during these years. This suggests that the distance in living standards between the classes widened at the turn of the century. It also underlines how very different the world of the unskilled, frequently immigrant, family still was from that of the artisans and aristocracy of labor. The children from skilled families had a better chance of surviving infancy than did those whose fathers toiled in the labor gangs. The disproportionate number of infant deaths occurring during the summer months implicates the urban environment itself as an underlying cause of much of this mortality. Inadequate sanitation and water supplies in the poorer districts, combined with lower standards of living, meant that many poor infants perished each summer through diarrhea. Middle-class babies living in suburban homes with sewers, piped water, and iceboxes or refrigerators were largely protected from the rapid increase in mortality that accompanied hot weather.

The formalization of social services, the institution of mandatory school attendance requirements, and the intervention into family life that occurred in these years tell as much about the perceptions of the middle class as they do about the needs of the working class. When residences had been more heterogeneous, charity and help were provided through direct or daily contact, but the physical distance led to the employment of paid charity and welfare workers. The poor became a job for hired agents and an undifferentiated mass to those who were ignorant of their daily circumstances. It became all too easy to attribute poverty and distress to personal or ethnic characteristics—fecklessness, alcoholism, ignorance of "American" customs—rather than to examine the root causes of pov-erty—the changing industrial structure, unsteady employment, and high levels of industrial mortality.[7]

The charitable and welfare agencies established during this period responded to genuine problems in the city. The number of instances of wife and child abuse reported to or observed by the Humane Society and the police or taken to the aldermen in all probability represented only a fraction of the actual incidents. The questions that cannot be answered from these data are: Did this form of abusive behavior increase as a result of urbanization and industrialization? Did the more fragmented nature of urban communities, characterized by a high degree of population mobility, remove traditional checks upon intrafamily violence? Did the service role played by women in the industrial economy lead men to feel they had a right to control women? The testimony presented in some of these cases supports the notion that men battered their wives when they did not meet their domestic expectations. It remains an open question whether reformers were reacting to a change in behavior patterns within families or to a new ideology of family relationships.[8]

New immigrants and the working class preferred self-help and local means of justice, such as the aldermen, to the new charity and welfare agencies, a preference that indicated the extent to which they rejected the Progressive image of themselves as dependent or needing cultural guidance from the suburbs. The inability to earn a living because of unsteady work for men, a lack of suitable employment or child-care facilities for women, particularly widows, the absence of kin who might help older or widowed residents, and the low wages paid to unskilled workers, rather than unwillingness to work, caused distress.

Urbanization and industrialization as they occurred in Pittsburgh increased inequality between the classes and the dichotomy of roles between the sexes. The measures of inequality between the sexes as reflected in gender roles were qualitatively different from those between the classes. Women's standard of living was essentially the same as men's within a class or ethnic group. The sexes shared their environment, and thus overcrowding and lack of sanitation and domestic conveniences were common to both. They might be more noticeable to women at home all day, however, than they were to men, who spent much of their time away from the household. Nonenvironmental discrepancies between the sexes were more apparent. Mortality levels varied between the sexes, for males were more vulnerable at many levels, both in infancy and adulthood. Accidental and occupational mortality rates were much higher for men than women, especially because of the nature of Pittsburgh's industries and the lack of safeguards in the workplace. Although there were some discrepancies in the educational rates of males and females, these were narrower than those between the classes.

Increasing numbers of young proletarian women moved into the labor force in these years seeking short-term jobs rather than the long-term occupations of their brothers. The expectation that women would work only briefly was a self-fulfilling prophecy. The reasons for this are not difficult to find. The majority (albeit a declining proportion) labored as domestic servants, working long hours for low pay and limited independence. The new employments for women in sweatshops and factories were frequently boring, repetitive, and poorly paid. Their wages and working conditions were poor, so that even those moving into white-collar jobs at the turn of the century (teachers excepted) found it difficult to be self-supporting on their income. In laboring homes where men were withdrawn from the daily affairs of the household by their long working hours, women were in charge of the family. Thus young women viewed marriage as the primary way to achieve some measure of autonomy in the stratified employment environments of their times. Employment outside the home increased in this era, but women's low wages and limited job prospects made it into a temporary expedient only. Women turned from the world of work, where they contributed their wages back to their families, to the creation of their own families. As a result working-class women spent only a fraction of their lives in the public worlds of school and employment and much longer in the private world of their own home. Their brothers also had limited time in school, but spent the rest of their lives in the comradeship of other men either at work or in various leisure pursuits including fishing and hunting clubs or drinking in the many taverns around the mills.

It was the structure of Pittsburgh's economy rather than the urban environment that differentiated the male and female experience. As long as the steel mills dominated the city's economy and excluded women from work inside them, women's employment in Pittsburgh could be seen as peripheral to the driving forces of the economy. Nevertheless women were chained to the continuous production processes of steel and glass as securely as if they were the pourers of molten metal and blowers of viscous glass. As the length of the working week increased for men and the numbers of skilled jobs were reduced through the introduction of new technologies, so the needs of the family unit forced women to devote themselves exclusively to supporting the men who trudged home exhausted from the mill. Women could not become ancillary wage earners. Only taking in boarders and thus being the "housewife" for several men permitted working-class women to earn additional income to balance the family budget.

Industrialization changed the nature of fatherhood as well as motherhood. Previous generations of fathers had been responsible for their sons' training and frequently worked with them. Many of Pittsburgh's industrial workers grew up on farms, where their fathers taught them the skills needed for agricultural life.[9] Others had been trained by their fathers through industrial apprenticeships, been taken on as helpers, then had worked their way up to the ranks of the iron or glass works. But employment in the steel mills mitigated against close contact between fathers and sons and lessened fathers' ability to train sons. The unreasonable hours of labor required of the men made them near strangers to their children. Being a good provider meant being out of the house; only short time at the mills, illness, or the aftermath of an accident left a father at home. The absence of apprenticeships in the steel mills and the growing desire on the part of skilled workers to educate their sons for the expanding white-collar job market also reduced the paternal role in child raising.

The same forces that drew fathers apart from their children reinforced maternal responsibilities. With husbands working such long hours and asleep for many of their nonworking hours, mothers had a concomitantly greater role to play in looking after the children. Women had to balance their maternal role with that of earning additional income through taking in boarders, for these activities competed for their attention. One approach was not to take lodgers when the children were small. This, of course, restricted income at precisely the time when family needs were greatest and ancillary wage earners fewest. The urgent nature of the demands upon proletarian women left them with little time to engage in activities outside the home, although they snatched moments of relaxation and informal contact with other women while pumping water, shopping, or chatting in the courtyards.

Pittsburgh's industrial environment promoted a familial rather than an individual approach to achievement for steel mill families. Children were drawn into the labor force since an unskilled worker's income was insufficient to sustain the family and there were no jobs that would permit women to combine housekeeping and child care. Women viewed themselves as part of a family economy in which they gave domestic services in return for support provided by men. Almost no white women held jobs after marriage, although some black women did. If women brought cash into the household, they did so through domesticity, by taking in boarders. This reemphasized the domestic nature of women's contributions to their families.

The hallmark of women's lives in the Steel City was segregation. It was this segregation that differentiated their lives from those of their maternal forebears. Industrialization decisively separated home from workplace so that women and men no longer observed each other's daily tasks. Women could not "help" their men at work as they had done in the past. It was difficult for women to combine productive economic labor and child rearing once production moved decisively outside the home.[10] Pittsburgh's highly gender-specific workplaces represent an extreme example of the sexual separation of women's and men's lives in the nineteenth and early twentieth centuries. By contrast, both colonial and rural America were replete with examples of women who took over the family business, farm, or plantation in their husband's absence. Of course women's lives were very different from men's in the eighteenth as well as the nineteenth centuries. The role reversal or interchange consisted of women helping at men's jobs, rarely the reverse. Women from the earlier period primarily had a domestic existence, bounded by a continual round of childbearing and child care. Though men's lives were oriented primarily toward the production of whatever commodities sustained the family, they were also "domestic" in that workplace and residence were the same and fathers usually trained their sons. Men's activities also had a public face that women's acquired very infrequently.[11] Yet women could and did step into the breach created by the absence of male kin. Anne Firor Scott, writing of three colonial women from disparate class and geographical backgrounds, suggests the extent to which women could be involved in business affairs despite a succession of pregnancies and the responsibilities of motherhood. One had a small shop, another kept her husband's business accounts, and the third ran several plantations.[12] Accounts of subsistence agriculture highlight women's involvement in procuring a cash income through dairying, raising chickens, and making butter.[13]

There are no instances where women stepped into their husband's work boots in late nineteenth-century Pittsburgh; it simply did not happen in the iron and steel mills. In these years gender roles became exaggerated as the distinctions hardened between work that brought in money and service that tended the domestic hearth and made the home habitable. Married women's contribution to the family economy consisted of providing domestic services to her husband and her family, in increasing isolation. As the children were pressed into school and the labor force, mothers labored on their own in the home with sole responsibility for the domestic side of family life. Her ancillary helpers took jobs in other women's homes, in shops, and factories in order to make cash contributions to the family. Women had informal contact with kin and neighbors, keeping an eye on one another's children, helping at births, and lending what aid they could in family crises. But the high rates of mobility in the city lessened the mutual dependence among neighbors and placed greater responsibilities upon family members. New laws restricted the extent to which women could rely upon their daughters to help around the house by mandating school attendance. The immigrant woman who followed the custom of her mothers and used her daughter to mind the younger children while she got on with the washing and baking violated the prescribed social order of her new country, which required that the daughter go to school.

Middle-class women's activities acquired the public face in this era that working-class women's lacked. Freed from the pressures to produce goods and services in the home by the growing consumer economy and the labor of domestic servants, affluent women entered into a wide range of social, political, and cultural affairs. They joined organizations such as the Women's Christian Temperance Union and the General Federation of Women's Clubs. They raised funds for charity, although they rarely went among the poor themselves by the close of this era. Some agitated for increased political rights for women, while others took a more conservative view. The municipal housekeeping movement transferred the concerns of the household into the community, legitimizing women's political activities by reference to their special abilities, particularly their presumed maternal nature. Middle-class women thus acquired horizons beyond the home, although domestic events concerned them most closely.[14] Working-class women rarely ventured beyond their own home and neighborhood. In general, their extrahousehold activities revolved around church and church-sponsored lodges. Particularly for newcomers adjusting to the urban world, their families' struggles for survival left them little time to become involved with the world beyond their immediate concerns. Their world remained steadfastly private, encompassed in a few blocks rather than ranging freely across the city or beyond.

The pace of life in the mills demanded a strict routine from the men and imposed a similarly strict routine upon the women, whose domestic labors made it possible for men to devote themselves completely to their work. Social pressure from every level of society reinforced the rigidly polarized roles of breadwinner and housewife. The family strategy for survival required specialization: husbands earned while wives managed resources. Women had responsibility for purchasing food, managing the home, keeping it clean in order to ensure the children's health and well-being, and saving to buy a house and to tide the family through rough times. Their culture held women solely responsible for the harmony of human relationships. Both husband and the popular press blamed the female partner if the marriage broke down, the food was inadequate, or the children got into trouble.

The vast majority of Pittsburgh's population moved into the city from rural areas, experiencing a revolution in how they earned their living and how they lived. In Pittsburgh men moved into industry, but most women did not. The divisions of labor between the sexes did not begin with the Industrial Revolution—far from it. If anything, the situation in Pittsburgh was an adaptation to a new world through a continuation and heightening of existing gender roles. Some young women took industrial jobs on the fringes of Pittsburgh's metal and glass industries, or in food processing, or in the various sweatshops that expanded at the turn of the century. For them the world of the home, through marriage, represented an escape from poorly paid, highly fragmented labor. The external world was not financially attractive to them in the long term because the conditions and prospects were so poor. Throughout this era the dominant experience for women remained domestic labor, either as servants or in their own homes.

To paraphrase Joan Kelly, was the Industrial Revolution a revolution for women?[15] On the evidence from Pittsburgh, the answer can only be a qualified yes. The result of all the transitions examined here is that in many spheres industrialization in the Steel City exaggerated gender roles for proletarian women. It excluded married ones from economic activity and channeled unmarried ones into household labor, although this was breaking down by the turn of the century. The consumer benefits of the new society, household and municipal technology, went in this era to middle-class women and rarely, if at all, to their less affluent sisters. Working-class men moved into industry, sustained by the domestic labors of their wives. The Industrial Revolution took men out of their homes and away from their families for long periods, making it difficult for them to participate fully in family life. It thus contributed to a division of labor in which women cared for their families while men earned the money to support them. Pittsburgh's lopsided economy and the appalling working conditions and hours in the mills were extreme examples of forces at work throughout industrial society in this era. In order to survive in such an environment, the family required maximum effort from all members in rigidly defined gender roles. The Industrial Revolution did not create those roles, but in Pittsburgh it refined and etched the contrasts between women and men throughout their lives.

Abbreviations

AAISW   Amalgamated Association of Iron and Steel Workers, *Journal of Proceedings*

AIS   Archives of Industrial Society, Hillman Library, University of Pittsburgh

BIS   Pennslyvania Bureau of Industrial Statistics, *Annual Report,* Harrisburg

PAIP   Pittsburgh Association for the Improvement of the Poor, *Annual Report,* Carnegie Library of Pittsburgh

WPHS   Western Pennsylvania Humane Society, Investigation Reports of Cruelty to Animals and Children

Introduction

1   Paul U. Kellogg, "The Pittsburgh Survey," *Charities and the Commons* 2 (January 1909): 524.

2   S. J. Kleinberg, "The Systematic Study of Urban Women," in Milton Cantor and Bruce Laurie, eds., *Class, Sex, and the Woman Worker* (Westport, Conn., 1977). Ileen A. DeVault, "Sons and Daughters of Labor: Class and Clerical Work in Pittsburgh, 1870–1910s" (Ph.D. Dissertation, Yale University, 1985) correctly notes the expansion of female employment in Pittsburgh in this era. She compares Pittsburgh's female labor force participation ratio to that of the nation as a whole and concludes that it exceeded the national average (p. 64). It did, but the comparison that is more relevant is that of Pittsburgh with other large U.S. cities. The female labor force participation rate in Pittsburgh was well below the urban average. The national average is lower, of course, because rural women had lower employment levels than urban women.

3   Harry Braverman, *Labor and Monopoly Capital: The Degradation of Work in the Twentieth Century* (London, 1974), pp. 282–83.

4   For analyses of employment and the family economy, see Daniel J. Walkowitz, *Worker City, Company Town: Iron and Cotton Worker Protest in Troy and Cohoes, New York, 1855–1884* (Urbana, Ill., 1978); Tamara Hareven, *Family Time and Industrial Time* (Cambridge, 1982); John T. Cumbler, *Working Class Community in Industrial America: Work, Leisure, and Struggle in Two Industrial Cities, 1880–1930* (Westport, Conn., 1979); Jonathan Prude, *The Coming of Industrial Order: Town and Factory Life in Rural Massachusetts, 1810–1860* (Cambridge, 1983); Thomas Dublin, *Women at Work* (New York, 1979).

321

5 Diana Gittins, *Fair Sex: Family Size and Structure, 1900–1939* (London, 1982), p. 29.

6 There are many studies of U.S. cities in this period. Among those that consider the issue of gender: Olivier Zunz, *The Changing Face of Inequality: Urbanization, Industrial Development, and Immigrants in Detroit, 1880–1920* (Chicago, 1982); Elizabeth H. Pleck, *Black Migration and Poverty: Boston, 1865–1900* (New York, 1979); John Bodnar, *Workers' World: Kinship, Community, and Protest in an Industrial Society, 1900–1940* (Baltimore, 1982); Michael Haines, "Poverty, Economic Stress and the Family in a Late Nineteenth Century American City," and Claudia Goldin, "Family Strategies and the Family Economy in the Late Nineteenth Century," both in Theodore Hershberg, ed., *Philadelphia, Work, Space, Family and Group Experience in the Nineteenth Century* (New York, 1981); John Modell, "An Ecology of Family Decisions: Suburbanization, Schooling and Fertility in Philadelphia, 1880–1920," *Journal of Urban History (1980): 397–418.*

7 General theoretical structures underlying this discussion include: Samuel P. Hays, "The Changing Political Structure of the City in Industrial America," *Journal of Urban History* (1974): 6–38 and Hays, *American Political History as Social Analysis* (Knoxville, Tenn., 1980); David Montgomery, *Workers' Control in Industrial America: Studies in the History of Work, Technology, and Labor Struggles* (Cambridge, 1979); Joan Scott and Louise Tilly, *Women, Work and Family* (New York, 1978); Gerda Lerner, *The Majority Finds Its Past: Placing Women in History* (New York, 1979); Tamara K. Hareven, "The Historical Study of the Family in Urban Society," *Journal of Urban History* (1975): 365–89.

8 Stuart Galishoff, *Safeguarding the Public Health, Newark, 1895–1918* (Westport, Conn., 1975); and Judith W. Leavitt, *The Healthiest City: Milwaukee and the Politics of Health Reform* (Princeton, N.J., 1982) provide particularly relevant comparisons. Also see John Duffy, *A History of Public Health in New York City* (New York, 1968).

9 Katherine Stone, "The Origins of Job Structure in the Steel Industry," *Review of Radical Political Economics* (1974): 113–73.

10 Samuel P. Hays, *Response to Industrialism* (Chicago, 1957), and Robert Wiebe, *The Search for Order, 1877–1920* (London, 1967) delineate the tensions of this period.

11 John Bodnar, Roger Simon, and Michael P. Weber, *Lives of Their Own: Blacks, Italians, and Poles in Pittsburgh, 1900–1960* (Urbana, Ill., 1982), focus on the newcomers to Pittsburgh in this era.

12 Lincoln Steffens, *The Shame of the Cities* (Cambridge, Mass., 1948).

13 These volumes were Elizabeth Butler, *Women and the Trades: Pittsburgh, 1907 – 1908* (New York, 1909); Margaret Byington, *Homestead: The House-*

holds of a Mill Town (New York, 1910): Crystal Eastman, *Work Accidents and the Law* (New York, 1910); John Fitch, *The Steel Workers* (New York, 1910); Paul U. Kellogg, ed., *The Pittsburgh District, The Civic Frontage* (New York, 1914); Kellogg, ed., *Wage Earning Pittsburgh* (New York, 1914).

14 Kellogg, "Pittsburgh Survey," p. 525.

15 John F. McClymer, "The Pittsburgh Survey, 1907–1914: Forging an Ideology in the Steel District," *Pittsburgh History* (1974): 169–86.

16 Catherine Reiser, *Pittsburgh's Commercial Development, 1800–1850* (Harrisburg, Pa., 1951); Stefan Lorant, ed., *Pittsburgh: The Story of an American City* (Garden City, N.Y., 1964); Michael F. Holt, *Forging a Majority: The Formation of the Republican Party in Pittsburgh, 1848–1860* (New Haven, Conn., 1969); Roy Lubove, *Twentieth Century Pittsburgh: Government, Business, and Environmental Change* (New York, 1969); Joel A. Tarr, *Transportation Innovation and Changing Spatial Patterns: Pittsburgh, 1850–1910* (Pittsburgh, 1972).

17 Bodnar, Simon, and Weber, *Lives;* Peter R. Shergold, *Working Class Life: The "American Standard" in Comparative Perspective, 1899–1913* (Pittsburgh, 1982); Francis G. Couvares, *The Remaking of Pittsburgh: Class and Culture in an Industrializing City, 1877–1919* (Albany, N.Y., 1984).

18 Dorothy Thompson, "Women and Nineteenth Century Radical Politics: A Lost Dimension," in Juliet Mitchell and Ann Oakley, eds., *The Rights and Wrongs of Women* (London, 1976), pp. 112–38, posits that public work alongside other women gave women an interest in politics and working-class affairs outside the home.

19 Norman Dennis, Fernando Henriques, and Clifford Slaughter, *Coal Is Our Life: An Analysis of a Yorkshire Mining Community* (London, 1956) discuss the implicit contract between spouses in single-employer communities. "The strict sexual division of labour in Ashton, emphasized by the nature of mining, has extensions in the range of social contacts and the ideas available to the two sexes" (p. 204). Women met their husbands' domestic needs although the support they received could be variable.

20 Corinne Azen Krause, "Urbanization Without Breakdown: Italian, Jewish, and Slavic Women in Pittsburgh, 1900–1945" *Journal of Urban History* (1978): 291–306.

21 See, for example, Michael Katz, *Poverty and Policy in American History* (New York, 1983); Roy Lubove, *Poverty and Social Welfare in the United States* (New York, 1972).

22 Ethel Spencer, *The Spencers of Amberson Avenue: A Turn-of-the-Century Memoir* (Pittsburgh, 1983), documents upper-class life at the turn of the century. Despite having seven children, Mrs. Spencer participated in various club activities. She was materially assisted in household chores by a cook, chambermaid, nurse, and laundress. All but the last were resident servants (p. 38). For biblio-

graphic treatments of women's changing roles, see Joan Scott, "Women in History," *Past and Present* (1983): 141–57, who reviews recent scholarship on women. Also see E. William Monter, Joan W. Scott, and Kathryn K. Sklar, *Recent United States Scholarship on the History of Women* (Washington, D.C., 1980).

23   Ruth Schwartz Cowan, *More Work for Mother: The Story of Household Technology from the Open Hearth to the Microwave* (New York, 1983); Joan Scott, "The Mechanization of Women's Work," *Scientific American* (1982): 167–87.

24   Elizabeth Butler, "Sharpsburg: A Typical Waste of Childhood," in Kellogg, *Wage Earning Pittsburgh,* and Lila Ver Planck North, "Pittsburgh Schools," in Kellogg, *Pittsburgh District,* epitomize this approach. For general historical treatments see Walter I. Trattner, *Crusade for the Children* (Chicago, 1970); David B. Tyack, *The One Best System: A History of American Urban Education* (Cambridge, Mass., 1974); and Carl F. Kaestle and Maris Vinovskis, *Education and Social Change in Nineteenth Century Massachusetts* (Cambridge, Mass., 1980).

25   Montgomery, *Workers' Control,* discusses the attitudes of skilled workers. On the development of the family wage ideology, see Martha May, "Bread before Roses: American Workingmen, Labor Unions and the Family Wage," in Ruth Milkman, ed., *Women, Work and Protest: A Century of Women's Labor History* (London, 1985), pp. 1–21.

26   Both Virginia Yans McLaughlin, *Family and Community: Italian Immigrants in Buffalo, 1880–1930* (Ithaca, N.Y., 1977), and Elizabeth H. Pleck, "A Mother's Wage: Income Earning among Married Italian and Black Women, 1896–1911," in Michael Gordon, ed., *The American Family in Social Historical Perspective,* 2d ed., (New York, 1978), pp. 490–510, emphasize the importance of cultural values in determining women's employment patterns.

27   Glen Elder, Jr., *Children of the Great Depression* (Chicago, 1974); Elder, "Family History and the Life Course," in Tamara Hareven, ed., *Transitions: The Family and the Life Course in Historical Perspective* (New York, 1978).

28   John Bodnar, *The Transplanted: A History of Immigrants in Urban America* (Bloomington, Ind., 1985), pp. 117–68, discusses fraternal and church organizations among immigrant groups.

29   My thinking on the nature of class has been powerfully influenced by Montgomery, *Workers' Control,* and Herbert Gutman, *Work, Culture, and Society in Industrializing America* (New York, 1977). David Gordon, Richard Edwards, and Michael Reich, *Segmented Work, Divided Worker* (Cambridge, 1982), discuss proletarianization and homogenization of the labor force.

30   Stephan Thernstrom, *Poverty and Progress* (New York, 1970), pp. 90–94; Clyde Griffen and Sally Griffen, *Natives and Newcomers: The Ordering of Opportunity*

in Mid-Nineteenth Century Poughkeepsie (Cambridge, Mass., 1978), pp. 54–56.

31 The field work for the Pittsburgh Survey was conducted primarily in 1907 and 1908. Byington, *Homestead.*

32 Lubove, *Twentieth Century Pittsburgh,* p. 14.

1 Iron and Steel in Pittsburgh's Economy

1 James Parton first so described Pittsburgh in the *Atlantic Monthly* 21 (1868): 17–35. Lincoln Steffens used it also in *The Shame of the Cities* (Cambridge, Mass., 1948), p. 147.

2 William Kornblum, *Blue Collar Community* (Chicago, 1974), p. 4.

3 For the history of the Amalgamated Association of Iron and Steel Workers, see David Brody, *Steelworkers in America: The Nonunion Era* (Cambridge, Mass., 1960); John Bennett, "Iron Workers in Woods Run and Johnstown: The Union Era, 1865–1895," (Ph.D. dissertation, University of Pittsburgh, 1977); Jesse S. Robinson, *The Amalgamated Association of Iron, Steel and Tin Workers* (Baltimore, 1920).

4 Catherine Reiser, *Pittsburgh's Commercial Development, 1800–1850* (Harrisburg, Pa., 1951), pp. 45–51; Stefan Lorant, ed., *Pittsburgh: The Story of an American City* (Garden City, N.Y., 1964), p. 64; Richard C. Wade, *The Urban Frontier: The Rise of Western Cities, 1790–1830* (Cambridge, Mass., 1959), p. 11; John M. Swank, "The Iron and Steel Industries in Pennsylvania," in BIS, 1881–1882, p. 28; Henry O. Evans, *Iron Pioneer: Henry W. Oliver* (New York, 1942), p. 29; BIS, 1878–79, p. 94.

5 BIS, 1876–1877, p. 171.

6 U.S. Census, Twelfth Census, 1900, vol. 7, *Manufactures,* pt. 2 (Washington, D.C., 1902), pp. 871–72, and vol. 2, *Population,* pt. 2 (Washington, D.C., 1902), pp. 582–85.

7 U.S. Census, Ninth Census, 1870, vol. 1, *Population* (Washington, D.C., 1872), p. 795; U.S. Census, Tenth Census, 1880, vol. 18, *Report on the Social Statistics of Cities,* pt. 1 (Washington, D.C., 1886), pp. 871–72; U.S. Census, Twelfth Census, 1900, vol. 2, *Population,* pt. 2 (Washington, D.C., 1902), pp. 582–85.

8 Peter R. Shergold, *Working Class Life: The "American Standard" in Comparative Perspective, 1899 – 1913* (Pittsburgh, 1982), p. 71.

9 Peter Temin, *Iron and Steel in Nineteenth Century America: An Economic Inquiry* (Cambridge, Mass., 1964), pp. 51, 139. BIS, 1894, pp. D1–D128 also gives a detailed account of the changes in the iron industry. See John Fitch, *The Steel Workers* (New York, 1910), pp. 24–25, on the industry at the turn of the century.

10 *National Labor Tribune*, 22 August 1895.

11 Fitch, *Steel Workers*, p. 33; Daniel J. Walkowitz, *Worker City, Company Town: Iron and Cotton Worker Protest in Troy and Cohoes, New York, 1855–1884* (Urbana, Ill., 1978), p. 35.

12 Temin, *Iron and Steel*, p. 17.

13 Fitch, *Steel Workers*, p. 33.

14 James J. Davis, *The Iron Puddler: My Life in the Rolling Mills and What Came of It* (Indianapolis, Ind., 1922), p. 86.

15 Swank, "Iron and Steel," p. 35; *Steelworkers*, Brody, p. 8.

16 R. R. Wright, Jr., "One Hundred Negro Steel Workers," in Paul U. Kellogg, *Wage-Earning Pittsburgh* (New York, 1914), p. 101.

17 Bennett, "Iron Workers," p. 3. According to Bennett, the skilled workers in the Amalgamated held key positions in the mills because they, not the bosses, trained new workers in the 1850s and 1860s. Members' concern over the effect of increased mechanization on their jobs is displayed in AAISW, 1885, p. 1577. Also see Walkowitz, *Worker City*, p. 5; Bennett, "Iron Workers," p. 17; and Brody, *Steelworkers*, p. 31, on mechanization.

18 John Bodnar, *Immigration and Industrialization: Ethnicity in an American Mill Town, 1870–1940* (Pittsburgh, 1977), pp. 3–4; Temin, *Iron and Steel*, p. 131; BIS, 1880, pp. 63–64.

19 Temin, *Iron and Steel*, pp. 275, 154.

20 BIS, 1876, pp. 153, 170–73; U.S. Census, Thirteenth Census, 1910, vol. 10, *Manufactures*, pt. 3 (Washington, D.C., 1913), p. 207.

21 James Howard Bridges, *The Inside History of the Carnegie Steel Company: A Romance of Millions* (New York, 1903), pp. 204–05.

22 J. Russell Smith, *The Story of Iron and Steel* (New York, 1927), p. 31.

23 Davis, *Iron Puddler*, p. 106, describes his activities as a puddler by saying that it took him the best part of half an hour to stir the molten iron into balls.

24 Temin, *Iron and Steel*, p. 139. AAISW, 1885, p. 1577.

25 Robinson, *Amalgamated*, pp. 127–28; BIS, 1885, p. 183; AAISW, 1885, p. 1577.

26 Paul Stanley Wagner, "Natural Gas Comes to Pittsburgh" (M.A. thesis, University of Pittsburgh, 1949), pp. 15–30, 53–55. Pittsburgh's industries began using natural gas in 1875. AAISW, 1885, pp. 1577–78; BIS, 1894, pp. D101–D102.

27 Brody, *Steelworkers*, chaps. 1–3, focuses on employers' attitudes, technological changes, and the defeat of the unions in the Pittsburgh district. Captain William R. Jones quoted in ibid., p. 35. On mill magnates' attitudes, see also Fitch, *Steel Workers*, pp. 166–69; Robinson, *Amalgamated*, p. 74; Margaret Byington, *Homestead: The Households of a Mill Town* (New York, 1910), pp. 171–72.

28 Fitch, *Steel Workers*, pp. 168–69; Thomas Bell, *Out of This Furnace* (Pittsburgh, 1976), p. 167.

29　Quoted in Fitch, *Steel Workers*, pp. 14–15.

30　For an exposition of this type of role segregation in the modern era, see Michael Young and Peter Willmott, *The Symmetrical Family* (New York, 1973), pp. 184–86.

31　These conclusions are drawn from the brief accounts of strikes and the outcomes in BIS, 1873–1900, esp. 1887, pp. 171–90, F19–F49; 1890, pp. C1–C31; 1892, pp. D1–D11; and 1895, pp. 224–45.

32　AAISW, 1878, pp. 117–22; BIS, 1892, pp. D1–D11. For a full account of the Homestead strike, see Leon Wolff, *Lockout: The Story of the Homestead Strike of 1892: A Study of Violence, Unionism, and the Carnegie Steel Empire* (New York, 1965).

33　Fitch, *Steel Workers*, p. 297; Bennett, "Iron Workers," p. 73; Robinson, *Amalgamated*, p. 19.

34　Among the large number of mobility studies, several are of particular comparative interest. Walkowitz's analysis of ironworkers at mid-century, *Worker City*, is most germane. So, too, is Bodnar's account of mobility rates in Steelton, Pennsylvania, *Immigration* (pp. 51–75), between 1880 and 1905. Michael P. Weber, *Social Change in an Industrial Town: Patterns of Progress in Warren, Pennsylvania, from Civil War to World War I* (University Park, Pa., 1976), found that unskilled and semiskilled workers who stayed in the small oil boom town did tend to move up the occupational hierarchy between 1870 and 1910 (pp. 42–56). John Bodnar, Roger Simon, and Michael P. Weber, *Lives of Their Own: Blacks, Italians, and Poles in Pittsburgh, 1900–1960* (Urbana, Ill., 1982), examines the connection between ethnicity, persistence, and upward mobility in Pittsburgh for the twentieth century.

35　The sources for these remarks, as for all quantitative references, are the U.S. Censuses for the relevant years. *British* refers to individuals born in England, Scotland, and Wales; *Irish* to those born in Ireland.

36　*Irish Pennsylvanian*, 15 August 1891.

37　Fitch, *Steel Workers*, p. 148.

38　Bodnar, Simon, and Weber, *Lives*, pp. 60–63, 132.

39　Fitch, *Steel Workers*, pp. 148–49.

40　*Pittsburgh Press*, Roto, 1 September 1971. Fitch, *Steel Workers*, pp. 142–47.

41　For an overview of the experiences of black steelworkers, see Wright, "Negro Steel Workers." Byington, *Homestead*, pp. 38–40, compares the experiences of black and white steelworkers in Homestead. For additional analysis see Dennis C. Dickerson, *Out of the Crucible: Black Steelworkers in Western Pennsylvania, 1875–1980* (Albany, N.Y., 1986).

42　Ira Reid, "The Negro in the Major Industries and Building Trades of Pittsburgh" (M.A. thesis, University of Pittsburgh, 1925), p. 31.

43　Helen A. Tucker, "The Negroes of Pittsburgh," in Paul U. Kellogg, *Wage-*

Earning Pittsburgh (New York, 1914), p. 428, says that "early in the '70s a few colored men found work in some of the mills. One of the first to employ Negroes was the Black Diamond Mill on Thirtieth Street. There were a few here before 1878. In that year, through a strike, Negro puddlers were put in, and since then the force of puddlers has been made up largely of Negroes."

44 AAISW, 1882, pp. 924–25; 1883, p. 1074; 1884, p. 1469; 1885, pp. 1678–79; Wright, "Negro Steel Workers," pp. 106–07. Bodnar, Simon, and Weber, *Lives*, pp. 55–82, discuss the differential ability of blacks, Italians, and Poles to obtain employment for relatives and friends.

45 Robinson, *Amalgamated*, p. 55. The William Martin Papers, Darlington Library, University of Pittsburgh, contain a number of references to wages paid in Pittsburgh's mills. A letter dated 22 August 1892 stated that laborers at Homestead earned $1.35 per day, helpers averaged $1.75 to $2.75 and fitters $2.00 to $3.00 per day. In a letter dated 23 September 1891, Martin said that helpers in a Pittsburgh mill earned $1.75 to $2.00 a day and unskilled made about $1.35. Puddlers earned about $4.00 per day and rollers $8.00 to $10.00 daily.

46 U.S. Industrial Commission, *Report*, vol. 13 (Washington, D.C., 1901), pp. 460, 503. Arthur Shadwell, *Industrial Efficiency: A Comparative Study of Industrial Life in England, Germany, and America*, vol. 1 (London, 1906), p. 333, found that rollers and heaters earned about seven times more than laborers. See Shergold, *Working Class Life*, pp. 42–51. The estimates of earnings are based on tabular data in BIS, 1874, p. 530; 1880, pp. 209–10; 1885, pp. 60–75; 1890, pp. 484–93; 1884, E82–83. See Brody, *Steelworkers*, pp. 54–68, on the instability of wages in iron and steel, and Fitch, *Steel Workers*, pp. 153, 167, on wage cuts. AAISW, 1885, p. 1624.

47 The phrase is that of a Carnegie Company partner deriding the Amalgamated, quoted in Brody, *Steelworkers*, p. 54.

48 Frick quoted by Brody, ibid., pp. 56–57; Byington, *Homestead*, pp. 42–43.

49 Fitch, *Steel Workers*, pp. 166–67; Brody, *Steelworkers*, pp. 39–40; and Temin, *Iron and Steel*, pp. 169–93, all discuss economies of scale and industrial organization in the steel industry.

50 All statistics are derived from U.S. Census, Eleventh Census, 1890, vol. 1 *Population*, pt. 2 (Washington, D.C., 1897), pp. 630–743 for 1890; and a 10 percent sample of the 1880 manuscript census for Pittsburgh.

51 Walkowitz, *Worker City*, pp. 149–51, discusses unemployment in Troy, N.Y. For a general history of unemployment, see John A. Garraty, *Unemployment in History: Economic Thought and Public Policy* (New York, 1978).

52 Alan Dawley, *Class and Community: The Industrial Revolution in Lynn* (Cambridge, Mass., 1976), p. 85.

53 Louise Odencrantz, *Italian Women in Industry* (New York, 1919).

54 Byington, *Homestead*, p. 42.

55 U.S. Commissioner of Labor, *Eighteenth Annual Report 1903*, pt. 1 (Washington, D.C., 1903), p. 556.

56 BIS, 1874, pp. 526–27.

57 *Irish Pennsylvanian*, 15 August 1891.

58 Kingsley House Association, *Third Annual Report* (Pittsburgh, 1896), pp. 22–28.

59 Young and Willmott, *Symmetrical Family*, pp. 80–83.

60 Elizabeth H. Pleck, "A Mother's Wages: Income Earning among Married Italian and Black Women, 1896–1911," in Nancy Cott and Elizabeth H. Pleck, *A Heritage of Her Own* (New York, 1979), p. 367, states that in 1910, 10 percent of the female labor force were married. "In 1900, the rate of wage earning was 26 percent for married black women and 3.2 percent for married white women." These are national figures. The rate of employment for married women was, as she shows, much higher in the cities, although it varied significantly by ethnicity and economic opportunities available (p. 372).

61 Miriam Cohen, "Italian-American Women in New York City, 1900–1950: Work and School," in Milton Cantor and Bruce Laurie, eds., *Class, Sex, and the Woman Worker* (Westport, Conn., 1977). Bodnar, *Immigration*, p. 143, describes the labor of Slavic women during the Great Depression in Harrisburg. Tamara Hareven, *Family Time and Industrial Time* (Cambridge, 1982), found that 23 percent of the married women in Manchester, N.H. were in the labor force (pp. 194–95).

62 Byington, *Homestead*, p. 107.

63 U.S. Census, Twelfth Census, 1900, *Special Report: Occupations at the Twelfth Census* (Washington, D.C., 1904), pp. 678–81.

64 Elizabeth Butler, *Women and the Trades: Pittsburgh, 1907–1908* (New York, 1909), pp. 209–10.

65 Massachusetts Bureau of Statistics and Labor, *Sixth Annual Report* (Boston, 1875), p. 358.

66 John Modell, Frank F. Furstenberg, Jr., and Theodore Hershberg, "Social Change and Transitions to Adulthood in Historical Perspective," in Michael Gordon, ed., *The American Family in Social Historical Perspective*, 2d ed. (New York, 1978), pp. 312–14.

67 Shergold, *Working Class Life*, p. 84.

68 Benjamin F. Jones, Diary, 27 September 1876 and 22 January 1877, AIS.

69 BIS, 1885, pp. 156–184, passim.

70 John Mason to the editor, *National Labor Tribune*, 2 January 1875. Mason's letter was captioned "From a laborer."

71 Between 34 and 44 percent of the recipients of relief from the Pittsburgh Association for the Improvement of the Poor between 1880 and 1896 were born in the United States, whereas between 10 and 31 percent were British, and 24 to 38

percent were Irish. About 13 percent were German born, but only 2 to 3 percent were Polish or Italian. (Figures compiled from PAIP, 1880–96.)

72 See Crystal Eastman, *Work Accidents and the Law* (New York, 1910), pp. 49–75; Fitch, *Steel Workers*, pp. 57–74; and compare Bodnar, *Immigration*, p. 38, and Walkowitz, *Worker City*, p. 109.

73 BIS, 1882, pp. 116–17.

74 AAISW, 1883, p. 1123.

75 Quoted in Brody, *Steelworkers*, p. 32. AAISW, 1884, p. 1466. Fitch, *Steel Workers*, p. 181, wrote, "But even if men prefer to work on Sundays simply because they are greedy for extra pay, it cannot properly be cited as an excuse for the practice."

76 Pittsburgh Department of Public Safety, *Report of the Bureau of Health, 1893* (Pittsburgh, 1893), p. 100.

77 Pittsburgh death certificates, 1870–1900; U.S. Census, Eleventh Census, 1890, vol. 4, *Report on Vital and Social Statistics in the United States* pt. 2 (Washington, D.C., 1896), passim. The death certificates were examined every fifth year. All remarks about mortality in Pittsburgh are based upon them. U.S. Census, Twelfth Census, 1900 vol. 2, *Population*, pt. 2, (Washington, D.C., 1902): pp. 122–48, and vol. 4, *Vital Statistics*, pt. 2, (Washington, 1902): pp. 26–53.

78 These conclusions are based on a sample of the death certificates for the city of Pittsburgh for every fifth year between 1870 and 1900. The years were chosen to coincide with the intervals of the U.S. Census and the depressions that occurred during the middle of each decade. The crude death rate dropped from 24.1 in 1871 to 18.8 in 1900 for all large U.S. cities. It declined from 22 in 1870 to 20 in 1900 for Pittsburgh. The 1871 figure is higher than the 1870 figure because of an improved registration system. See Frederick L. Hoffman, "The General Death Rate of Large American Cities, 1871–1904," *Quarterly Publication of the American Statistical Association* 10 (1906): 1–75, and Pittsburgh Board of Health, *Annual Report, 1873*, p. 39.

79 Unless otherwise attributed, all death rates are based on the death certificates sample. Accidental and violent deaths have been grouped together in keeping with the convention established by the International Statistical Classification of Diseases, Injuries, and Causes of Death. See Henry S. Shryock and Jacob S. Siegel, *The Methods and Materials of Demography*, vol. 2 (Washington, D.C., 1975), p. 406. For a contrary view see Paul Uselding, "In Dispraise of the Muckrakers: United States Occupational Morality, 1890–1910," *Research in Economic History* (1 (1976): 348–49.

80 The early death certificates listed only the final cause of death but rarely were explicit about contributory causes. Later death certificates gave primary, secondary, and tertiary causes of death, enabling the researcher to trace the sequence of events resulting in the individual's death. For a general analysis of accidental

mortality, see Albert P. Iskrant and Paul V. Joliet, *Accidents and Homicide* (Cambridge, Mass., 1968). Roger Lane, *Violent Death in the City* (Cambridge, Mass., 1979), pp. 35–52, discusses accidental deaths in Philadelphia and also finds that many fewer females than males succumbed.

81 Eastman, *Work Accidents*, p. 14.

82 Ibid. Eastman found that, of the 526 fatal work accidents in Allegheny County, Pa., between 1 July 1906 and 30 June 1907, 24 percent happened to railroad workers, 14 percent to miners, 37 percent to steelworkers, and the rest to other occupations. On the variation by job type within the railroad industry, see Walter Licht, *Working for the Railroad* (Princeton, N.J., 1983).

83 *Pittsburgh Dispatch*, 6 July 1890.

84 *National Labor Tribune*, 14 June 1892.

85 On depressions in the steel industry, see Brody, *Steelworkers*, p. 39; Bodnar, *Immigration*, pp. 85–86; Fitch, *Steel Workers*, pp. 160–61.

86 Eastman, *Work Accidents*, p. 14 found that 47 percent of the work accidents occurred among the Austro-Hungarian and Italian workers. Herbert Gutman, *Work, Culture, and Society in Industrializing America* (New York, 1977, p. 31. Eastman, *Work Accidents*, p. 65, tells of a Slav who protested the dangers; the foremen said it did not matter if he were killed. He went, afraid to lose his job, and died.

87 *National Labor Tribune*, 22 August 1895.

88 Bell, *Furnace*, p. 54. Bell's fictional account of this accident matches the published account.

89 Interview with Ann Haver, 25 December 1976.

90 This account of the hazards of railroading is drawn from Eastman, *Work Accidents*, ch. 2. Also see Licht, *Working*, ch. 5.

91 *Commoner and Glass Worker*, 12 January 1889.

92 Fitch, *Steel Workers*, p. 68. Eastman, *Work Accidents*, p. 58, lists the private railroads of the steel industry: the Union Railroad of the Carnegie Steel Company, the Monongahela Connecting Railroad of the Jones and Laughlin, the McKeesport Connecting Railroad of the National Tube Company, etc.

93 George Orwell, *The Road to Wigan Pier* (London, 1937), describes the dangers and unpleasantness of coal mining in Britain. Also see Katherine A. Harvey, *The Best Dressed Miners: Life and Labor in the Maryland Coal Region, 1835–1910* (Ithaca, N.Y., 1969), pp. 38–42, for conditions in the Maryland coal mines which, according to Harvey, were considerably safer than other mines; yet as late as 1905 miners there labored by the naked flame of their lamps in up to a foot of water (p. 42).

94 BIS, 1878–79, pp. 401–655 provides a complete analysis of coal mining accidents in Pennsylvania. *National Labor Tribune*, 10 July 1880.

95 *National Labor Tribune*, 21 February 1874.

96 By "J. P., Houtzdale, Pa.," in *National Labor Tribune*, 11 September 1880. Houtzdale is about twenty miles north of Altoona, Pa.

97 *National Labor Tribune*, 14 June 1879; *Commoner and Glass Worker*, 12 January 1889.

98 *National Labor Tribune*, 23 October 1880. The accident occurred at the "Seaham Colliery, County Durham, North of England," and a poem about the accident accompanied an editorial praising the miner who stayed with the dying lad, stating that "the theme was worthy of the poet's pen."

99 *Commoner and Glass Worker*, 17 March 1888.

100 *National Labor Tribune*, 22 August 1887.

101 *Commoner and Glass Worker*, 23 October 1887. *National Labor Tribune*, 27 November 1873, carried an account of water screens that kept puddlers "comparatively comfortable." Ibid., 7 March 1874 and 11 July 1874, requested inspections of steam boilers. See also "Letter from a Committee of 12 Workmen," in Troy, N.Y., *Evening Standard*, 23 December 1878, reprinted in *National Labor Tribune*, 4 January 1879, regarding boilers in the steel works; *National Labor Tribune*, 22 May 1880, containing an account of a paper read at a district meeting concerning the benefits accruing to "boiler, heater, and manufacturer alike" from the use of patented shields that protected the workers from the heat of the furnaces.

102 *National Labor Tribune*, 8 March 1900. Walter I. Trattner, *Crusade for the Children* (Chicago, 1970), p. 74, notes that the Pennsylvania state commissioner of labor fought with mine operators who opposed requirements for documentary proof of age for child workers and declared that most mine accidents resulted from the workers' carelessness.

103 Pittsburgh death certificates, 1895; Eastman, *Work Accidents*, pp. 169–73. *National Labor Tribune*, 8 March 1900.

104 James Timberlake, *Prohibition and the Progressive Movement* (Cambridge, Mass., 1965), pp. 67–75; David S. Beyer, "Safety Provisions in the United States Steel Corporation," *Survey*, 7 May 1910.

105 Brody, *Steelworkers*, p. 91, notes that before 1900 steel companies employed liability insurance firms, which were not concerned with seeing justice done for the working man or his family.

106 Eastman, *Work Accidents*, p. 69.

107 U.S. Immigration Commission, *Reports: Immigrants in Industries, Iron and Steel Manufacturing*, vol. 8 (Washington, D.C., 1911), pp. 139–51. The Pennsylvania judiciary ruled that "the right of recovery for death does not extend to dependent relatives who are non-resident and alien" (Eastman, *Work Accidents*, p. 65).

108 *Commoner and Glass Worker*, 23 October 1887.

109 *National Labor Tribune,* 8 March 1890; Fitch, *Steel Workers,* pp. 195–96.
110 Eastman, *Work Accidents,* pp. 132–43, 119.

2 Population Growth and Mobility

1 U.S. Census, Twelfth Census, 1900, vol. 1, *Population,* pt 1 (Washington, D.C., 1901), pp. 430–33; George Littleton Davis, "Greater Pittsburgh's Commercial and Industrial Development, 1850–1900" (Ph.D. dissertation, University of Pittsburgh, 1951), p. 51. The Municipal Planning Association was formed in 1920. The Allegheny Conference on Community Development, founded by Andrew Mellon in 1943, worked closely with the Pennsylvania Economy League, Western Division (founded 1935), and the Pittsburgh Regional Planning Association (founded 1938) to promote the Pittsburgh Renaissance. See Roy Lubove, ed., *Pittsburgh* (New York, 1976), p. 178; Lubove, *Twentieth-Century Pittsburgh: Government, Business, and Environmental Change* (New York, 1969), pp. 27–28.

2 Board of Trade of London, *Cost of Living in American Towns: Report of an Inquiry* (London, 1911), p. 337.

3 Stefan Lorant, ed., *Pittsburgh: The Story of an American City* (Garden City, N.Y., 1964), pp. 20–26, gives an account of the battle in 1755 in which General Braddock lost his life and Colonel George Washington fought.

4 In James Howard Bridges, *The Inside History of the Carnegie Steel Company: A Romance of Millions* (New York, 1903), pp. 85–86. Bill Jones was Captain William R. Jones, manager of the Edgar Thomson Works.

5 Margaret Byington, *Homestead: The Households of a Mill Town* (New York, 1910), pp. 4–5, provides an account of the development of the steel industry in Homestead. Joel Tarr, "Growth, Stability and Decline in an Urban Area: One Hundred Years of Hazelwood" (paper presented at the Social Science History Association, Columbus, Ohio, 1978), details the development of the community that grew up around the steel mill in that somewhat isolated section of Pittsburgh.

6 U.S. Census, Ninth Census, 1870, vol. 1, *Population,* (Washington, D.C., 1872), p. 244; U.S. Census, Twelfth Census, 1900, vol. 2, *Population,* pt. 2, (Washington, D.C., 1902), pp. 582–85.

7 Kathleen Neils Conzen, *Immigrant Milwaukee: Accommodation and Community in a Frontier City* (Cambridge, Mass., 1976); Stephan Thernstrom, *Poverty and Progress: Social Mobility in a Nineteenth-Century City* (New York, 1970); Howard Gitelman, *Workingmen of Waltham: Mobility in American Urban Industrial Development, 1850–1890* (Baltimore, 1974); Dean R. Esslinger, *Immigrants and the City: Ethnicity and Mobility in a Nineteenth-Century Mid-Western Community* (Port Washington, N.Y., 1975), focus on Germans and Irish

in their respective cities. Daniel J. Walkowitz, *Worker City, Company Town: Iron and Cotton Worker Protest in Troy and Cohoes, New York, 1855–1884* (Urbana, Ill., 1978), and John Bodnar, *Immigration and Industrialization: Ethnicity in an American Mill Town, 1870–1940* (Pittsburgh, 1977), analyze ethnicity in Troy and Cohoes, N.Y., and Steelton, Pa., respectively. Also see Victor Greene, *The Slavic Community on Strike: Immigrant Labor in Pennsylvania Anthracite* (Notre Dame, Ind., 1968). Of particular interest in the literature on black migration patterns are: Claude V. Kiser, *Sea Island to City* (New York, 1969); David Katzman, *Before the Ghetto: Black Detroit in the Nineteenth Century* (Urbana, Ill., 1973); Florette Henri, *Black Migration: Movement North, 1900–1920* (New York, 1975); Carter G. Woodson, *A Century of Negro Migration* (New York, 1969).

8   Lubove, *Twentieth-Century Pittsburgh*, pp. 27–28.

9   For a detailed ethnic distribution of household heads, see S. J. Kleinberg, "Technology's Stepdaughters: The Impact of Industrialization upon Working Class Women, Pittsburgh, 1865–1890" (Ph.D. dissertation, University of Pittsburgh, 1973), p. 44.

10 Abraham Epstein, *The Negro Migrant in Pittsburgh* (Pittsburgh, 1918), passim. Paul J. Lammermeier, "Urban Black Family of the Nineteenth Century: A Study of the Black Family Structure in the Ohio Valley, 1850–1880," *Journal of Marriage and Family* (August 1973): 445, calculated that the proportion of skilled workers in the black population declined from 16.6 percent to 8.8 percent in those years. Blacks also complained of hostility from union members (the skilled iron- and steelworkers) once they had obtained jobs within the mill. AAISW, 1884, p. 1469. R. R. Wright, Jr., "One Hundred Negro Steel Workers," in Paul U. Kellogg, ed., *Wage-Earning Pittsburgh* (New York, 1914), also provides a mixed portrait of the experiences of blacks in the mills.

11 Alois B. Koukol, "A Slav's a Man for A' That," in Kellogg, *Wage-Earning Pittsburgh*, p. 64. Ewa Morawska, " 'For Bread with Butter': Life-worlds of Peasant Immigrants from East Central Europe, 1880–1914," *Journal of Social History* (Spring 1984): 387–404, provides an overview of the world from which many of Pittsburgh's immigrants came and their strategies in the New World.

12 James J. Davis, *The Iron Puddler: My Life in the Rolling Mills and What Came of It* (Indianapolis, Ind., 1922), p. 51. Davis was typical of his generation of iron puddlers, learning his trade as a helper under the watchful eye of older relatives. See David Montgomery, *Workers' Control in Industrial America: Studies in the History of Work, Technology, and Labor Struggles* (Cambridge, 1979), p. 11.

13 Byington, *Homestead*, p. 206. Helen Z. Lopata, "The Polish American Family," in Charles H. Mindel and Robert W. Habenstein, *Ethnic Families in America: Patterns and Variations* (New York, 1976), describes the Polish

immigrants as making frequent trips across the Atlantic to escort family members to the United States. Family and friends acted as intermediaries with the social system (pp. 16–19).

14 U.S. Census, Twelfth Census, 1900, vol. 2, *Population*, pt. 2 (Washington, D.C., 1902), pp. 310–48. At the other extreme, the male to female ratio in Fall River, Mass., was 92:100; it was 90:100 in New Orleans and Washington, D.C.

15 Thomas Bell, in *Out of This Furnace* (Pittsburgh, 1976), pp. 14–20, captures two patterns in his fictional portrayal of life among Pittsburgh's Hungarian immigrants. Kracha sent for his wife; later Dubik sent for his sweetheart. In both couples, the men moved outside the immediate ethnic community by working, but the women remained within it. In 1900, 89 percent of black women and 58 percent of black men were employed in the "domestic and personal service" category of the census. U.S. Census, Twelfth Census, 1900, *Special Report: Occupations at the Twelfth Census* (Washington, D.C., 1904), pp. 678–83. Ira Reid, "The Negro in the Major Industries and Building Trades of Pittsburgh" (M.A. thesis, University of Pittsburgh, 1925), p. 8, found that one-third of all black men in 1910 were domestic servants, excluding unspecified laborers whom the 1900 census included in the domestic service category.

16 All statistics are derived from a 10 percent sample of the 1860 manuscript census for Pittsburgh, and U.S. Census, Twelfth Census, 1900, vol. 2, *Population*, pt. 2, pp. 310–48.

17 Ibid. Slavic immigrants in Pittsburgh told social surveyors that they wished to return to the old country, though some who did found conditions less congenial than they remembered. See Koukol, "A Slav," p. 67. John Bodnar, Roger Simon, and Michael P. Weber, *Lives of Their Own: Blacks, Italians, and Poles in Pittsburgh, 1900–1960* (Urbana, Ill., 1982), pp. 120–21, suggest that age and length of stay in Pittsburgh accounted for persistence among northern-born blacks, about one-third of whom remained in the city between 1900 and 1905.

18 Sam Bass Warner, Jr., *Streetcar Suburbs: The Process of Growth in Boston, 1870–1900* (New York, 1971), discusses the development of transportation systems and class homogeneity.

19 Michael F. Holt, *Forging a Majority: The Formation of the Republican Party in Pittsburgh, 1848–1860* (New Haven, Conn., 1969), pp. 31–33, 334. Joel Tarr, *Transportation, Innovation, and Changing Spatial Patterns in Pittsburgh, 1850–1934* (Chicago, 1978), pp. 1–5. Howard Storch, "Changing Functions of the Center City, Pittsburgh, 1850–1912" (seminar paper, Department of History, University of Pittsburgh, 1966), pp. 1–5.

20 Holt, *Forging a Majority*, p. 32.

21 Warner, *Streetcar Suburbs*, p. 5.

22 Mary Darlington, Scrapbook, Darlington Library, University of Pittsburgh,

clipping of the obituary of Elizabeth F. Denny, patron of many local charities in the middle decades of the nineteenth century. Mrs. Denny, widow of a lawyer, Harmar Denny, died 18 January 1878.

23 Tarr, *Transportation, 1850–1934,* p. 5.

24 Edward Ewing Pratt, "Industrial Causes of Congestion of the Population in New York City," *Columbia University Studies in History* (New York, 1911), pp. 116–18.

25 Byington, *Homestead,* p. 35.

26 Interview with John B., 3 March 1976, Pittsburgh Oral History Project, cited in Bodnar, Simon, and Weber, *Lives,* p. 71.

27 Tarr, *Transportation, 1850–1934,* pp. 47–53, provides maps of Pittsburgh's transit systems. For photographs see Stefan Lorant, ed., *Pittsburgh: The Story of an American City* (Garden City, N.Y., 1964), pp. 192–93, 225.

28 Holt, *Forging a Majority,* pp. 30–31; 1880 census sample; U.S. Census, Eleventh Census, 1890, vol. 1, *Population,* pt. 1 (Washington, D.C., 1895), p. 945.

29 Elizabeth Butler, *Women and the Trades: Pittsburgh, 1907–1908* (New York, 1909), pp. 334–38.

30 1880 census sample.

31 Board of Trade of London, *Cost of Living,* p. 339; 1880 census sample; Willard Glazier, "The Great Furnace of America," in Lubove, *Pittsburgh,* p. 23; J. Cutler Andrews, "The Civil War and Its Aftermath," in Lorant, *Pittsburgh,* pp. 143, 153; Gerald W. Johnson, "The Muckraking Era," in ibid., pp. 268–70.

32 1880 census sample.

33 J. Davis, *Iron Puddler,* p. 62.

34 Howard P. Chudacoff, *Mobile Americans: Residential and Social Mobility in Omaha, 1880–1920* (New York, 1972), p. 25.

35 The death certificates for the city of Pittsburgh, 1870–1905, AIS. I was granted access for them only for 1870–1900.

36 Thernstrom, *Poverty and Progress,* p. 86.

37 Chudacoff, *Mobile Americans,* p. 41. Clyde Griffen and Sally Griffen, *Natives and Newcomers: The Ordering of Opportunity in Mid-Nineteenth Century Poughkeepsie* (Cambridge, Mass., 1978), p. 16; Stephan Thernstrom, *The Other Bostonians: Poverty and Progress in the American Metropolis, 1880–1920* (Cambridge, Mass., 1973), pp. 222–25; Thomas Kessner, *The Golden Door: Italian and Jewish Immigrant Mobility in New York City, 1880–1915* (New York, 1972).

38 Bodnar, Simon, and Weber, *Lives,* p. 121.

39 David Brody, *Steelworkers in America: The Nonunion Era* (Cambridge, Mass., 1960), p. 87.

40 AAISW, 1885, p. 1577.

41 This reflects similar patterns found by other analysts of mobility. See Griffen and Griffen, *Natives and Newcomers*, p. 25, for ethnic persistence rates, and p. 16 for occupational breakdown. The Philadelphia Social History Project generated a number of studies of mobility. Stephanie W. Greenberg, "Industrialization in Philadelphia: The Relationship between Industrial Location and Residential Patterns, 1880–1930" (Ph.D. dissertation, Temple University, 1977); and Alan N. Burstein, "Residential Distribution and Mobility of Irish and German Immigrants in Philadelphia, 1850–1880" (Ph.D. dissertation, University of Pennsylvania, 1975), are of particular relevance.

42 Byington, *Homestead*, p. 135. Peter R. Shergold, *Working Class Life: The "American Standard" in Comparative Perspective, 1899–1913* (Pittsburgh, 1982), pp. 39–40, states that new immigrants were the first to be fired at the mills; many left the city altogether. U.S. Congress, Senate, *Reports of the Immigration Commission*, Senate Document no. 633 (Washington, D.C., 1911), suggested that about half the immigrants in this era eventually returned to their country of origin, and that during the depression of 1907–1908 many more left than arrived.

43 AAISW, 1886, p. 1736.

44 Board of Trade of London, *Cost of Living*, p. 498.

45 Koukol, "A Slav," p. 77. Alexis Sokoloff, "Medieval Russia in the Pittsburgh District?" in Kellogg, *Wage-Earning Pittsburgh*, p. 94, wrote that the Russians and "the rest of the Slavs" lived as though in the United States temporarily. "They expect to go back home."

46 Michael Anderson, *Family Structure in Nineteenth-Century Lancashire* (Cambridge, 1971), p. 150.

47 Shergold, *Working Class Life*, p. 40.

48 Anderson, *Family Structure*, p. 41, found that 14 percent of the men and 19 percent of the women over the age of 10 in 1861 were living in the same house as in 1851, and that the turnover was higher during depressions.

49 Carolyn Sutcher Schumacher, "School Attendance in Nineteenth-Century Pittsburgh: Wealth, Ethnicity, and Occupational Mobility of School Age Children, 1855–1865" (Ph.D. dissertation, University of Pittsburgh, 1977), p. 193. The importance of teaching as a profession for women can be estimated from Richard M. Bernard and Maris A. Vinovskis, "The Female School Teacher in Antebellum Massachusetts," *Journal of Social History* (March 1977): 332–45. They found that only 2 percent of the white working women in their sample were teachers but that about 20 percent had been teachers at some point in their working lives. Though late nineteenth-century Pittsburgh little resembles antebellum Massachusetts, the data are suggestive.

50 On the growing importance of white-collar work after 1900, see W. Elliot Brownlee and Mary M. Brownlee, *Women in the American Economy: A Documentary History, 1675–1929* (New Haven, Conn., 1976), pp. 31–33.

51 Davis, *Iron Puddler*, p. 51. Bell, *Furnace*, pp. 14–25. The role of the family in migration has been discussed in detail by Tamara Hareven, "Family Time and Industrial Time: Family and Work in a Planned Corporation Town, 1900–1914," in Hareven, ed., *Family and Kin in Urban Communities, 1700–1930* (New York, 1977).

52 Koukol, "A Slav," p. 74, recounts Andrew Antonik's accident at the Homestead Mill and its aftermath.

53 Griffen and Griffen, *Natives and Newcomers*, pp. 22–23, found that older workers continued to move in and out of the city in search of work. "The continuing movement in search of jobs among the unskilled who had achieved no security for their old age was yet another of the familiar patterns citizens recognized in the volatility of people in the community."

54 Michael P. Weber, *Social Change in an Industrial Town: Patterns of Progress in Warren, Pennsylvania, from Civil War to World War I* (University Park, Pa., 1976), p. 36, shows that in Warren, native whites had higher persistence rates than the foreign born. Richard J. Hopkins, "Status, Mobility, and the Dimensions of Changes in a Southern City: Atlanta, 1870–1910," in Kenneth J. Jackson and Stanley K. Schultz, eds., *Cities in American History* (New York, 1977), p. 228, found that "Black Atlantans changed residence within the city as often as most whites, but blacks left the city less often than all whites." Griffen and Griffen, *Natives and Newcomers*, p. 25, found blacks had lower persistence rates than whites.

55 G. Dale Greenwald, "Germans in Pittsburgh, 1850, 1880, 1930: Residency, Occupations, and Assimilation" (seminar paper, Department of History, Carnegie-Mellon University, 1976), pp. 18, 23.

56 A similar pattern of labeling individuals by who owned their country rather than their language group exists in the marriage records for Pittsburgh in 1900. Marriage dockets, Allegheny County, 1900.

57 Crystal Eastman, *Work Accidents and the Law* (New York, 1910), p. 14.

58 Bodnar, Simon, and Weber, *Lives*, p. 121.

59 Wright, "Negro Steel Workers," pp. 98–99, states that almost all the black steel workers in Pittsburgh were natives of the South and only 6 were over 50 years of age. Bodnar, Simon, and Weber, *Lives*, p. 129. Morawska, "For Bread," pp. 395–96, points out that it was the earnings of wives taking in boarders and children's work outside the home that helped consolidate the position of Eastern European immigrants in Johnstown, Pa., at the beginning of the twentieth century.

3 Home and Neighborhood

1 U.S. Census, Twelfth Census, 1900, vol. 1, *Population*, pt. 1 (Washington, D.C., 1901), pp. 430–33. The role of women in taking in boarders has been explored by Tamara Hareven, *Family Time and Industrial Time* (Cambridge, Mass., 1982), pp. 159–66, passim.

2 F. Elisabeth Crowell, "Painter's Row: The Company House," in Paul U. Kellogg, ed., *The Pittsburgh District: The Civic Frontage* (New York, 1914), p. 131.

3 *Harper's New Monthly Magazine*, December 1880, p. 57.

4 The best published collection of photographs of Pittsburgh during this era is in Stefan Lorant, ed., *Pittsburgh: The Story of an American City* (Garden City, N.Y., 1964). The Pennsylvania Division, Carnegie Library of Pittsburgh, has a photographic file containing most of the photographs in Lorant's book and many others culled from a wide variety of sources. Some of the photographs in Lorant, *Pittsburgh*, have been retouched to emphasize the detail that the smoke obliterated. One on p. 193 shows workers' housing; in the original in the Pennsylvania Division, the mills are barely visible; in the book they have been outlined and darkened, as were the houses and the horsecar. Also see Lorant, *Pittsburgh*, pp. 170–75.

5 The "Plan of Birmingham and East Birmingham, 1872," a map in the possession of Carnegie Library of Pittsburgh, shows that iron- and glassworks had preempted the flat land along the river, and some of the glass houses had moved several blocks back from the river. Most of the residents living near these industrial establishments were laborers, semiskilled and skilled industrial workers. The occupations of the household heads were located in the U.S. Census, Ninth Census, 1870, manuscript census for Birmingham. This district became part of the city of Pittsburgh in 1873.

6 BIS, 1886, p. 20.

7 Michael F. Holt, *Forging a Majority: The Formation of the Republican Party in Pittsburgh, 1848–1860* (New Haven, 1969), p. 30, says that in the 1850s most unskilled workers "with families could still afford to rent their own cottages." D. A. Sanborn, *Insurance Map of the Business and Manufacturing Parts of Pittsburgh, West and South Pittsburgh, Allegheny and Birmingham, Pennsylvania, 1871* (New York, 1871). A good summary of housing conditions in Pittsburgh after the turn of the century can be found in Emily Wayland Dinwiddie and F. Elisabeth Crowell, "The Housing of Pittsburgh's Workers," in Kellogg, ed., *Pittsburgh District*, pp. 87–123.

8 U.S. Census, Ninth Census, 1870, vol. 1, *Population*, (Washington, D.C., 1872), p. 600; U.S. Census, Eleventh Census, 1890, vol. 1, *Population*, pt. 1

(Washington, D.C., 1895), p. 945. Unless otherwise noted, all statistics of population density are drawn from these two sources.

9   Population density decreased in the Fourth Ward in the last decades of the century.

10   The total number of dwellings per acre was derived by dividing the number of acres in each ward by the number of dwellings.

11   The number of people per dwelling was derived by dividing the population of the ward by the number of dwellings.

12   The Sanborn *Insurance Map* is located in the Pennsylvania Division of the Carnegie Library, Pittsburgh.

13   Ruby Ross Goodnow and Rayne Adams, *The Honest House: Presenting Examples of the Usual Problems Which Face the Home-Builder Together with an Exposition of the Simple Architectural Principles Which Underlie Them: Arranged Especially in Reference to Small House Design* (New York, 1914). The house sizes given in this book, aimed at the home builder, ranged from 1,250 square feet for a Philadelphia duplex to 3,000 square feet for a Manchester, Mass., three-story stucco house (pp. 132–72). All references to house sizes in the Third Ward are derived from the Sanborn *Insurance Map* and the 1870 census.

14   Michael Young and Peter Willmott, *The Symmetrical Family* (New York, 1973), passim.

15   BIS, 1883, pp. 112–15.

16   S. J. Kleinberg, "Housing and Privacy: Contrasts Between the Working and Middle Classes," in Edward Papenfuse, ed., *Proceedings of the Second Maryland Conference on Local History,* Annapolis, 1978 (forthcoming).

17   Carroll D. Wright, *Seventh Special Report of the Commissioner of Labor: The Slums of Great Cities: New York, Baltimore, Chicago, and Philadelphia* (Washington, D.C., 1894), pp. 584–94.

18   Ibid., p. 84. Other contemporary housing studies include Edith Elmer Wood, *The Housing of the Unskilled Wage Earner: America's Next Problem* (New York, 1919); Janet Kemp, *Housing Conditions in Baltimore* (New York, 1907); U.S. Congress, Senate, *Reports Relating to Affairs in the District of Columbia: The President's Home Commission* (Washington, D.C., 1910); and E. P. Goodrich and George B. Ford, *Housing Report to the City Plan Commission of Newark, New Jersey* (Newark, 1913).

19   Margaret Byington, *Homestead, The Households of a Mill Town* (New York, 1910), p. 202.

20   Board of Trade of London, *Cost of Living in American Towns: Report of an Inquiry* (London, 1911), pp. 352–53.

21   Abraham Oseroff, *Survey of Workingmen's Homes in the Soho District of Pittsburgh: A Study of Civic Neglect in the Heart of a Great City* (Pittsburgh, 1914), unpaginated.

22 Peter R. Shergold, *Working Class Life: The "American Standard" in Comparative Perspective, 1899–1913* (Pittsburgh, 1982), p. 149. Oseroff, *Workingmen's Homes*, noted that the Chamber of Commerce Housing Committee developed a plan for building small, sanitary dwellings for the working class that "seems practical." The problem with model housing was that it rarely returned sufficiently on the capital to make it a worthwhile investment.

23 *People's Monthly*, June 1871.

24 PAIP, 1880, p. 11; *Pittsburgh Commercial Gazette*, 19 January 1880.

25 *National Labor Tribune*, 5 April 1900.

26 Paul U. Kellogg, "Community and Workshop," in Kellogg, ed., *Wage-Earning Pittsburgh* (New York, 1914), p. 20.

27 F. Elisabeth Crowell, "Tammany Hall: A Common Rookery," in Kellogg, *Pittsburgh District*, pp. 136–38.

28 Pittsburgh Board of Health, *Annual Report* (Pittsburgh, 1876), p. 27.

29 See the photographs by Peter Krumel in Lorant, *Pittsburgh*, pp. 252–53.

30 New York Bureau of Municipal Research, *The City of Pittsburgh, Pennsylvania: Reports of a Survey of the Department of Health* (Pittsburgh, 1913), pp. 26–30.

31 Florence Larrabee Lattimore, "Three Studies in Housing and Responsibility: Skunk Hollow, the Squatter," in Kellogg, *Pittsburgh District*, p. 128.

32 Thomas Bell, *Out of This Furnace* (Pittsburgh, 1976), p. 168. Mihal Dobrejcak, "relit his pipe against the privy's smell and went outside."

33 Robert Layton in U.S. Congress, Senate, Committee on Education and Labor, *Report upon the Relations between Labor and Capital* (Washington, D.C., 1885), vol. 1, pp. 27, 22.

34 BIS, 1883, pp. 112–15.

35 *National Labor Tribune*, 20 December 1890.

36 R. R. Wright, Jr., "One Hundred Negro Steel Workers," in Kellogg, *Wage-Earning Pittsburgh*, p. 102.

37 Helen A. Tucker, "The Negroes of Pittsburgh," *Charities and the Commons*, 3 January 1909.

38 Ibid.

39 About 50 percent of the foreign-born whites in Pittsburgh in 1930 owned their own homes as compared with 17 percent of all blacks. Black home ownership levels were 33 percent of those of foreign-born whites in 1900, rising to 40 percent in 1930. John Bodnar, Roger Simon, and Michael P. Weber, *Lives of Their Own: Blacks, Italians, and Poles in Pittsburgh, 1900–1960* (Urbana, Ill., 1982), p. 159.

40 Bell, *Furnace*, p. 144.

41 Oseroff, *Workingmens' Homes*.

42 Pittsburgh Christian Social Service Union, The Methodist Episcopal Church Union, and Other Co-operating Agencies, *The Strip: A Socio-Religious Survey of*

a Typical Problem Section of Pittsburgh, Pennsylvania (Pittsburgh, 1915), p. 27.

43   BIS, 1886, p. 20.

44   *Harper's Weekly,* 15 February 1871. Layton in Senate Committee on Education and Labor, *Labor and Capital,* p. 29. John Fitch, *The Steel Workers* (New York, 1910), p. 58.

45   Paul Stanley Wagner, "Natural Gas Comes to Pittsburgh" (M.A. thesis, University of Pittsburgh, 1949), pp. 15–30, 53–55.

46   W. C. Rice, "Midland: A Forerunner of Modern Housing Development for Industrial Sections," in Kellogg, *Wage-Earning Pittsburgh,* pp. 410–13, describes Midland Steel Company's efforts to provide housing for its workers in a new industrial town, thirty-seven miles southwest of Pittsburgh on the Ohio River. It provided for the segregation of the foreign born and blacks from native-born whites.

47   H. W. D. English, *Annual Report of the President of the Pittsburgh Chamber of Commerce* (Pittsburgh, 1908).

48   Crowell, "Painter's Row," pp. 130–34.

49   Board of Trade of London, *Cost of Living,* p. 354.

50   Layton in Senate Committee on Education and Labor, *Labor and Capital,* p. 27; Sanborn, *Insurance Map;* and U.S. Census, Ninth Census, 1870, manuscript census.

51   Byington, *Homestead,* pp. 202–03.

52   Ibid. See Massachusetts Bureau of the Statistics of Labor, *Sixth Annual Report* (Boston, 1875), for similar contrasts between the strata of the working class. It found ironworkers living in "moderately furnished" rooms, a machine shop laborer in a "poorly furnished" house, and a roller residing with wife and two children in a well-furnished five-room tenement. Robert Coit Chapin, *The Standard of Living Among Workingmen's Families* (New York, 1910), p. 96, found similar discrepancies for the post-1900 period.

53   The William Martin Papers, Darlington Library, University of Pittsburgh. Although Martin lived in Columbus, Ohio, at the time he kept some of these records, his spending patterns reflect those of Pittsburgh's skilled working-class families in view of the mobility among iron- and steelworkers and the fixed tonnage scales under which they labored.

54   Photographic file, Pennsylvania Division, Carnegie Library of Pittsburgh. Also see the photographs by Lewis Hine for the Pittsburgh Survey published in Byington, *Homestead;* Kellogg, *Pittsburgh District,* and Kellogg, *Wage-Earning Pittsburgh.* A photographer, Solomon Butcher, captured the significance of the parlor organ in an 1888 picture of a Custer County, Neb., family. They posed around their organ with livestock, wagons, and corrals in the background. The photographer noted that the family did not want to "show the sod

house to friends back East, but the young lady and mother wanted to prove they owned an organ." See William R. Current and Karen Current, *Photography and the Old West* (New York, 1979).

55 Layton in Senate Committee on Education and Labor, *Labor and Capital*, p. 20.

56 See the Lewis Hine photograph of a "Front Room" opposite p. 56 in Byington, *Homestead*.

57 Alan Dawley, *Class and Community: The Industrial Revolution in Lynn* (Cambridge, Mass., 1976), p. 105.

58 WPHS, 6 June 1888.

59 This is a composite description drawn from the photographs in the files of the Humane Society and the PAIP and those taken by Lewis Hine for the Pittsburgh Survey.

60 Michael Anderson, *Family Structure in Nineteenth-Century Lancashire* (Cambridge, 1971), p. 34, describes the poverty of the textile workers of Lancashire. Antonia Bergeron, who started working in the Amoskeag mill when she was 15 (in 1895), described how her mother set up housekeeping: "She bought some secondhand clothes, an old stove, some beds and mattresses, and she set up housekeeping." Quoted in Tamara Hareven and Randolph Langenbach, *Amoskeag: Life and Work in an American Factory City* (New York, 1978), pp. 58, 60.

61 John J. O'Connor, *The Cost of Living Studies in Pittsburgh* (Pittsburgh,, 1914), p. 7.

62 *People's Monthly*, February 1872; *National Labor Tribune*, 2 January 1875.

63 BIS, 1883, pp. 112–15.

64 Ibid., 1886, p. 19.

65 Byington, *Homestead*, p. 52.

66 Board of Trade of London, *Cost of Living*, p. 351.

67 Frank Hatch Streighthoff, *The Standard of Living among the Industrial People of America* (Boston, 1911), p. 18.

68 On boarding and lodging generally see John Modell and Tamara Hareven, "Urbanization and the Malleable Household: An Examination of Boarding and Lodging in American Families," *Journal of Marriage and the Family* 35 (1973): 467–79.

69 1880 census sample.

70 Oseroff, *Workingmen's Homes;* Byington, *Homestead*, p. 143.

71 Shergold, *Working Class Life*, pp. 86–88, discusses the various contemporary estimates of the extent of the boarding population. Bodnar, Simon, and Weber, *Lives*, based their calculations on a 20 percent sample of the black, Italian, and Polish families in the 1900 manuscript census.

72 Glen Elder, Jr., "Family History and the Life Course," in Tamara Hareven, ed., *Transitions: The Family and the Life Course in Historical Perspective* (New

York, 1978), p. 52, states that "boarding helped to stabilize family income by replacing the earnings of a departed offspring with the payments of a guest, and enabled wives to earn money for their domestic labor."

73 This discussion of boarding in the family life cycle is based upon Bodnar, Simon, and Weber's sample, *Lives,* pp. 103–06.

74 Bell, *Furnace,* p. 152. Mary's boarders added about $30.00 a month to the family income and enabled the Dobrejcaks to get out of debt.

75 Byington, *Homestead,* p. 148.

76 Bodnar, Simon, and Weber, *Lives,* p. 102.

77 Shergold, *Working Class Life,* p. 89.

78 Ewa Morawska, " 'For Bread with Butter": Life-worlds of Peasant Immigrants from East Central Europe, 1880–1914," *Journal of Social History* (Spring 1984): 395, calculated that boarders in Johnstown, a steel mill town in western Pennsylvania dominated by the Cambria Iron Company, contributed $20–25 a month, or about two-thirds to three-fourths the husband's earnings. The discrepancy between these figures and those cited by Shergold is, to some extent, accounted for by Shergold's practice of averaging the contribution over all families who took in boarders. Since the Slavs and Italians took in more boarders than most groups, the contribution to the family income, especially given the husband's low wage, would have been proportionately higher.

79 *National Labor Tribune,* 17 January 1874; 18 April 1875; 26 June 1875; 2 January 1875; 2 July 1875; 25 July 1890.

80 *People's Monthly,* September 1871.

81 Upton Sinclair captured the immigrants' fervor for home ownership in *The Jungle* (New York, 1906), pp. 123, 151. *The Labor Enquirer,* 18 January 1887, published in Chicago, lauded home ownership as providing cultural benefits to the working class.

82 U.S. Census, Twelfth Census, 1900, vol. 2, *Population,* pt. 2 (Washington, D.C., 1902), pp. 709–10, 737, 753. The census first investigated home ownership in 1890.

83 Morawska, "For Bread," p. 397. Bodnar, Simon, and Weber, *Lives,* p. 159.

84 Howard P. Chudacoff, *Mobile Americans: Residential and Social Mobility in Omaha, 1880–1920* (New York, 1972), pp. 116–18.

85 Byington, *Homestead,* pp. 60–61.

86 Edith Abbott, *The Tenements of Chicago, 1908–1935* (Chicago, 1936), p. 37.

87 The least expensive homes advertised in the Pittsburgh region cost about $1,000 for a three-room frame house in the Thirty-first Ward. The Mellon Brothers' Lumber Yard advertised homes on easy monthly payments for $1,100 for a four-room frame house in the Twenty-first Ward. *Commoner and Glass Worker,*

17 March 1888; 7 April 1888; 28 April 1888. On black home ownership in the twentieth century, see Bodnar, Simon, and Weber, *Lives,* p. 159. By the middle of the twentieth century, 56 percent of Allegheny County's black population, concentrated in East liberty, Lower North Side, and the Hill District, lived in substandard housing, compared with 20 percent of the white population. Roy Lubove, ed., *Pittsburgh* (New York, 1976), p. 179.

88 For a general account of technological developments, see Sigfried Giedion, *Mechanization Takes Command: A Contribution to Anonymous History* (New York, 1948).

89 Sam Bass Warner, Jr., *Streetcard Suburbs: The Process of Growth in Boston, 1870–1900* (New York, 1971), p. 31, implies that public utilities were distributed on an equal basis since they were needed "to cover the whole city at once." This was manifestly not true in Pittsburgh.

90 Pittsburgh Public Works Department, *The City of Pittsburgh and Its Public Works* (Pittsburgh, 1916), p. 19.

91 *The Municipal Record Containing the Proceedings of the Select and Common Councils of the City of Pittsburgh,* 1868–1900, contained lists of the streets paved, water pipes installed, sidewalks laid, gas lamps erected, etc. The overwhelming impression from reading these accounts and plotting the distribution pattern on maps is that working-class neighborhoods received fewer services than middle-class ones. The services they did enjoy came at a later date than those in more affluent areas.

92 U.S. Census, Tenth Census, 1880, vol. 18, *Report on the Social Statistics of Cities,* pt. 1 (Washington, D.C., 1886), pp. 866–67. It is worth remembering that pundits hailed the motor car as a means of decreasing urban pollution when it was first introduced, the pollution being that of horse droppings and the flies they attracted.

93 Pittsburgh Board of Health, *Annual Report* (Pittsburgh, 1873), pp. 19–20; ibid., 1873–1887 (Pittsburgh, 1874–1888), passim.

94 Pittsburgh City Controller, *Annual Report* (Pittsburgh, 1895), pp. 12–14.

95 *National Labor Tribune,* 18 July 1874.

96 The Board of Health inspected working-class districts and reported annually on the nuisances found there, those cleaned up by the board and those where the owners or occupants were ordered to set matters to rights. Pittsburgh Board of Health, *Annual Reports, 1873–1887* (Pittsburgh, 1874–1888), passim.

97 For a general history of urban water systems, see Joel A. Tarr and Francis C. McMichael, "Water and Wastes," *Water Spectrum* (Fall 1978): 18–25; Pittsburgh Public Works Department, *City of Pittsburgh,* p. 19; Pittsburgh Water Commission, *Annual Report, 1872* (Philadelphia, 1873), p. 5; ibid., *Annual Report, 1873* (Philadelphia, 1874), p. 4.

98 Pittsburgh Superintendent of Water Works, *Annual Report, 1877–1878* (Pittsburgh, 1878), p. 5.

99 Ibid., p. 3–4. *Pittsburgh Commercial Gazette*, 19 June 1888.

100 *Pittsburgh Commercial Gazette*, 18 July 1877.

101 Pittsburgh Superintendent of Water Works, *Annual Report, 1878–1879* (Pittsburgh, 1879), p. 5.

102 Caroline Davidson, *A Woman's Work Is Never Done: A History of Housework in the British Isles, 1650–1950* (London, 1982), pp. 18–20.

103 B. Rosenkrantz, *Public Health and the State: Changing Views in Massachusetts, 1842–1936* (Cambridge, Mass., 1972), pp. 99–108. Alison Ravetz, "Modern Technology and an Ancient Occupation: Housework in Present-day Society," *Technology and Culture* (Spring 1965): 256–60.

104 Pittsburgh Department of Public Safety, *Annual Report, 1889* (Pittsburgh, 1890), p. 78.

105 Martin Papers, Darlington Library, University of Pittsburgh.

106 Byington, *Homestead*, p. 54. Pittsburgh Council of the Churches of Christ, *The Uptown: A Socio-Religious Survey of a Section of Pittsburgh, Pennsylvania* (Pittsburgh, 1917), p. 11.

107 Goodnow and Adams, *Honest Hosue*, p. 24.

108 William Henry Matthews, *Pamphlet Illustrative of Housing Conditions in Neighborhoods Popularly Known as the Tenement House Districts of Pittsburgh* (Pittsburgh, 1907), p. 5; Crowell, "Painter's Row," p. 132; Emily Dinwiddie and F. Elizabeth Crowell, "The Housing of Pittsburgh's Workers," in Kellogg, *Pittsburgh District*, p. 95.

109 Dinwiddie and Crowell, "Housing," pp. 108–09.

110 Board of Trade of London, *Cost of Living*, p. 349.

111 *Commoner and Glass Worker*, 13 February 1887. Pittsburgh Bureau of Health, *Annual Report, 1888* (Pittsburgh, 1888), p. 3. A city government reorganization in 1887 entailed some name changes among the departments.

112 *Commoner and Glass Worker*, 24 December 1887; 1 January 1888; 7 January 1888; 4 February 1888; *Every Saturday*, 18 March 1871, p. 263; "Report of the Mayor to the Select Council," in *Municipal Record, 1884* (Pittsburgh, 1884), pp. 127–28; *Municipal Record, 1885* (Pittsburgh, 1885), pp. 85–87, 212, 235; David Brody, *Steelworkers in America: The Nonunion Era* (Cambridge, Mass., 1960), p. 103.

113 Pittsburgh Board of Health, *Annual Report, 1879* (Pittsburgh, 1879), pp. 20–23. The map of the sewer system appended to this report shows no sewers in many of the working-class districts.

114 Crosby Gray, *The Past, Present and Future Sanitation of Pittsburgh* (Pittsburgh, 1889), p. 69; Pittsburgh Department of Public Safety, *Annual Report, 1889* (Pittsburgh, 1889), p. 44; ibid., *1890* (Pittsburgh, 1890), p. 66.

115 Pittsburgh Department of Public Safety, *Annual Report, 1907* (Pittsburgh, 1908), p. 138.

116 Dinwiddie and Crowell, "Housing," p. 93.

117 Photographic Collection, Pennsylvania Division, Carnegie Library of Pittsburgh. Roy Lubove, *Twentieth Century Pittsburgh: Government, Business, and Environmental Change* (New York, 1969), p. 143.

118 Matthews, *Pamphlet*, pp. 5–12.

119 This situation was not, of course, unique to Pittsburgh. On the sanitation of New York City, see John Duffy, *A History of Public Health in New York City, 1866–1966* (New York, 1974). General studies of tenements and sanitation include: Roy Lubove, *The Progressives and the Slums: Tenement House Reform in New York City* (Pittsburgh, 1962); Robert Hunter, *Tenement Conditions in Chicago* (Chicago, 1901); John F. Sutherland, "Housing the Poor in the City of Homes: Philadelphia at the Turn of the Century," in Allen F. Davis and Mark H. Haller, eds., *The Peoples of Philadelphia* (Philadelphia, 1973), pp. 175–201. See in particular Frank E. Wing, "Thirty-five Years of Typhoid," and Emily Dinwiddie and F. Elisabeth Crowell, "The Housing of Pittsburgh's Workers," both in Kellogg, *Pittsburgh District*.

120 Pittsburgh Board of Health, *Annual Report, 1875* (Pittsburgh, 1875), p. 12.

121 Ibid., pp. 14, 19–20; *Annual Report, 1878* (Pittsburgh, 1878), p. 22.

122 Pittsburgh Department of Public Safety, *Annual Report for 1895* (Pittsburgh, 1895), p. 421.

123 S. J. Kleinberg, "Escalating Standards: Women, Housework, and Household Technology in the Twentieth Century," in Frank Coppa and Richard Harmond, eds., *Technology in the Twentieth Century* (Dubuque, Iowa, 1983).

124 Edward Meeker, "The Improving Health of the United States, 1850–1915," *Explorations in Economic History* 9 (1972): 373.

125 Robert Higgs, "Cycles and Trends of Mortality in Eighteen Large American Cities, 1871–1900," *Explorations in Economic History* 16 (1979): 381–408; Judah Matras, *Populations and Societies* (New York, 1973), p. 241. The role of quality of urban life as a factor in mobility has been discussed by Jeffrey G. Williamson, "Was the Industrial Revolution Worth It? Disamenities and Death in Nineteenth-Century British Towns," *Explorations in Economic History* 19 (1982): 221–45. C. E. A. Winslow, *The Evolution and Significance of Modern Public Health Campaigns* (New Haven, Conn., 1923), found a sharp rise in water filtration at the end of the nineteenth century. J. J. Cosgrove, *History of Sanitation* (Pittsburgh, 1909), found that almost all cities had sewer connections by 1907, but as late as 1890 less than half the dwellings in cities were actually connected to the sewer systems. See Meeker, "Improving Health," p. 372; also Charles Chapin, *Municipal Sanitation in the United States* (Providence, R.I., 1900). For a more affirmative analysis of the distribution of municipal technology, see

Jon C. Teaford, *The Unheralded Triumph: City Government in America, 1870–1900* (Baltimore, Maryland, 1984).

126 Thomas McKeown, *The Modern Rise of Population* (New York, 1976), posits that medicine contributed little to declining mortality in the nineteenth century, but improved diet led to a fall in tuberculosis mortality. See T. McKeown and R. G. Record, "Reasons for the Decline of Mortality in England and Wales in the Nineteenth Century," *Population Studies* 16, no. 2 (1962): 94–122; Charles Chapin, *Changes in Type of Contagious Diseases* (Chicago, 1926); Samuel Preston, *Mortality Patterns in National Populations* (New York, 1976). Gretchen Condran and Rose Cheney, "Mortality Trends in Philadelphia: Age- and Cause-specific Death Rates, 1870–1930," *Demography* 19 (1982): 105–09, provide a brief review of the literature.

127 Frederick L. Hoffman, "The General Death Rate of Large American Cities, 1871–1904," *Quarterly Publication of the American Statistical Association* 10 (1906): 1–75. All conclusions about death in Pittsburgh are based upon a sample of the death certificates for the city, drawn every fifth year between 1870 and 1900. Class attributions are based on husband's or father's occupation as cross-referenced with the appropriate city directory, if none was listed on the death certificate.

128 *National Labor Tribune*, 8 January 1876.

129 Rosenkrantz, *Public Health*, traces the efforts to improve health in Massachusetts. See Lubove, *Progressives* and *Twentieth Century Pittsburgh*, on the reform process generally and in Pittsburgh. Pittsburgh Board of Health, *Annual Report, 1879* (Pittsburgh, 1879), pp. 10–11.

130 Carl Dauer, Robert F. Kerns, and Leonard M. Schuman, *Infectious Diseases* (Cambridge, Mass., 1968), p. 39; U.S. Census, Eleventh Census, 1890, vol. 4, *Report on Vital and Social Statistics in the United States*, pt. 2 (Washington, D.C., 1896), pp. 66–74.

131 Pittsburgh Board of Health, *Annual Report, 1880* (Pittsburgh, 1880), p. 21.

132 *National Labor Tribune*, 7 February 1880.

133 *Commer and Glass Worker*, 12 January 1889.

134 Pittsburgh Department of Public Safety, *Report of the Bureau of Health, 1910* (Pittsburgh, 1910), p. 299.

135 E. E. Lanpher and C. F. Drake, *City of Pittsburgh, Pa.: Its Water Works and Typhoid Fever Statistics* (Pittsburgh, 1930), pp. 31–33.

136 *National Labor Tribune*, 26 September 1885.

137 Wing, "Typhoid," pp. 63–86. Lanpher and Drake, *Pittsburgh*, p. 33.

138 There were 337 deaths in New York, 251 in Boston, and 245 in Pittsburgh, per 100,000 residents. U.S. Census, Eleventh Census, 1890, *Report on Vital and Social Statistics*, pp. 66–74.

139 Death certificates, 1900; Fitch, *Steel Workers*, p. 68.

4 Childhood and Education

1 For a fuller articulation of the concept of life cycle, see Glen Elder, Jr., "Age Differentiation and the Life Course," *Annual Review of Sociology* (1975): 165–90, Paul C. Glick and Robert Parke, "New Approaches in Studying the Life Cycle of the Family," *Demography* 2 (1965): 187–202; and John Modell, Frank F. Furstenberg, Jr., and Theodore Hershberg, "Social Change and Transitions to Adulthood in Historical Perspective," in Michael Gordon, ed., *The American Family in Social Historical Perspective*, 2d ed. (New York, 1978), pp. 192–219.

2 Bernard Wishy, *The Child and the Republic* (Philadelphia, 1968); Glen Elder, Jr., *Children of the Great Depression* (Chicago, 1974); John Demos, *A Little Commonwealth* (New York, 1970); Richard L. Rapson, "The American Child as Seen by British Travelers, 1845–1935," *American Quarterly* 17 (1965); 520–34; John Demos and Virginia Demos, "Adolescence in Historical Perspective," *Journal of Marriage and the Family* 31 (1969): 632–38; Joseph Ketts, *Rites of Passage: Adolescence in America* (New York, 1977); Glen Elder, Jr., "Family History and the Life Course," *Journal of Family History* 2 (1977): 276–304, all examine childhood and adolescence.

3 M. C. Wylie, "Comparative Statement of Births and Deaths, 1873–1900 Inclusive," in *Annual Report of the Department of Public Health* (Pittsburgh, 1910), p. 392; death certificates, Pittsburgh, 1870–1900.

4 These summary comments are based upon an analysis of the 1880 census and the 1886 and 1900 marriage dockets for Pittsburgh.

5 The inadequacy of death registration systems throughout the United States makes comparison with other cities difficult before the twentieth century. Infant death rates in the Steel City exceeded those in Massachusetts, a highly urbanized state, where the infant death rate peaked in the 1870s. They were also higher and declined more slowly than in Philadelphia. In 1910, Pittsburgh ranked tenth among large U.S. cities in infant mortality, but by this time it had amalgamated with Allegheny City, a union that lowered overall mortality levels. Except for Washington, D.C., manufacturing dominated the economies of all those cities with high infant death rates. Some, like Pittsburgh, Johnstown, Pa., and Detroit, were heavy industry cities, whereas the rest of the "top ten" were centers of light industry: Lowell, Holyoke, Fall River, New Bedford, and Lawrence in Massachusetts, and Manchester, N.H. Washington, D.C., stood alone among southern cities in having an adequate death registration system, but some other southern cities had exceptionally high infant death rates. U.S. Department of Commerce, Bureau of the Census, *Historical Statistics of the United States, Colonial Times to 1970*, pt. 1. (Washington, D.C., 1975), p. 57; Rose A. Cheney, "Seasonal Aspects of Infant and Childhood Mortality: Philadelpia, 1865–1920," *Journal of*

Interdisciplinary History 14 (1984): 561–85; U.S. Census Bulletin 109, *Mortality Statistics, 1910* (Washington, D.C., 1911), pp. 191–92.

6 The ideal way to determine class-based mortality would be to compare the death and birth certificates for a given year. However, birth certificates for Pittsburgh are not available to researchers because they indicate legitimacy and illegitimacy. For another method of determining family mortality rates, see Daniel Scott Smith, "Differential Mortality in the United States before 1900," *Journal of Interdisciplinary History* 13 (1983): 735–59.

7 Robert M. Woodbury, "Economic Factors in Infant Health," *Journal of the American Statistical Association* 19 (1924): 137–55. Also see Gretchen Condran and Rose Cheney, "Mortality Trends in Philadelphia: Age- and Cause-Specific Death Rates, 1870–1930," *Demography* 19 (1982): 116; Gretchen Condran and Eileen Crimmins, "Mortality Differentials Between Rural and Urban Areas of States in the Northeastern United States, 1890–1900," *Journal of Historical Geography* 6, no. 2 (1980): 179–202. U.S. Census, Eleventh Census, 1890, vol. 4, *Report on Vital and Social Statistics in the United States* pt. 2, (Washington, D.C., 1896) analyzes mortality within major urban areas.

8 Emma Duke, *Infant Mortality: Results of a Field Study in Johnstown, Pa., Based on Births in One Calendar Year* (Washington, D.C., 1915), p. 46.

9 These conclusions are based on a sample of the death certificates for the city of Pittsburgh for every fifth year between 1870 and 1900. U.S. Census, *Historical Statistics*, pt. 1, p. 60, gives 162.4 deaths per 1,000 infants for death-registration areas only. The years were chosen to coincide with the intervals of the U.S. Census and the depression that occurred during the middle of each decade.

10 This classification scheme follows that of the International Statistical Classification of Diseases, Injuries, and Causes of Death. See Henry S. Shryock and Jacob S. Siegel, *The Methods and Materials of Demography*, vol. 2 (Washington, D.C., 1975), p. 406.

11 Robert Higgs, "Cycles and Trends of Mortality in Eighteen Large American Cities, 1871–1900," *Explorations in Economic History* 16 (1979): 381–408, argues that improvements in living standards coupled with public health measures led to declining mortality levels in U.S. cities. This seems not to have been the case for Pittsburgh's infants; compare Condran and Cheney, "Mortality Trends," p. 97–123.

12 Duke, *Infant Mortality*, p. 35.

13 Virginia Yans McLaughlin, *Family and Community: Italian Immigrants in Buffalo, 1880–1930* (Ithaca, N.Y., 1977), p. 101.

14 Woodbury, "Economic Factors," p. 43.

15 Antony S. Wohl, *Endangered Lives: Public Health in Victorian Britain* (London, 1983), pp. 15–16.

16 It is important to remember that middle-class babies comprised a disproportionately small share of all categories of infant deaths. Woodbury, "Economic Factors," p. 151.

17 Richard W. Wertz and Dorothy C. Wertz, *Lying-In: A History of Childbirth in America* (New York, 1977), p. 133; Duke, "Infant Mortality," pp. 31–34.

18 Warren S. Thompson and P. K. Whelpton, *Population Trends in the United States* (New York, 1969), p. 252.

19 Condran and Cheney, "Mortality Trends," p. 114; Samuel Preston, *Mortality Patterns in National Populations* (New York, 1976), p. 111; Woodbury, "Economic Factors," 137–55.

20 Sir Arthur Newsholme, *Elements of Vital Statistics* (London, 1899), p. 120.

21 See John Knodel and Hallie Kintner, "The Impact of Breast Feeding Patterns on the Biometric Analysis of Infant Mortality," *Demography* 14 (1977): 391–409.

22 L. Emmet Holt, *Diseases of Infancy and Childhood* (New York, 1914), p. 345; Cheney, "Seasonal Aspects," p. 564; Wohl, *Endangered Lives*, chap. 2; Wertz and Wertz, *Lying-In*, pp. 144–50.

23 Pittsburgh Department of Public Safety, *Report of the Bureau of Health 1894, 1891* Pittsburgh, 1891), p. 141.

24 L. B. Cook, C. E. Clement, and B. J. Davis, "The Milk Supply: A Study Conducted by the Dairy Division, United States Department of Agriculture, May 23 to June 16, 1913," in Duke, *Infant Mortality*, pp. 89–92.

25 Pittsburgh Department of Public Safety, *Report of the Bureau of Health, 1894,* pp. 136–37; ibid., 1895, p. 141.

26 Harvey Levenstein, "Artificial Feeding of Infants in America, 1880–1920," *Journal of American History* 70 (1983): 75–94.

27 Woodbury, "Economic Factors," p. 15.

28 Pittsburgh death certificates sample, 1895–1900; Levenstein, "Artificial Feeding," p. 83.

29 Duke, *Infant Mortality*, pp. 39–41. Frank E. Wing, "Thirty-five Years of Typhoid," in Paul U. Kellogg, ed., *The Pittsburgh District: The Civic Frontage* (New York, 1914), p. 82. A British government study conducted in 1910 found that about four-fifths of working-class mothers breast fed their babies. See Carol Dyhouse, "Working Class Mothers and Infant Mortality in England, 1895–1914," *Journal of Social History* 12 (1978): 255.

30 Class was determined by tracing the child's father through the city directory to obtain occupation. Despite having name and address, 27 percent were untraceable. Thus it is possible that the distinctions between skilled and unskilled workers' children are to some extent an artifact of the data.

31 Woodbury, "Economic Factors," p. 18, puts these deaths down to improper feeding.

32 Duke, *Infant Mortality*, p. 83–84.

33 Levenstein, "Artificial Feeding," p. 79; Wohl, *Endangered Lives*, p. 22; F. B. Smith, *The People's Health, 1830–1910* (London, 1979), pp. 92–93.

34 H. W. Jones, et al., *Blakiston's New Gould Medical Dictionary* (Philadelphia, 1951), p. 212.

35 These figures are based on an analysis of the addresses of decedents contained in the Pittsburgh death certificates, 1870–1900.

36 See Duke, *Infant Mortality*, p. 53; Woodbury, "Economic Factors," pp. 137–55.

37 Pittsburgh Board of Health, *Annual Report, 1879* (Pittsburgh, 1879), p. 10.

38 *National Labor Tribune*, 6 October 1877; 16 May 1874.

39 Ibid., 7 August 1875.

40 David Stannard, "Death and the Puritan Child," in Stannard, ed., *Death in America* (Philadelphia, 1975), p. 19.

41 Ivy Pinchbeck and Margaret Hewitt, *Children in English Society*, vol. 1 (London, 1969), p. 7.

42 Michael Anderson, *Family Structure in Nineteenth-century Lancashire* (Cambridge, 1971), p. 69. On Mortality levels in France and Britain, see Joan Scott and Louise Tilly, *Women, Work, and Family* (New York, 1978), p. 102.

43 Daniel Scott Smith, "Child Naming Patterns and Family Structure Change: Hingham, Massachusetts, 1650–1880," *Newberry Paper in Family and Community History*, 1977, no. 1.

44 Interview with Michael Haver, 24 August 1976. Also see E. H. Hunt, *British Labour History, 1815–1914* (London, 1981), p. 47 on the prevalence of this custom in England. Hunt, citing Lady F. Bell, *At the Works* (1907), p. 194 suggests that some parents accepted infant mortality.

45 *Commoner and Glass Worker*, 11 August 1888; *National Labor Tribune*, 5 September 1885; 24 July 1880.

46 *National Labor Tribune*, 15 May 1874.

47 Department of Charities, newspaper clipping, 14 March 1901, AIS.

48 The proportion of infants buried in the poor ground is based upon a sample of the daybooks at St. Mary's Cemetery, Pittsburgh. I looked at every fifth year between 1850 and 1900. The percentage of pauper burials declined over the latter half of the century because of the development of the separate burial ground for stillborn infants in 1890 and the increased tendency of Southern and Eastern European immigrants to use other cemeteries as these developed.

49 *Commoner and Glass Worker*, 19 January 1889. *People's Monthly*, November 1871; July 1871; June 1872. The picture on the "Household Page" showed a girl of 6 or 8 years hanging the wash inside the kitchen with the caption "Lucy—I help Mamma to Wash."

50 This contrasts with the description presented by Karen Mason, Maris Vinovskis,

and Tamara Hareven, "Women's Work and the Life Course in Essex County, 1880," in Hareven, ed., *Transitions: The Family and the Life Course in Historical Perspective* (New York, 1978), p. 198, where the majority of daughters worked after leaving school. Compare Claudia Goldin, "The Family and Household Economy in a Late Nineteenth Century American City, Philadelphia, 1880," (paper presented at the Social Science History Association, Ann Arbor, Michigan, 1977).

51 Beulah Kennard, "The Playgrounds of Pittsburgh," in Kellogg, *Pittsburgh District*, p. 311. Victor Greene, *The Slavic Community on Strike: Immigrant Labor in Pennsylvania Antracite* (Notre Dame, Ind., 1968), p. 44, states that children helped their "exhausted mother" with her chores.

52 Samuel Thayer Rutherford, "The Department of Charities of the City of Pittsburgh, 1888–1923" (M.A. thesis, University of Pittsburgh, 1938), pp. 7–20.

53 Lloyd de Mause, "The Evolution of Childhood," in de Mause, ed., *The History of Childhood* (New York, 1974), p. 52; Anderson, *Family Structure*, p. 70. For a general study of child abuse, see David G. Gil, *Violence against Children: Physical Child Abuse in the United States* (Cambridge, Mass., 1970).

54 These conclusions are based upon WPHS, 1888–89. The completeness of the records partially compensates for the limited number. Another historical source for the study of child abuse is the newspaper columns that reported crime drata. In the nineteenth century these brief articles contained frequent referencc to abusive behavior but focused on wifc abuse.

55 Alan Dawley, *Class and Community: The Industrial Revolution in Lynn* (Cambridge, Mass., 1976), p. 45.

56 WPHS, 23 August 1888; 15 August 1888; 15 July 1888. The agent of the Humane Society believed a whipping to make children "mind" was acceptable as long as restraint was used.

57 Compare Anderson, *Family Structure*, p. 68. Nancy Tomes, "A Torrent of Abuse: Crimes of Violence Between Working Class Men and Women in London, 1840–1875," *Journal of Social History* 2 (1978): 332–33, points both to the alcoholic consumption that frequently preceded abuse and to the use of the neighbors for protection. WPHS, 5 November 1888; 23 May 1889.

58 WPHS, 8 August 1888; 27 February 1889; 15 December 1888; de Mause, "Evolution of Childhood," pp. 42–43. For an extended consideration of family violence, see Elizabeth Pleck, *Domestic Tyranny: The Making of American Social Policy Against Family Violence from Colonial Times to the Present* (New York, 1987). Unfortunately this excellent study appeared too late for comparison with the conclusions presented here.

59 *National Labor Tribune*, 20 March 1880.

60 *Commoner and Glass Worker*, 22 December 1888.

61 Margaret Byington, *Homestead. The Households of a Mill Town* (New York, 1910), p. 147. Michael Young and Peter Willmott, *The Symmetrical Family* (New York, 1973), p. 75, state that "it is reasonable to think that tiredness sufficient to reduce output per hour is also tiredness sufficient to reduce 'output' at home, too, that is to detract at an accelerating rate from the amount of energy which a man has available for his wife and children." *National Labor Tribune*, 13 March 1880.

62 Described in Henry O. Evans, *Iron Pioneer: Henry W. Oliver* (New York, 1942), p. 37.

63 Byington, *Homestead*, p. 64; Thomas Bell, *Out of This Furnace* (Pittsburgh, 1976), p. 168.

64 Byington, *Homestead*, p. 181.

65 Kennard, "Playgrounds," p. 308.

66 Young and Willmott, *Symmetrical Family*, p. 38.

67 Robert Layton, in U.S. Congress, Senate, Committee on Education and Labor, *Report upon the Relations Between Labor and Capital* (Washington, D.C., 1885), vol. 1, pp. 27, 31. For pictures of suburban homes in Pittsburgh, see Stefan Lorant, *Pittsburgh: The Story of an American City* (New York, 1964), pp. 192, 268–69; and Photographic Archive, Pennsylvania Division, Carnegie Library of Pittsburgh.

68 Pittsburgh Department of Public Safety, *Third Annual Report*, (Pittsburgh, 1891), pp. 483–606, passim; Photographic Archives, Pennsylvania Division, Carnegie Library of Pittsburgh; interview with Michael Haver, 24 August 1976. Mr. Haver grew up in the Soho district of Pittsburgh. In 1915 a drunken streetcar driver ran over his sister, who died from her injuries. Although witnesses attested to the driver's condition, the family decided not to bring suit as a result of threats from the company's lawyers.

68 Layton in Senate Committee on Education and Labor, *Labor and Capital*, pp. 27, 31. For pictures of suburban homes in Pittsburgh see Lorant, *Pittsburgh*, pp. 192, 268–269, and Photographic Archive, Pennsylvania Division, Carnegie Library of Pittsburgh.

69 *People's Monthly*, September 1871; *Commoner and Glass Worker*, 7 May 1886; Pittsburgh Department of Public Safety, 1891, 483–606, passim.

70 Florence Larrabee Lattimore, "Three Studies in Housing and Responsibility: Skunk Hollow, the Squatter," in Kellogg, *Pittsburgh District*, p. 127. Leroy Scott, "Little Jim Park," *Charities and the Commons*, 8 February 1909, pp. 911–12; the park was destroyed before the publication of F. Elizabeth Crowell, "Painter's Row: The Company House," in Kellogg, *Pittsburgh District*. Francis G. Couvares, *The Remaking of Pittsburgh: Class and Culture in an Industrializing City, 1877–1919* (Albany, N.Y., 1984), p. 119.

71 Kennard, "Playgrounds," p. 307. Mel Sidenberg, Lois Mulkearn, and James W. Hess, "Two Hundred Years of Pittsburgh's History," in Lorant, *Pittsburgh*, p. 470.

72 Interview with Michael Haver, 26 August 1976.

73 Kennard, "Playgrounds," p. 311, passim. Lattimore, "Three Studies," p. 129, shows a marvelous photograph captioned "Play in Skunk Hollow: The Ball Team" with eight boys lined up with their baseball equipment. There is a horse-drawn wagon in the background and a toddler in the foreground.

74 Kennard, "Playgrounds," pp. 310–16. For a map of the Pittsburgh park system in 1914, see ibid., opposite p. 321.

75 Paul Boyer, *Urban Masses and Moral Order in America, 1820–1920* (Cambridge, Mass., 1978), p. 243.

76 On the expansion of education see Michael Katz, *The Irony of Early School Reform: Educational Innovation in Mid-Nineteenth Century Massachusetts* (Cambridge, Mass., 1968), and Katz, *Class, Bureaucracy and the Schools: The Illusion of Educational Change in America* (New York, 1971) on the values of the U.S. educational establishment as they developed in the nineteenth century. Carolyn Sutcher Schumacher, "School Attendance in Nineteenth Century Pittsburgh: "Wealth, Ethnicity, and Occupational Mobility of School Age Children" (Ph.D. dissertation, University of Pittsburgh, 1977). Schumacher's work is based upon the attendance and school records of the city of Pittsburgh and includes an excellent analysis of high school attendance patterns during the second half of the century (p. 11). Richard Kristufek, "The Immigrant and the Pittsburgh Public School, 1870—1940" (Ph.D. dissertation, University of Pittsburgh, 1975), pp. 30–32.

77 1880 census sample; U.S. Census, Twelfth Census, 1900, vol. 2, *Population*, pt. 2 (Washington, D.C., 1902), pp. 388–97.

78 Michael Katz, "Who Went to School," *History of Education Quarterly* 12 (1972): 432–54. William M. Landes and Lewis C. Soloman, "Compulsory Schooling Legislation: An Economic Analysis of Law and Social Change in the Nineteenth Century," *Journal of Economic History* 32 (1972): 54–91, point out that northeastern states generally formulated compulsory education laws when the proportion of school attendance approached 80 percent.

79 U.S. Census, Ninth Census, 1870, vol. 1 *Population* (Washington, D.C., 1872), p. 795; U.S. Census, Twelfth Census, 1900, *Special Report: Occupations at the Twelfth Census* (Washington, D.C., 1904), pp. 678–83; Pittsburgh Superintendent of Public Schools, *Annual Report* (Pittsburgh, 1933), p. 11; Byington, *Homestead*, p. 126. Timothy L. Smith, "Immigrant Social Aspirations and American Education, 1880–1930," *American Quarterly* 21 (1969): 523–43.

80 Kathleen Neils Conzen, *Immigrant Milwaukee: Accommodation and Community*

in a Frontier City (Cambridge, Mass., 1976), p. 91; Goldin, "Family and Household Economy," p. 10.

81 All 1880 school attendance statistics are derived from the 1880 census sample for Pittsburgh. Where employment was available for children, poorer working-class families sent their children to work at an earlier age than in Pittsburgh. Daniel J. Walkowitz, *Worker City, Company Town: Iron and Cotton Worker Protest in Troy and Cohoes, New York, 1855–1884* (Urbana, Ill., 1978), p. 115; describes the cotton mill as "employment and financial refuge" for the widowed and unskilled family. In Cohoes children left school at the age of 12 to seek employment in the cotton mills. Schumacher, "School Attendance," p. 78, states that at midcentury poorer Pittsburgh boys were "almost always less likely to be in school."

82 Goldin, "Family and Household Economy," p. 14 also found among Philadephia families that the absence of the father thrust many children into the labor force. Among the Lancashire textile workers Anderson analyzed, younger children seemed to give a larger portion of their earnings to their parents and older ones kept more for themselves. Michael Anderson, *Family Structure in Nineteenth-Century Lancashire* (Cambridge, 1971), pp. 124–32.

83 PAIP, 1886, p. 12.

84 *National Labor Tribune*, 1 April 1876.

85 1880 census sample; U.S. Census, Twelfth Census, 1900, vol. 2, *Population*, pt. 2 (Washington, D.C., 1902), pp. 388–97; Schumacher, "School Attendance," p. 62.

86 Goldin, "Family and Household Economy," pp. 10–18; 1880 census sample. Conzen, *Milwaukee*, p. 92, suggests that the continued immigration of lower-class Germans into Milwaukee during the 1850s explained their lower school attendance rates.

87 Schumacher, "School Attendance," pp. 32–32.

88 1880 census sample. U.S. Census, Twelfth Census, 1900, vol. 2, *Population*, pt. 2 (Washington, D.C., 1902), pp. 388–97. Schumacher suggests that poorer blacks may have continued in elementary school classes past the age of 15 and that those with more wealth kept their children home because there was no high school facility open to blacks at this time.

89 U.S. Immigration Commission, quoted in Kellogg, *Pittsburgh District*, pp. 295–96; Elizabeth Butler, "Sharpsburg: A Typical Waste of Childhood," in Kellogg, *Wage-Earning Pittsburgh*, pp. 286–90.

90 Byington, *Homestead*, p. 126.

91 Schumacher, "School Attendance," p. 70.

92 U.S. Immigration Commission, *The Children of Immigrants in Schools*, vol. 5, (Washington, D.C., 1909), pp. 30–33. Pittsburgh's high schools officially were

desegregated, but, as will be shown below in chap. 5, employment prospects for black high school graduates were poor generally.

93 Louise Odencrantz, *Italian Women in Industry* (New York, 1919), p. 251, found that less than 5 percent of the young Italian women she surveyed who had attended school in New York City had gone to high school. Butler, "Sharpsburg," p. 284, states that German and Irish Catholic schools offered some advanced work. Virginia Yans McLaughlin, *Family and Community: Italian Immigrants in Buffalo, 1880–1930* (Ithaca, N.Y., 1977), p. 49; Byington, *Homestead,* pp. 154–55. John Bodnar, Roger Simon, and Michael P. Weber, *Lives of Their Own: Blacks, Italians, and Poles in Pittsburgh, 1900–1960* (Urbana, Ill., 1982), p. 97, suggest that Italians were more skill-conscious than Poles.

94 Butler, "Sharpsburg," pp. 281, 297, 299.

95 Lila VerPlanck North, "Pittsburgh Schools," in Kellogg, *Pittsburgh District,* pp. 228–31; *Report of the Parish Schools of Pittsburgh Diocese* (Pittsburgh, 1909), passim.

96 North, "Pittsburgh Schools," p. 230. John Bodnar, *Immigration and Industrialization: Ethnicity in an American Mill Town, 1870–1940* (Pittsburgh, 1977), p. 89, states that attempts to Americanize immigrant children included the memorization of the "Battle Hymn of the Republic," "Columbia, the Gem of the Ocean," and the Pledge of Allegiance.

97 The Sixth Diocese Synod in 1893 appointed a school board and a board of examiners. The superintendent of the Catholic schools of Pittsburgh established a sample curriculum and furnished copies of it to all the schools under his supervision. North, "Pittsburgh Schools," pp. 233–39 passim.

98 T. Smith, "Immigrant Social Aspirations," p. 239, states that early parochial schools stressed learning English as much as preservation of Old World culture. In Chicago's Polish Catholic schools in 1901, students studied religion, Polish language, and history and also had geography and U.S. history, bookkeeping, and algebra instruction in English. This would seem to suggest an emphasis on the preservation of cultural values combined with a recognition of New World Skills. Anti-Slavic sentiment remained a problem in the Pittsburgh district well into the twentieth century. A University of Pittsburgh undergraduate from Alliquippa, Pa., reported that Slavic students were made to sit in the back of the classroom in the 1950s and felt ridiculed by teacher and Anglo-Saxon students. (Anonymous interview, Pittsburgh, 21 March 1970) Bell, *Furnace,* p. 223. Also see Bodnar, Simon, and Weber, *Lives,* p. 96.

99 Odencrantz, *Italian Women,* p. 205; Bodnar, *Immigration,* p. 130.

100 Barbara Holsopple, "The Germans," *Pittsburgh Press,* Roto, Special Number, September 1971; 1880 census sample; U.S. Census, Twelfth Census, 1900, vol. 2, *Population,* pt. 2 (Washington, D.C., 1902), 388–97.

101 Schumacher, "School Attendance," pp. 166, 189, traced 677 boys and 207 girls in Pittsburgh's high schools in 1890. Ileen A. Devault, "Sons and Daughters of Labor: Class and Clerical Work in Pittsburgh, 1870s–1910s" (Ph.D. dissertation, Yale University, 1985), pp. 205–07.

102 Kristufek, "Immigrant," p. 45.

103 Superintendent of Pittsburgh Public Schools, *Thirty-second Annual Report* (Pittsburgh 1900), p. 59; U.S. Immigration Commission, *Children of Immigrants in Schools,* vol. 5; North, "Pittsburgh Schools," p. 273.

104 Report of the vice president of the Kindergarten Association to the Superintendent of schools, in Pittsburgh Superintendent of Schools, *Twenty-sixth Annual Report* (Pittsburgh, 1894), p. 40; Marvin Lazerson, "Urban Reform and the Schools: Kindergartens in Massachusetts, 1870–1915," in Michael Katz, ed., *Education in American History: Readings on the Social Issues* (New York, 1973), pp. 223–24; Superintendent of Schools, 1894, pp. 40–44.

105 Kristufek, "Immigrant," p. 38; North, "Pittsburgh Schools," p. 291; Byington, *Homestead,* p. 122, quoting a Homestead school board member.

106 Lazerson, "Urban Reform," pp. 222–23.

107 Kingsley House Association, *Second Annual Report* (Pittsburgh, 1895), p. 6.

108 Lazerson, "Urban Reform," p. 228; Kristufek, "Immigrant," p. 44.

109 Quoted by David Tyack, "Bureaucracy and the Common School: The Example of Portland, Oregon, 1851–1913," in Katz, *Education,* p. 166.

110 Quoted in Kristufek, "Immigrant," p. 18.

111 Pittsburgh Superintendent of Schools, *Fifth Annual Report* (Pittsburgh, 1876), p. 186.

112 Kristufek, "Immigrant," pp. 27–35, passim; BIS, 1875–75, p. 430; Pittsburgh Superintendent of Schools, *Seventh Annual Report* (Pittsburgh, 1876), p. 40; Kingsley House Association, *First Annual Report* (Pittsburgh, 1894), p. 5.

113 *Commoner and Glass Worker,* 12 March 1886.

114 James J. Davis, *The Iron Puddler: My Life in the Rolling Mills and What Came of It* (Indianapolis, Ind., 1922), p. 91.

115 John A. Fitch, *The Steel Workers* (New York, 1910), p. 12.

116 Byington, *Homestead,* p. 126.

117 AAISW, 1882, p. 972.

118 Bodnar, *Immigration,* p. 12.

119 Kristufek, "Immigration," pp. 29–37.

120 Pittsburgh Superintendent of Schools, *Thirty-eighth Annual Report* (Pittsburgh, 1906).

121 For the background of the school reorganization, see Samuel P. Hays, "The Politics of Reform" in Municipal Government in the Progressive Era," *Pacific Northwest Quarterly* 5 (October 1965): 157–69.

122   Kristufek, "Immigrant," p. 70.
123   BIS, 1889, p. 2E.

5   Women's Work

1   E. P. Thompson, *The Making of the English Working Class* (New York, 1963), p. 416.
2   Joan Jensen, *With These Hands: Women Working on the Land* (Old Westbury, N.Y., 1981). Rolla M. Tyron, *Household Manufactures in the United States, 1640–1860* (Chicago, 1917), details women's domestic manufacturing activities.
3   Joan Scott and Louise Tilly, *Women, Work and Family* (New York, 1978), p. 3.
4   Alice Kessler-Harris, *Out to Work: A History of Wage Earning Women in the United States* (New York, 1982), chap. 3.
5   Carl Degler, *At Odds: Women and the Family in America from the Revolution to the Present* (New York, 1980), p. 74.
6   Bernard Wishy, *The Child and the Republic* (Philadelphia, 1968), pp. 28–30.
7   Neil Smelser, *Social Chane and the Industrial Revolution* (Chicago, 1959); Michael Anderson, *Family Structure in Nineteenth-Century Lancashire* (Cambridge, 1971); Caroline F. Ware, *The Early New England Cotton Manufacture: A Study in Industrial Beginnings* (New York, 1931); Tamara Hareven, *Family Time and Industrial Time* (Cambridge, 1982).
8   Anderson, *Family Structure*, p. 131; Scott and Tilly, *Women*, pp. 135–36.
9   S. J. Kleinberg, "The Systematic Study of Urban Women," in Milton Cantor and Bruce Laurie, eds., *Class, Sex, and the Woman Worker* (Westport, Conn., 1977); Elizabeth H. Pleck, "A Mother's Wage: Income Earning Among Married Italian and Black Women, 1896–1911," in Michael Gordon, ed., *The American Family in Social Historical Perspective*, 2d ed. (New York, 1978). Virginia Yans McLaughlin *Family and Community: Italian Immigrants in Buffalo, 1880–1930* (Ithaca, N.Y., 1977), argues strongly that cultural heritage determined female employment patterns among Italian immigrants in Buffalo.
10   All remarks about females employed in 1900 here and below are based upon calculations made from U.S. Census, Twelfth Census, 1900, *Special Report: Statistics of Women at Work* (Washington, D.C., 1904), hereafter cited as *Women at Work*. Those for Pittsburgh in 1880 are derived from the manuscript census sample for that year.
11   For a history of Troy see Daniel J. Walkowitz, *Worker City, Company Town: Iron and Cotton Worker Protest in Troy and Cohoes, New York, 1855–1884* (Urbana, Ill., 1978).
12   Degler, *At Odds*, p. 390, notes that one-fourth of all married black women had jobs.

13 *Women at Work*, p. 146. Howard N. Rabinowitz, "Southern Urban Development, 1860–1900," in Blaine Brownell and David R. Goldfield, eds., *The City in Southern History* (Port Washington, N.Y., 1977), p. 117. Black women's comments on their employment have been collected by Gerda Lerner, ed., *Black Women in White America: A Documentary History* (New York, 1973).

14 Claudia Goldin, "Female Labor Force Participation: The Origin of Black and White Differences, 1870–1880," *Journal of Economic History* 37 (March 1977): 87–112; Pleck, "Mother's Wage," passim.

15 McLaughlin, *Family and Community, p. 53.*

16 Kessler-Harris, *Out to Work,* p. 123.

17 *Women at Work*, passim; Hareven, *Family Time,* p. 189.

18 See Rosalyn Terborg-Penn, "Survival Strategies Among African-American Women Workers: A Continuing Process," in Ruth Milkman, ed., *Women, Work, and Protest* (Boston, 1985), pp. 139–55.

19 *Women at Work;* David Katzman, *Seven Days a Week: Women and Domestic Service in Industrializing America* (New York, 1978), p. 70, shows a sharp decline among second-generation Irish women working as domestic servants.

20 McLaughlin, *Family and Community,* p. 105; Pittsburgh marriage dockets, 1900.

21 1880 census sample; *Women at Work;* Miriam Cohen, "Italian-American Women in New York City, 1900–1950: Work and School," in Milton Cantor and Bruce Laurie, eds., *Class, Sex, and the Women Worker* (Westport, Conn., 1977). Elizabeth Pleck, "Two Worlds in One," *Journal of Social History* 10 (1976): 178–95, shows the range of black and Italian wives' contributions to household income along with that of children and lodgers, with a broad spread by type of city for Italians but much less variation among blacks. Elyce Rotella, *From Home to Office: U.S. Women at Work, 1870–1930* (Ann Arbor, Mich., 1980), pp. 17–26, discusses married women's labor force participation in the early twentieth century by size of city.

22 Letter from a Negro nurse, 25 January 1912, reprinted in Lerner, *Black Women,* p. 228.

23 For overviews of changing female employment patterns see Kessler-Harris, *Out to Work;* Degler, *At Odds,* chaps. 15–17; Rotella, *From Home to Office;* Valerie Kincade Oppenheimer, *The Female Labor Force in the United States* (Berkeley, Calif., 1970); Leslie Woodcock Tentler, *Wage-Earning Women: Industrial Work and Family Life in the United States, 1900–1930* (New York, 1979); Claudia Goldin, "The Changing Economic Role of Women: A Quantitative Approach," *Journal of Interdisciplinary History* 13, no. 4 (1983): 707–33.

24 U.S. Commissioner of Labor, *Sixth Annual Report* (Washington, 1890), pp. 603–06, based on a survey of Pennsylvania employers in trade and industry. Edith Abbott, *Women in Industry* (New York, 1910), pp. 3–4.

25 See Elizabeth Beardsley Butler, *Women and the Trades: Pittsburgh, 1907–1908* (University of Pittsburgh Press, 1984), pp. vii–xlv, for an analysis of Butler's work by Maurine W. Greenwald. As she points out, *Women and the Trades* documents both women's employment and "the concerns and prejudices of middle class female reformers" in the Progressive era (p. xv).

26 Ibid., p. 27.

27 Ibid., p. 20; U.S. Census, Thirteenth Census, 1910, vol. 4, *Occupations* (Washington, D.C., 1914), pp. 590–92.

28 McLaughlin, *Family and Community,* p. 209.

29 Michael F. Holt, *Forging a Majority: The Formation of the Republican Party in Pittsburgh, 1848–1860* (New Haven, Conn., 1969), p. 20; U.S. Census, Tenth Census, 1880, vol. 18, *Social Statistics of Cities,* pt. 1 (Washington, D.C., 1886), pp. 871–72; U.S. Commissioner of Labor, *Eleventh Annual Report* (Washington, D.C., 1896), pp. 633–34; U.S. Census, Twelfth Census, 1900, *Special Report: Occupations at the Twelfth Census* (Washington, D.C., 1904), pp. 681–83.

30 All statistical data come from the U.S. Census for the relevant year (see note 29). The 1880 material is based upon the 10 percent census sample.

31 For a somewhat different categorization of women's jobs, see Patricia Branca, "A New Perspective on Women's Work: A Comparative Typology," *Journal of Social History* (1978): 129–53. Katzman, *Seven Days,* and Faye Dudden, *Serving Women: Household Service in Nineteenth-Century America* (New York, 1983), discuss this lack of autonomy.

32 Barbara Mayer Westheimer, *We Were There: The Story of Working Women in America* (New York, 1977), pp. 234–35.

33 *Women at Work,* p. 117; Robert Smuts, *Women and Work* (New York, 1959), p. 20.

34 Kessler-Harris, *Out to Work,* p. 128.

35 Oppenheimer, *Female Labor Force,* p. 80; Abbott, *Women in Industry,* pp. 119, 140–41. On unemployment levels, see U.S. Census, Eleventh Census, 1890, vol. 1, *Population,* pt. 2 (Washington, D.C., 1897), pp. 712–13; U.S. Census, Twelfth Census, 1900, *Special Report: Occupations,* pp. 682–83.

36 *Women at Work,* passim. Margery Davies, *A Woman's Place is at the Typewriter: Office Work and Office Workers, 1870–1930* (Philadelphia, 1982), provides a detailed examination of white-collar work for women in this era.

37 *Women at Work,* pp. 286–87.

38 BIS, 1894, pp. A76–A133; *Women at Work,* p. 286. Hareven, *Family Time,* found women textile workers had high turnover rates.

39 Annie MacLean, *Wage-Earning Women* (New York, 1910), p. 63.

40 Sylvia Sachs, "The Jews," *Pittsburgh Press,* Roto, Special Number, September 1971, pp. 44–46; MacLean, *Wage-Earning Women,* p. 65.

41 Sachs, "Jews," pp. 44–46; Butler, *Women and the Trades*, p. 296.

42 Kessler-Harris, *Out to Work*, pp. 135–38 discusses this aspect of women's retail employment.

43 *Women at Work*, pp. 92, 374–75; Elizabeth Butler, *Saleswomen in Mercantile Stores: Baltimore, 1909* (New York, 1912); Butler, "Work of Women in the Mercantile Houses of Pittsburgh," *Annals of the American Academy of Political and Social Science* 33 (March 1909), pp. 102–13; Butler, *Women and the Trades*, pp. 306–7.

44 *Pittsburgh Commercial Gazette*, 31 July 1888; BIS, 1894, p. A41; Pennsylvania Legislature Act, 2 May 1905, Section 7, P L no. 226.

45 Butler, *Women and the Trades*, pp. 300–01, 306.

46 Ibid., p. 43. McLaughlin, *Family and Community*, p. 255, also found Polish women well represented in the ranks of factory labor.

47 Board of Trade of London, *Cost of Living in American Towns: Report of an Inquiry* (London, 1911), p. 347.

48 U.S. Commissioner of Labor, *Eleventh Annual Report*, p. 632.

49 Butler, *Women and the Trades*, chaps. 2, 3.

50 Tentler, *Wage-Earning Women*, p. 76.

51 Elizabeth Butler, "The Stogy Industry in Pittsburgh," *Survey*, 4 July 1908, p. 434; Board of Trade of London, *Cost of Living*, p. 346.

52 U.S. Census, Tenth Census, 1880, vol. 18, *Social Statistics of Cities*, pt. 1 (Washington, D.C., 1886), p. 872; U.S. Commissioner of Labor, *Eleventh Annual Report*, p. 632.

53 U.S. Census, Twelfth Census, 1900, *Special Report: Occupations*, pp. 678–83.

54 Abbott, *Women in Industry*, p. 188.

55 Board of Trade of London, *Cost of Living*, p. 346. Tentler, *Wage-Earning Women*, p. 41, cites a New York State Factory Investigation Commission report noting the poor ventilation in tobacco, chemical, textile, and artificial flower workshops. Butler, "Stogy Industry," p. 448; Abbott, *Women in Industry*, p. 209.

56 Butler, *Women and the Trades*, pp. 86, 90, 94. Abbott, *Women in Industry*, describes the hostility of the Cigarmakers' International to women in the industry and to the machinery they used.

57 U.S. Commissioner of Labor, *Eleventh Annual Report*, p. 603.

58 Tentler, *Wage-Earning Women*, p. 34.

59 Butler, *Women and the Trades*, pp. 210–21.

60 Kessler-Harris, *Out to Work*, pp. 142–51, provides a succinct review of this process.

61 *Commoner and Glass Worker*, 1 September 1888.

62 U.S. Congress, Senate, *Report on the Condition of Women and Child Wage*

Earners in the United States, vol. 3, *The Glass Industry* (Washington, D.C., 1910), pp. 283–86.

63 Statistics derived from a 10 percent sample of the 1880 manuscript census for Pittsburgh. Butler, *Women and the Trades*, pp. 240–42.

64 *National Labor Tribune*, 14 February 1885.

65 Letter from "Populist," in Pittsburgh, *National Labor Tribune*, 21 April 1895.

66 Abbott, *Women in Industry*, p. 207.

67 *National Labor Tribune*, 15 November 1900.

68 Elizabeth F. Baker, *Protective Legislation with Special Reference to Women in the State of New York*, Columbia University Studies in History, Economics, and Public Law 116, no. 2 (1925): 261–67. For a general history of protective legislation, see Judith A. Baer, *The Claims of Protection: The Judicial Response to Women's Labor Legislation* (Westport, Conn., 1978).

69 *Commoner and Glass Worker*, 1 September 1888.

70 In 1930, 34 percent of all women workers in Pittsburgh were domestics, and 26 percent were clerical workers. By 1940, 31 percent did housework, and 39 percent did paper work. U.S. Census, Fifteenth Census, 1930, vol. 4, *Population: Occupations by States* (Washington, D.C., 1933), pp. 1429–30; U.S. Census, Sixteenth Census, 1940, vol. 3, *The Labor Force: Occupation, Industry, Employment, Income*, pt. 5 (Washington, D.C., 1943), pp. 29–31.

71 Butler, *Women and the Trades*, analyzes women's commercial and industrial employment and ignores domestic service altogether, giving the impression that Pittsburgh was "many workshops; and in these workshops women stand beside men" (p. 17). In fact, women and men worked together in few of the limited trades open to women in the Steel City. As the Louis Hine photographs included in this volume show, women worked with other women, and the occasional man present in the women's workrooms was there as supervisor, as a machine fixer, or transferring items from one workroom to another.

72 Theresa McBride, *The Domestic Revolution* (London, 1976), describes household service as a modernizing occupation for women, but in Pittsburgh, where men worked in labor gangs in the steel mills, domestic service remained a traditional occupation. Various reformers, as Katzman, *Seven Days*, p. 251, notes, attempted to incorporate systems and relations found in factory and shop work that "would attract more women into household service."

73 Scott and Tilly, *Women, Work, and Family*, p. 153.

74 Lucy Maynard Salmon, *Domestic Service* (New York, 1901), pp. 140–66, details the industrial and social disadvantages of domestic service.

75 *Irish Pennsylvanian*, 29 August 1891.

76 1880 census sample; *Women at Work*, passim. Elizabeth H. Pleck, *Black Migration and Poverty: Boston 1865–1900* (New York, 1979), pp. 124–30, finds a similar situation in Boston at this time.

77 Helen A. Tucker, "The Negroes of Pittsburgh," in Paul U. Kellogg, ed., *Wage-Earning Pittsburgh* (New York, 1914), pp. 430–31. Also see Mary White Ovington, *Half a Man: The Status of the Negro in New York* (1911; reprint, New York, 1969), chap. 6.

78 *Women at Work*, passim. Katzman, *Seven Days*, focuses on the special problems black women encountered.

79 Isabel Eaton, "Special Report on Negro Domestic Service in the Seventh Ward, Philadelphia," in W. E. B. DuBois, *Philadelphia Negro* (1899; reprint, New York, 1967), p. 431.

80 Katzman, *Seven Days*, p. 67. *Women at Work*, passim.

81 WPHS, 14 December 1888.

82 Thomas Bell, *Out of This Furnace* (Pittsburgh, 1976), pp. 136–37, believes that service helped accustom rural women to urban mores. $1.65 per day was the average income of Slavic mill workers in Homestead. See Margaret Byington, *Homestead: The Households of a Mill Town* (New York, 1910), p. 79.

83 Salmon, *Domestic Service*, p. 137.

84 1880 census sample. For the employers' viewpoint, see Ethel Spencer, *The Spencers of Amberson Avenue: A Turn-of-the-Century Memoir* (Pittsburgh, 1983).

85 Pleck, *Black Migration*, pp. 135–37; PAIP, 1879; 1880 census sample; Sigfried Giedeon, *Mechanization Takes Command: A Contribution to Anonymous History* (New York, 1948), pp. 571–75.

86 There are two excellent studies of prostitution: Ruth Rosen, *The Lost Siterhood: Prostitution in America, 1900–1918* (Baltimore, 1982); Judith Walkowitz, *Prostitution and Victorian Society: Women, Class and the State* (Cambridge, 1980).

87 James Forbes, "The Reverse Side," in Kellogg, *Wage-Earning Pittsburgh*, p. 349.

88 Rudolf I. Coffee, "The Pittsburgh Morals Efficiency Commission," in Kellogg, *Wage-Earning Pittsburgh*, pp. 501–09.

89 1880 census sample; Denise Fisher, "Working Women in Ward One, Pittsburgh, Pa., 1880" (unpublished paper, Department of History, University of Pittsburgh, 1969).

90 Katzman, *Seven Days*, p. 213.

91 Marion Goldman, "Prostitution and Virtue in Nevada," *Society* 10 (1972): 34.

92 Forbes, "Reverse Side," p. 355.

93 Frances A. Keller, "Opportunities for Southern Negro Women in Northern Cities," *Voice of the Negro* 11 (1905). Katzman, *Seven Days*, pp. 213–14, discusses this aspect of black women's employment. Claude V. Kiser, *Sea Island to City* (New York, 1969), p. 49, writing of the 1920s, points out that Negro prostitutes were more likely than whites to be arrested.

94   1880 census sample; *Pittsburgh Commercial Gazette*, 17 July 1888.

95   *Commoner and Glass Worker*, 2 October 1887.

96   WPHS, 7 August 1889; 31 August 1888; 18 September 1889; 4 October 1888; 27 March 1889; 14 December 1888; 14 March 1889; 5 April 1889.

97   Ida Cohen Selavan, "The Social Evil in an Industrial Society: Prostitution in Pittsburgh, 1900–1925" (unpublished paper, Department of History, University of Pittsburgh, 1971).

98   Coffee, "Morals Efficiency Commission," pp. 508–09.

99   Ibid.

100 Forbes, "Reverse Side," p. 349.

101 Ibid., p. 364.

102 Quoted in Leon Wolff, *Lockout: The Story of the Homestead Strike of 1892: A Study of Violence, Unionism, and the Carnegie Steel Empire* (New York, 1965), p. 236.

103 Forbes, "Reverse Side," p. 364.

104 Butler, *Women and the Trades*, p. 306.

105 Sachs, "Jews," pp. 44–46; Butler, *Women and the Trades*, pp. 302–03.

106 BIS, 1894, p. A42.

107 Ruth Rosen and Sue Davidson, eds., *The Maimie Papers* (Old Westbury, N.Y., 1979), p. 12. Maimie highlights the financial logic behind prostitution when she observes that she can make the same wages in an afternoon that factory women make in a week.

108 Abbott, *Women in Industry*, pp. 308–09, citing Davis R. Dewey's report for the census of 1900. Butler, *Women and the Trades*, p. 237. Also see Ronnie Steinberg, *Wages and Hours: Labor and Reform in Twentieth-Century America* (New Brunswick, N.J., 1982).

109 Salmon, *Domestic Service*, p. 100. Clyde Griffen and Sally Griffen, *Natives and Newcomers: The Ordering of Opportunity in Mid-Nineteenth-Century Poughkeepsie* (Cambridge, Mass., 1978), p. 240, discuss teachers' salaries in detail, finding that high school teachers were paid more than those at the elementary level.

110 Degler, *At Odds*, p. 380.

111 BIS, 1874–75, p. 55.

112 Katzman, *Seven Days*, p. 304.

113 Salmon, *Domestic Service*, pp. 98–102; Lerner, *Black Women*, p. 226; Katzman, *Seven Days*, p. 306.

114 Salmon, *Domestic Service*, p. 101; Faye E. Dudden, *Serving Women: Household Service in Nineteenth-Century America* (Middletown, Conn., 1983), p. 221.

115 Alice Kessler-Harris, "Between the Real and the Ideal" presented at the Organization of American Historians, Denver, 1974.

116 Butler, *Women and the Trades*, p. 338; BIS, 1894, pp. All 115–33.
117 Elizabeth Butler, "Sharpsburg: A Typical Waste of Childhood," in Kellogg, *Wage-Earning Pittsburgh*, p. 291.
118 Butler, *Women and the Trades*, pp. 134–35, 338.
119 PAIP, 1879–1880, pp. 11–12.
120 Speech by a striking laundry worker, Mollie Coll, as reported in *Commoner and Glass Worker*, 24 March 1888.
121 Butler, *Women and the Trades*, p. 163.
122 *Commoner and Glass Worker*, 6 November 1887; 13 March 1887; 28 January 1888; 14 February 1888; 21 February 1888; 10 March 1888; 24 March 1888; 7 April 1888; 14 April 1888; 28 April 1888.
123 U.S. Commissioner of Labor, *Sixth Annual Report* (Washington, D.C., 1890), p. 601. Compare Carole Turbin, "And We Are Nothing But Women: Irish Working Women in Troy," in Carol Berkes and Mary Beth Norton, eds., *Women of America* (Boston, 1979), pp. 203–20.
124 Butler, *Women and the Trades*, p. 171.

6 Children's Work

1 Many studies point to this; of particular interest are Tamara Hareven, *Family Time and Industrial Time* (Cambridge, 1982); Virginia Yans McLaughlin, *Family and Community: Italian Immigrants in Buffalo, 1880–1930* (Ithaca, N.Y., 1977); Donald Cole, *Immigrant City: Lawrence, Massachusetts, 1845–1901* (Chapel Hill, N.C., 1963); Elizabeth H. Pleck, *Black Migration and Poverty: Boston, 1865–1900* (New York, 1979).
2 David Montgomery, *Workers' Control in Industrial America: Studies in the History of Work, Technology, and Labor Struggles* (Cambride, 1979), p. 77.
3 BIS, 1874–75, pp. 373–74; S. J. Kleinberg, "Success and the Working Class," in Thomas D. Clark, ed., *Onward and Upward: Essays on the Self-Made American* (Bowling Green, Ohio, 1979).
4 Michael Katz, *The Irony of Early School Reform: Education and Innovation in Mid-Nineteenth-Century Massachusetts* (Cambridge, Mass., 1968). On the child labor debates, see Walter I. Trattner, Crusade for the Children (Chicago, 1970).
5 1880 census sample; U.S. Census, Twelfth Census, 1900, *Special Report: Occupations at the Twelfth Census* (Washington, D.C., 1904), pp. 682–83. Unless otherwise noted, all occupational data come from these sources and will not be noted separately.
6 *National Labor Tribune*, 13 February 1877.
7 Karen Mason, Maris Vinovskis, and Tamara Hareven, "Women's Work and the

Life Course in Essex County, 1880," in Hareven, ed., *Transitions: The Family and the Life Course in Historical Perspective* (New York, 1978); Claudia Goldin, "The Changing Economic Role of Women: A Quantitative Approach," *Journal of Interdisciplinary History* 13, no. 4 (1983): 707–33.

8   Elizabeth Butler, *Women and the Trades: Pittsburgh, 1907–1908* (New York, 1909), pp. 21, 62, 83, 124, 129. John Bodnar, Roger Simon, and Michael P. Weber, *Lives of Their Own: Blacks, Italians, and Poles in Pittsburgh, 1900–1960* (Urbana, Ill., 1982), p. 99.

9   BIS, 1874–75, p. 375; 1877–78, p. 634.

10 Owen Lovejoy, "Child Labor in the Glass Industry," *Annals of the American Academy of Political and Social Science* 27 (1906): 300–11; John William Larner, Jr., "The Glass House Boys: Child Labor Conditions in Pittsburgh's Glass Factories, 1890–1917," *Western Pennsylvania Historical Magazine* 48 (1965): 362–63.

11 Margaret Byington, *Homestead: The Households of a Mill Town* (New York, 1910), p. 118.

12 BIS, 1889, pp. E3, E12, E8.

13 *Commoner and Glass Worker*, 3 November 1887.

14 BIS, 1889, pp. E3–E12.

15 Thomas Bell, *Out of This Furnace* (Pittsburgh, 1976), p. 211.

16 1880 census sample; U.S. Census, "Twelfth Census, 1900, vol. 2, *Population*, pt. 2 (Washington, D.C., 1902), pp. 669–83.

17 Stephen Thernstrom, *Poverty and Progress: Social Mobility in a Nineteenth-Century City* (New York, 1970), p. 108, dates the narrowing of the opportunity for laborers' sons in Newburyport, Mass., to 1870.

18 Mary E. Richmond and Fred S. Hall, *A Study of Nine Hundred and Eighty-Five Widows Known to Certain Charity Organization Societies in 1910* (New York, 1913), pp. 30–31. Pittsburgh's high rate of accidental mortality among unskilled workers in particular meant that the majority of orphaned children came from the lower echelons of the working class. Pittsburgh death certificates, 1870–1900.

19 Stephen Thernstrom, *The Other Bostonians: Poverty and Progress in the America Metropolis, 1880–1920* (Cambridge, Mass., 1973), p. 240; Clyde Griffen and Sally Griffen, *Natives and Newcomers: The Ordering of Opportunity in Mid-Nineteenth-Century Poughkeepsie* (Cambridge, Mass., 1978); John Bodnar, *Immigration and Industrialization: Ethnicity in an American Mill Town, 1870–1940* (Pittsburgh, 1977); Howard Gitelman, *Workingmen of Waltham: Mobility in American Urban Industrial Development, 1850–1890* (Baltimore, 1974); Michael P. Weber, *Social Change in an Industrial Town: Patterns of Progress in Warren, Pennsylvania, from Civil War to World War I* (University Park, Pa., 1976).

20   Carolyn Sutcher Schumacher, "School Attendance in Nineteenth-Century Pittsburgh" (Ph.D. dissertation, University of Pittsburgh, 1977), p. 166.

21   Pittsburgh Superintendent of Schools, *Annual Report* (Pittsburgh, 1933), p. 11.

22   U.S. Census, Ninth Census, 1870, vol. 1, *Population,* p. 795; U.S. Census, Twelfth Census, 1900, *Special Report: Occupations,* pp. 678–83.

23   Elizabeth Butler, "Sharpsburg: A Typical Waste of Childhood," in Paul U. Kellogg, ed., *Wage-Earning Pittsburgh* (New York, 1914), pp. 295–302.

24   Lovejoy, "Child Labor," p. 301.

25   Quoted in Lovejoy, "Child Labor," p. 301; Larner, "Glass House Boys," pp. 362–63.

26   WPHS, 21 November 1888; Lovejoy, "Child Labor," p. 309.

27   Trattner, *Crusade,* p. 77; Lovejoy, "Child Labor," p. 309.

28   *Pittsburgh Leader,* 10 March 1907.

29   Helen Grimes, "The Civic Club Aims to Abolish Child Labor," Civic Club Papers, 1909, AIS. Butler, "Sharpsburg," p. 297, recites the following example in 1908 of parents attempting to evade the minimum age regulations: John V., 12 years old, an Italian boy who lived in a rear house in Glasshouse Row, had been working in the adjoining factory for a year. His mother had taken him to the squire to get his certificate, which the squire refused, saying, "You know that boy isn't fourteen. Now if you don't put him back in school, I'll prosecute you." The result was that John worked without a certificate instead of with one.

30   Florence Kelley, "Factory Inspection in Pittsburgh," in Kellogg, *Wage-Earning Pittsburgh,* p. 202.

31   *Pittsburgh Dispatch,* 30 April 1909.

32   As Kelley, "Factory Inspection," p. 202, pointed out, this opened the doors for blackmail and defeated the intent of the law. U.S. Census, Thirteenth Census, 1910, vol. 4, *Occupations* (Washington, D.C., 1914), p. 591. There were also 134 14- and 15-year-old boys working in the glass houses in that year.

33   Compare this situation with that of Manchester, N.H., where children's entrance into the textile mills was delayed by child labor laws. See Hareven, *Family Time,* p. 187.

34   U.S. Census, Twelfth Census, 1900, *Special Report: Occupations,* pp. 680–81.

35   For earlier employment patterns for women, see Michael F. Holt, *Forging a Majority: The Formation of the Republican Party in Pittsburgh, 1848–1860* (New Haven, Conn., 1969), p. 20. U.S. Census, Ninth Census, 1870, vol. 1, *Population,* p. 795. Thirty-four Pittsburgh women worked in Allegheny City textile factories in 1870.

36   Joan Scott and Louise Tilly, *Women, Work, and Family* (New York, 1978), p. 104. Claudia Goldin, "The Family and Household Economy in a Late Nineteenth-Century American City, Philadelphia, 1880," (paper presented at the

Social Science History Association, Ann Arbor, Mich., 1977), p. 14, documents the same tendency in Philadelphia.

37 U.S. Census, Tenth Census, 1880, vol. 18, *Social Statistics of Cities,* pt. 1 (Washington, D.C., 1886), pp. 871–72; U.S. Census, Twelfth Census, 1900, *Special Report: Occupations,* pp. 428–71.

38 Ileen DeVault, "Sons and Daughters of Labor: Class and Clerical Work in Pittsburgh, 1870s–1910s" (Ph.D. dissertation, Yale University, 1985), pp. 211–14, analyzes the educational prospects of widow's daughters.

39 Of all black female children living with their parents, 84 percent were under 15 in 1880, and only 71 percent of the black male children were in this age group. By comparison, 72 percent of all native white female and 75 percent of the native white male children were as young as that. The only explanation for the disparity is the widespread employment of young black women as servants.

40 Schumacher, "School Attendance," pp. 74–76, 189.

41 In 1930, 34 percent of Pittsburgh's women workers were domestics while 26 percent were clerical staff. By 1940 domestic servants declined to 31 percent and clerical workers increased to 39 percent. U.S. Census, Fifteenth Census, 1930, vol. 4, *Population, Occupations by States* (Washington, D.C., 1933), pp. 1429–30; U.S. Census, Sixteenth Census, 1940, vol. 3, *The Labor Force: Occupation, Industry, Employment Income,* pt. 5 (Washington, D.C., 1943), pp. 29–31.

42 Isabel Eaton, "Special Report on Negro Domestic Service in the Seventh Ward, Philadelphia," in W. E. B. DuBois, *Philadelphia Negro* (1899; reprint, New York, 1967), p. 431, found that 17 percent of the black women servants were under 20; 43 percent were 21–30; 23 percent were 31–40; 15 percent were over 41, and 1 percent were of unknown age. She also states (p. 429) that over 90 percent of the black women working throughout Pennsylvania in 1890 were domestic servants.

43 On ethnicity and domestic service see David Katzman, *Seven Days a Week: Women and Domestic Service in Industrializing America* (New York, 1978), p. 70.

44 Butler, "Sharpsburg," *passim.*

45 Byington, *Homestead,* p. 118; interestingly she itemizes the labor of sons (p. 160) but not of daughters (p. 201).

46 Leslie Woodcock Tentler, *Wage-Earninging Women: Industrial Work and Family Life in the United States, 1900–1930* (New York, 1979), pp. 84–93.

47 Mary White Ovington, *Half a Man: The Status of the Negro in New York* (1911; reprint, New York, 1969).

48 Abraham Epstein, *The Negro Migrant in Pittsburgh* (Pittsburgh, 1918), p. 24.

49 Bodnar, Simon, and Weber, *Lives,* pp. 92–93.

50 WPHS, 27 February 1888; 13 December 1888.
51 Butler, *Women and the Trades*, p. 346.
52 Faye Dudden, *Serving Women: Household Service in Nineteenth-Century America* (New York, 1983), p. 222, suggests that the ability to accumulate cash recommended service to immigrant daughters who wished to send remittances home.

7 Marriage and Family

1 The literature on marriage, family relations, and sex roles has grown voluminously in the last decade. My thinking on these topics has been shaped by the work of Tamara Hareven, whose analysis of the relationship between industrial structure and family life have appeared in "Family Time and Industrial Time: Family and Work in a Planned Corporation Town, 1900–1914," in Hareven, ed., *Family and Kin in Urban Communities, 1700–1930* (New York, 1977), and Hareven, "The Family as Process: The Historical Study of the Family Cycle," *Journal of Social History* 7 (1974): 322–29. See also Joan Scott and Louise Tilly, "Women's Work and the Family in Nineteenth-Century Europe," *Comparative Studies in Society and History* 17 (1975): 36–64; Scott and Tilly, *Women, Work and Family* (New York, 1978); Gerda Lerner, "The Lady and the Mill Girl: Changes in the Status of Women in the Age of Jackson," *Midcontinent American Studies* 10 (1969): 5–14; Edward Shorter, *The Making of the Modern Family* (New York, 1975); Charles Rosenberg, "Sexuality, Class and Role in Nineteenth-Century America," *American Quarterly* 25 (1973): 131–53; Michael R. Haines, "Fertility, Marriage and Occupation in the Pennsylvania Anthracite Region, 1850–1880," *Journal of Family History* 2 (1977): 28–55; Elizabeth Pleck, "Two Worlds in One," *Journal of Social History* 10 (1976); 178–95; Mary P. Ryan, *Womanhood in America* (New York, 1975); John Modell and Tamara Hareven, "Urbanization and the Malleable Household: An Examination of Boarding and Lodging in American Families," in Michael Gordon, ed., *The American Family in Social Historical Perspective* 2d ed., (New York, 1978); Herbert Gutman, *The Black Family in Slavery and Freedom* (New York, 1976); Laurence A. Glasco, "Life Cycles and Household Structure of American Ethnic Groups: Irish, Germans, and Native-Born Whites in Buffalo, New York, 1855," *Journal of Urban History* 1 (1975): 339–64. Carl Degler, *At Odds: Women and the Family in America from the Revolution to the Present* (New York, 1980).

2 On family relationships in mining and heavy industrial centers, see Haines, "Fertility"; Joan Scott, *The Glass Workers of Carmaux* (Cambridge, Mass., 1974); Katherine A. Harvey, *The Best Dressed Miners: Life and Labor in the Maryland Coal Region, 1835–1910* (Ithaca, N.Y., 1969); Victor Greene, *The*

Slavic Community on Strike: Immigrant Labor in Pennsylvania Anthracite (Notre Dame, Ind., 1968); Daniel J. Walkowitz, *Worker City, Company Town: Iron and Cotton Worker Protest in Troy and Cohoes, New York, 1855–1884* (Urbana, Ill., 1978); Elizabeth Jameson, "Imperfect Unions: Class and Gender in Cripple Creek, 1894–1904," in Milton Cantor and Bruce Laurie, eds., *Class, Sex, and the Woman Worker* (Westport, Conn., 1977); John Bodnar, *Immigration and Industrialization: Ethnicity in an American Mill Town, 1870–1940* (Pittsburgh, 1977); and compare Michael Anderson, *Family Structure in Nineteenth-Century Lancashire* (Cambridge, 1971); Elizabeth Pleck, "A Mother's Wages: Income Earning among Married Italian and Black Women, 1896–1911," in Gordon, *American Family;* Virginia Yans McLaughlin, "Italian Women and Work," and Miriam Cohen, "Italian-American Women in New York City, 1900–1950: Work and School," both in Cantor and Laurie, *Woman Worker.*

3   Alan Dawley, *Class and Community: The Industrial Revolution in Lynn* (Cambridge, Mass., 1976), p. 5.
4   *Commoner and Glass Worker,* 25 November 1885.
5   Scott and Tilly, *Women.*
6   Degler, *At Odds,* pp. 48–50.
7   S. J. Kleinberg, "Technology and Women's Work," *Labor History* 17 (1976): 58–76; Ruth Schwartz Cowan, *More Work for Mother: The Story of Household Technology from the Open Hearth to the Microwave* (New York, 1983); Susan Strasser, *Never Done: A History of American Housework* (New York, 1982).
8   Lerner, "Lady and Mill Girl."
9   Pleck, "Two Worlds," p. 187. See Barbara Welter, "The Cult of True Womanhood, 1820–1860," *American Quarterly* 19 (1966): 151–74; on domesticity see Kathryn Kish Sklar, *Catherine Beecher; A Study in American Domisticity* (New York, 1973.
10 For an analysis of employment patterns correlated with industrial types, see S. J. Kleinberg, "Systematic Study of Urban Women" in Milton Cantor and Bruce Laurie, eds., *Class, Sex, and the Woman Worker* (Westport, Conn., 1977). On the sporadic nature of female employment, see Hareven, "Family Time"; Scott and Tilly, *Women.*
11 For a sociological statement of the steel mill rhythm as it influences working-class family life see William Kornblum, *Blue Collar Community* (Chicago, 1974).
12 This discussion of the asymmetrical family type draws heavily upon Michael Young and Peter Willmott, *The Symmetrical Family* (New York, 1973). Young and Willmott themselves follow some of the concepts developed by Elizabeth Bott, *Family and Social Network: Roles, Norms, and External Relationships in Ordinary Urban Families* 2d ed., (New York, 1971). Margaret Byington, in her study of steel mill families for the Pittsburgh Survey, *Homestead: The House-*

holds of a Mill Town (New York, 1910), developed some of these themes of role segregation.

13 Paul Laurie, "The Light of the House: A Tale of Our Mills," *People's Monthly,* June 1871.

14 Bell, *Out of This Furnace* (Pittsburgh, 1976), p. 22.

15 Quoted in Barbara Holsopple, "The Slavic People," *Pittsburgh Press,* Roto, Special Number, September 1971.

16 On recreational patterns see Gareth Stedman Jones, "Working Class Culture and Working Class Politics: Notes on the Remaking of a Working Class," *Journal of Social History* 7 (1974): 460–508.

17 *People's Monthly,* June 1871.

18 *National Labor Tribune,* 22 March 1900.

19 *Commoner and Glass Worker,* 1 September 1888.

20 *National Labor Tribune,* 16 January 1875.

21 Ibid., 13 February 1875.

22 Ibid., 3 April 1875.

23 *Irish Pennsylvanian,* 22 August 1891.

24 Allegheny County marriage dockets, 1886. U.S. Census, Twelfth Census, 1900, vol. 2, *Population,* pt. 2 (Washington, D.C., 1902), p. 569. For national data see David Hackett Fischer, *Growing Old in America* (New York, 1977).

25 John Bodnar, Roger Simon, and Michael P. Weber, *Lives of Their Own: Blacks, Italians, and Poles in Pittsburgh, 1900–1960* (Urbana, Ill., 1982), p. 100; Tamara Hareven, *Family Time and Industrial Time* (Cambridge, 1982), pp. 172–75. Pittsburgh data developed from U.S. Census, Twelfth Census, 1900, vol. 2, *Population,* pt. 2 (Washington, D.C., 1902), p. 569.

26 Census sample, 1880.

27 Haines, "Fertility," pp. 34–35, correlates low female employment with early marriage, high marital rates, and high fertility. Alice Kessler-Harris, *Out to Work: A History of Wage-Earning Women in the United States* (New York, 1982), p. 225, highlights the painful choice some immigrant women made to remain single in order to write or organize sister workers. See Degler, *At Odds,* pp. 160–61, on middle-class professional women.

28 U.S. Census, Twelfth Census, 1900, vol. 2, *Population,* pt. 2 (Washington, D.C., 1902), p. 569.

29 Allegheny County marriage dockets, 1886 and 1900. For 1886 I analyzed all marriages where one partner resided within the city of Pittsburgh and where the marriage ceremony had been performed. ($N=1360$) I then attempted to trace ethnic and occupational relationships by using place of birth and the information given in the docket or available by looking at the wife's name in the city directory. Unfortunately for my purposes, race was not a category on the dockets, hence the

reliance upon census data in 1880. I sampled every tenth marriage in 1900 ($N=264$).

30 The following analysis is based upon the information recorded in the marriage dockets and 1880 census sample. Compare Bodnar, *Immigration*, p. 131.

31 Compare Walkowitz, *Worker City*, pp. 117–18.

32 W. E. B. DuBois, *Philadelphia Negro*, (1899; reprint, New York, 1967), pp. 361, 367.

33 Elizabeth H. Pleck, *Black Migration and Poverty: Boston, 1865–1900* (New York, 1979), pp. 116–17, differentiates the black experience in Boston from that in other cities, the high rate of intermarriage there reflecting the degree to which blacks were assimilated in 1900.

34 Since the marriage dockets gave both name and address, I traced the occupation of the women or, much more typically, their father's, through the city directory. In the case of common names, identification was considered correct only if the name and address matched in directory and docket.

35 Robert Layton in U.S. Congress, Senate, Committee on Education and Labor, *Report upon the Relations between Labor and Capital* (Washington, D.C., 1885), vol. 1, p. 20.

36 Crystal Eastman, *Work Accidents and the Law* (New York, 1910), chaps. 9 and 10, highlights this problem of "sliding" by skilled workers as they grew older. This will be discussed in chap. 8, below.

37 It proved more difficult to trace individuals from the 1900 marriage dockets for several reasons. The city directory for 1900 unfortunately had several sections missing or so badly mutilated as to be unusable. The large number of recent Slavic immigrants who married also complicated tracing. Many of the women had no male relatives resident in the United States, and if they were under age, "permission" for their marriage was given by the courthouse clerk or someone with a different last name and address from the bride.

38 Bell, *Furnace*, p. 138.

39 *Commoner and Glass Worker*, 29 January 1886; *National Labor Tribune*, 26 April 1890.

40 Jones, "Working Class Culture," p. 491.

41 1880 census sample; U.S. Census, Twelfth Census, Special Report, 1900, *Occupations at the Twelfth Census* (Washington, D.C., 1904), pp. 682–83.

42 Elizabeth Butler, *Women and the Trades: Pittsburgh, 1907–1908* (New York, 1909), pp. 133–34, tells of an injured miner whose mother and sister supported the family making jeans at $1.10 per dozen.

43 Joseph Hill, *Women in Gainful Occupations, 1870 to 1920* (Washington, D.C., 1929), passim.

44 Byington, *Homestead*, p. 120.

45 Allegheny County marriage dockets, 1886 and 1900; Corinne Azen Krause, "Urbanization Without Breakdown. Italian, Jewish, and Slavic Women in Pittsburgh, 1900–1945," *Journal of Urban History* (1978): 13.

46 1880 census sample.

47 U.S. Census, Sixteenth Census, 1940, vol. 4, *Population: Differential Fertility for States and Large Cities* (Washington, D.C., 1943), pp. 15, 156. See Degler, *At Odds,* chap. 19, for discussion of fertility limitation in this era.

48 1880 census sample. U.S. Census, Sixteenth Census, 1940, *Differential Fertility for States and Large Cities,* tables 36 and 38, p. 57; compare the number of children under 5 and ages 5–9 living in black and white households. Wilson H. Grabill, Clyde V. Kiser, and Pascal K. Whelpton, *The Fertility of American Women* (New York, 1958), p. 57.

49 *National Labor Tribune,* 19 January 1889.

50 1880 census sample; U.S. Census, 1900, Twelfth Census, 1900. *Special Report: Occupations at the Twelfth Census* (Washington, 1904), p. 682.

51 Richard W. Wertz and Dorothy C. Wertz, *Lying-In: A History of Childbirth in America* (New York, 1977), pp. 47–48, trace the reasons for the shift to physician attendants at the deliveries of middle-class women.

52 Bell, *Furnace,* p. 140.

53 Emma Duke, *Infant Mortality: Results of a Field Study in Johnstown, Pa., Based on Births in One Calendar Year* (Washington, D.C., 1915), p. 44.

54 Ibid., p. 33.

55 Byington, *Homestead,* p. 172.

56 John Fitch, *The Steel Workers* (New York, 1910), pp. 2–3.

57 Byington, *Homestead,* pp. 64–65.

58 *National Labor Tribune,* 17 July 1880; 2 May 1895.

59 *National Labor Tribune,* 7 February 1885.

60 *People's Monthly,* September 1871.

61 *National Labor Tribune,* 7 February 1885.

62 *Commoner and Glass Worker,* 22 December 1888.

63 As one woman told Margaret Byington, "The only time 'the mister' notices anything about the house is when I wash the curtains" (*Homestead,* p. 108).

64 Joann Vanek, "Time Spent in Housework," *Scientific American,* November 1974, pp. 116–20; Ruth Schwartz Cowan, "The Industrial Revolution in the Home: Household Technology and Social Change in the United States," *Technology and Culture* 17 (1976): 1–26. Also see Cowan, *More Work.*

65 Elizabeth Bacon, "The Growth of Household Conveniences in the United States, 1865–1900" (Ph.D. dissertation, Radcliffe College, 1942), p. 247; Sigfried Giedion, *Mechanization Takes Command: A Contribution to Anonymous History*

(New York, 1948); Central District and Printing Telegraph Company, *List of Subscribers,* 1878 and 1886.

66 Byington, *Homestead,* pp. 38, 60. In later years women's attempts to cope with the relative deprivation of household conveniences occasionally took the form of labor union militancy. A most eloquent exposition of women's role in unionizing in a men's work environment is found in *Salt of the Earth,* a movie about the Mine, Mill, and Smelter Workers' struggle in New Mexico during the early 1950s. The women's desire for better living conditions (indoor water, modern kitchens, etc.) and their attendant militancy contributed significantly to the strike effort. According to Clinton Jencks, former organizer for Mine, Mill, and Smelters, later professor of economics at San Diego State University, the miners refused to take the women's interest in the strike seriously and did so only when it seeemed doomed to failure.

67 Byington, *Homestead,* pp. 85–86.

68 Cowan, *More Work,* p. 6.

69 *People's Monthly,* September 1871.

70 Ruth Moynihan, *Abigail Scott Duniway: Rebel for Rights* (New Haven, Conn., 1983), p. 69, notes a similar phenomenon among male pioneers in the West who ignored their wives' fatigue.

71 Byington, *Homestead,* p. 108. Lee Rainwater, Richard P. Coleman, and Gerland Handel, *Workingman's Wife* (1959, reprint, New York, 1968), p. 173, in discussing working-class consumption patterns, state that hesitancy in making major purchases resulted from the "essential fear that the future will not treat them more fortunately than has the present and may even threaten them with financial disasters." See Ann Oakley, *The Sociology of Housework* (New York, 1974); Hannah Gavon, *The Captive Wife* (London, 1966).

72 Thorstein Veblen, *The Theory of the Leisure Class* (New York, 1967).

73 For an overview see S. J. Kleinberg, "Escalating Standards: Women, Housework, and Household Technology in the Twentieth Century," in Frank Coppa and Richard Harmond, eds., *Technology in the Twentieth Century* (Dubuque, Iowa, 1983).

74 Bacon, "Household Conveniences," pp. 25–29, 98–103. Prices from *Commoner and Glass Worker,* 1885–88. For pictures of these homes see Paul U. Kellogg, ed., *The Pittsburgh District: The Civic Frontage* (New York, 1914); and Byington, *Homestead.* Working-class homes built during these years sometimes had a hole cut in the ceiling that permitted the heat to rise to the upper floor from the kitchen. This arrangement was typical of the houses along the railroad tracks in Skunk Hollow near Boundary Way in the Fourteenth Ward. The middle-class homes built at the end of the nineteenth century typically had central heating or individual room gas fireplaces known as Taylor Burners.

75 Bacon, "Household Conveniences," pp. 25, 219–20.

76 Isabella Campbell's husband beat her to death over suspected infidelities. The description comes from the investigating officer's report of the scene of the crime. *Pittsburgh Daily Gazette*, 11 January 1870.

77 Bacon, "Household Conveniences," p. 104.

78 *Commoner and Glass Worker*, 15 December 1888.

79 Ibid.

80 *Pittsburgh Gazette*, 14 January 1870.

81 Byington, *Homestead*, p. 87.

82 I am grateful to Mrs. Weir of Wright Street on the South Side for her description of clothes washing at the turn of the century. She made the process graphically comprehensible to a person brought up in the age of the electric washing machine.

83 *Commoner and Glass Worker*, 15 December 1888.

84 *People's Monthly*, July 1871.

85 *Commoner and Glass Worker*, 15 December 1888.

86 *People's Monthly*, June 1872.

87 *Commoner and Glass Worker*, 22 December 1888.

88 *Commoner and Glass Worker*, 5 January 1889.

89 *Commoner and Glass Worker*, 29 December 1888.

90 Degler, *At Odds*, p. 201; *Commoner and Glass Worker*, 22 December 1888.

91 Byington, *Homestead*, p. 33; Kornblum, *Blue Collar Community*, p. 33.

92 Francis G. Couvares, *The Remaking of Pittsburgh: Class and Culture in an Industrializing City, 1877–1919* (Albany, N.Y., 1984), pp. 73–74.

93 *Commoner and Glass Worker*, 7 October 1887.

94 Peter R. Shergold, *Working Class Life: The "American Standard" in Comparative Perspective, 1899–1913* (Pittsburgh, 1982), pp. 120–27, contains a thorough review of working-class shopping patterns.

95 *Commoner and Glass World*, 7 April 1988.

96 *Pittsburgh Post*, 20 April 1881, price list for Chautauqua Ice Company; U.S. Department of Labor, *Bulletin*, July 1907, pp. 175–328.

97 Byington, *Homestead*, chap. 5; Board of Trade of London, *Cost of Living in American Towns: Report of an Inquiry* (London, 1911), p.356.

98 Interview with Michael Haver, 25 December 1976.

99 Holsopple, "Slavic People," p. 24.

100 U.S. Commissioner of Labor, *Eighteenth Annual Report*, pt. 1 (Washington, D.C., 1903), p. 556. These figures are Pennsylvania-wide, but Byington, *Homestead*, p. 204, confirms them for the Pittsburgh district.

101 Kingsley House Association, *Third Annual Report* (Pittsburgh, 1896).

102 *National Labor Tribune*, 25 September 1880.

103 These findings resemble those of Henry Mayhew, who remarked of the London

costermongers that "the wife is considered an inexpensive servant and the disobedience of a wish is punished with blows." Henry Mayhew, *London Labour and the London Poor,* (London, 1861), vol. 1, p. 43.

104 *People's Monthly,* May 1872.

105 WPHS, 9 January 1889.

106 Alexis Sokoloff, "Medieval Russia in the Pittsburgh district," in Paul U. Kellogg, ed., *Wage-earning Pittsburgh* (New York, 1914), p. 89. Agnes Smedley, *Daughter of Earth* (Old Westbury, N.Y., 1973), suggests that poverty engendered brutality within the family and that both women and men accepted this violence as inevitable. She paints a brutal picture of the relations between spouses in this autobiographical novel.

107 WPHS, 21 February 1889; Sokoloff, "Medieval Russia," pp. 88–89.

108 Allegheny City magistrates' dockets, 25 September 1888.

109 WPHS, 6 October 1888; 5 November 1888.

110 *Pittsburgh Post,* 9 July 1977, 20 July 1877. I examined the brief articles in the Pittsburgh newspapers' crime and local occurrences columns, 1868–93 and the magistrates' docket books for Allegheny City, 1888–93, which indicated that the major reason for women's suits against their husbands were nonsupport and physical abuse.

111 On divorce in this era see Elaine Tyler May, "The Pressure to Provide: Class, Consumerism, and Divorce in Urban America, 1880–1920," *Journal of Social History* 12 (1978): 180–93.

112 *National Labor Tribune,* 25 June 1875.

113 Scott and Tilly, *Women,* p. 54, state that in preindustrial households, women's power stemmed from "the fact that they managed household expenditures for food." I am arguing here that in late nineteenth-century Pittsburgh this power was delegated by their husbands and that the choice between peas and potatoes was not a significant one, except insofar as the woman had to please her husband and make do on whatever sums he gave her.

114 Allegheny City magistrates' dockets, 1888–93 passim.

115 Byington, *Homestead,* p. 108.

116 *National Labor Tribune,* 29 August 1895.

117 *People's Monthly,* June 1871.

118 *National Labor Tribune,* 16 January 1875.

119 1880 census sample; Byington, *Homestead,* p. 201; Abraham Oseroff, *Survey of Workingmens' Homes in the Soho District of Pittsburgh: A Study of Civic Neglect in the Heart of a Great City* (Pittsburgh, 1914), unpaginated.

120 Byington, *Homestead,* p. 201.

121 Ibid., p. 142. Shergold, *Working Class Life,* pp. 86–88, puts a lower figure on the income derived from housing lodgers.

122 Bodnar, Simon, and Weber, *Lives*, pp. 00, describe the timing and valuation of boarding for principal ethnic groups in 1900.

123 Sokoloff, "Medieval Russia," pp. 88–89; Greene, *Slavic Community*, p. 44.

124 Byington, *Homestead*, p. 100.

125 Bell, *Furnace*, pp. 151, 173.

126 Greene, *Slavic Community*, p. 44.

127 *Commoner and Glass Worker*, 19 January 1889.

128 *National Labor Tribune*, 18 July 1874.

129 David Montgomery, *Workers' Control in Industrial America: Studies in the History of Work, Technology, and Labor Struggles* (Cambridge, 1979), p. 13.

130 Couvares, *Remaking of Pittsburgh*, p. 23.

131 *National Labor Tribune*, 9 July 1881.

132 Ibid., 1890.

133 Ibid.

134 *Irish Pennsylvanian*, 15 August 1891.

135 E. E. LeMasters, *Blue-Collar Aristocrats: Life-Style at a Working Class Tavern* (Madison, Wis., 1975) discusses the male-centeredness of the modern working-class tavern.

136 *People's Monthly*, September 1871.

137 Fitch, *Steel Workers*, pp. 61, 227.

138 AAISW, 1877, p. 53.

139 Ibid., 1885, p. 1613.

140 Ibid., 1877, p. 53.

141 Byington, *Homestead*, p. 140; Bodnar, *Immigration*, p. 80.

142 Kornblum, *Blue Collar Community*, p. 75.

143 Sokoloff, "Medieval Russia," p. 89; Shergold, *Working Class Life*, p. 201; David Brody, *Steelworkers in America: The Nonunion Era* (Cambridge, Mass., 1960), p. 106.

144 *People's Monthly*, September 1871.

145 Byington, *Homestead*, p. 109.

146 Holsopple, "Slavic People," p. 24.

147 Greene, *Slavic Community* p. 48; Bodnar, *Immigration*, p. 79.

148 Greek Catholic Union Yearbook, AIS; *Emerald Vindicator*, 15 March 1885; *Pittsburgh Commercial Gazette*, 27 January 1887; *Emerald Vindicator*, 15 April 1885; Byington, *Homestead*, pp. 115–16.

149 *National Labor Tribune*, 3 April 1875; AAISW, 1880, pp. 421–22, and *Report of the Second Annual Reunion Held at Beaver Fair Grounds* (Pittsburgh, 1881); John Bennett, "Iron Workers in Woods Run and Johnstown: The Union Era, 1865–1895" (Ph.D. dissertation, University of Pittsburgh, 1977), p. 120.

150 Leon Wolff, *Lockout: The Story of the Homestead Strike of 1892: A Study of*

Violence, Unionism, and the Carnegie Steel Empire (New York, 1965), p. 33. MacLean, *Wage-Earning Women* (New York, 1910), p. 137; Byington, *Homestead*, p. 151; Bell, *Furnace*, p. 152.

151 Herbert Gutman, *Work, Culture, and Society in Industrializing America* (New York, 1977), p. 39.

152 *Commoner and Glass Worker*, 19 January 1889.

153 Francis G. Couvares, "The Triumph of Commerce," in Michael H. Firsch and Daniel Walkowitz, eds., *Working Class American Society* (Urbana, Ill., 1983), pp. 123–52, discusses the way in which recreation became a cultural battlefield in Pittsburgh.

154 Byington, *Homestead*, p. 65.

155 Interview with Ann Haver, 25 December 1976.

156 Brody, *Steelworkers*, pp. 107–8; Bell, *Furnace*, pp. 152–53; Krause, "Urbanization," p. 26, quoting "Mrs. V." Compare Young and Willmott, *Symmetrical Family*, p. 30.

157 Louise Odencrantz, *Italian Women in Industry* (New York, 1919), p. 203.

158 *Pittsburgh Commercial Gazette*, 4 June 1888; *Commoner and Glass Worker*, 7 May 1886.

159 *Commoner and Glass Worker*, 25 August 1888.

160 Ibid., 7 May 1886.

161 PAIP, 1881.

162 Kingsley House Association, *Seventh Annual Report* (Pittsburgh, 1899), p. 18.

163 Bell, *Furnace*, pp. 126–29.

164 In *Pittsburgh Press*, Roto, 1 September 1971.

165 McLaughlin, *Family and Community*, pp. 144–50, found that efforts by Buffalo's settlement houses to involve Italian women met with limited success, in part because the husbands opposed these threats to their authority and because the women themselves preferred not to leave their homes.

166 Odencrantz, *Italian Women*, pp. 34, 167; Holsopple, "Slavic People," p. 12; Clarke Thomas, "Area Greeks Find Heritage Everywhere," *Pittsburgh Press*, Roto, 4 October 1973.

167 Anderson, *Family Structure*, chap. 10.

168 Kingsley House Association, *Seventh Annual Report*, p. 23; AAISW, *Journal of Proceedings*, 1879, pp. 267–68; *National Labor Tribune*, 15 May 1880; 31 May 1890; Byington, *Homestead*, pp. 160–64; Holsopple, "Slavic People," p. 10. I have found no literary evidence for working-class women's friendships similar to that located by Carroll Smith-Rosenberg for middle-class women in the nineteenth century. Carroll Smith-Rosenberg, "The Female World of Love and Ritual: Relations between Women in Nineteenth-Century America," *Signs* 1 (1975): 1–31. That such friendships did exist among working-class women is

suggested by Alice Kessler-Harris, "Organizing the Unorganizable. Three Jewish Women and Their Union," *Labor History* 17 (1976): 5–23. It is difficult to see, however, how illiterate women would have sustained contact over distance, as did Smith-Rosenberg's middle-class women and Kessler-Harris's working-class Jewish trade union organizers through their correspondence.

169 *Pittsburgh Post,* 18 June 1868. Murder trial testimony provides evidence for a high degree of female interaction in Pittsburgh's tenement courts. In 1868, Louis Lane, a laborer, was accused of poisoning his wife. The neighbors testified that they had been in the Lanes' house frequently, that Henrietta Lane had borrowed a broom from Emily Reed, that Mrs. Grace Allison had given Mrs. Lane a cup of water when she did not feel well. While this is not evidence of close friendships, it suggests that working-class women helped one another and were involved with one another's lives.

170 WPHS, 26 February 1889.

171 Richard J. Gelles, *The Violent Home: A Study of Physical Aggression Between Husbands and Wives* (Beverley Hills, Calif., 1972), p. 124, found that violence "is prevalent when the husband's occupational status is low." Nancy Tomes, "A Torrent of Abuse: Crimes of Violence Between Working Class Men and Women in London, 1840–1875," *Journal of Social History* 2 (1978): 331–32, found that money frequently was a factor in marital quarrels and abuse in London during the middle of the nineteenth century.

172 Compare Kathleen Neils Conzen, *Immigrant Milwaukee: Accommodation and Community in a Frontier City* (Cambridge, Mass., 1976), p. 157. Jones, "Working Class Culture," pp. 486–87, posits that stricter division of labor between the sexes came as the girl children were forced into school and wives found it more difficult to work outside the home without the housekeeping and child-minding services of their older children. Men's social life tended to take place outside the home and the women's within it.

173 Greene, *Slavic Community,* p. 44; *People's Monthly,* January 1872; Charles H. Anderson, *The Political Economy of Social Class* (Englewood Cliffs, N.J., 1974), p. 319.

8 The Final Stages of the Life Cycle

1 See Daniel J. Walkowitz, *Worker City, Company Town: Iron and Cotton Worker Protest in Troy and Cohoes, New York, 1855–1884* (Urbana, Ill., 1978), pp. 112–15, for a comparison of widowhood in an area that provided both iron and textile employment.

2 Conclusions are drawn from a 10 percent sample of the 1880 manuscript census and 1870 and 1900 Pittsburgh death certificate sample.

3   David Hackett Fischer, *Growing Old in America* (New York, 1977); W. Andrew Achenbaum, *Old Age in the New Land: The American Experience Since 1790* (Baltimore, 1978); Carole Haber, *Beyond Sixty-Five: The Dilemma of Old Age in America's Past* (Cambridge, 1983). For a general history of retirement, see William Graebner, *A History of Retirement* (New Haven, Conn., 1980).

4   Fischer, *Growing Old*, pp. 222–23.

5   Graebner, *Retirement*, p. 24, cites the example of machinists who dyed their hair. Brian Gratton, *Urban Elders: Family, Work, and Welfare Among Boston's Aged, 1890-1950* (Philadelphia, 1986), p. 5, concludes that Boston's older men did not suffer diminished occupational prestige.

6   Susan Tamke, "Human Values and Aging: The Perspective of the Victorian Nursery," in Stuart F. Spicker, Kathleen M. Woodward, and David D. Van Tassel, eds., *Aging and the Elderly: Humanistic Perspectives in Gerontology* (Atlantic Highlands, N.J., 1978), p. 64.

7   Conclusion is based upon analysis of poems, short stories, and articles appearing in *National Labor Tribune*, 1874–1900; *Commoner and Glass Worker*, 1886–90; and *Irish Pennsylvanian*, 1891.

8   *National Labor Tribune*, 25 October 1875.

9   Ibid., 2 May 1874.

10 On the attitude toward old age in the eighteenth and early nineteenth century, see Daniel Scott Smith, "Old Age and the 'Great Transformation,' A New England Case Study," in Spicker, Woodward, and Van Tassel, *Aging*, p. 299.

11 *Irish Pennsylvanian*, 29 August 1891.

12 *National Labor Tribune*, 8 March 1890.

13 Ibid., 8 March 1890.

14 1880 census sample; U.S. Census, Twelfth Census, 1900, vol. 2, *Population*, pt. 2 (Washington, D.C., 1902), pp. 679–91, 895.

15 Abraham Epstein, *Facing Old Age* (New York, 1922), p. 59.

16 Pennsylvania Commission on Old Age Pensions, *Report* (Harrisburg, 1919), p. 101. Epstein, *Old Age*, p. 62, suggests that children had to choose between helping their parents and providing for their own offspring.

17 John A. Fitch, *The Steel Workers* (New York, 1910), p. 183.

18 Bell, *Out of This Furnace* (Pittsburgh, 1976), pp. 167, 223.

19 *National Labor Tribune*, 18 April 1874.

20 Josephine McIlvain, "Twelve Blocks: A Study of One Segment of the South Side of Pittsburgh, 1880–1915," (unpublished paper, AIS).

21 *Pittsburgh Dispatch*, 26 September 1904.

22 Jesse S. Robinson, *The Amalgamated Association of Iron, Steel, and Tin Workers* (Baltimore, 1920), p. 75; David Brody, *Steelworkers in America: The Nonunion Era* (Cambridge, Mass., 1960), pp. 89–90.

23 Achenbaum, *Old Age,* p. 68.

24 Fitch, *Steel Workers,* p. 183.

25 Nevertheless Graebner, *Retirement,* pp. 44–49, finds by the twentieth century that employers also discriminated against older white-collar workers.

26 Epstein, *Old Age,* p. 84.

27 J. A. Ryan, *A Living Wage,* pp. 155–56, cited in Lee Welling Squier, *Old Age Dependency in the United States* (New York, 1912), p. 41.

28 1880 census sample; U.S. Census, Twelfth Census, 1900, *Compendium of the Twelfth Census* (Washington, D.C., 1902), p. 122.

29 Marriage dockets, 1886, 1900. Compare Joan Scott and Louise Tilly, *Women, Work, and Family* (New York, 1978), pp. 27, 52, on the limited prospects for remarriage among widows in France in the seventeenth and eighteenth centuries. U.S. Census, Twelfth Census, 1900, vol. 2, *Population,* pt. 2 (Washington, D.C., 1902), pp. 682–83.

30 Helen Znaniecki Lopata, *Widowhood in an American City* (Cambridge, Mass., 1973), p. 17.

31 Mary Richmond and Fred Hall, *A Study of 985 Widows* (New York, 1913), pp. 14–15.

32 Letter from Rose Miller in *National Labor Tribune,* 31 July 1875; 21 August 1875.

33 *National Labor Tribune,* 10 May 1890.

34 *National Labor Tribune,* 17 June 1876.

35 Bell, *Furnace,* p. 214.

36 Michael Anderson, *Family Structure in Nineteenth-Century Lancashire* (Cambridge, 1971), p. 32.

37 City of Pittsburgh, Department of Charities clipping, 1901, in Department of Charities File, AIS. This incident can serve as a warning to those who try to trace people. The same person appeared in three separate newspaper clippings as Ellen Silefsky, Helen Salinsky, and Nellie Solinski. I could find none of these names in the city directories.

38 PAIP, 1879. Anderson, *Family Structure,* p. 50.

39 Richmond and Hall, *Widows,* pp. 23–27.

40 U.S. Census, Twelfth Census, 1900, *Special Report: Statistics of Women at Work* (Washington, D.C., 1904), pp. 286–89, hereafter cited as *Women at Work.*

41 J. M. Gusky Orphanage Home, Minute Book, 1881–1893, AIS.

42 Florence Lattimore, "Pittsburgh as a Foster Mother," in Paul U. Kellogg, ed., *The Pittsburgh District: The Civic Frontage* (New York, 1914), pp. 377–80.

43 *Women at Work,* pp. 286–89; *Pittsburgh Commercial Gazette,* 31 July 1888; WPHS, 1 December 1888; 9 May 1889.

44 *Women at Work,* p. 287; PAIP, 1879–1900.

45   Agnes Smedley, *Daughter of Earth* (Old Westbury, N.Y., 1973), poignantly portrays how laundry work wore out her mother.
46   WPHS, 31 May 1888; 23 November 1889; 19 July 1889; 28 February 1889.
47   *National Labor Tribune*, 5 March 1881.
48   PAIP, 1917, p. 36.
49   *Commoner and Glass Worker*, 6 November 1887.
50   Allegheny City magistrates' dockets, 28 December 1888; WPHS, 6 October 1888.
51   Richmond and Hall, *Widows*, pp. 15–16, detail the amounts of insurance left to widows and the price of funerals. The funeral took two-thirds of the insurance money, leaving these poor families approximately $56 after the burial of the breadwinner.
52   Mary White Ovington, *Half a Man: The Status of the Negro in New York* (1911; reprint, New York, 1969), p. 78, suggests that because black youths worked away from home, they felt less obligation to contribute to it.
53   Anderson, *Family Structure*, pp. 55–56. Michael Katz, *Poverty and Policy in American History* (New York, 1983), p. 86, maintains that relatives were more likely to provide for elderly of the same sex.
54   City of Pittsburgh, Department of Charities clipping, 1901, AIS.
55   *Commoner and Glass Worker*, 23 June 1888.
56   *National Labor Tribune*, 24 September 1881.
57   1880 census sample.
58   Achenbaum, *Old Age*, pp. 77–78.
59   1880 Census sample.
60   Ibid., 1860.
61   Squier, *Dependency*, p. 12.
62   Scott and Tilly, *Women*, p. 106, state that when children left home and parents' earning capacity declined, the parents might be reduced to penury.
63   *National Labor Tribune*, 8 January 1881.
64   WPHS, 17 June 1889.
65   *Pittsburgh Daily Gazette*, 25 January 1870.
66   Epstein, *Old Age*, pp. 58–62. It is interesting that reformers such as Epstein perceived this allocation of resources as depriving the coming generation. It reflects the Progressives' emphasis on youth as well as their willingness to intervene in all manner of family relationships.
67   WPHS, 15 July 1889. For a general analysis of the poorhouse in this era, see Katz, *Poverty and Policy*, pt. 1.
68   WPHS, 9 May 1889.
69   John Newton Boucher, *A Century and a Half of Pittsburgh and Her People* (Pittsburgh, 1908), pp. 270–73, 432–39; Board of Commissioners of Public

Charities of the State of Pennsylvania, *Sixth Annual Report* (Harrisburg, 1876), p. 104; Samuel Thayer Rutherford, "The Department of Charities of the City of Pittsburgh, 1888–1923" (M.A. thesis, University of Pittsburgh, 1938), p. 34.

70 WPHS, 23 May 1889.

71 Pennsylvania Commissioners of Public Charities, *Sixth Annual Report*, p. 32.

72 See photographs in Katz, *Poverty and Policy*, pp. 189, 199.

73 Rutherford, "Department of Charities," p. 82.

74 Board of Managers, Home for Aged Protestant Women, *Eighth Annual Report* (Pittsburgh, 1879), pp. 22–23.

75 See Haber, *Beyond Sixty-Five*, chap. 5, for an overview of the development of such homes.

76 Home for Aged Protestant Women, *Eighth Annual Report*, p. 23.

77 Katz, *Poverty and Policy*, p. 122.

78 Home for Aged Protestant Women, *Eighth Annual Report*, p. 23.

79 Ibid.

80 Ibid.

81 R. E. Diffenbacher, *Directory of the City of Pittsburgh*, 1880, 1888, 1895. Compare, John Bodnar, *Immigration and Industrialization: Ethnicity in an American Mill Town, 1870–1940* (Pittsburgh, 1977), p. 104.

82 Graebner, *Retirement*, pp. 128–29.

83 Brody, *Steelworkers*, p. 90.

84 Epstein, *Old Age*, pp. 148–49, citing the Pennsylvania Commission on Old Age survey.

85 Diffenbacher, *Directory*, 1887–1888, p. 79.

86 Boucher, *Century and a Half*, p. 443.

87 J. M. Kelly, *Handbook of Greater Pittsburgh* (Pittsburgh, 1898), pp. 11–21.

88 U.S. Census, Twelfth Census, 1900, vol. 2, *Population*, pt. 2, p. 140, and U.S Census, Twelfth Census, 1900, *Compendium of the Twelfth Census* (Washington, D.C., 1902), p. 122.

89 Achenbaum, *Old Age*, p. 80, states that about 2 percent of the elderly lived in almshouses at this time.

90 PAIP, 1879–80, p. 12. Statistical conclusions drawn from ibid., 1879–80 to 1899–1900.

91 Women's Christian Association of Pittsburgh and Allegheny, *Seventh Annual Report*.

92 The proportion of widows surrounding the mill areas was much higher than the national average.

93 Maris A. Vinovskis, "Angels' Heads and Weeping Willows: Death in Early America," in Michael Gordon, ed., *The American Family in Social Historical Perspective*, 2d ed. (New York, 1978), pp. 546–63.

94 Marriage dockets, 1885–86, 1900.

95 *National Labor Tribune*, 2 August 1900.

96 Ann Douglas, "Heaven Our Home: Consolation Literature in Northern United States, 1830–1880," *American Quarterly* 26 (1974): 515.

97 *National Labor Tribune*, 25 April 1895; *Commoner and Glass Worker*, 21 April 1888; 8 September 1888; *National Labor Tribune*, 3 January 1885; 17 July 1880.

98 *National Labor Tribune*, 23 August 1900; *Commoner and Glass Worker*, 31 December 1887; *National Labor Tribune*, 5 December 1885.

99 *National Labor Tribune*, 12 December 1885.

100 Ibid., 25 July 1874; *Commoner and Glass Worker*, 17 December 1887; *Pittsburgh Press*, 15 April 1875.

101 W. Scott Newcomer, ed., *The Keystone State Echo in Commemoration of the Golden Jubilee Anniversary of the Funeral Directors Association of the State of Pennsylvania* (Pittsburgh, 1931), pp. 81, 107.

102 *National Labor Tribune*, 8 March 1900.

103 Ibid., 17 January 1885. Stanley French, "The Cemetery as Cultural Institution: The Establishment of Mount Auburn and the 'Rural Cemetery Movement,' " in David Stannard, ed., *Death in America* (Philadelphia, 1975), pp. 69–91. The Uniondale Cemetery in Pittsburgh advertised itself as having beautifully located grounds with a grand view. *Pittsburgh Press*, 7 May 1870. The characterization of individual graves as "singles" comes from the cemetery workers. These conclusions are based on the day books from Allegheny Cemetery, 1870–1900; St. Mary's Cemetery, 1847–1900; and South Side Cemetery, 1873–1900.

104 *National Labor Tribune*, 5 September 1874; *Commoner and Glass Worker*, 5 January 1889.

105 This figure is derived from a sample of day books, St. Mary's Cemetery, 1850–1900. French, "Cemetery," p. 78.

106 Charles O. Jackson, "Death in American Life," in Charles O. Jackson, ed., *Passing: The Vision of Death in America* (Westport, Conn., 1977), p. 230.

107 William Martin paid for his cemetery plot in small annual installments. Martin Scrapbook, Darlington Library, University of Pittsburgh. *National Labor Tribune*, 8 March 1900; Greek Catholic Union, *Diamond Jubille, 1967*, p. 35, AIS; AAISW, 1878, p. 158; Robinson, *Amalgamated*, p. 65.

108 St. Mary's, Allegheny, and South Side cemeteries, Pittsburgh.

109 *National Labor Tribune*, 11 April 1874.

110 Robert W. Habenstein and William M. Lamers, "The Pattern of Late Nineteenth-Century Funerals," in Jackson, *Passing;* interview with Michael Haver, 25 December 1976.

111 Milton M. Allison, "Iffly: Ghost Town," *Western Pennsylvania Historical Magazine* 35 (June 1952): 99; interview with Michael Haver, 25 December 1976; *Pittsburgh Post*, 31 Mary 1900.

112 *National Labor Tribune*, 21 November 1885.

113 *Commoner and Glass Worker,* 10 December 1887.

114 Ibid., 15 December 1888; *National Labor Tribune,* 17 January 1885; 23 January 1885. On Armstrong's funeral see Francis G. Couvares, *The Remaking of Pittsburgh: Class and Culture in an Industrializing City, 1877–1919* (Albany, N.Y., 1984), pp. 74–74; *Commoner and Glass Worker,* 2 October 1887.

115 *National Labor Tribune,* 8 March 1883. Habenstein and Lamers, "Funerals," p. 94; *Commoner and Glass Worker,* 10 December 1887.

116 Habenstein and Lamers, "Funerals," p. 97; *Commoner and Glass Worker,* 28 January 1888; Elizabeth Stuart Phelps, *The Gates Ajar* (New York, 1869). Picture of a child's funeral belonging to Mrs. Dorothy Puhatch, obtained through her cousin, Mrs. Ann Haver. *National Labor Tribune,* 30 August 1900.

117 Interview with Michael Haver, 25 December 1976.

9 The Response to Urban Industrial Life

1 For general histories of philanthropy see James Leiby, *A History of Social Welfare and Social Work in the United States* (New York, 1978); Paul Boyer, *Urban Masses and Moral Order in America, 1820–1920* (Cambridge, Mass., 1978); Walter I. Trattner, *From Poor Law to Welfare State* (London, 1979); Michael Katz, *Poverty and Policy in American History* (New York, 1983). Katz provides a particularly useful analysis of historians' writings on social welfare. Robert Wiebe's seminal work, *The Search for Order, 1877–1920* (London, 1967), explores the emerging middle class's efforts to remake the hurly-burly of American urban society into an ordered bureaucracy.

2 Boyer, *Urban Masses,* p. 46; David Rothman, *Conscience and Convenience: The Asylum and Its Alternatives in Progressive America* (Boston, 1980), analyzes the limitations of Progressive reform, particularly the ability of reformers to foresee the consequences of their actions for the abridgment of liberty and intervention into the behavior of the poor. However, such intervention did not begin with the Progressives. Jacobus Ten Brock, *Family Law and the Poor* (Westport, Conn., 1971), demonstrates that it has a long history. See Frances Fox Piven and Richard Cloward, *Regulating the Poor* (New York, 1971), on political manipulation of the poor. For comments on Piven and Cloward, see Walter I. Trattner, ed., *Social Welfare or Social Control: Some Historical Reflections on Regulating the Poor* (Knoxville, Tenn., 1983).

3 Analyses of charity and social welfare in U.S. cities at the end of the nineteenth century include Nathan Huggins, *Protestants against Poverty: Boston's Charities, 1870–1900* (Westport, Conn., 1971); Robert Bremner, *From the Depths: The Discovery of Poverty in the United States* (New York, 1956); Allen F. Davis, *Spearheads for Reform: The Social Settlements and the Progressive Movement, 1890–1914* (New York, 1967); Roy Lubove, *The Professional*

Altruist: The Emergence of Social Work as a Career, 1880–1930 (Cambridge, Mass., 1965).

4 Detailed analysis of these agencies can be found in S. J. Kleinberg, "Technology's Stepdaughters: The Impact of Industrialization upon Working Class Women, Pittsburgh, 1865–1890" (Ph.D. dissertation, University of Pittsburgh, 1973).

5 On the changing forms of Pittsburgh government, see Clarence Barclay Duncan, "Evolution of the Government of Pittsburgh" (M.A. thesis, University of Pittsburgh, 1929); Samuel Thayer Rutherford, "The Department of Charities of the City of Pittsburgh, 1888–1923" (M.A. thesis, University of Pittsburgh, 1938); Samuel P. Hays, "The Politics of Reform in Municipal Government in the Progressive Era," *Pacific Northwest Quarterly* 5 (October 1965): 157–69. The role of the City Council in providing services is documented in *The Municipal Record: Minutes of the Proceedings of the Select and Common Councils of the City of Pittsburgh, 1868–1901*.

6 *Emerson Company, Report on the Department of Charities* (New York, 1913). Raymond A. Mohl, "Abolition of Outdoor Public Relief," in Trattner, *Social Welfare*, places such efforts in their national perspective. Department of Charities, *Annual Report*, 1895, p. 313; Rev. R. M. Little, "Modern Charity in Pittsburgh," *Presbyterian Banner*, 19 November 1908; 3 December 1908.

7 Michael Anderson, *Family Structure in Nineteenth-Century Lancashire* (Cambridge, 1971), pp. 62–67.

8 Allegheny City magistrates' hearing books, 1887–93. The testimony given before the magistrates indicates a high degree of familial interaction. The account of one murder, that of a puddler's wife by her estranged husband, showed some aspects of this interaction. Mrs. O'Neil took in boarders after separating from her husband, who abused her. Her sister visited her after Mr. O'Neil told Patrick McGee (his wife's brother) that he wanted the divorce proceedings withdrawn. Mrs. O'Neil sent for her mother to be with her during this time of crisis. The marital crisis sparked intervention, then, by brother, sister, sister-in-law and mother. *Commercial Gazette*, 8 February 1888. Also see WPHS, 21 February 1888; Allegheny City magistrates' hearing book, 21 November 1887; WPHS, 23 March 1889.

9 *National Labor Tribune*, 8 March 1900; Thomas Bell, *Out of This Furnace* (Pittsburgh, 1976), Joan Scott and Louise Tilly, *Women, Work, and Family* (New York, 1978), pp. 143–44.

10 *National Labor Tribune*, 15 May 1880.

11 Kingsley House Association, *Seventh Annual Report* (Pittsburgh, 1900), p. 23.

12 *National Labor Tribune*, 31 May 1890.

13 AAISW, 1879, pp. 267–68; 1886, p. 6; *National Labor Tribune*, 25 December 1880. The Amalgamated adopted a national death benefit system in 1903, but by that time it was not a force in the steel industry in Pittsburgh. Jesse S. Robinson,

The Amalgamated Association of Iron, Steel, and Tin Workers (Baltimore, 1920), p. 74.

14 *Commoner and Glass Worker*, 13 November 1887; 18 January 1888; 17 November 1888.

15 *National Labor Tribune*, 3 July 1875; 31 October 1895; 7 November 1895. Of various donations received by the national office of the AAISW, William Martin, secretary of the union, wrote, "These donations are evidence of the charitableness of our craft." AAISW, 1882, p. 904. In 1888, David Malory, who had his arm torn off at the Vesuvius Iron Works, received one day's pay from each fellow worker, $1,500 in all. *Commoner and Glass Worker*, 2 November 1888. Daniel J. Walkowitz, *Worker City, Company Town: Iron and Cotton Worker Protest in Troy and Cohoes, New York, 1855–1884* (Urbana, Ill., 1978), p. 172; Alan Dawley, *Class and Community: The Industrial Revolution in Lynn* (Cambridge, Mass., 1976), p. 57; and John Bennett, "Iron Workers in Woods Run and Johnstown: The Union Era, 1865–1895" (Ph.D. dissertation, University of Pittsburgh, 1977), p. 170, all note the presence of working-class benevolent organizations or informal contributions in Troy, N.Y., Lynn, Mass., and Johnstown, Pa., respectively.

16 *National Labor Tribune*, 7 November 1874; 11 January 1890; 22 February 1890; *Commoner and Glass Worker*, 22 December 1888; 14 September 1888.

17 George H. Thurston, *Directory of Pittsburgh and Allegheny Cities, 1856–57* (Pittsburgh, 1856) and ibid., 1865–66 (Pittsburgh, 1865); Iron World, *Pittsburgh, Allegheny and Birmingham Business Directory*, 1872 (Pittsburgh, 1872); J. F. Diffenbacher, *Directory of Pittsburgh and Allegheny Cities, 1887* (Pittsburgh, 1887); Lou Gunnerman, *Twin City Reference Book*, (Pittsburgh, 1877).

18 Kathleen Neils Conzen, *Immigrant Milwaukee: Accommodation and Community in a Frontier City* (Cambridge, Mass., 1976), pp. 161, 169; *Emerald Vindicator*, 1 May 1885; 15 March 1885. The *Emerald Vindicator*, 1885–89, published in Pittsburgh, styled itself as "the friend and advocate of all deserving Catholic Associations." It was devoted "to the advancement of the Emerald Beneficial Association of North America and Catholic interests generally."

19 John W. Larner, Jr., "A Community in Transition: Pittsburgh's South Side, 1880–1920" (seminar paper, Department of History, University of Pittsburgh, 1961); Diffenbacher, *Directory, 1895*, passim.

20 Helen Znaniecki Lopata, *Widowhood in an American City* (Cambridge, Mass., 1973), p. 19; *Schwabischen Unterstutzungs-Verein von Pittsburgh und Allegheny*, 1885–1906, membership book, AIS.

21 Amended Articles of Incorporation of Greek Catholic Union of Russian Brotherhoods of the U.S.A. (Pittsburgh, 1914) passim; Greek Catholic Union, *Diamond Jubilee, 1967*, AIS; Rev. A. Pekar, OSBM, "Our Past and Present, Historical

Outlines of the Byzantine Ruthenian Metropolitan Provine" (Pittsburgh, 1974).

22 Margaret Byington, *Homestead: The Households of a Mill Town* (New York, 1910), pp. 154–55.

23 "Croatian Fraternal Union of America, 1894–1969," manuscript, AIS. John Bodnar, *Immigration and Industrialization: Ethnicity in an American Mill Town, 1870–1940* (Pittsburgh, 1977), p. 103, notes that Croatians and Slovenes organized a sick and death benefit society at the urging of a visiting Slovene priest from Joliet, Ill.

24 Robinson, *Amalgamated*, p. 13; John Fitch, *The Steel Workers*, (New York, 1910), p. 195. In 1881, the National Tube Works in McKeesport, Pa., established a cooperative insurance fund, but it "utterly failed, greatly from the migratory character of a large part of our laborers and from the subscriptions being voluntary." BIS, 1887, p. B18.

25 William R. Martin Papers, Darlington Library, University of Pittsburgh, Receipts Scrapbook.

26 Bell, *Furnace*, p. 182; Byington, *Homestead*, pp. 90–91.

27 Pittsburgh Christian Social Service Union, The Methodist Episcopal Church Union, and Other Cooperating Agencies, *The Strip: A Socio-Religious Survey of a Typical Problem Section of Pittsburgh, Pennsylvania* (Pittsburgh, 1915), p. 32. Louise Odenkrantz, *Italian Women in Industry* (New York, 1919), pp. 200–01.

28 Eric H. Monkkonen, *The Dangerous Class: Crime and Poverty in Columbus, Ohio, 1860–1885* (Cambridge, Mass., 1975), provides an insightful investigation into the relationship between poverty and crime.

29 H. V. Blaxter and Allen H. Kerr, "The Aldermen and Their Courts," in Paul U. Kellogg, ed., *The Pittsburgh District: The Civic Frontage* (New York, 1914), pp. 139–41. Katz, *Poverty and Policy*, p. 198, states that "magistrates' courts often turned into forums for the resolution of working class domestic difficulties."

30 Lists of aldermen's names were found in the city directories for 1870, 1880, and 1889. The names were traced backward through the preceding directories until an occupation other than alderman was listed. The aldermen's address changes were traced in the same manner.

31 Arthur Burgoyne, *All Sorts of Pittsburghers* (Pittsburgh, 1892), passim.

32 The activities of the aldermen were traced through the *Pittsburgh Daily Gazette* and the *Pittsburgh Commercial Gazette* for 1868, 1870, 1877, 1880, 1888, and 1893.

33 Of all aldermanic cases, 20 percent involved neighbors, whereas 10 percent of the mayoral cases did so. About half the aldermanic cases and one-third the mayoral cases involved women.

34 *Pittsburgh Daily Gazette*, 28 June 1870; 8 June 1888; 29 June 1868; 11 January 1870; 20 January 1870.

35 *Pittsburgh Commercial Gazette*, 8 June 1888; *Pittsburgh Daily Gazette*, 29 June 1868; 28 January 1870.

36 The divorce actions had to be initiated in Circuit Court. *Pittsburgh Daily Gazette* and *Pittsburgh Commercial Gazette*, 1868, 1870, 1877, 1880, 1888, 1893, passim.

37 *Pittsburgh Daily Gazette*, 1870, passim. Allegheny County magistrates' hearing books, 21 December 1888.

38 Blaxter and Kerr, "Alderman," pp. 140–51; *Pittsburgh Commercial Gazette*, 12 July 1877. John C. Reilly, proprietor of a livery stable, was appointed to fill the term of Alderman Samuel McMasters, who was convicted of arranging abortions.

39 Mazella Cox v. Joseph Wilkins, Jacob Witmer, Michael Sweeny, Jerry Thomas, and Patrick Down, Allegheny County magistrates hearing books, 20 November 1887.

40 Samuel P. Hays, "The Changing Political Structure of the City in Industrial America," *Journal of Urban History* 1 (1974): 19–20, discusses professionalization in various aspects of Pittsburgh government during the late nineteenth and early twentieth centuries.

41 Katz, *Poverty and Policy*, p. 205.

42 Trattner, *Poor Law*, p. 95.

43 Anthony M. Platt, *The Child Savers: The Invention of Delinquency* (Chicago, 1973), p. 4, notes that their programs diminished the civil liberties and privacy of youth. WPHS, *History of the Society* (typescript, 1961); *Handbook of Greater Pittsburg (sic)*, (Pittsburgh 1909), pp. 10–11; Katz, *Poverty and Policy*, p. 194.

44 WPHS, *History of the Society*.

45 The use of paid agents represents a shift in female philanthropy from the direct involvement in the lives of the poor. See Keith Melder, "Ladies Bountiful," *New York History* 48 (1967): 231–55, and contrast with John Rousmaniere, "Cultural Hybrid in the Slums," *American Quarterly*, 20 (1970): 45–66.

46 All data regarding the Humane Society's activities come from its manuscript casework records for 1889–91. These are particularly valuable because they detail the workings and mentality of the society and its agents.

47 Katz, *Poverty and Policy*, p. 196; Leiby, *History*, p. 194. For general histories of the temperance movement, see Joseph R. Gusfield, *Symbolic Crusade* (Urbana, Ill., 1966); James Timberlake, *Prohibition and the Progressive Movement* (Cambridge, Mass., 1965).

48 PAIP, 1878, p. 23; WPHS, *Ninth Annual Report*, 1884, passim; Leiby, *History*, 114–16.

49 Children's Temporary Home, *Annual Report*, 1890, p. 38.

50 WPHS, 1889–1891; Children's Temporary Home, *Annual Report*, 1890, p. 38.

51 Pittsburgh and Allegheny Home for the Friendless, *Tenth Annual Report*

(Pittsburgh, 1871), pp. 1, 6, 9; PAIP, 1880, p. 13; 1881, p. 10; 1882, pp. 13–23; WPHS, 8 November 1890.

52 WPHS, 27 May 1889; 29 August 1888; 15 October 1890.

53 Ibid., 16 April 1888; 5 April 1885; 26 April 1889; 1 May 1889.

54 Ibid., 27 August 1888; 8 September 1888; 10 August 1889; 6 September 1888; 7 November 1889.

55 *Handbook of Greater Pittsburg* [sic], (Pittsburgh, 1909), p. 10.

56 WPHS, 18 June 1889; 20 January 1889.

57 Ibid., 6 March 1889; 23 August 1888; 15 September 1888; 24 July 1889; 14 November 1889.

58 Ibid., 6, 13, 15 June 1889.

59 Katz, *Poverty and Policy,* pp. 210–11.

60 Florence Larrabee Lattimore, "Three Studies in Housing and Responsibility: Skunk Hollow, the Squatter," in Kellogg, *Pittsburgh District,* p. 341. The court also placed children out and committeed 398 to institutions in 1907. For divergent analyses of juvenile courts see Rothman, *Conscience and Convenience;* Platt, *Child Savers;* Joseph M. Hawes, *Children in Urban Society* (New York, 1971).

61 For a fuller account of antebellum charity in Pittsburgh, see Cecelia F. Bucki, "The Evolution of Poor Relief Practice in Nineteenth Century Pittsburgh" (seminar paper, Department of History, University of Pittsburgh, 1977).

62 John Newton Boucher, *A Century and a Half of Pittsburgh and Her People* (Pittsburgh, 1908), p. 270. Boyer, *Urban Masses,* p. 121, roots the growth of the nineteenth-century charity movement in an effort to exert moral influence over the largely non-Protestant urban masses. Catholics responded with suspicion and their own organizations.

63 AAISW, 1878, p. 117.

64 Boucher, *Century,* p. 441.

65 For example, Mrs. Harmar Denny was, according to her obituary in 1878, "identified with every Allegheny County benevolent enterprise." Mary Darlington, Scrapbook, Darlington Library, University of Pittsburgh. In 1875, Louise Herron was a member of the Women's Christian Association and was first vice president of the Temporary Home for Destitute Women; Mrs. Samuel McKee, wife of a lumber merchant, was a life member of the Women's Christian Association, a manager of the Temporary Home for Destitute Women, the Home for Aged Protestant Women, and Sheltering Arms. Numerous other examples of multiple membership exist. Women's Christian Association of Pittsburgh and Allegheny, *Seventh Annual Report,* (Pittsburgh, 1875), passim.

66 PAIP, 1880, pp. 4, 12.

67 Ibid., pp. 4–7. Lubove, *Professional Altruist,* documents this transition from the professionals' perspective.

68 J. F. Diffenbacher, *Directory,* 1875, 1896, passim.

69 Letter from the Legal Aid Society to the Board of Directors of the Civic Club, 1899, and newspaper clipping, 1908, Civic Club of Pittsburgh File, AIS; Roy Lubove, "The New York Association for Improving the Condition of the Poor," *New York Historical Society Quarterly* 43 (1959): 307–27.

70 There were about twenty orphanages in Pittsburgh and several other institutions that boarded children and thirteen homes for aged, widowed, or destitute women in 1896. Diffenbacher, *Directory,* 1896.

71 PAIP, 1875, p. 20; 1895, p. 13.

72 PAIP, "Solving the Problem" (Typescript in possession of PAIP, 1915).

73 PAIP, 1880, p. 17; 1895, p. 13.

74 Peter R. Shergold, *Working Class Life: The "American Standard" in Comparative Perspective, 1899–1913* (Pittsburgh, 1982), p. 40, found that aid went first to U.S. citizens.

75 PAIP, 1880, p. 17; 1885, p. 17; 1890, p. 12. Ibid., 1895, p. 13 reported the religious affiliation or lack thereof for its relief recipients. During these years, 3,134 laborers, 2,245 washerwomen and servants, 428 seamstresses, and 418 millworkers received assistance. Though the number of washerwomen and servants receiving relief fluctuated somewhat with the economic cycle, that of millworkers and laborers was strongly affected by business downturns. In 1890, 426 laborers received assistance, but in 1895, 1,131 did so. For washerwomen and servants the comparable figures are 459 and 562.

76 PAIP, 1880, pp. 11–17. The phrase is drawn from the title of Allen F. Davis's book.

77 This review of Dr. Coit's activities is based upon interviews with his daughter Lady Flemming, née Virginia Coit, 12 July 1977, 20 December 1977; the Stanton Coit Papers, British Humanist Association; and Davis, *Spearheads,* pp. 8–12.

78 J. M. Kelly, *Handbook of Greater Pittsburgh* (Pittsburgh, 1898), p. 13.

79 Philip Rosen, "Thirty Years at Kingsley House" (seminar paper, History Department, Carnegie Mellon University, 1969.)

80 William Mathews, *Adventures in Giving* (New York, 1939), pp. 70–73.

81 Ibid., p. 7.

82 Rev. Riley McMillan Little, "Modern Charity in Pittsburgh," *Presbyterian Banner,* 19 November 1908, pp. 4–7, 20.

83 PAIP, 1880, pp. 4, 12.

84 Kingsley House Association, Minutes of the Executive Committee, Pittsburgh, Pennsylvania, January 1910.

85 Rosen, "Thirty Years," pp. 4–8.

86 Women's Christian Association, *Seventh Annual Report, 1875* (Pittsburgh,

1875), passim; Pittsburgh and Allegheny Home for the Friendless, *Tenth Annual Report* (Pittsburgh, 1871), and *Twentieth Annual Report* (Pittsburgh, 1881); PAIP, 1880; 1890.

87 For comparison with male organizations see Donald H. Doyle, "The Social Functions of Voluntary Associations in a Nineteenth Century American Town," *Social Science History* 1 (1977): 333–55.

88 PAIP, 1880, pp. 4–7; Women's Christian Association, 1881, p. 51.

89 Beulah Kennard, "The Playgrounds of Pittsburgh," in Kellogg, *Pittsburgh District*, pp. 306–24.

90 *Commoner and Glass Worker*, 10 March 1888.

91 Byington, *Homestead*, p. 78.

92 Davis, *Spearhead*, pp. 86–87 highlights some of the problems confronting settlement house workers in their dealings with their working-class immigrant neighbors.

93 Compare Bodnar, *Immigration*, p. 3; Bennett, "Iron Workers," p. 159, and Dawley, *Class and Community*, pp. 112–19, on charity and its uses in Steelton and Johnstown, Pa., and Lynn, Mass.

94 *National Labor Tribune*, 2 February 1875, 6 March 1875, 15 March 1875.

95 Ibid., 15 February 1879.

96 *Irish Pennsylvanian*, 15 August 1891.

97 *Commoner and Glass Worker*, 21 April 1888.

98 Byington, *Homestead*, p. 178; Fitch, *Steel Workers*, p. 226.

99 *National Labor Tribune*, 20 February 1875; 3 July 1875; 3 October 1895.

100 The Irene Kaufmann Settlement, responding to the needs and interests of the Jewish community that gave it birth, hosted meetings with the Tobacco Workers, Bakers, Tailors, Brooms, Peddlars, and Stogy Makers' unions. Raymond McClain, "The Immigrant Years: The Irene Kaufmann Settlement, 1895–1915" (unpublished paper, Department of History, Carnegie Mellon University, 1969). For a general history of labor–settlement house relations, see Davis, *Spearhead*, chap. 6, who finds New York, Boston, and Chicago settlements more favorably disposed toward working-class organizations. Though they lost some contributions, they also had more diversified support than Kingsley House. Also see Katz, *Poverty and Policy*, p. 194.

101 Lubove, *Professional Altruist*, p. 16.

102 The PAIP was caught between the old and new styles of philanthropy. The Pittsburgh Survey attacked it as an "unregenerate charitable institution" (see Roy Lubove, *Twentieth Century Pittsburgh: Government, Business and Environmental Change* (New York, 1969), p. 25). It was partially superseded by the Associated Charities, formed at the behest of the Civic Club. In 1911 the women of the board voluntarily became the women's auxiliary, ceding power to a new

all-male board of trustees. They apparently resented relinquishing their position and the formalization of record keeping. (PAIP, minute books, 1911).

10 Conclusion

1 John Bodnar, Roger Simon, and Michael P. Weber, *Lives of Their Own: Blacks, Italians, and Poles in Pittsburgh, 1900–1960* (Urbana, Ill., 1982), p. 93, confirm this description for Polish steel millworkers and Italians, who were more trade- and craft-oriented. They find that a different pattern prevailed among blacks, few of whom were able to find work in the mills.

2 Compare Francis G. Couvares, *The Remaking of Pittsburgh: Class and Culture in an Industrializing City, 1877–1919* (Albany, N.Y., 1984); David Montgomery, *Workers' Control in Industrial America: Studies in the History of Work, Technology, and Labor Struggles* (Cambridge, 1979).

3 Mary Richmond and Fred Hall, *A Study of 985 Widows* (New York, 1913), found that in 44 percent of the families headed by widows, children made contributions to the family income.

4 John Bodnar, *Workers' World: Kinship, Community, and Protest in an Industrial Society, 1900–1940* (Baltimore, 1982), p. 168.

5 Compare Alice Kessler-Harris, *Out to Work: A History of Wage-Earning Women in the United States* (New York, 1982), chap. 5.

6 Roy Lubove, *The Progressives and the Slums: Tenement House Reforms in New York City* (Pittsburgh, 1962). For case studies of housing in other cities, see E. P. Goodrich and George B. Ford, *Housing Report to the City Plan Commission of Newark, New Jersey* (Newark, 1913); Janet Kemp, *Housing Conditions in Baltimore* (New York, 1907); James B. Ford et al., *Slums and Housing* (Cambridge, Mass., 1936); Carroll D. Wright, *Seventh Special Report of the Commissioner of Labor: The Slums of Great Cities: New York, Baltimore, Chicago, and Philadelphia* (Washington, D.C., 1894); Edith Abbott, *The Tenements of Chicago, 1908–1935* (Chicago, 1936).

7 Nathan Huggins, *Protestants Against Poverty: Boston's Charities, 1870–1900* (Westport, Conn., 1971), chap. 7, highlights the growing physical and cultural distance between the rich and poor.

8 Richard J. Gelles, *The Violent Home: A Study of Physical Aggression Between Husbands and Wives* (Beverly Hills, Calif., 1972), emphasizes the use of violence to control the wife's or child's behavior.

9 Jonathan Prude, *The Coming of Industrial Order: Town and Factory Life in Rural Massachusetts, 1810–1860* (Cambridge, 1983), describes fathering in agricultural and early industrial America.

10 Joan Scott and Louise Tilly, *Women, Work, and Family* (New York, 1978), p.

47. Mary Beth Norton, *Liberty's Daughters* (Boston, 1980), chap. 8 and 9, and Linda Kerber, *Women of the Republic* (Chapel Hill, N.C., 1980), chap. 9, document the changing attitudes toward women and the emphasis on domesticity and maternality that accompanied industrialization. Nancy Cott, *The Bonds of Womanhood* (New Haven, Conn., 1977), p. 205, discusses the concept of "Woman's Sphere," believing that the majority of women upheld this concept to increase their status.

11 John Mack Faragher, *Sugar Creek: Life on the Illinois Prairie* (New Haven, Conn., 1986).

12 Anne Firor Scott, *Making the Invisible Woman Visible* (Urbana, Ill., 1984), pp. 3–33.

13 Joan Jenson, *With These Hands: Women Working on the Land* (Old Westbury, N.Y., 1981).

14 Carl Degler, *At Odds* (New York, 1983), chap. 13.

15 Joan Kelly, *Women, History, and Theory* (Chicago, 1984), pp. 19–50, "Did Women Have a Renaissance?"

Selected Bibliography

The documentation for this study comes from two groups of sources: those written by the working class and those written about them or enumerating them. The first category is the smaller of the two but contains important collective expressions of popular sentiment. Much of this material can be found in newspapers published by or aimed at trade union members and English-speaking laborers. There are also collections of publications of fraternal and mutual assistance organizations of many immigrant groups in Pittsburgh, as well as rather short-lived immigrant newspapers. Although it is true that few members of the working class left memoirs or papers for the historians' benefit, some trade union officials did so. These give insight into the thoughts and feelings of the aristocracy of labor. They also highlight the discrepancies between their standard of living and those of both the middle class and unskilled workers.

The major working-class newspapers published in Pittsburgh, the *National Labor Tribune* and *Commoner and Glass Worker,* focused on matters that concerned union members, old rather than new immigrants, and skilled rather than unskilled workers. Nevertheless, they had some sensitivity to the problems of the unskilled and newly arrived. They also carried social and household advice columns, thus broadening their appeal to include the women who did not work outside the home. The Amalgamated Association of Iron and Steel Workers published the proceedings of its meetings, detailing the anxieties of its members and the losing battle they fought to maintain their control over production and their status. The Pennsylvania Bureau of Industrial Statistics provides a more general account of working conditions, industrial relations, and workers' attitudes. The bureau also conducted surveys, publishing the results of its investigations into such diverse matters as strikes, attitudes toward child labor, and the employment of women.

The materials written about the working class come from disparate sources including social surveys, charitable records, and city, state, and federal government records. The quantitative portrait of working-class women and their families is drawn from the federal manuscript census returns for Pittsburgh in 1860, 1870, 1880, and 1900, from the published census volumes, and from the documents of municipal and charitable agencies. Of the various municipal records, the Pittsburgh death certificates are among the most central to this work. They brought home the appalling wastage of life wrought by the steel mills, railroad, coal mines, and unsanitary neighborhoods. For the summer months, there was page after page of infant deaths due to marasmus, inanition, and summer complaint, almost all in working-class districts. Throughout the year young men perished from burns and other mill accidents, from broken bones and the ensuing pneumonia, and from typhoid fever. Yet the death certificates also contain information of an entirely unexpected sort. They serve as a reminder to researchers to be sensitive to the variety of uses to which data can be put, some of them clearly not intended by the originators of those data. Not all death certificates of this era did so, but those from Pittsburgh contain information that enables historians to trace geographical mobility, namely, residence at the time of death, length of residence at that address, previous residence, and place of birth. Among other things it was possible to compare male and female mobility for the population involved.

There are two excellent collections of Pittsburghiana, a general one in the Pennsylvania Division of the Carnegie Library of Pittsburgh and a more specific one, focusing on industrial society, in the Archives of Industrial Society in the Hillman Library of the University of Pittsburgh. The AIS houses industrial records, research papers by students of the history departments of the University of Pittsburgh and Carnegie Mellon University, local government records, church and charitable society papers, and personal papers. There is also a collection of personal papers and memorabilia at the University of Pittsburgh's Darlington Library.

What follows is a list of the primary source documents consulted. The secondary source materials are cited in the notes and so are not repeated here. Unless the location of unpublished material is specified, it is in the possession of the body named.

Manuscripts and Reports of Charitable, Fraternal, and Welfare Associations

Catholic Diocese of Pittsburgh. *Report of the Parish Schools*. Pittsburgh, 1909.

Civic Club of Pittsburgh. Collected Papers. 1899–1910. AIS.

Columbian Council of Jewish Women. *Report of the Immigrant Aid Committee Regarding the Conditions of Immigrant Girls*. Pittsburgh, 1906.

Croatian Fraternal Union of America. Papers. 1894–1969. AIS.

Darlington, Mary. Scrapbook. Darlington Library, University of Pittsburgh.

East Liberty Problems Survey. 1919. AIS.

Greek Catholic Union of Russian Brotherhoods of the U.S.A. *Amended Articles of Incorporation*. Pittsburgh, 1914. AIS.

————. *Diamond Jubilee*. Pittsburgh, 1967. AIS.

Home for Aged Protestant Women. *Annual Reports*. 1871–79. Carnegie Library of Pittsburgh.

Jones, Benjamin, F. Diary. AIS.

Joseph M. Gusky Orphanage Home. Minute Book. 1881–93. AIS.

Martin, William. Papers. Darlington Library, University of Pittsburgh.

Pittsburgh and Allegheny Home for the Friendless. *Annual Reports*. 1871–91. Carnegie Library of Pittsburgh.

Pittsburgh Association for the Improvement of the Poor. *Annual Reports*. 1875–1905. Carnegie Library of Pittsburgh.

Pittsburgh Free Dispensary. *Annual Reports*. 1880–87. Carnegie Library of Pittsburgh.

Protestant Orphan Asylum of Pittsburgh and Allegheny. *Ninth Annual Report*. Pittsburgh, 1871.

Schwabischen Unterstutzungs-Verein von Pittsburgh und Allegheny. *Mitgleidschaft Buch*. 1885–1905. AIS.

Western Pennsylvania Humane Society. Investigation Reports of Cruelty to Animals and Children. 1888–91. WPHS.

———. *History*. Pittsburgh, 1969. WPHS.

———. *Annual Reports*. 1875–1900. WPHS.

Women's Christian Association of Pittsburgh. *Annual Reports*. 1868–1900. Carnegie Library of Pittsburgh.

Cemetery Association Records

Allegheny Cemetery, Pittsburgh. 1843–1910.

St. Mary's Cemetery, Pittsburgh. 1847–1910.

South Side Cemetery, Pittsburgh. 1873–1910.

Newspapers
(Years surveyed are indicated in parentheses.)

Amalgamated Association of Iron and Steel Workers. *Journal of Proceedings* (1876–1905).

American Glass Review (1885–86).

Charities and the Commons (1907–11).

Commoner and Glass Worker (1887–1900).

Emerald Vindicator (1885–89).

Every Saturday (1870–71).

Harpers' New Monthly Magazine (1878–80).

Irish Pennsylvanian (1891).

National Labor Tribune (1874–1910).
People's Monthly (1871–75).
Pittsburgh Commercial Gazette (1877–88).
Pittsburgh Daily Gazette (1868–93).
Pittsburgh Daily Post (1877–1907).
Pittsburgh Press (1971–73).

Government Documents

Allegheny City. Magistrates dockets. 1884–93.
Allegheny County. Marriage dockets. 1886, 1900.
Kelly, J. M. *Official Handbook, Compendium and Historical Sketch of the Bureau of Highways and Sewers of the Department of Public Works.* Pittsburgh, 1898.
Massachusetts Bureau of Labor Statistics. *Annual Reports.* 1874–80.
Pennsylvania Bureau of Industrial Statistics. *Annual Reports.* 1872–1907.
Pennsylvania Commissioners of Public Charities. *Annual Reports.* 1870–1900.
Pittsburgh City Controller. *Annual Report.* 1895.
Pittsburgh City Council. *Municipal Record: Proceedings of the Common and Select Council of the City of Pittsburgh.* 1868–1900.
Pittsburgh Fire Department. *Annual Reports.* 1870–88.
Pittsburgh Public Health Department. *Annual Reports.* 1873–1910.
Pittsburgh Public Safety Department. *Annual Reports.* 1888–1907.
Pittsburgh Public Works Department. *Annual Reports.* 1888–89.
———. *The City of Pittsburgh and Its Public Works.* 1916.
Pittsburgh Superintendent of Schools. *Annual Reports.* 1871–1933.
Pittsburgh Water Commission. *Annual Reports.* 1872–79.
United States. Bureau of the Census. Eighth Census, 1860. (Manuscript census for Pittsburgh.)
———. Ninth Census, 1870. (Manuscript census for Pittsburgh.)
Vol. 1, *Population.* Washington, D.C., 1872.
———. Tenth Census, 1880. (Manuscript census for Pittsburgh.)
Vol. 1, *Population.* Washington, D.C., 1883.
Vol. 2, *Manufactures.* Washington, D.C., 1883.
Vol. 18, *Social Statistics of Cities.* Pt. 1. Washington, D.C., 1886.
———. Eleventh Census, 1890.
Vol. 1, *Population.* Pt. 1. Washington, D.C., 1895. Pt. 2. Washington, D.C., 1897.
Vol. 4, *Report on Vital and Social Statistics in the United States.* Pt. 2. Washington, D.C., 1896.
———. Twelfth Census, 1900. (Manuscript census for Pittsburgh.)
Compendium of the Twelfth Census. Washington, D.C., 1902.

Vol. 1, *Population*. Pt. 2. Washington, D.C., 1901.

Vol. 2, *Population*. Pt. 2. Washington, D.C., 1902.

Vol. 4, *Vital Statistics*. Pt. 2. Washington, D.C., 1902.

Vol. 7, *Manufactures*. Pt. 1. Washington, D.C., 1906.

Special Report: Occupations at the Twelfth Census. Washington, D.C., 1904.

Special Report: Statistics of Women at Work, 1900. Washington, D.C., 1904.

————. Thirteenth Census, 1910.

Vol. 1, *Population*. Washington, D.C., 1915.

Vol. 4, *Occupations*. Washington, D.C., 1914.

Vol. 10, *Manufactures*. Pt. 3. Washington, D.C., 1913.

————. Fourteenth Census, 1920.

Vol. 1, *Population*. Washington, D.C., 1921.

Vol. 4, *Occupations*. Washington, D.C., 1923.

————. Fifteenth Census, 1930.

Vol. 4, *Occupations by States*. Washington, D.C., 1933.

————. Sixteenth Census, 1940.

Vol. 3, *The Labor Force: Occupation, Industry, Employment, Income*. Pt. 5. Washington, D.C., 1943.

Vol. 4, *Population: Differential Fertility for States and Large Cities*. Washington, D.C., 1943.

United States Commissioner of Labor. *Sixth Annual Report*. Washington, D.C., 1890.

————. *Eleventh Annual Report*. Washington, D.C., 1896.

United States Congress. Senate. *Report of the Condition of Women and Child Wage Earners in the United States*. Vol. 3, *The Glass Industry*. Washington, D.C., 1910.

————. Committee on Education and Labor. *Report upon the Relations Between Labor and Capital*. 5 vols. Washington, D.C., 1885.

Directories

Caldwell, J. M. *Pittsburgh Business Directory*. Pittsburgh, 1868.

Central District and Printing Telegraph Company. Telephone Exchanges, *List of Subscribers Connected with the Central Office*. Pittsburgh, 1878, 1885.

J. F. Diffenbacher. *Directory of Pittsburgh and Allegheny Cities*. 1877, 1880, 1886, 1888, 1890, 1895, 1900, 1905.

Gunnerman, Lou. *Twin City Reference Book*. Pittsburgh, 1877.

Iron World. *Pittsburgh, Allegheny, and Birmingham Business Directory*. 1872. Pittsburgh, 1872.

Thurston, George. *Directory of Pittsburgh and Allegheny*. 1856–1857, 1865–66, 1870–71.

Maps and Photographs in the Carnegie Library of Pittsburgh

Anon. *New Map of the Cities of Pittsburgh, Allegheny, Birmingham and Adjacent Boroughs*. Pittsburgh, 1869.

Anon. *Plan of Birmingham and East Birmingham*. Pittsburgh, 1872.

Busch, Edward. *Atlas of the Cities of Pittsburgh, Allegheny, and Adjoining Boroughs from Actual Surveys and Official Records*. Philadelphia, 1872.

Lee, Alex Y. *Map of the Industries of Pittsburgh and Allegheny City, no. 2, Showing the Location of the Public Buildings, Street Car Lines, Hotels, Mills and Other Manufacturers*. Pittsburgh, 1884.

Lorant, Stefan. Photographic Collection.

Neeper, Alex M. *Maps and Descriptions of the Election Districts of Pittsburgh and Allegheny*. Pittsburgh, 1886.

Sanborn, D. A. *Insurance Map of the Business and Manufacturing Parts of Pittsburgh, West and South Pittsburgh, Allegheny and Birmingham, Pennsylvania, 1871*. New York, 1871.

Index

PITTSBURGH SERIES IN SOCIAL AND LABOR HISTORY
Maurine Weiner Greenwald, Editor

And the Wolf Finally Came: The Decline of the American Steel Industry
John P. Hoerr

The Correspondence of Mother Jones
Edward M. Steel, Editor

Don't Call Me Boss: David L. Lawrence, Pittsburgh's Renaissance Mayor
Michael P. Weber

The Shadow of the Mills: Working-Class Families in Pittsburgh, 1870–1907
S. J. Kleinberg

The Speeches and Writings of Mother Jones
Edward M. Steel, Editor

The Steel Workers
John A. Fitch

Trade Unions and the New Industrialisation of the Third World
Roger Southall, Editor

What's a Coal Miner to Do? The Mechanization of Coal Mining
Keith Dix

Women and the Trades
Elizabeth Beardsley Butler

OTHER TITLES IN THE SERIES

The Emergence of a UAW Local, 1936–1939: A Study in Class and Culture
Peter Friedlander

Homestead: The Households of a Mill Town
Margaret F. Byington

The Homestead Strike of 1892
Arthur G. Burgoyne

Immigration and Industrialization: Ethnicity in an American Mill Town, 1870–1940
John Bodnar

Out of This Furnace
Thomas Bell

Steelmasters and Labor Reform, 1886–1923
Gerald G. Eggert

Steve Nelson, American Radical
Steve Nelson, James R. Barrett, & Rob Ruck

Working-Class Life: The "American Standard" in Comparative Perspective, 1899–1913
Peter R. Shergold